# WILLIE MAYS
## FIVE TOOLS

EDITED BY BILL NOWLIN AND GLEN SPARKS

ASSOCIATE EDITORS: LEN LEVIN AND CARL RIECHERS

Society for American Baseball Research, Inc.
Phoenix, AZ

Willie Mays Five Tools
Edited by Bill Nowlin and Glen Sparks
Associate editors Len Levin and Carl Riechers

Front cover art: Mike Schacht, courtesy of Linda Schacht
Back cover photos: SABR/The Rucker Archive;
photograph in San Francisco shirt courtesy of the National Baseball Hall of Fame

*Book design by Gilly Rosenthol*

ISBN 978-1-960819-03-1 (paperback)
ISBN 978-1-960819-02-4 (ebook)
Library of Congress Control Number (LCCN): 2023904437



Cronkite School at ASU
555 N. Central Ave. #416
Phoenix, AZ 85004
Phone: (602) 496-1460
Web: www.sabr.org
Facebook: Society for American Baseball Research
Twitter: @SABR

## TABLE OF CONTENTS


1 Introduction
*by Glen Sparks*

4 Willie Mays
*by John T. Saccoman*

29 The Embodiment of the Negro Leagues
*by Jake Bell*

40 Tracking Down Willie Mays's 1948 Game Log
*by Tom Thress*

43 The Negro Leagues Beyond 1948, and the Adventures of a Boy Named Willie
*by Alan Cohen*

47 Willie Mays in Trenton
*by Steven M. Glassman*

54 Willie Mays Had a Spectacular – But Short – Stay in Minneapolis
*by Stew Thornley*

59 Willie Mays at the Polo Grounds
*by John J. Burbridge Jr.*

65 Willie Mays – All-Time All-Star
*by Jason Horowitz*

71 Willie Mays and Ted Williams face off
*by Bill Nowlin*

73 Mantle vs. Mays
*by David Kaiser*

77 Willie Returns to New York
*by Robert F. Garratt*

85 Willie Mays Night at Shea Stadium
*by Thomas J. Brown, Jr.*

90 The Defensive Excellence of Willie Mays
*by Mark Simon*

99 "Now Playing in…" - Willie Mays' Other Positions
*by Steven M. Glassman*

103 Willie Mays – the leader in extra-inning home runs
*by Bill Nowlin*

110 Roomie: The Relationship Willie Mays and Monte Irvin Shared
*by Duke Goldman*

122 Frightening Pitchers with Giant Willies: The Slugging Duo of Willie Mays and Willie McCovey
*by Gordon Gattie*

127 Fatherly Willie Mays Took Bobby Bonds and Barry Bonds Under His Wing
*by Richard Cuicchi*

133 Willie Mays and his Managers
*by Mark S. Sternman*

139 Willie and the Giants: Why the Greatest Player won only Three Pennants
*by David Kaiser*

143 That One Time When Willie Mays Wasn't Perfect
*by Rob Neyer*

148 The Unlikely Celebrity: The "Say Hey Kid" in Song and on Screen
*by Bob LeMoine*

156 Say Hey Forever
*by Brent Kallestad*

## SELECTED GAMES

158 Mays Singles Home the Winner in Extra Innings in Game One of the Negro American League Championship Series
*by Jeb Stewart*

162 Mays' Two-Out Double in the Ninth Saves the Day for the Black Barons — Game Two of the Negro American League Championship Series
*by Jeb Stewart*

165 Mays Leads the Black Barons to Postseason Victory - Game Three of the 1948 Negro League World Series
*by Richard J. Puerzer*

168 May 1, 1951 - Willie Mays Has Three Hits, Makes Spectacular Catch in Millers Home Opener
*by Dave Lande*

171 May 28, 1951 – His First National League Hit Was a Towering Homer
*by Richard Bogovich*

175 August 15, 1951: "It was the most perfectest throw I ever made"
*by Dan Fields*

177 April 18, 1952: Mays Makes His Greatest Catch – No, Not That One
*by Glen Sparks*

181 May 27, 1952: Willie Mays leads Giants over Dodgers as Army induction approaches
*by John Fredland*

186 May 24, 1954: Willie Mays's Two Homers, Three Hits, and Four RBIs Sink Phillies
*by Howard Rosenberg*

189 September 26, 1954: Willie Mays Says "Hey" to the National League Batting Title
*by Frederick C. Bush*

192 September 29, 1954: Willie Mays makes 'The Catch'
*by Gregory H. Wolf*

196 September 25, 1955: Willie Mays ties Johnny Mize's Giants record with 51st home run
*by Tim Odzer*

199 July 10, 1956: A Tale of the Kid and the Man and the Say Hey Kid and the Commerce Comet
*by Alan Cohen*

202 May 18, 1957: Mays Steals Four Bases, Homers against Redlegs
*by Glen Sparks*

206 September 29, 1957: End of an era as Giants play final home game in New York
*by Stephen V. Rice*

209 April 26, 1958: Mays 'Seals' the Win with Homer
*by Daniel Winkler*

212 May 13, 1958: Mays Completes Torrid Stretch against Rival Dodgers
*by Glen Sparks*

216 September 28, 1958: Mays vies for an improbable batting title on the season's final day
*by James Forr*

219 July 11 & 13, 1960: Willie Mays hits for the cycle in All-Star doubleheader
*by Mike Huber*

223 September 15, 1960: Giants top Phillies behind three triples by Willie Mays
*by Bob Webster*

226 April 30, 1961: The Say Hey Kid's four-homer game
*by Nelson "Chip" Greene*

230 June 29, 1961 - Mays hits three homers, including the game-winner in the 10th
*by Theo Tobel*

233 June 1, 1962: "Hey You Guys, Where You Been?"
*by Alan Cohen*

236 September 30, 1962: Mays' 8th-Inning HR Forces 3-Game Playoff for NL Pennant
*by Paul Hofmann*

239 October 1, 1962: Mays and Pierce Lead Giants to Win in Game One of Tiebreaker Series
*by Brian M. Frank*

243 October 3, 1962: The Giants Win the Pennant, Part Two!
*by Tim Otto*

247 July 2, 1963: Marichal outduels Spahn in 16-inning thriller
*by Lou Hernández*

251 July 9, 1963: The Say Hey Kid Steals the Show
*by Craig Garretson*

254 August 7, 1965: A Revitalized Willie Mays Homers Twice and Drives in Five En Route to MVP Award
*by Chad Moody*

258 September 8, 1965: Willie Mays swats two home runs, closes in on Number 500, as Giants take first place
*by Mike Huber*

262 October 3, 1965: Mays Breaks Giants' Record with 52nd HR, Calls It a Day
*by Jake Bell*

266 August 17, 1966: "That one kind of sang itself out of the park": Mays passes Foxx with 535th career homer
*by Creg Stephenson*

270 September 22, 1969: Mays Hits His 600th Homer and Frank Torre Can Go Home Now
*by Luis Blandon*

275 July 18, 1970: Willie Mays joins the 3,000-hit club
*by Douglas Jordan*

279 May 14, 1972: Willie Mays Homers in New York Mets Debut
*by Kevin Larkin*

282 August 17, 1973: Mays's 660th and final HR goes for naught in nailbiter loss
*by Kurt Blumenau*

286 October 14, 1973: Say "Oh, No!" to "Say Hey" One Last Time: Willie Mays Helps Mets Prevail in 12 Innings in World Series Game Two
*by Frederick C. Bush*

290 Contributor biographies

# INTRODUCTION

BY GLEN SPARKS

**THE ACTRESS AND** noted Giants baseball fan Tallulah Bankhead once said, "There have only been two geniuses in the world – Willie Mays and Will Shakespeare."[1] This book focuses on the first of those two great men.

Willie Howard Mays Jr. could do it all. To many, he is the greatest baseball player of all time, greater even than Babe Ruth. He was, as scouts and other baseball people like to say, a five-tool player and the best five-tool player at that. He could hit for average, hit for power, run, field, and throw.

Buck, as some called Mays, batted .301 lifetime over his 23 big-league seasons and topped the .300 mark 10 times. He led the National League with a .345 average in 1954, the first of his two MVP campaigns. On July 18, 1970, he bounced a single through the left side of the infield at Candlestick Park for his 3,000th career hit. Mays retired with 3,293 hits. "I was able to hit to all fields," he said. "I learned to get a lot of hits to right and right-center. You can't pull everything or you're in trouble."[2]

Mays blasted 660 home runs for the Giants and Mets and led the National League in this category four times. He hit a career-high 52 in 1965, his second MVP season. Willie knocked at least 30 home runs in a season 11 times. When he retired, only Ruth and Henry Aaron had more homers. Through 2022, he was sixth on the all-time list.

He stole 338 bases, finished atop the leaderboard four straight years (1956-59), and reached the 30-homer, 30-stolen-base milestone in 1956 and 1957. He swiped at least 20 bags seven times, including in 1971, his age-40 season. As another indication of his great speed, Mays topped the circuit in triples three times and hit 20 in 1957.

Baseball's "Say Hey Kid" may be most famous for his defense. He won a Gold Glove for 12 straight seasons. He assuredly would have won more, but the award was not given out before 1957. Fans and baseball people tell stories of the amazing way that Mays patrolled center field and his famous basket catches. What was his greatest catch? Many say it was his grab against Vic Wertz in the 1954 World Series. Yes, that was a good one. Mays, though, said he made an even better catch off a Bobby Morgan line drive in early 1952. "Defense was my thing," Mays wrote in his book *24*, published in 2020 and co-written with John Shea. "You might go on a streak at the plate and have some down days. But defense, you have to bring it every day."[3]

The 24-time All-Star has said many times that the throw he made on the Wertz liner was better than the catch. In one game against the rival Los Angeles Dodgers in 1966, Mays recalled that he "almost threw for the cycle." He doubled pitcher Don Drysdale off first base, threw out the speedy Willie Davis trying to sprint from first to third on Ron Fairly's double, and nailed Maury Wills at home. "I had another guy at second, but Tito (Fuentes) dropped the ball. He felt bad about it, but I told him, 'Don't worry, that's baseball.'"[4]

Mays grew up outside Birmingham, Alabama, the son of Willie Mays Sr. or "Cat," a top ballplayer in the local industrial league. Willie attended Fairfield Industrial School and took classes for a career in the laundry business. He also joined his dad on the ballfield. Willie signed to play professional baseball with the Chattanooga Choo Choos, a minor-league club in the Negro Leagues, and soon earned a promotion to the Birmingham Black Barons of the Negro National League. The New York Giants signed him in 1949. Giants scout Ed Montague said, "This was the greatest young player I had ever seen in my life or my scouting career."

Willie Mays was part of that early wave of African American players who fought through bigotry following decades of segregation. He made his big-league debut just a few years after the Brooklyn Dodgers' Jackie Robinson broke baseball's shameful color line. Mays, along with Robinson, Don Newcombe, Roy Campanella, Larry Doby, and others changed baseball forever with their talent and determination. Willie Howard Mays Jr. elicited smiles and awe from fans at ballparks across the country.

It seems amazing that Mays won just the two MVP Awards. He deserved many more. Willie led the National League in Wins Above Replacement (WAR, admittedly a statistic created after Mays retired) nine times. Five times he posted an OPS (on-base plus slugging percentage) above 1.000, a superstar-level performance. So, why did the writers ignore Mays in the MVP voting? One reason is the final standings. The Giants won three pennants during Mays' time with the team and that includes his rookie campaign of 1951, when he was promoted to the big club in late May and began his career in a 1-for-26 slump. (He still won Rookie of the Year honors.)

So often, the Giants played second fiddle in the National League pennant race to the Dodgers and St. Louis Cardinals. Mays' club did beat out the Dodgers for the 1962 pennant, but that was the year Maury Wills set a major-league record by stealing 104 bases. Even so, Mays led the NL with a 10.5 WAR, while Wills finished at 6.0, an admirable figure but one not really as good as Wille's. The statistically inclined sportswriter Rob Neyer says, "Mays was terribly neglected in the MVP voting" and adds, "Mays was probably the best player in the league six, seven, or eight times and just wasn't going to win because the Giants weren't winning the league." Neyer also says, "It's not difficult to make the case that Mays is even better than his WAR."[5] Durocher said it this way: "If somebody came and hit .450, stole 100 bases, and performed miracles in the field every day, I'd still look you in the eye and say Willie was better."[6]

This book will add to the many already written about Mays, who remains an icon nearly 50 years after his retirement. *Five Tools* features dozens of articles that are original to the book. These include game stories that describe how Mays could take over a baseball game through both his talent and his baseball genius. Other pieces focus on Mays' relationship with his managers, his days as a minor leaguer in Minneapolis, and more. Members of the Society for American Baseball Research (SABR) contributed all the articles as a way to both highlight and bring new perspectives on one of baseball's most legendary players.

## NOTES

1 www.artspander.com/articles/say-hey-says-it-all-about-willie.

2 Willie Mays and John Shea, *24: Life Stories and Lessons from the Say Hey Kid* (New York: St. Martin's, 2020), 246-47.

3 Mays and Shea, 240.

4 Mays and Shea, 243.

5 Mays and Shea, 270.

6 Bruce Herman, *Hall of Fame Players: Cooperstown* (Lincolnwood, Illinois: Publications International, 2007), 121.

# WILLIE MAYS

BY JOHN T. SACCOMAN

*If somebody came up and hit .450, stole 100 bases, and performed a miracle in the field every day, I'd still look you right in the eye and tell you that Willie was better. He could do the five things you have to do to be a superstar: hit, hit with power, run, throw and field. And he had the other magic ingredient that turns a superstar into a super Superstar. Charisma. He lit up a room when he came in. He was a joy to be around.*

– Leo Durocher, Mays' first major-league manager[1]

MANY CONTEMPORARY PLAYERS and writers agree with Leo Durocher's assessment of Willie Mays as the best all-around player in baseball history. Mike Lupica, longtime columnist for the *New York Daily News,* quoted the late Boston columnist George Frazier on the combination and star power of an athlete like Mays. "That guy has some Willie Mays in him, the same way you used to say this singer or that had some Elvis in him."[2] Former teammate and manager Bill Rigney said about Mays, "All I can say is that he is the greatest player I ever saw, bar none."[3] In baseball's never-ending attempts to somehow order its gods, Mays is the only contender whose proponents rarely use statistics to make their case. It is as if Mays' 660 home runs and 3,283 hits somehow sell the man short, that his wonderful playing record is almost beside the point. With Mays it is not merely what he did – but *how he did it.* He scored more than 2,000 runs, nearly all of them, it would seem, after losing his cap flying around third base. He is credited with more than 7,000 outfield putouts, many exciting, some spectacular, a few breathtaking. How do you measure that? An artist and a genius, for most of his 22 seasons in the big leagues, you simply could not keep your eyes off Willie Mays.

The great ballplayer's father, William Howard Mays, was named after William Howard Taft, who was the US president when he was born in 1912. The elder Mays worked in the steel mills of Westfield, Alabama, outside Birmingham. Nicknamed "Cat," he was a semipro baseball player for the Westfield team in the Tennessee Coal and Iron League. Cat's father, Willie's grandfather, Walter Mays, was a sharecropper and pitcher. Cat's wife, Anna (Sattlewhite) Mays, was a high-school athlete who ran track and who led her basketball team to three consecutive state championships.[4]

Anna gave birth to the third-generation Mays ballplayer, Willie Howard Mays, on May 6, 1931. According to Charles Einstein, the author of several books with and about Mays, a former Birmingham Black Barons teammate once said of Willie Mays, "His momma had but one."[5] In truth, Anna died in 1953 giving birth to her 11th child, but that was long after she and Cat had split up and she was married to a man named Frank McMorris.

It has often been reported that Cat put a baseball in Willie's crib and that Willie learned to walk at six months, ambling toward a baseball sitting on a chair. Despite these stories, Mays claims that his father did not push him to be a ballplayer.

Willie stayed with his father after his parents separated. When he was 10 years old, the family moved from a company-owned house in Westfield to Fairfield, another suburb of Birmingham. Cat was now a Pullman porter on the Birmingham-to-Detroit train, and Willie was virtually raised by Anna's two young orphaned sisters, Aunt Sarah and Aunt Ernestine.

In Mays' several first-person retellings of his childhood, he never stressed childhood difficulties, but of course he had plenty of hardships growing up as an African American in the Deep South during the Depression. He did assert that "there were times that I went to school without any shoes."[6]

*Don Zimmer insisted that Willie Mays could have been in All-Star at any position. Courtesy Jerry Coli/ Dreamstime.*

As was typical for poor families at this time, the Mays household included a friend of Cat's from the mills, "Uncle" Otis Brooks, as well as several cousins. However, with Cat back working in the mills for $2.60 a day, when there was work, and Ernestine working as a waitress, Mays recalled, "[E]veryone pulled together."[7]

Willie attended Fairfield Industrial High School, where he was trained to be a cleaner or presser for a laundry. He starred as a football quarterback and averaged 20 points per game in basketball. The school did not have a baseball team, so he played second base and center field alongside his father on the Fairfield Industrial League team and the semipro Gray Sox. Needless to say, both teams were solely African American, as were their opponents and their fans. These games drew as many as 6,000 fans.

Willie excelled in the Industrial League and, briefly in 1947, for a Negro minor-league team called the Chattanooga Choo-Choos, essentially a farm team for the Birmingham Black Barons of the Negro American League. When he turned 16, Cat introduced him to Piper Davis, the manager of the Black Barons. Davis became very influential in Mays' life. That was the year Jackie Robinson broke the color barrier with the Brooklyn Dodgers, but Mays asserts that the bigger breakthrough came in 1946, when Robinson broke into White baseball with the Montreal Royals in the Brooklyn Dodgers' farm system. Mays much later remarked, "Every time I look at my pocketbook, I see Jackie Robinson."[8]

Cat Mays, Piper Davis, and Willie's high-school principal insisted that Mays should graduate from high school, so he played only in the Black Barons' weekend home games until the school year was over. Ineligible to play high-school sports, he was by far the youngest player on the defending champions of the Negro American League.

Even at 16 years old, Mays played the outfield like a more experienced player. According to Piper Davis, "Nobody ever saw anybody throw a ball from the outfield like him, or get rid of it so fast."[9]

In his first professional appearance, batting seventh and playing left field in the nightcap of a doubleheader at Birmingham's Rickwood Field – shared with the (White) Birmingham Barons of the Southern Association – Mays had two hits off Chet Brewer, whom he called "one of the best pitchers in the league."[10] He moved to center field when the regular, Bobby Robinson, broke his leg. Upon his recovery, Robinson found himself in left field.

According to the Seamheads.com database, Mays batted .239 with 11 RBIs and one stolen base in 21 games with the Black Barons.[11] Mays recalled his first meeting with Satchel Paige: "[D]uring the first meeting with the legend, I got a double off Paige my very first time up. I stood on second, dusted myself off, feeling pretty good. Paige walked toward me. 'That's it, kid.' ... My next three times up I went whoosh, whoosh, whoosh. ..."[12]

Even at the tender age of 17, Mays came up big in big spots. In the Negro American League playoff series against the Kansas City Monarchs,

*One early scouting report lamented that Willie Mays could not hit a curveball. SABR/The Rucker Archive.*

his two-out, bases-loaded single in the bottom of the 11th broke a 4-4 tie and gave the Black Barons a Game One victory. His double in the bottom of the ninth in Game Two drove in future Giants teammate Artie Wilson with the tying run that sent the contest into extra innings. Another ninth-inning double in Game Three seems to have preceded a game-winning homer by teammate Jimmy Zapp, but the details are sketchy. What is not sketchy is that the Black Barons won three consecutive one-run games before the series moved to Kansas City. Birmingham won in eight games (Game Five had ended in a tie) and moved on to the Negro League World Series.

Mays played in the final Negro League World Series, in 1948, when the Black Barons lost to the Homestead Grays. In Game Three of the Series, he is credited with having made two sparkling defensive plays, chasing down a Bob Thurman fly in the fourth and gunning down Buck Leonard trying to go from first to third in the sixth. A scorching hit through the box in the ninth drove in Bill Greason with the winning run for a 4-3 Birmingham victory, although it is not clear if it was a single or an error by the second baseman. Mays was credited with the RBI. Leonard, a power-hitting first baseman on that Grays squad, had this scouting report on his 17-year-old opponent: "He could run and he could throw. He wasn't hitting so good, because at that time he couldn't hit a curveball."[13]

According to the *Biographical Encyclopedia of Negro League Baseball*, Mays batted .311 in 75 games for the Black Barons in 1949, and he continued to tear the cover off the ball in 1950, starting the year batting .330 and slugging .547. With more major-league teams developing an interest in signing young Black players, Mays was obviously attracting attention.

After the 1949 season Dodgers catcher Roy Campanella led a barnstorming team in the South. In a game between the barnstormers and the Black Barons, Mays threw Larry Doby out at the plate after catching a fly ball near the center-field fence. This impressed Campy, and he begged the Dodgers to send scouts down to sign Mays. The scouting report filed by Wid Matthews echoed Buck Leonard: "The kid can't hit the curveball."[14]

In a 1954 letter to Tim Cohane, the sports editor of *Look* magazine, Giants scout Eddie Montague stated that he was scouting the Black Barons first baseman, Alonzo Perry, for the Giants' Sioux City Class-A club, when Mays caught his eye. He said, "[T]his was the greatest young player I had ever seen in my life or my scouting career."[15]

Leo Durocher wrote in his book *Nice Guys Finish Last* that Montague reported, "[T]hey got a kid playing center field practically barefooted that's the best ballplayer I ever looked at. You better send somebody down there with a barrelful of money and grab this kid."[16]

Mays concludes in his autobiography, *Say Hey*: "Montague was in our little house in Fairfield, and I signed my first professional contract. Since I was a

*Willie Mays and Mets manager Casey Stengel enjoy a laugh. Courtesy National Baseball Hall of Fame.*

minor, my father signed too. ... I got a $4,000 signing bonus and a salary of $250 a month."[17]

Instead of Sioux City, Mays was sent to Trenton of the Class-B Interstate League. Race played a role in that shift; Sioux City did not want a Black player because there was an uproar over the recent burial of a Native American in a "Whites Only" cemetery there. Even so, Mays was the first African American to play in the Interstate League.[18] He thought the level of competition in the Interstate League was far below what he had seen with the Black Barons. "No league that included Satchel Paige and Josh Gibson was a Class B league," he said.[19]

Before he could leave Birmingham, Mays gave a friend some money to take his date to the prom. That taken care of, Mays played his first game in June in Hagerstown, Maryland, one of the league cities below the Mason-Dixon Line. His manager at Trenton, Chick Genovese, started him in center field.

In a 1996 interview with a nonprofit organization that recognizes achievers, Mays recalled: "I was the first black in that particular league. And we played in a town called Hagerstown, Maryland. I'll never forget this day, on a Friday. And they call you all kind of names there, 'nigger' this, and 'nigger' that. I said to myself ... 'Hey, whatever they call you, they can't touch you. Don't talk back.'"[20]

He also recalled staying at a Blacks-only hotel across town from the team's hotel, and five of his new White teammates coming to his room to check on him: "About two o'clock in the morning, three players came through the window, and they slept on the floor. One of my right fielders, Hank Rowland, one of the catchers, Herb Perelto, and another guy, Bob Easterwood, slept on the floor until about six o'clock in the morning."[21]

Mays experienced collapses from fatigue late in the year after several consecutive doubleheaders. He played all-out, running hard on the bases and in the field, and by his own admission "expended more energy than the average player on worrying and thinking."[22] He would collapse in similar fashion several times over the course of his career, but doctors never found a medical cause for it, according to Mays.

After going hitless in his first four games in Hagerstown, Mays wound up with 108 hits in 81 games, batting .353 with 55 RBIs. Clearly, he was ready for a higher level of competition.

In 1951 Mays trained with the Giants' top minor-league club, the Minneapolis Millers of the American Association. The major-league team trained in Lakeland, Florida, and their minor-league camp was in nearby Sanford. A game was arranged between the team's two top farm clubs, Minneapolis and Ottawa, because Leo Durocher wanted to see Mays play, though the Giants' hierarchy would not bring him to the major-league camp.

In the arranged match, Mays hit a double and a long home run. Durocher began lobbying for Mays to play for the Giants immediately, but owner Horace Stoneham resisted. He said Mays was going into military service "any minute." Stoneham had his way and Mays began the season with Minneapolis as planned.

The New York Giants won two of their first three games but then lost 11 in a row, while Mays collected 12 hits in his first week with Minneapolis and played a spectacular center field. Durocher's pleading for Mays intensified. Mays, unaware of this, played still better.

In May Minneapolis was in Sioux City to play an exhibition against the Giants' farm club there. The Millers had an offday, and Mays went to a movie theater. Between features, the house lights went on and the manager announced, "If Willie Mays is here, would he please immediately report to his manager at the hotel."[23]

Manager Tommy Heath informed Mays that he had been called up to the Giants. Mays' response: "Tell Leo I'm not coming."[24] Heath called, and Durocher laid into Mays on the phone. Mays told him that he didn't feel that he could hit big-league pitching. Durocher, speechless for perhaps the first time in his life, finally broke his silence and asked Mays what he was hitting. Mays answered, ".477."

*Willie Mays liked to play stickball with the neighborhood kids during his time with the New York Giants. Courtesy National Baseball Hall of Fame.*

(He had a current 16-game hitting streak and a .799 slugging percentage, and was on a pace to score more than 150 runs and drive in 120.) Durocher asked, very quietly but with some scatological punctuation, "Do you think you can hit .250 for me?" Mays responded in the affirmative.[25] He was on the next plane to meet the team in Philadelphia. Stoneham bought an ad in the *Minneapolis Tribune* to assuage the local fans' outrage at losing their young star.

The Giants were 17-19, in fifth place, on May 25, the day Mays joined the team at Shibe Park. Durocher immediately installed the 20-year-old in center field. The Giants won all three of the games in Philadelphia, though Mays was hitless in his first 12 at-bats. Despite his batting woes, when the team returned to the Polo Grounds, Mays' first home game saw him batting third against the Boston Braves and their star southpaw Warren Spahn. In his first at-bat, he hit Spahn's offering atop the left-field roof for a home run, his first major-league hit.

After the homer, Mays went on a 0-for-13 slide, leaving him hitting .038 (1-for-26). At this point, in an often-told story, Mays sat in front of his locker, crying, after taking the collar again. Coaches Freddie Fitzsimmons and Herman Franks sent for Durocher. Mays again said he couldn't hit big-league pitching. Durocher replied, "As long as I'm the manager of the Giants, you are my center fielder. ... You are the best center fielder I've ever looked at."[26] Then he told Mays to hitch up his pants more to give himself a more favorable strike zone; he proceeded to go on a 14-for-33 tear.

For a 20-year-old from the Deep South, living in Manhattan could have been overwhelming. The Giants took good care of him, setting him up in the Harlem rooming house of David and Anna Goosby at St. Nicholas Avenue and 155th Street, not far from the Polo Grounds. Mays, still very much a big kid, ate many meals there, and Anna washed his clothes. Neighbors often waited outside for him to arrive home.

Outfielder Monte Irvin, a Negro League veteran, was assigned as the rookie's roommate and protector. Mays recalled that Irvin looked after him like a big brother. In fact, Mays recalled, "He was a guy that was sort of like my father. ... There was a park by his house there, we would go out and just talk, nothing specific, just talk, mostly about life."[27]

His stickball-playing reputation was forged in those early days. As *New York Daily News* columnist David Hinckley wrote, "If you were a 14-year-old New York kid in the summer of 1931, you couldn't just round up some of your musical pals, knock on Irving Berlin's window and have Irv come out and write a few songs with you. If you were a 14-year-old aspiring vocalist in the summer of 1941, you couldn't just grab a couple of tenors, knock on Frank Sinatra's window and have Frank come join you for a round of harmony. If you were a 14-year-old kid in the summer of 1951, you couldn't just knock on Willie Mays' window at 9 o'clock in the morning and have him come out and play an hour of stickball with you. Well, actually, you could."[28] In fact, the games were followed by a trip to the soda shop – Mays' treat. As Hinckley wrote, this was not some publicity stunt; he actually played. On August 30, 1951, Mays hit two home runs in one game against the Pirates at the Polo Grounds, and then homered in a stickball game later that day.

Mays later recalled encounters with his old stickball teammates while he was working for Bally's Casino in Atlantic City in the 1980s and '90s. Someone might say, "Do you remember me? I'm one of the kids that you bought the ice cream for on 155th St. and St. Nicholas (Avenue)." Mays said that, on such occasions, a "smile comes to my face. ... That's a very, very good thing."[29]

In addition to his stickball exploits, Mays also babysat for Durocher's 6-year-old adopted son, Chris. It was not always clear who was babysitting whom. On road trips they would eat together, play catch, go to movies, and read comic books. Police in Cincinnati once stopped them to ask what a White child was doing with a Black man. A call to Durocher cleared up the matter.

On the field, it did not take long for Mays' game to warrant superlatives. One of the many outstanding defensive plays of his rookie season came at Pittsburgh. Rocky Nelson hit a shot to deepest center field, and Mays tracked it down looking over his shoulder, but the ball hooked away from his glove. He caught the ball barehanded on the dead run. The Pirates' general manager, Branch Rickey, called it "the finest catch I have ever seen."[30]

Others would say that a double play he initiated against the Dodgers with a spectacular catch of Carl Furillo's slicing line drive and a whirling throw to nab Billy Cox at the plate, preserving a tie, was the best. Dodgers manager Chuck Dressen said, "I'd like to see him do it again."[31]

The Giants were playing better, but the Dodgers were running away with the league. On August 11 the Giants were in second place, 13 games behind the Dodgers, 8½ games further behind than when Mays joined the club. This deficit merely set the stage for the Giants' miraculous 37-7 stretch to catch the Dodgers, and Bobby Thomson's famous home run to win the best-of-three tiebreaker. Mays was kneeling in the on-deck circle when Thomson hit his homer in the bottom of the ninth in Game Three, and by his own admission, was still frozen there as Thomson rounded second. The 20-year-old was on his way to the World Series.

A few days later, Mays met his idol, Joe DiMaggio, during warm-ups as the Giants readied to face the Yankees, but the Giants were out of miracles and lost in six games. Mays batted .182 in his first World Series.

Mays had made good on his vow to hit .250, winning the NL Rookie of the Year award with 20 home runs, 68 RBIs, and a .274 batting average in 121 games. Durocher wrote, "Just to have him [Mays] on the club, you had 30 percent of the best of it before the ballgame started. In each generation, there are one or two players like that, men who are winning players because of their own ability and their own ... magnetism."[32]

On his return to the Jim Crow South after the season, the first place he visited was the Woolworth lunch counter where Aunt Ernestine worked. He ordered a glass of water while her back was turned, and when she saw who it was, she chided the Rookie of the Year, "Junior, you know colored can't sit down at the counter in here."[33]

Starting the 1952 season, Mays batted just .236 in 34 games before he was drafted into the US Army, an obligation that would keep him out of the major leagues until 1954. Red Smith chronicled Mays' last game before his military call-up, in Brooklyn's Ebbets Field: "[T]here was a fine, loud cheer for Willie. This was in Brooklyn, mind you, where 'Giant' is the dirtiest word in the language."[34] At the time of his departure, the Giants were in first place, with a 2½-game lead over the Dodgers. The Giants promptly lost eight of ten and were never a factor in the pennant race.

The Army sent Mays to Fort Eustis, Virginia, and assigned him to play baseball for the most part. According to Mays, Durocher kept an eye on him from afar, chiding him when he stole a base with his team leading and sending him money from time to time. The August 13, 1953, edition of *Jet* magazine reported that Mays broke a bone in his foot sliding into third base in an Army game and would wear a cast for five weeks.[35] Mays recalled that he also sprained his ankle in a basketball game, prompting another call from Durocher, telling him to stay off the court.

During his time in the service, his mother, Anna, died, and Mays harbored some bitterness that he wasn't allowed to resume his playing career to support all his half brothers and -sisters, since his stepfather was unemployed.

Mays estimated that he played 180 games while in the service. When he returned to the Giants in the spring of 1954, he was a half-inch taller and 10 pounds heavier, 5-feet-11 and 180 pounds. When Mays showed up at the Giants' camp in Phoenix on March 1, the consensus among New York writers seemed to be, "Here comes the pennant," despite the Dodgers' 105 wins in 1953. *Newsweek* predicted in its April 5 issue that Mays could mean the difference between "the second division and the pennant in 1954."

This optimism is remarkable; how is it possible that one player could make up the 35 games and four places in the standings that the Giants finished behind the Dodgers? His major-league résumé up to that time, in 155 games, included a .266 batting average, a .459 slugging percentage, and 24 home runs – an impressive start to a career, but nothing to make one think he could take a mediocre team past the Dodgers, a group that included Jackie Robinson, Duke Snider, and Roy Campanella. On the other hand, Mays had yet to celebrate his 23rd birthday.

Many were not impressed with Mays' numbers. In an article about Mays written after his retirement, Roger Angell of the *New Yorker* recalled a spring-training wager with Cleveland columnist Whitey Lewis, who claimed that Mays would not bat .300 for the season. Angell also quoted Indians coach Red Kress saying that "Willie was flat-out overrated." Lewis sent a check for $20 on September 1 – as Angell described it, "a lovely concession speech."[36]

In Mays' favor was this bottom-line statistic: In the 155 regular-season games for which he had been on the major-league roster (including the '51 playoff series with the Dodgers), the Giants' record was 107-48, a .690 winning percentage. Whether or not it was a coincidence, writers and teammates clearly associated Mays with winning.

Bobby Thomson, who played center field before Mays' arrival in 1951 and again while Mays was in the Army, was now expendable, and the Giants traded him to the Boston Braves for left-handed hurler Johnny Antonelli. Antonelli was just 24 and finished a solid 12-12 for Milwaukee in 1953. The Giants needed another starter, but few would have predicted that Antonelli would lead the league in ERA and win 21 games, one of the key reasons the Giants won 97 games and captured the pennant. The main reason was the center fielder, who became the player Leo Durocher confidently suggested that he would be.

Before the 1954 season, Durocher predicted a .300, 30-home-run season for Mays, and he reached the second of those milestones by midseason, playing the first half of the season on a home-run tear. With Mays batting .326 and ahead of Ruth's 60-homer pace when he hit his 36th on July 28, Durocher asked him to stop trying for the fences and go for base hits for the good of the team. Mays hit only five more homers the rest of the year, but batted .379 down the stretch.

The Giants were in fifth place in a tight race on May 22, but took over the top spot by June 15, and led by 5½ games at the All-Star break. Although the Dodgers hung tough all season, the Giants clinched the pennant in the final week and won by five games. Willie Mays was back in the World Series, this time as a certified star.

And batting champion. Going into the final day of the season, teammate Don Mueller was hitting a league-leading .3426, the Dodgers' Duke Snider .3425, and Mays .3422. Mueller finished 2-for-6, Snider 0-for-3 and Mays 3-for-4. After the games, Mays was batting .345, Mueller .342, and Snider .341. In addition to his batting title, Mays hit 41 home runs, drove in 110 runs, and led the league in triples (13) and slugging percentage (.667). To put this statistic into perspective, consider the period from 1931 through 1992, bracketed between two live-ball eras. In those 62 seasons, only two other National Leaguers bested Mays' slugging percentage: Stan Musial (.702 in 1948) and Henry Aaron (.669 in 1971). Mays also played in his first All-Star Game, and after the season, sportswriters named him the league's Most Valuable Player, at 23. He is the third youngest National Leaguer to receive the award.

But Mays' season was not over, and the legend-making was not over either.

On September 29, 1954, the Giants hosted the Indians in the first game of the World Series at the Polo Grounds, New York's Sal Maglie hooking up with Cleveland's Bob Lemon. With the score tied, 2-2, in the top of the eighth inning, the Indians put their first two runners on. Although Maglie had allowed just seven hits, Vic Wertz, the next batter, had already tripled and singled twice. Accordingly, Durocher brought in left-hander Don Liddle to face the left-handed-swinging Wertz. Wertz hit a 2-and-1 pitch, a shoulder-high fastball, to deep center field, directly over Mays' head. No matter.

*Amazingly, Willie Mays won just two MVP awards. He finished in the top six in voting 12 times. Courtesy National Baseball Hall of Fame.*

He sprinted directly away from the batter and ran it down in the deepest part of the park, catching it over his shoulder like a receiver taking a long pass from his quarterback. The film clip of this catch is one of baseball's most famous.[37]

At least as impressive as the catch was what happened next: As Arnold Hano described it in *A Day in the Bleachers*: "[He] whirled and threw like some olden statue of a Greek javelin hurler. ... What an astonishing throw. ... This was the throw of a giant, the throw of a howitzer made human." Larry Doby had tagged up and made it to third; a man of Doby's baserunning ability could have conceivably advanced two bases tagging up on a ball hit that deeply in the spacious Polo Grounds. Meanwhile, as Hano described it, the other runner, Al Rosen, "scampered back to first."[38]

Liddle, having retired Wertz, was relieved by Marv Grissom after Cleveland manager Al Lopez sent up a right-handed hitter. Later, in the clubhouse, Liddle reportedly said, "Well, I got my man."[39]

Many observers believed that play was the defining moment in the Series. The catch clearly saved the first game, as the Giants prevailed, 5-2, in the 10th inning, and may have provided the momentum they needed to sweep heavily favored Cleveland in four games. The October 14, 1954, issue of *Jet* magazine quotes New York sportswriter Dan Daniel as writing that all great catches "fade out of the book as the Mays classic moves to the top." Lopez called it "the best I ever saw."

Mays himself felt that other catches he made were better. For example, he mentions one in Ebbets Field in 1952 on a ball hit by Bobby Morgan. Mays remembered this catch in a 1996 interview:

"I made a catch in Ebbets Field, off of a guy by the name of Bobby Morgan. And it was in the seventh inning, two men on, [two out,] a ball was hit over the shortstop – over the line – over the shortstop. Now you've got to visualize this. Over the shortstop. I go and catch the ball in the air. I'm in the air like this, parallel. I catch the ball, I hit the fence. Ebbets Field was so short that if you run anywhere you're going to hit a fence. So I catch the fence, knock myself out. And the first guy that I saw – there were two guys – when I open my eyes, was Leo and Jackie. And I'm saying to myself, 'Why is Jackie out here?' Jackie came to see if I caught the ball, and Leo came to see about me. So I'm saying to myself, 'This guy is thinking very cool.' I'm talking about Jackie now. He wasn't even on the field, he was in the dugout. Now this is my thinking, he may have a different reason. That was my best catch, I think. It was off of Bobby Morgan in Ebbets Field. I caught a lot of balls barehanded, which I felt was good, but that was my best catch, I think."[40]

Mays also recalled a catch he made in Trenton in 1950. He said that Lou Heyman of Wilmington hit a ball 405 feet to dead center and he caught it barehanded, bounced off the wall, and threw the ball all the way home on the fly.

All in all, 1954 was a fine season. There were more to come.

Back home in Birmingham, Mays' Aunt Sarah died in 1954. He continued to send a good portion of his salary, soon to be $25,000, to his 10 half-siblings and to Cat and Aunt Ernestine. Whether it was from grief or the Alabama heat, Mays almost fainted at Sarah's funeral.

Between the 1954 and 1955 seasons, Mays played in the Puerto Rican League for the Santurce Crabbers, managed by Giants coach Herman Franks. He was in the same outfield as the young and relatively unknown Roberto Clemente, a daunting prospect for opposing pitchers and baserunners. Mays batted a league-leading .393 for the Crabbers, who won the Caribbean Series for Puerto Rico that year. Mays recounted that he played for the team as a favor to Franks and Giants owner Horace Stoneham, whose friend owned the team. However, Mays had grown tired after playing 250 games in 10 months and took six weeks off to rest before the Giants' spring training in 1955.

The champion Giants fell to a disappointing third place in 1955, despite Mays' 51 home runs, 127 RBIs, and .319 batting average. He was the seventh player in baseball history to hit more than 50 homers in a season, and Durocher actually had told him to start trying for the fences, contradicting the instructions of the previous year. He also led the NL in triples and slugging average and was second in stolen bases with 24 in 28 attempts, a success rate of better than 85 percent.

Leo Durocher's personality and outspokenness, tolerated in the pennant- and World Series-winning seasons, grew stale when the team finished in third place. The club announced that he would be replaced by former infielder Bill Rigney for 1956.

Durocher recalled the last game that he and Mays were on the same team. On the final day of the season, during a doubleheader against the Philadelphia Phillies in the Polo Grounds, Durocher called Mays into a small bathroom just off the dugout. Leo told him, "You are the best ballplayer I ever saw. ... I'm telling you this because I won't be back next season." Mays said, "But you won't be here to help me." Durocher said, "Willie Mays don't need help from anybody," and then kissed him on the cheek.[41]

Even at this early stage, Mays' throwing arm was recognized as the best in the game. The *New Yorker* wrote on July 10, 1954, that it took Mays three years to learn his famous basket catch, with his hands waist-high and the "gloved hand turned out." He said his Trenton manager, Genovese, first suggested it, and he perfected it while he was in the Army. Some considered it showboating, but Mays felt that it helped him keep his eye on the ball and position his feet to throw. He led the NL in outfield assists in 1955 with 23, and in double plays with 8.

Mays was widely recognized as the best all-around player in the National League during the 1950s. His defensive prowess and howitzer throwing arm were already established. After he won the batting title in 1954 and hit 51 homers in 1955, the highest total in the National League since Ralph Kiner's 54 in 1949, he led the league in steals four years in a row beginning in 1956. His 40 steals that year were the most in the majors since 1944. His four-year totals (40, 38, 31, 27) were punctuated by a 78 percent success rate.

On May 6, 1956, his 25th birthday, Mays stole four bases in a 5-4 Giants victory. The next year *New York Times* writer John Drebinger credited Mays with "returning" the stolen base to baseball and compared his baserunning derring-do to that of Ty Cobb. He wrote, "Perhaps, by reason of Willie's spark ... more players soon may be goaded into trying to bring back what was once one of baseball's most picturesque plays."[42]

The stolen base returned to prominence in no small part because of the emergence of players from the Negro Leagues, which showcased a style more suited to the Deadball Era, with much basestealing and "inside baseball." Meanwhile, the White major leagues played a more "station to station" style. During the years 1946-1960 the average team stole fewer than 40 bases per season, 75 percent less than in the Deadball Era.

Mays' impact on the game went beyond his on-field exploits. Baseball historian Jules Tygiel wrote that "Mays, with his indisputable excellence, convinced all but the most stalwart resisters to integration of the need to recruit African-Americans."[43]

In his memoir of 50-plus years in the game, Don Zimmer, a contemporary of Mays who began his career as a shortstop for the Brooklyn Dodgers (and also Mays' teammate on the Santurce team), summed up the prevailing opinion of Mays:

"In the National League in the 1950s, there were two opposing players who stood out over all the others – Stan Musial and Willie Mays. ... I've always said that Willie Mays was the best player I ever saw. ... [H]e could have been an All Star at any position."[44]

The 1956 season was marked by Mays' marriage to the former Margherite Wendell. She had been married twice before, once to a member of the singing group the Ink Spots. In 1958 Mays and Margherite adopted a five-day-old baby whom they named Michael, but the marriage would be troubled.

On the field, Mays was slightly less brilliant in 1956, with "only" 36 home runs, 84 RBIs, and a .296 batting average, for a team that dropped to sixth place. The next season he increased his average to .333, while recording 35 home runs and 97 RBIs. Besides his stolen bases, Mays became the fourth player in the twentieth century to amass 20 or more doubles, triples, and home runs in the same season. He also won the first of 12 consecutive Gold Gloves in that award's inaugural year.

During the 1957 season, the unemployed Leo Durocher publicly criticized the Giants and Rigney, while still praising his old center fielder. Mays recalled, "After the article came out, I had to apologize for Leo. I admit ... that there was a coolness between me and Rigney. We didn't give each other a chance."[45]

The Sporting News *named Willie Mays Player of the Decade for the 1960s. SABR/The Rucker Archive.*

In their final home game at the Polo Grounds, on September 29, 1957, the Giants lost to the last-place Pirates, 9-1. Mays had two of the team's six hits. After the season the Giants left New York for San Francisco while the Dodgers moved to Los Angeles, depriving New York of National League ball for the first time since 1882.

The new city did not exactly greet Mays with open arms. After Soviet leader Nikita Khrushchev was warmly received there, Frank Conniff of the Hearst newspapers commented, "San Francisco is the damnedest city I ever saw in my life. They cheer Khrushchev and boo Mays."[46]

Mays recalled that a real-estate broker withdrew his offer on a home because of pressure from other homeowners in the neighborhood. Mayor George Christopher apologized and offered to share his home with Mays and Margherite. In mid-November, they moved into the original house; almost immediately someone threw a brick through a window.

Much has been made of the city's less-than-warm reception. Charles Einstein suggested three factors: "Mays was the hated embodiment of New York. ... He had the temerity to play center field in Seals Stadium, where the native-born DiMaggio had played it in his minor-league days. Also, Mays was Black. The brick that crashed through his window almost as soon as he moved in had to reflect at least one of these viewpoints, if not all three."[47] Relations between Mays and manager Rigney continued to be strained, and Rigney did not help matters when he predicted to the San Francisco media before the 1958 season that Mays would break Babe Ruth's record of 60 home runs in a season. He didn't come close, and that, coupled with the ascendancy of rookie first baseman Orlando Cepeda, likely resulted in Cepeda's being voted the team's MVP by the fans. Here are their statistics for 1958:

Mays: 152 G, 29 HR, 96 RBI, .347 BA, 121 R
Cepeda: 148 G, 25 HR, 96 RBI, .312 BA, 88 R

Mays' explanation of Cepeda's victory in the fan vote: "The fans were disappointed that I hadn't hit 61 home runs, and Orlando was theirs from scratch."[48]

Cepeda's performance brought him the NL Rookie of the Year Award. However, Mays' numbers, by some measures, were the best in the league. He led the league in runs scored and stolen bases while winning another Gold Glove; in addition, he almost won the batting title as well. Going into the last game of the season, he was neck-and-neck with the eventual winner, Phillies Hall of Famer Richie Ashburn. Rigney batted Mays leadoff in the final game, hoping to give him more at-bats and a shot at the title. He went 3-for-5, including a double and a home run, but Ashburn finished 3-for-4 and wound up at .350.

Mays' 1958 was a streaky season; he was batting .400 by early June, followed by a .274 pace through August. A "nervous exhaustion," which troubled him occasionally throughout his career, was reappearing. He was so tired that during a road trip to Philadelphia he was admitted to a New York hospital and was told there was nothing physically wrong, but that he needed to rest.

In 1959 Mays had his first brushes with serious injury. In spring training, he cut his leg on Red Sox catcher Sammy White's shin guard, requiring 35 stitches and a two-week recuperation. With the team in first place in early August, Mays broke his right pinkie sliding back to first base after a long single. While he still hit 16 more homers the rest of the way, the Giants as a team tailed off, finishing in third place, four games behind the Los Angeles Dodgers, who went on to win the World Series. Mays hit 34 home runs and batted .313.

Chicago Cub Ernie Banks won back-to-back NL MVP awards in 1958 and 1959. Looking back, he said, "When I was in the Big Leagues, there was a tremendous amount of great ballplayers, but the guy who stood head and shoulders above them all was Willie Mays. He was so exciting – not only exciting to the fans, but to the teams he played with – the Giants – and against. He was just amazing."[49]

After struggling their final years in New York, the San Francisco Giants began to introduce a string of players who would form the core of one of the finest squads never to win a championship – the Giants of the 1960s. After Cepeda in 1958, Willie McCovey came up in 1959, winning the Giants their third Rookie of the Year award in nine years. Mays and McCovey would form as potent a left-right power duo as ever played together. They were joined by third baseman Jim Davenport, shortstop Jose Pagan, catcher Tom Haller, and second baseman Chuck Hiller, pitchers Juan Marichal and Gaylord Perry, and three outfielder brothers from the Dominican Republic, Felipe, Matty, and Jesus Alou.

The Giants sported a 902-704 record from 1960 to 1969; the most successful team of the '60s, the Baltimore Orioles, won 911 games. But San Francisco played in only one World Series, losing to the Yankees in 1962 in seven games. By way of comparison, the Los Angeles Dodgers, who finished 24½ games behind the Giants during the decade, won the World Series in 1963 and 1965 behind star pitchers Sandy Koufax and Don Drysdale, and stolen-base king Maury Wills.

The problem with recounting Mays' career is that the great statistics begin to run together. Although he won two MVP Awards, in 1954 and 1965, he could have won virtually any year in between as well, since he seemed to have the same season every year. He won a Gold Glove 12 times, though they didn't create the award until Mays' fifth season. He played in 24 All-Star Games, and these were not just token appearances – he started 18 games in center field, and 11 times played the entire game. By midcareer he was not merely a star player, but was often considered *the star*, the greatest player ever.

Felipe Alou, who played alongside Mays, played against such luminaries as Frank Robinson and Hank Aaron, and managed Barry Bonds, said, "[Mays] is number one, without a doubt. ... [A]nyone who played with him or against him would agree that he is the best."

The game that may have been Mays' greatest took place on April 30, 1961, against the Milwaukee Braves at County Stadium in Milwaukee. The night before, Mays and roommate McCovey ate a midnight snack of room-service spare ribs. Mays experienced sharp stomach pains and called for team trainer Doc Bowman. When Mays arrived at the ballpark, he took batting practice but reported feeling very weak. Using teammate Joey Amalfitano's lighter bat, he homered in his first two at-bats against Lew Burdette. After lining out against Moe Drabowsky in the fifth inning, he hit another round-tripper off lefty Seth Morehead in the sixth. Finally, in the eighth inning, he hit his fourth home run of the day, off Don McMahon. He finished 4-for-5 with 8 RBIs and missed a chance for a fifth homer when the top of the ninth ended with him on deck. After the fourth homer, McCovey quipped, "How 'bout some more ribs?"[50]

Two months later, on June 29, Mays once again showed his all-around abilities in leading the Giants to a doubleheader sweep at Philadelphia. In the first game, he hit three homers, including the game-winner in the 10th inning of the first game, becoming the fourth player with three or more home runs twice in one season. In the nightcap Mays tripled and doubled, while also gunning down a runner at the plate in one of three double plays in which he would participate in the season. Overall, just another Mays season: 40 home runs, 123 RBIs, .308 batting average, leading the league in runs scored with 129.

On January 31, 1962, Mays signed a contract for $90,000 for the coming season. Once again, 11 years after the "Shot Heard 'Round the World," the Giants and Dodgers tied for first place and, 3,000 miles west, Mays and Leo would again be involved in a "sudden death" series, this time with Durocher as the third-base coach for Los Angeles.

The pennant race turned on July 17, when the Dodgers' Sandy Koufax, 14-5 and leading the league in strikeouts and ERA, left his start with a circulatory problem in his finger – he would miss two months, and would be largely ineffective when he returned in late September. The Dodgers had a one-game lead when Koufax went down, but valiantly held on.

Mays had his own health woes. In the second inning of a September 12 game in Cincinnati, Mays, feeling hot and dizzy, fainted in the dugout. Revived by Doc Bowman, he was carried away on a stretcher and sent to a hospital. He was diagnosed with tension and exhaustion, and rest was prescribed. Manager and former teammate Alvin Dark insisted that Mays rest until he was ready to return, despite the pennant fight, and he missed three games. In his first game back, Mays hit a three-run home run in Forbes Field off the Pirates' Elroy Face.

On the last day of the season, the Giants needed to beat the expansion Houston Colt .45s and hope the Dodgers lost to the Cardinals to force a tie. Batting in the eighth inning of a 1-1 tie, Mays hit his 47th home run to secure the 2-1 victory. In Los Angeles, the Dodgers cooperated by losing 1-0 to a Curt Simmons five-hitter.

In the first game of the best-of-three tiebreaker series, Mays finished 3-for-3 with two home runs and a walk, pacing the Giants to an 8-0 victory. His 49 home runs gave him the major-league title for the first time since 1955; the two in the extra tiebreaker games allowed him to pass Harmon Killebrew, who had 48 round-trippers.

The Giants lost the second game, 8-7, leaving 13 runners on base. Durocher, coaching for the Dodgers, reportedly wore the same T-shirt he wore in 1951 on the day of Thomson's homer. Mays finished 1-for-5, but gunned down Maury Wills at third base in the sixth inning.

In the clincher the Giants trailed 4-2 when the team came to bat in the top of the ninth. The team rallied for four runs on two singles, four walks, and an error. Mays' line-drive single off pitcher Ed Roebuck's glove was right in the middle of the inning, southpaw Billy Pierce retired the Dodgers one-two-three in the ninth, with Mays catching the final out.

The Giants and Yankees met in the World Series for the seventh time, but the first since the Giants moved west. The Yankees won in seven games. Mays was left on base carrying the winning run when McCovey lined out to end the Series. Mays batted .250, scoring three runs, driving in one, and stealing one base.

After the World Series, Mays checked into Mount Zion Hospital in San Francisco to see if there was a reason for his physical collapses. Three days of tests produced no conclusive diagnosis; however, Mays undeniably had a great deal on his plate at that time. Besides the pennant race, he was in the middle of a divorce from Margherite. She had filed a separate-maintenance suit in 1961 and the couple, deep in debt, nearly filed for bankruptcy. Arnold Hano wrote a story for *Sport* in August 1963, under the headline "Willie Mays: His Loneliness and Fulfillment." The Mays he presented was not satisfied with his life and spent most of his evenings alone. He quoted Mays: "I'm lonely. I want to have a family of my own. I have a son and love him, but Michael lives with his mother in New York, and I get to see him only once or twice a year. I want a wife who will love me for myself, because I am Willie Mays, a person, not Willie Mays, a good ballplayer."[51]

On the field he was the same old Mays. In 1962 he managed 49 homers and 141 RBIs (the most in his career) and batted .304. He slugged .615 and stole 18 bases in 20 attempts. He just missed out on his second MVP Award, losing one of the Award's closest ballots, 209-202, to Maury Wills.

Before the 1963 season, Mays got a raise to $105,000 ($5,000 more than Mickey Mantle), making him the highest-paid player in baseball. His health issues did not go away, however, and the strain continued to show. On a trip to Chicago, Mays broke down crying in his hotel room and had the shakes. Doc Bowman gave him sleeping pills and Alvin Dark brought Mays to his room to sleep that night.

Despite his troubles off the field, Mays maintained a high level of play. In the July 2 game against the Braves, he homered in the 16th inning, providing the only run in a 1-0 Giants win. Juan Marichal bested Warren Spahn. Both pitchers went the distance.

In the All-Star Game, Mays went 1-for-3, drove in two runs, scored two, and stole two bases in the 5-3 NL victory. He also made a spectacular running catch in the eighth inning, depriving Joe Pepitone of an extra-base hit. These efforts earned him the game's MVP Award, established the previous year. Mays also garnered the Award in 1968, becoming the first player to win it twice.

The Giants wound up 11 games out of first in 1963, but no one could blame the center fielder: 157 G, 38 HR, 103 RBIs, .314 BA, 115 R.

Alvin Dark clearly viewed his player with great affection. Mays received a note shortly after Dark was named to manage the Giants in 1961: "Just a note to say that knowing you'll be playing for me is the greatest privilege and thrill any manager could ever hope to have."[52]

The Giants averaged 91.5 wins each year over Dark's four seasons as manager, and featured one of the most powerful offenses in NL history. However, the 1964 season would prove to be Dark's downfall and leave a blot on his reputation.

The controversy began in May when a quote from Dark appeared in a book by Jackie Robinson, *Baseball Has Done It*: "Older people in the South have taken care of the Negroes. They feel they have a responsibility to take care of them. That's my opinion of how things are."[53]

In an attempt to defend himself from media criticism, Dark expressed the view that he would play "nine colored players on the field at one time as long as they can win." However, he also expressed the view that integration was "being rushed too fast."[54]

A few days after the story broke, Dark called Mays into his office and named him the Giants' first captain since Dark himself had left the team as a player in 1956, and the first African American captain in major-league history. Mays took responsibility for mediating between Dark and many of the Giants' Latin players, particularly Cepeda. In July the racial and ethnic tensions exploded when Dark was quoted by Stan Isaacs of the newspaper *Newsday*: "We have trouble [atrocious mistakes] because we have so many Spanish-speaking and Negro players on the team. They are just not able to perform up to the white ballplayer when it comes to mental alertness."[55]

Elsewhere in the article, Dark exempted his new captain from this opinion, but every Black and Latin player met in Mays' hotel room in Pittsburgh to discuss the situation. According to an account in Charles Einstein's *Willie's Time*, Mays, ever the voice of reason, quelled a potential rebellion. He told the players that changing managers during the season had been disastrous in 1960 and it would be disastrous again. Likely working with some inside information from his friends in the Giants brain trust, including vice president Charles Feeney and coach Herman Franks, he also told the players that Dark would not be back the next season, and that, notwithstanding what the manager had said, all of them had gotten a fair shake from him. When Cepeda vowed, "I'm not going to play another game for that son of a bitch," Mays replied, "Don't let the rednecks make a hero out of him."[56] For his part, Mays did not speak to Dark for the remaining two months of the season, and beyond.[57]

In *Willie's Time*, Charles Einstein quoted Mays' real feelings about Dark from that meeting in the Pittsburgh hotel room. Mays said to his teammates:

"I know when [Dark] helped me and I know why. ... [H]e likes money. That preacher's talk that goes with it, he can shove up his ass. I'm telling you he helped me. And he's helped everybody here. I'm not playing Tom to him when I say that. He helps us because he wants to win, and he wants the money that goes with winning. Ain't nothing wrong with that."[58]

The Giants finished in fourth place, only three games back. Dark was fired on the last day of the season.

Herman Franks, a Durocher crony, was named manager for 1965, and Mays was given much latitude as a field general, almost an assistant manager. When asked why, Franks responded, "Because he knows more about those things than I do. You got any hard questions?"[59] The new manager also was a successful investor and helped Mays recover financially, steering him toward solid investments.

On the field, the Giants responded to the firing of Alvin Dark by contending for another pennant in 1965, losing to the Dodgers by just two games. Though Mays turned 34 that season, he hit a career-high 52 home runs, leading the NL in on-base percentage (for the first time) and slugging percentage. Along the way, he won his second MVP Award, 11 years after his first.

One of Mays' 52 homers was the 500th of his career, on September 13 in the Houston Astrodome, a 450-foot liner to center off Don Nottebart. He was only the fifth player to hit 500 home runs, following Babe Ruth, Jimmie Foxx, Mel Ott, and Ted Williams. No National Leaguer had hit 50 in a season since Mays in 1955.

The pennant race was marred by one of the ugliest incidents in baseball history. On August 22 the Giants' Juan Marichal had knocked down two Dodgers hitters early in the game when he came to bat to lead off the bottom of the third inning against Dodgers ace Sandy Koufax. After Dodgers catcher John Roseboro, in a bit of retaliation, whistled the ball past Marichal's ear on his return throw to Koufax, Marichal shouted at Roseboro. When the catcher started to get out of his crouch to go after him, the enraged Marichal hit Roseboro over the head with his bat. Naturally, both benches emptied. Mays ran from the dugout to Roseboro's aid and cradled Roseboro's head in his hands, with blood staining Mays' uniform and tears streaming down his face. After play resumed, the next two batters made out, two men walked, and Mays hit a three-run homer, one of his NL-record 17 round-trippers that month.

Roseboro's account of Mays' role in the incident is particularly telling. "I guess Mays was more of a ballplayer than he was a Giant," he wrote in his autobiography, *Glory Days With the Dodgers, and Other Days With Others.* "He was a sensitive guy, a good buddy, and he didn't like what his teammate had done to me. … Mays may have been shook, but he hit his fourth homer of the four game series [after the incident]. …"[60]

Marichal was suspended for eight days and fined $1,750. League President Warren Giles said Mays' conduct was "fine and decent. … This man was an example of the best in any of us."[61] On later road trips that season, Mays received rousing ovations in Pittsburgh, Chicago, Philadelphia, and, of course, New York. In Los Angeles the Giants were booed lustily, but during his first at-bat, Mays received a tremendous standing ovation, despite the rivalry and the pennant race.

Initially, the Giants went into a tailspin, going 4-8 in the first 12 games after the incident. Then they won 14 games in a row, and by September 16 they were in first place, 4½ games ahead of Los Angeles. But the Dodgers won 13 straight in late September to take the pennant by two games. Marichal, the Giants' best pitcher, finished the year with a 22-13 record, but likely missed two starts because of his suspension.

Mays' MVP seasons in 1954 and 1965 form excellent bookends for the story of his career. He was

*Speed was another one of Willie Mays' five tools. Here, he slides safely home. SABR/The Rucker Archive.*

a perennial MVP contender, and many of those 12 seasons are indistinguishable from one another. The 1954 season was his first full year with the Giants, his first and only world championship and batting title, but his first of 13 consecutive seasons of 150 or more games, his first of 12 consecutive seasons of 100 or more runs scored, the first of five consecutive years of 400 or more outfield putouts, and the first of 20 consecutive years making the National League All-Star team. In addition, Mays led the league in slugging for the first of five times in his career. He led the league in on-base percentage for the first time in his career in 1965 (he would lead in that category once more), but the home-run and slugging titles in 1965 would be his last.

The All-Star Game was considered Mays' greatest stage. He played in 24 midsummer classics, tied for the most of any major leaguer. (Two All-Star Games were played each year from 1959 through 1962 to fatten the players' pension fund. Both Hank Aaron and Stan Musial also played in 24 All-Star Games.) Mays led the NL to a 17-6-1 record in his All-Star Game career, batting .307 in those contests, with 23 hits in 75 at-bats, 2 doubles, 3 triples, 3 home runs, and 20 runs scored. It is interesting to contrast these numbers with his postseason stats: In 25 career postseason games, he hit one homer, drove in 10 runs, and batted .247.

Mays enjoyed his last great season in 1966. He turned 35 that year and played in 152 games, hit 37 homers, drove in 103 runs, and scored 99, levels he would never reach again. He batted .288 (he would never top .300 the rest of his career) and captured his 10th straight Gold Glove, one for every season the award had existed. His 103 RBIs marked his eighth consecutive season with 100 or more, at the time an NL record, although he never led the league in that category. In each of 12 seasons, 1954-1965, he had led the league in at least one major offensive category. For the rest of his career Mays topped the leader board only in walks and on-base percentage in 1971.

Mays continued his assault on the career home-run record, passing Ted Williams (521) in June 1966 and Jimmie Foxx (534) in August. The day after tying Foxx, Mays hit number 535 off the Cardinals' Ray Washburn, putting him in second place on the all-time list, 179 behind Babe Ruth. Mays recalled, "Until I actually got that 'close' at 535, I don't think I gauged how monumental his record was."[62]

The Giants remained in the race until the last day of the season. Along with his other accomplishments, Mays may have helped to prevent a large-scale race riot. Rumors swirled about a potential riot in the predominantly black Hunter's Point section of San Francisco, and in an attempt to give the people something indoors to do, a game previously not on the TV schedule was added. Mays encouraged fans via radio ads to stay home and watch an important televised game from Atlanta. In *Willie's Time*, Charles Einstein wrote, "Mayor John Shelley told Horace Stoneham afterward that nothing else could have prevented all-out rioting and looting.... The TV did it."[63]

The aging center fielder battled flu-like symptoms for much of 1967. In July he was hospitalized again for five days after leaving a game with fever and the shakes. He said he never felt strong the rest of the year. In an August contest, the Braves intentionally walked Jim Ray Hart to pitch to Mays. He hit a run-scoring single. At age 36, he finished with a .263 batting average and 22 home runs. Both figures were his lowest in any full season to that point.

In 1968, the "Year of the Pitcher," the NL won the All-Star Game, 1-0, with its 37-year-old leadoff batter scoring the only run, in the first inning. Mays was starting only because of an injury to Pete Rose. He singled, moved to second on an errant pickoff throw, got to third on a wild pitch, and scored on a double play. It was his last hit in All-Star competition, though he would bat at least once in every midsummer classic until his retirement. As mentioned previously, Mays received his second All-Star Game MVP Award for his efforts, a throwback to the "inside baseball" of his Negro League days.

Mays continued to approach milestones. He ended the 1968 season one steal shy of 300, 13 homers shy of 600, and 188 hits shy of 3,000. His numbers: 148 G, 23 HRs, 79 RBIs, .289 BA, 84 R.

The 1969 season was frustrating for Mays; the Giants finished in second place for the fifth straight year, this time three games behind Atlanta. Manager Clyde King briefly experimented with Mays in the leadoff spot, a position foreign to him, as he had batted third almost exclusively for much of his career. He accepted this move as a team player would, but not before protesting to King that, at age 38, the duties of a leadoff hitter would have him, in his own words, "too tired" before the season was half over. He had other run-ins with King and, coupled with a knee injury, it made for an unhappy year. The Giants' brass might have agreed with Mays; King was fired after 42 games the next season.

The highlight of Mays' 1969 season may have come on September 22, when he became the second man to hit 600 career home runs, reaching the milestone and delivering the game-winning RBI in a pinch-hitting appearance against San Diego's Mike Corkins. He also surpassed 300 stolen bases for his career.

Prior to the 1970 season, *The Sporting News* named Mays Player of the Decade for the 1960s. He started strong, hitting 19 home runs by the All-Star break. On July 18 Mays singled off Montreal pitcher Mike Wegener for his 3,000th career hit. Play was halted for a ceremony, attended by Monte Irvin, Carl Hubbell, and Stan Musial, the NL career hits leader at the time. All fans were given a free ticket to another game that season, and the Giants presented Mays' son, Michael, with a four-year college scholarship. Mays finished with 28 home runs and a .291 average, his best numbers since 1966. The team finished 16 games behind, in third place.

In 1971 Mays experienced a renaissance both professionally and personally. Manager Charlie Fox used him as an additional coach to instruct the outfielders. Fox said, "Willie Mays is the greatest player I saw or heard of."[64]

Mays hit his 629th career homer on the first pitch he saw on Opening Day. He hit home runs in the first four games of the season, the first time any player had done that. He had a .336 average at the end of May and 14 home runs by the All-Star break, and the Giants were in first place in the NL West for good by the end of April.

On May 6, his 40th birthday, Mays was honored at a banquet attended by such luminaries as Hank Aaron and Joe DiMaggio. Aaron once said that Mays was a greater ballplayer than he, although he saw himself as the stronger hitter. DiMaggio once told a young ballplayer to strive for perfection on the baseball field, and that, while that is impossible, Willie Mays came the closest. Commissioner Bowie Kuhn read a telegram from President Nixon that included a line that Mays was "proof that people over the age of 30 could be trusted."[65]

By this time Mays was reaching or eclipsing some milestone once a week. In the opener of a May 30 twin bill, he hit his 638th career homer in a 5-4 defeat of the Expos. The next day, he scored his 1,950th run in a 2-1 victory over the Mets, passing Stan Musial as the all-time leading run scorer in National League history. On June 6 he hit his 22nd career extra-inning homer to lead the Giants to a 4-3 win over Philadelphia, earning the Giants a doubleheader split.

Helping the team any way he could, Mays worked the count more, leading the league in both walks and on-base percentage (.425). He played 84 games in center field and 48 at first base, to rest his legs. After he made several outstanding plays at first base in a game against the New York Mets, their manager, Gil Hodges, said, "I can't very well tell my players not to hit it to him. Wherever they hit it, he's there anyway."[66]

The Giants outlasted the Dodgers to win the Western Division by one game, but lost to the Pirates in the National League Championship Series. Mays hit his only postseason home run, a two-run blast off Bob Miller, in Game Two.

After the season Mays married Mae Louise Allen in Acapulco, after 10 years of off-and-on dating.

He originally got her phone number from Wilt Chamberlain.

The 1972 season began later than scheduled because of a player strike. While reticent in the past on commenting about controversial issues, he said this to the executive board of the union:

> I know it's hard being away from the game and our paychecks and our normal life. I love this game. It's been my whole life. But we made a decision … to stick together and until we're satisfied, we have to stay together. … [If] I have played my last game, it will be painful. But if we don't hang together, everything we've worked for will be lost.[67]

*Willie Mays retired with 3,283 hits and 660 home runs. Arguably the greatest player ever, he was awarded the Presidential Medal of Freedom in 2015. Courtesy National Baseball Hall of Fame.*

By now, Mays' salary was $160,000 a year, but he wanted a long-term contract from the Giants that would carry beyond his playing career. None was offered, and rumors began to surface that he would be traded. When the Giants reached Philadelphia in May 1972, New York sportswriter Red Foley informed him he would be traded to the Mets, though it took a few days to formalize the details. Mays would finish his career where he had started. He said, "When you come back to New York, you come back to paradise."[68] He was batting .184 after 19 games when he was traded to the Mets for minor-league pitcher Charlie Williams and $50,000. Horace Stoneham denied that any cash was included in the deal and maintained that he was giving Mays a financial future that the Giants, one of only a handful of family-owned teams left in the majors, could not. Upon joining the Mets, Mays immediately received a contract that would pay him $175,000 per year for the rest of his career and, after he retired, $50,000 a year to coach for the club.

Several days after the trade, the Giants retired Mays' uniform number 24.

Mays' first game for the Mets was against the Giants, on May 14, 1972, Mother's Day, at Shea Stadium. In the fifth inning he homered to break a 4-4 tie, and the Mets won, 5-4. Having the all-time great on the roster did not make manager Yogi Berra's job any easier. The fans wanted to see Mays, but the manager, of course, had to put the best lineup on the field. As a part-time player, Mays was third on the club in batting average and second in slugging, despite having the worst numbers of his career to this point: 88 G, 8 HRs, 22 RBIs .250 BA, and 35 R. All eight of his round-trippers were with the Mets, and he played 11 of his 69 games as a Met in 1972 at first base.

In preparing for spring training of 1973, Mays had old friend Herman Franks to watch him to see if anything was left in the tank. Franks told him he had one season left. When he had second thoughts about retirement in August, he consulted Franks, who told him to stick by his original decision.

He struggled at the start, hitting .118 in April, and did not drag his average over .200 until July 8. He informed the Mets he would retire at the end of the season, and that the club could announce it in September. He had knee problems that required draining fluid, and favoring one leg caused problems with the other. He also had cracked ribs.

The team wasn't doing much better, settling in last place all of July and August. They finally escaped the cellar on August 31 but finished 20-8 after that and captured an extremely compressed division.

On September 25 the club had a Willie Mays Night. He resisted the honor initially for fear it would distract the team in the middle of a pennant race. After a one-hour ceremony, many gifts, and an outpouring of affection from the fans at Shea, Mays made his farewell speech:

"I hope that with my farewell tonight, you'll understand what I'm going through right now. Something that I never feared: that I were ever to quit baseball. But, as you know, there always comes a time for someone to get out. And I look at these kids over there, the way they are playing, and the way they are fighting for themselves, and it tells me one thing: Willie, say goodbye to America. Thank you very much."[69]

In the League Championship Series, he made his first appearance on the field as a peacemaker, not a player. In Game Three, Reds left fielder Pete Rose's takeout slide into Mets shortstop Bud Harrelson ignited a brawl. Shea Stadium fans began heckling Rose in left field, and when a bottle flew from the stands toward him, Reds manager Sparky Anderson pulled his team off the field. The umpires threatened the Mets with a forfeit, so Mays, Berra, and Tom Seaver, among others, walked out to left and pleaded with the fans to let the game go on. The crowd settled down, and the Mets won, 9-2. Mays played only in the fifth and deciding game, but he made the most of the opportunity. He delivered a pinch-hit Baltimore chop single with the bases loaded in the home fifth, and later scored an insurance run in the Mets' 7-2 victory.

The story of Mays misplaying two balls in center field in the second game of the World Series against the Oakland A's is always used when the topic is a star athlete who plays too long past his prime. Exhibit B might be Mays' ultimately harmless stumble on the basepaths in the same game. What is often forgotten is what happened in the 12th inning, when he duped A's catcher Ray Fosse into calling for a fastball, telling him, "Ray, it's tough to see the balls with that background. I hope he doesn't throw me any fastballs."[70] He bounced a Rollie Fingers fastball over the pitcher's head and into center to drive in the winning run.

Mays' last career hit in his next-to-last career at-bat provided the game-winning RBI in a World Series game. In the clubhouse watching the game on TV when Mays came to the plate, Mets pitcher and former Giants teammate Ray Sadecki said, "He has to get a hit. This game was invented for Willie Mays a hundred years ago."[71]

The Mets lost the Series in seven games. Many of his teammates lauded his impact. Tug McGraw: "I guess I learned as much from Willie Mays as anybody." Jerry Koosman: "He was still our best player. I begged him not to retire." Tom Seaver: "Many of the New York writers made him out as a load we had to carry, but, quite the contrary, he helped us *carry* the load we had all the way down through the season, especially the last month and a half, when we got hot and put it all together."[72]

Mays' post-career years were much less publicly eventful, of course. After retiring as an active player, Mays was a "goodwill" coach for the Mets, working with the young players, visiting farm teams, and appearing at booster-club dinners. He also did public-relations work for the Colgate-Palmolive company for 12 years.

In 1979 the Baseball Writers Association of America elected Mays to the National Baseball Hall of Fame in his first year of eligibility. At his induction ceremony, he was eloquent and humble:

"What can I say? This country is made up of a great many things. You can grow up to be what you want. I chose baseball, and I loved every minute of it. I give you one word –love. It means dedication. You have to sacrifice many things to play baseball. I sacrificed a bad marriage and I sacrificed a good marriage. But I'm here today because baseball is my number one love."[73]

That fall he accepted a 10-year deal to do public-relations work for Bally's Casino in Atlantic City, to greet people and play golf, things he had done at the Dunes Hotel in Las Vegas for years. According to Mays, his agreement prohibited him from gambling within 100 miles of Bally's. Nevertheless, Commissioner Bowie Kuhn prohibited Mays and Yankees great Mickey Mantle, who had a similar job, from holding salaried positions with major-league clubs. While a number of owners, including the Yankees' George Steinbrenner and the Pirates' John Galbreath, had connections with horse racing, and despite the fact that Atlantic City did not (and does not) allow sports wagering, Kuhn forced two of the greatest names in baseball history to sever their ties with the game.

In 1981 *New York Daily News* writer Bill Madden interviewed Mays to mark his 50th birthday. Although saddened at his banishment, he was tending to his various business affairs, charitable efforts, and the Bally's job. Madden wrote: "And there was something about Willie Mays gave the fans more satisfaction than probably any other player of his time. Charisma is the way some other people would explain it. Mays has his own explanation as to why he is so beloved. "It's because I love people," he said. "You can't fool people. ... I loved what I was doing. ..."[74]

In March 1985, shortly after being named commissioner, Peter Ueberroth reinstated Mantle and Mays, saying, "They are two of the most beloved and admired athletes in the country today, and they belong in baseball."[75]

Giants general manager Al Rosen put Mays back in uniform as a spring-training instructor the next year. An All-Star third baseman for Cleveland in the 1950s, Rosen said, "From everything I ever witnessed, Mays was the finest player I ever saw. ... His presence is electric. ... [P]laying against him, you had the feeling you were playing against someone who was going to be the greatest of all time."[76]

At a ceremony in 1986 honoring McCovey, Mays received a five-minute standing ovation from the Candlestick faithful. In his remarks to the crowd on his special day, McCovey paid homage to his longtime teammate, "Willie Mays, it was an honor to wear the same uniform you wore."[77]

The 1990s saw Mays lose three men who were great influences in his life. In 1991 Leo Durocher died, and in 1997 Piper Davis died. Both were father figures to him. Then Mays' natural father, Cat, died in 1999 at age 88. Willie had set Cat up in an apartment in Harlem in 1954 and moved him out to Oakland in 1958. However, it seemed that the greatest tragedy for Mays was Mae's diagnosis of Alzheimer's disease before she even turned 60.

In 2006, Willie Mays remained a part-time consultant for the Giants. A surrogate father to Barry Bonds, his godson, he gave his blessing when Bonds passed him for third place on the all-time home-run list in 2004.

And the accolades kept coming. *Washington Post* writer Dave Sheinin, in a column about Mays' 90th birthday, wrote, "There can never be another like Mays, if only because the elements for his creation no longer exist. Baseball no longer holds the imagination of the country the way it did in the 1950s and '60s. ..."[78] Despite their political differences, Presidents Bill Clinton, George Bush, and Barack Obama, baby boomers all, idolized him and desired contact with him. Clinton, a frequent golf partner of the Say Hey Kid, said, "When you see [Willie Mays] do something you admire, the image of that makes a mockery of all forms of bigotry."[79] Bush, who named Mays the commissioner of the White House T-ball league, said, "When I was growing up, I wanted to be the Willie Mays of my generation."[80] When President Obama was elected as the first African American in the job, Mays sent him a note: "Dear Mr. President, Move on in. Your Friend, Willie Mays." Mays subsequently joined the president on Air Force One traveling to the 2009 All-Star Game.

When Peter Magowan, a Giants fan from the Polo Grounds days, purchased the team in 1993, one of his first acts was to give Mays a lifetime contract to be a part of the Giants organization. On the occasion of Mays' 80th birthday in 2011, Daniel Brown of the *San Jose Mercury News* wrote, "Magowan was surprised a few years ago when Mays approached him about a contract extension. 'Willie, it's a lifetime contract. You know what that means, right?' Magowan said. 'I know what it means. I still want an extension,' Mays replied."[81]

Mays had requested the extra year to ensure that Mae would be cared for once he was gone. On April 19, 2013, Mae died of complications from her Alzheimer's disease.[82]

In 2015 President Obama awarded him the Presidential Medal of Freedom,[83] and on August 27, 2022, the New York Mets retired Mays' uniform number 24. While not present at the Mets Old Timers Day ceremony in which the number retirement served as a surprise, Mays sent a statement that was read by the master of ceremonies, Mets announcer Howie Rose, which said in part, "you might lose a lot of details after so many years, but what I can never forget is the way it felt to be back in New York City playing for the fans. Mets fans always gave me the biggest ovations and the loudest "thank yous" ever. Today I return those thank yous from the bottom of my heart. Thank you, Mets!"[84]

When *The Sporting News* polled fans to name the All-Century team for the twentieth century, Mays placed second to Babe Ruth. He wrote the foreword for the book honoring the team: "It's a great honor to be named the No. 2 player in baseball history. … I have the satisfaction of knowing that when they call my name, everybody knows me. If you'd asked me when I was 15 in Birmingham if all this could happen, there's no way I would have said yes."[85]

## SOURCES


In addition to the sources cited in the Notes, the author consulted the following:

Honig, Donald. *The All Star Game* (St. Louis: The Sporting News Publishing Company, 1987).

Klima, John. *Willie's Boys: The 1948 Birmingham Black Barons, the Last Negro League World Series, and the Making of a Baseball Legend* (New York: John Wiley and Sons, Inc., 2009).

Museum of Living History, Academy of Achievement Interview with Willie Mays, February 19, 1996 (achievement.org).

*The Sporting News Selects Baseball's Greatest Players: A Celebration of the 20th Century's Best* (St. Louis: The Sporting News Publishing Company, 1998.)
blog.sfgate.com/giants/2013/04/19/willie-mays-wife-mae-dies-at-74/ (accessed January 6, 2013).

TV show, *The Sporting News 100,* interviewed by Bob Costas.

Lee, Anthony, Seton Hall University librarian (personal communication).


## NOTES

1 Leo Durocher, *Nice Guys Finish Last* (New York: Pocket Books, 1975), 385.

2 Mike Lupica, "A Baseball Giant," *New York Daily News,* May 8, 2011.

3 James S. Hirsch, *Willie Mays: The Life, the Legend* (New York: Simon & Schuster, 2010), 257.

4 Hirsch, 35.

5 Charles Einstein, *Willie's Time: A Memoir* (Carbondale: Southern Illinois University Press, 2004), 348.

6 Willie Mays with Lou Sahadi, *Say Hey: The Autobiography of Willie Mays* (New York: Simon & Schuster, 1988), 19.

7 Hirsch, 24.

8 https://www.baseball-almanac.com/players/player.php?p=robinja02 (accessed November 28, 2022).

9 Hirsch, 47.

10 Hirsch, 31.

11 https://www.seamheads.com/NegroLgs/player.php?playerID=mays-01wil (accessed November 28, 2022).

12 Mays, *Say Hey,* 31-32.

13 Mays, *Say Hey,* 43.

14 Bobby Thomson with Lee Heiman and Dan Gutman, *"The Giants Win the Pennant! The Giants Win the Pennant!"* (New York: Kensington Publishing Co., 1991), 107.

15 Willie Mays, as told to Charles Einstein, *My Life in and Out of Baseball* (New York: E.P. Dutton & Co., Inc, 1966), 29.

16 Durocher, 271.
17 Mays, *Say Hey*, 45.
18 Dateline-Hagerstown. *Trentonian* (Trenton, New Jersey), June 24, 1950.
19 Mays, *My Life in and Out of Baseball*, 32.
20 https://achievement.org/achiever/willie-mays/.
21 https://achievement.org/achiever/willie-mays/.
22 Mays, *Say Hey*, 52.
23 Hirsch, 77.
24 Mays, *My Life in and Out of Baseball*, 85.
25 Hirsch, 78.
26 Durocher, 273.
27 "Willie Mays remembers Mentor Monte Irvin," NPR.org, January 13, 2016. https://www.npr.org/sections/thetwo-way/2016/01/13/462945783/willie-mays-remembers-mentor-monte-irvin (accessed November 29, 2022).
28 David Hinckley, "Four-Sewer Man: Willie From The Block," *New York Daily News*, October 1, 2003.
29 John Benson and Tony Blengino, *Baseball's Top 100: The Best Individual Seasons of All Time* (Wilton, Connecticut: Diamond Library, 1997).
30 Mays, *Say Hey*, 83.
31 Hirsch, 125.
32 Durocher, 271.
33 Einstein, 65.
34 Red Smith, "A Chapter Closes," *New York Herald Tribune*, May 29, 1952: 21.
35 "Willie Mays Breaks Foot in Army Game," *Jet*, August 13, 1953.
36 Roger Kahn, *The Era: 1947-1957, When the Yankees, the Giants and the Dodgers Ruled the World* (New York: Ticknor and Fields, 1993), 320.
37 https://youtu.be/1vrsg_-dV7Q (accessed November 11, 2022).
38 Einstein, 107.
39 Hirsch, 196.
40 https://achievement.org/achiever/willie-mays/.
41 Gerald Eskenazi, *The Lip: A Biography of Leo Durocher* (New York: William Morrow and Company Inc., 1993), 283.
42 John Drebinger, "Stolen base Is Returned to Baseball by Willie the Wonder," *New York Times*, May 24, 1957: 37.
43 Robert Elias, ed., *Baseball and the American Dream: Race, Class, Gender and the National Pastime* (Armonk, New York: M.E. Sharpe, 2001), 183.
44 Don Zimmer with Bill Madden, *The Zen of Zim* (New York: T. Dunne Books, 2004), 162.
45 Mays, *Say Hey*, 142.
46 Einstein, 111.
47 Einstein, 111.
48 Mays, *Say Hey*, 151.
49 Art Rust, *Get That Nigger Off the Field: An Oral History of Black Ballplayers From the Negro Leagues to the Present* (Los Angeles: Shadow Lawn Press, 1992), 124.
50 Mays, *Say Hey*, 168.
51 Arnold Hano, "Willie Mays: His Loneliness and Fulfillment," *Sport*, August 1963.
52 Mays, *My Life in and Out of Baseball*, 204.
53 Jackie Robinson, *Baseball Has Done It* (Brooklyn, New York: Ig Publishing, 2005), 117.
54 Mays, *Say Hey*, 209.
55 Mays, *Say Hey*, 215.
56 Mays, *Say Hey*, 210.
57 Hirsch, 421.
58 Einstein, 210-11.
59 Einstein, 316.
60 John Roseboro, *Glory Days With the Dodgers and Other Days With Others* (New York: Atheneum Publishing, 1978), 8.
61 Einstein, 244.
62 Mays, *Say Hey*, 232.
63 Einstein, 253-54.
64 Einstein, 320.
65 Einstein, 321-22.
66 https://www.allgreatquotes.com/quote-173262/.
67 Geoffrey C. Ward and Ken Burns, *Baseball: An Illustrated History* (New York: Alfred A. Knopf, 1994), 426.
68 Mays, *Say Hey*, 253.
69 Peter Golenbock, *Amazin': The Miraculous History of Baseball's Most Beloved Team* (New York: St. Martin's Griffin, 2003), 309.
70 Mays, *Say Hey*, 257.
71 Hirsch, 529.
72 Golenbock, 308.
73 Hirsch, 535-36.
74 Bill Madden, "Happy 50 Willie Mays," *New York Daily News*, May 7, 1981.
75 Ron Fimrite, "Mantle and Mays," *Sports Illustrated*, March 25, 1985.
76 Mays, *Say Hey*, 274.
77 Gerald Astor, *The Baseball Hall of Fame 50th Anniversary Book* (New York: Prentice Hall, 1988), 272
78 Dave Sheinin, "Willie Mays Broke Barriers His Own Way," *Washington Post*, August 17, 2021. https://www.washingtonpost.com/sports/2021/08/17/willie-mays-baseball/ (accessed November 26, 2022).
79 Hirsch, 233.
80 George W. Bush, speech, July 30, 2006.

81 Daniel Brown, "Happy Birthday, Willie Mays," *San Jose Mercury News,* May 5, 2011.

82 https://blogs.mercurynews.com/giants/2013/04/19/pregame-notes-giants-announce-death-of-willie-mays-wife-of-41-years/(accessed 11/28/22).

83 https://obamawhitehouse.archives.gov/the-press-office/2015/11/16/president-obama-names-recipients-presidential-medal-freedom (accessed November 11, 2022).

84 Anthony DiComo, "Mets retire Willie Mays' No. 24 during Old Timers' Day," MLB.com, August 27, 2022. https://www.mlb.com/news/mets-retire-willie-mays-no-24 (accessed November 11, 2022).

85 *The Sporting News Selects Baseball's Greatest Players: A Celebration of the 20th Century's Best,* (St. Louis: The Sporting News Publishing Company, 1988).

# THE EMBODIMENT OF THE NEGRO LEAGUES

BY JAKE BELL

*"These men couldn't do what I did because they didn't have the chance. But they dreamed the dreams I did when they were 15, too. And they taught me and they gave me the combat training so that I could do it."*

– Willie Mays on the Birmingham Black Barons.[1]

PERFORMANCE CAN MEAN two things. Typically, when a baseball player is recognized for on-field performance, it's about success, execution, achievements, and excellence. But performance can also refer to spectacle, exhibition, presentation, putting on a show. Regardless of which definition one chooses, Willie Mays was one of baseball's greatest on-field performers.

At a time when major-league outfielders were taught to field groundballs on one knee, Mays charged them as if he was playing shortstop. He wore caps a size too big for his head so they would fly off when he ran the bases or chased down a fly ball, creating the illusion that he was moving faster. Every kid is taught the proper way to field a fly ball, but Mays was just as likely to catch the ball at his waist, over his shoulder, or barehanded. He made hard plays look easy, but also made easy plays look hard to keep fans in the stands on the edges of their seats, and he learned it all years before he ever stepped on a major-league diamond. "In the Negro Leagues, we were all entertainers," Mays reminisced. "And my job was to give the fans something to talk about each game."[2]

Mays was a multisport star in high school. In the fall, he was the starting quarterback for the Baby Hornets of Fairfield Industrial High School, a team that scrimmaged against college players. As a freshman, he made the team as a halfback, capable of breaking tackles and outrunning anyone on the field. The coach moved him under center because of his powerful arm and long fingers that let him effortlessly hurl accurate passes "sixty, seventy, eighty yards on a line," according to a childhood friend's recollection.[3]

In the winter he took his dominant athleticism to the basketball court, where he played with a quickness that few defenders could counter and a skyhook similar to the signature move that would take Kareem Abdul-Jabbar to the Basketball Hall of Fame decades later. Mays earned the top spot on the *Birmingham World* newspaper's all-county basketball team after winning the Jefferson County scoring title by averaging just over 20 points per game and leading his team to a state championship.[4]

But even though it was only his third-best sport, it was understood that Willie's future was in baseball. The Negro Leagues provided opportunity for Black athletes that neither football nor basketball could. With the exception of the Harlem Globetrotters, professional teams in both sports featured all-White rosters.[5] "There were no blacks in the majors, but guys were making money in Negro Leagues," Mays said. But then his outlook and his prospects changed. "It became real. I was in high school, about 15, when Jackie [Robinson] played his first year in Montreal."[6]

The only other job the teenage Mays pursued was washing dishes. He was hired by a cafeteria but walked away after only a few hours. He went home and told his father, William Howard Mays Sr., that baseball was his only career plan. The elder Mays, a mill worker whose quickness and reflexes playing outfield in the semipro Industrial League had earned him the nickname Cat, accepted his son's decision. "You play baseball," he agreed, "and I'll make sure you eat."[7]

Fairfield Industrial High didn't have a baseball team, so instead boys played on community teams. As a 10-year-old, Willie held his own on teams with 15-year-olds. As a seventh-grader, he joined Industrial League games when a team was missing players or the score was lopsided enough that neither team cared if a teen patrolled left field alongside Cat and other grown men. So, against other high-schoolers his own age, Mays was a force of nature.

Initially, Cat Mays had plans for his son to be a shortstop in the mold of Willie Wells. The legendary middle infielder was considered one of the greatest defensive shortstops ever but also won three home-run titles and led the Negro National League in all Triple Crown categories in 1930. That plan didn't work out, however, because the boy's arm was too strong. William "Cap" Brown, a first baseman for the Fairfield Gray Sox, a local sandlot team that showcased players who might one day play in the Industrial League, remembered, "He used to throw the ball down to me so hard it made my hand numb. I said, 'We've got to put this joker in the outfield.'"[8]

It's easy to understand how a coach would see the pitching mound as the best outlet to harness the teenager's rocket-like throwing ability – and, in fact, several major-league scouts would feel the same in the years to come – but it was the last place Cat wanted his son to be. "He didn't want me pitching or catching," Mays explained. "He always tried to make sure I didn't get hurt, and he wanted me to play every day. You can't play every day if you pitch or catch."[9]

The elder Mays also understood that a pitcher was vulnerable to the whims of his coach. An arm injury could end a pitcher's career in the blink of an eye, and Cat didn't trust high-school coaches, community volunteers, or sandlot managers to prioritize his son's longevity above their own short-term success. Most of the kids on those teams were destined to a life of backbreaking labor in steel mills or coal mines, so what difference would it make if a teenager tore some ligaments in his shoulder throwing too many pitches on the way to winning a regional championship?

Cat Mays understood that young Black men were disposable in America. After a game for the Fairfield Gray Sox, a local sandlot team meant to showcase players who might one day play in the Industrial League, Cat saw his concern justified. Manager Cle Holmes put Willie on the mound, where he pitched nine innings and hit the game-winning home run, only to collapse from exhaustion after crossing the plate. Cat laid out an ultimatum: If you want Willie Mays on your team, keep him off the mound. Holmes put the teen in center field, where his legend grew beyond Jefferson County, even to other states.

In Tennessee, the lore of Willie Mays reached the ear of Beck Shepherd, owner of the Chattanooga Choo Choos of the Negro Southern League. The team served as a minor-league feeder for the Birmingham Black Barons. Shepherd offered a contract for the 1948 season, but Willie couldn't join the team until he finished the school year. Cat drove his son to Chattanooga and dropped him off to join the team for the summer. Willie was initially penciled in at shortstop until he fielded a grounder in the hole and his throw took off the first baseman's glove. He was moved to center field.

When the Birmingham Black Barons visited Chattanooga for a game against the Black Lookouts, Mays spoke with manager Lorenzo "Piper" Davis in a hotel lobby. The veteran infielder had heard rumors of the teenage phenom but had more insight into the boy, having played with and against Cat Mays since the two were in high school. He warned Willie about losing his eligibility to play high-school sports if he was caught playing baseball for money, but the teenager didn't care. Understanding that the phenom had chosen his career path, Davis told Mays to have his father contact him if he was serious about playing ball for money.

In a June doubleheader in Memphis, Mays got attention after going a combined 5-for-7 with a home run as the Choo Choos swept the hometown Blue Sox.[10] The same article that praised Mays indicated that Chattanooga would be playing in several Midwest cities in the coming week, such as "Ipsilanti [*sic*], Detroit, Dayton, South Bend, and Grand Rapids." Bad weather on that trip forced several games to be canceled, which meant players, who were earning a percentage of the gate, didn't get paid. Mays would later recall eating "stale bread and sardines ... in Dayton, Ohio, at the time – I said to myself, if this ever gets over, I'm quitting."[11] When the team returned to Tennessee, Willie asked for bus fare home and never returned, ending his tenure as a Choo Choo after roughly a month.

Birmingham needed a fourth outfielder, and shortly after Mays returned from Chattanooga, Cat took his son to Rickwood Field for a tryout. Davis sent Willie out to shag fly balls. "I heard he had a good arm," Davis recounted. "Then I saw him throw."[12] Any questions Davis had about whether Mays belonged on the team vanished.

Officially, Mays made his first start in the second game of a Fourth of July doubleheader against the Memphis Red Sox. According to legend, after his impressive tryout, Mays sat on the bench with orders from Davis to "watch. Watch what's going on." After a Black Barons win in the first game, Davis wrote "MAYS, LF" batting seventh in his lineup card for the second half. When some players complained, Davis gave them the option of "take off the uniform if you want to."[13] After the game, Mays was offered a contract.

Unofficially, it's likely that he took part in some exhibition games played away from Birmingham prior to that doubleheader, using a fake name to preserve his eligibility to play high-school sports. The start shouldn't have surprised anyone and if it was a secret that Mays was on the team, it was a poorly kept one considering that the morning of the game, the *Birmingham News* reported:

> Willie Mays can pound the ball. ... Outfielder Mays, a youngster who joined the club recently, shows promise of being a topnotch player, too. He can field with the best of them and packs plenty of dynamite for a man of his size.[14]

Some players took issue with Mays getting a start, primarily Jimmy Zapp, the regular left fielder. The doubleheader marked the end of the first half of the season, and Birmingham had clinched a playoff spot by finishing with the best record in the Negro

American League. While the players saw the potential in Mays to be a superstar of tomorrow, he couldn't hit a breaking pitch today. A playoff team needed production, not potential.

Mays signed a contract that paid him $250 per month, plus a $50 bonus for every month that he batted over .300.[15] He wouldn't earn the bonus during his first season, but Mays managed to win over his teammates with his infectious energy and defensive mastery. "Mays was a happy-go-lucky kid," Zapp once said. "He didn't act like a kid on the field. That was the difference. He acted like a veteran on that ball field. Other than that, Mays was a baby."[16]

Davis would put him in as a defensive replacement for Bobby Robinson in center field, and when Robinson broke his leg, Mays became the regular starter. Even when he was batting below .200, he made an impact with his glove and arm.

First baseman Joe Scott recalled chasing a hit into the gap in right-center field. He got to the ball, but his momentum was taking him away from the diamond. Mays had also been running down the ball, and Scott relied on his teenaged teammate. "I sure couldn't throw as well as him ... so I just flipped it to him so he could throw it to second."[17] The runner retreated to first and settled for a single rather than challenge the high-schooler's arm.

Mays became so adept at covering the outfield that his teammates would get caught taking it easy. During one game, Davis chewed out left fielder Zapp and right fielder Ed Steele in the dugout for "running that boy's legs off."[18] When Mays was in center, the two corner outfielders played closer to the lines and for every ball in the gaps, they'd yell, "Come on, Willie!" and watch the teenager do what he did best.

On his first road trip, Mays learned that playing ball was not all it took to be a ballplayer. Davis did all he could to protect his prospect, having him room with the following day's starter since the pitcher wouldn't be out carousing the night before a start. "We had 25 guys on the club, and all 25 would put me to bed every night. I didn't get to meet many girls that way, but I got plenty of sleep," Mays later joked in his Hall of Fame speech.[19]

Davis and the rest of his teammates didn't want Mays to get a reputation. As quickly as word of his talent could spread, rumors of laziness, belligerence, complacency, drunkenness, or any other negative trait that White scouts might use to justify not giving him an opportunity to play in the majors would proliferate even faster. While some of them would one day play for White teams, the Black Barons recognized that Mays was positioned to do something none of them ever could, and they weren't going to let him spoil it.

Word of Mays' talent was, in fact, spreading. Two weeks after making his official debut, he was the third Birmingham hitter spotlighted in an article previewing a weekend series against the Cleveland Buckeyes in Ohio. After touting Artie Wilson, the Black Barons' shortstop, who was leading all of baseball with a .412 batting average, and Davis, who was hitting .373 and leading the team to a playoff berth as a first-year manager, the *Newark Advocate* predicted that "the new utility outfielder, Willie Mays, only turning 17 years of age, will be a sensation within the present baseball season."[20] When the team rolled into Chicago, Abe Saperstein was in the stands. The founder of the Harlem Globetrotters was now scouting for Bill Veeck's Cleveland Indians, but also had connections to the New York Giants. Davis made certain that Saperstein, who was there to report on Wilson, knew about Mays.

Among the highlights Saperstein may have caught was a long drive by Chicago American Giants catcher Quincy Trouppe to deep center field. He rounded first and sprinted into second for what he thought was an easy double, only to be tagged out by a waiting Wilson. "Mays got it," he informed the dumbfounded batter.[21]

A month earlier, Trouppe had contacted Mays after getting a hot tip about an up-and-coming outfielder with a tremendous arm. He offered him a tryout in Chicago. When Cat Mays sent the American Giants a letter asking for $300 a month, the team made clear that no teenager was worth that much money and passed. When Trouppe's hit went to the wall in center, Mays saw a chance to show what he was worth. He bolted in all the way from left, hollering at Robinson to let him take it, and rifled the ball to Wilson for the out, leaving Trouppe to reflect how the American Giants had let him slip through their fingers.

In Cleveland, Davis decided it was time for Mays to learn a new lesson. Mays dug in against veteran right-hander Chet Brewer, who drilled the young player with a fastball to the arm and sent him sprawling to the dirt. Davis shouted as he walked down from the third-base coaching box and even gave his crying outfielder a little kick, but didn't make any effort to help him to his feet.

"These men gave me my combat training," Mays reflected decades later. "And what was combat training in the Negro Leagues? It was getting knocked down and either laying in the dirt and crying or getting up again."[22]

"Boy, do you see first base?" Davis barked. "Get up and go down there, and the first chance you get, you steal second, and then third." Mays did as he was told and scored on a fly ball. When he returned to the dugout, Davis told him, "That's how you handle a pitcher."[23]

However, Davis may have been the one handling the pitcher. The two were old friends and former teammates and, though he never admitted it, it's more than likely Davis asked Brewer to plunk his rookie to see how Mays would react.[24] Both Brewer and Davis told this story for many years, laughing off the suggestion that they'd been in cahoots.

During a game against the Kansas City Stars, a feeder team for the Monarchs, another Negro League legend cast his eyes on Mays for the first time and saw the potential for greatness. Stars manager Cool Papa Bell, years past his prime, recognized much of his own playing style, his speed and defensive range, in Mays. But the teen had a powerful swing capable of clearing the most distant fences, which Bell never possessed, and while Bell was certainly capable of throwing out baserunners from the outfield, his arm strength paled compared with that of Mays. He begged the Monarchs to sign Mays away from Birmingham and let him tutor the young outfielder for a year.

Monarchs owner Tom Baird refused. The Ku Klux Klan member, who had purchased the team from founder J.L. Wilkinson earlier in the year, didn't trust Black players from the South[25] and wasn't going to spend hundreds of dollars for the services of an Alabama outfielder who hadn't even started his junior year of high school.

When the Monarchs and Black Barons met in August, the Monarchs proved too much for Birmingham and won the series, which led to a playoff series between the two for a bid to the Negro League World Series. But Mays showed that his hitting was improving. He slapped a leadoff single to start the third inning of the first game of the series and scored on a single by Wilson. And his talent was beginning to draw the attention of "White folks' ball."

The Black Barons derived their name from the city's White minor-league team, the Birmingham Barons, whose name was inspired by the coal and steel barons who built their wealth on the labor of families in and around Birmingham. The teams shared Rickwood Field, though the Barons owned the ballpark and the Black Barons paid them rent.

The Barons were the Double-A Southern Association affiliate of the Boston Red Sox. One might think this would give the Red Sox some sort of edge on courting Mays, but the team seemed to have no interest.

Barons GM Eddie Glennon pleaded with Boston's front office to send scouts who could watch Mays in action. They could arrive in town a few days early, take in a Black Barons game, and still have time to watch the Barons. Al LaMacchia, then a pitcher for the Barons, saw Mays play while recovering from a broken wrist, but his enthusiastic scouting report failed to spark any interest.

The Red Sox went on to be the last major-league team to integrate when they added Pumpsie Green to their 1959 roster, 13 years after Jackie Robinson signed with the Dodgers. LaMacchia summed it up nicely: "You'd have to be a horseshit scout to pass up Willie Mays."[26]

On their way home from a season-ending series against the American Giants, the team took a detour through Missouri. The Indians were playing the St. Louis Browns and Satchel Paige was starting for Cleveland on September 4. The Browns were one of only two teams in the majors that still had segregated seating,[27] so the team's view may not have been the greatest, but for the first time in his life Willie Mays got to see a Black player in a major-league game.

The Monarchs came to Birmingham to open the NAL championship series. Since the teams' last meeting, Mays had continued to improve his game. He was now the regular starting center fielder and had raised his average from .222 to .246 in the last month. Davis displayed his confidence in his rookie when he turned in his lineup card with "MAYS, CF" written in the cleanup spot.

The Black Barons won the series, with Mays contributing key hits, timely RBIs, and superlative defense. Birmingham went on to face the Homestead Grays, and though they lost the series four games to one, the one victory was a showcase for Willie Mays's talents. He robbed Bob Thurman of a sure double at the center-field fence, threw out Buck Leonard going from first to third on a single, and hit a comebacker through the pitcher's legs for the game-winning RBI in a 4-3 final.

With the season over and school back in session, many of Mays' classmates were upset that their star quarterback had abandoned their team.[28] The principal threatened to suspend Mays for not taking his education seriously, but Cat and Willie's aunt intervened and forged an agreement that school would come first and Willie would play only weekend home games the following spring.

Before leaving to play winter ball in Puerto Rico, Davis made a special arrangement for his rookie star. A barnstorming tour featuring Jackie Robinson and Roy Campanella would be coming through Birmingham, and Davis made sure Mays would be in center field for the locals. Mays doubled for one of his team's only two hits but demonstrated that he belonged on the same field as two men who would win four of the next seven National League MVP Awards.[29]

There was no official Rookie of the Year Award in the Negro Leagues, but that didn't stop Mays from being labeled such. The *Alabama Tribune* bestowed the title, and declared Davis the Manager of the Year.[30] When the team opened training camp the following March, "Willie Mays, the rookie find of last season" was listed among the returning veterans,[31] and when the school year was nearing its end, it was predicted that "fans will swarm into Rickwood tomorrow just to see the kid who was named as rookie of the year in 1948 turn on the astonishments."[32]

As the 1949 season approached, the team had undergone a few changes, the biggest of which was that Artie Wilson's contract had been sold to Cleveland. That move prompted a protest by the New York Yankees, which, in turn, played a role in the team that ultimately landed Mays.[33] The other big change was to be expected. Mays was the starting center fielder with Robinson now in left.

While front offices' opinions on the likelihood of his making the majors differed, Mays was known to every team. Even while playing only weekend home games, "Birmingham's school-going centerfielder," as the *Pittsburgh Courier* identified him, was making national news for making "a perfect throw [that] cut down [Jesse] Douglass [*sic*] at the plate trying to score after Lonnie Summers hoisted out."[34]

The Sunday before the final three days of the school year, the *Birmingham News* reminded fans that Mays, who had "become one of the sensations of Negro baseball ... and many figure he is marked for the majors in another year or so," would "become a full-fledged Baron, eligible to play games on the road as well as at home" after "school is out the coming Wednesday."[35] A charity game to raise money for a hospital to serve Birmingham's Black community was promoted with the promise that "fans will have a chance to see the sensational Willie Mays perform in the Black Barons centerfield. ... Many observers believe Mays is a clinch for future major league stardom."[36]

With school out, Mays could join the team for its Eastern road trip, where he would play center field for the first time and hit his first career home run, an inside-the-parker, in the New York Cubans' home ballpark, the Polo Grounds. Despite having been aware of Mays for almost a year, the New York Giants declined the chance to talk to him yet as they knew he was still untouchable. Major-league rules didn't allow teams to sign players until after they graduated from high school, but that didn't stop teams from looking at Mays.

Bill Maughn, a scout for the Boston Braves, remembered watching Mays throw out a runner on a ball fielded by Robinson. A batter banged a hit off the scoreboard in Rickwood Field, and Robinson scooped it up. Mays ran over yelling for the ball and "be-doggoned if the left fielder didn't shovel pass like a football player," he said with amazement. "The centerfielder threw out the runner trying to go from first to third."[37]

The White Sox also took interest when John Donaldson, a former Negro League pitcher and the first Black scout hired by a major-league team, rated Mays above his other top prospects, Ernie Banks and Elston Howard.

Glennon finally cornered a scout who'd come to assess the Barons and their competition and persuaded him to stick around one more day to see Mays. The scout graded Mays with an A or A+ in all five categories: hitting, power, running, throwing, and fielding. Scouts rarely gave A+ ratings, which translated to a prediction that the prospect would be a "superstar" and "a consistent MVP candidate and the best at his respective position in the major leagues"[38] in any category, much less all five.

The Red Sox did eventually make a move to get Mays, though indirectly. General manager Joe Cronin approached Davis and offered to buy his contract with an agreement that he could finish the 1949 season with the Black Barons and join Boston in 1950. The idea was that Mays would be more likely to go to a team where his mentor could be his roommate in the minor leagues.[39]

By mid-June, Mays was batting .421. When the Black Barons traveled to Kansas City for a rematch of the previous year's NAL championship, the *Kansas City Star* wrote, "Major league scouts have labeled Mays as the greatest young prospect they have seen in action."[40]

Mays was held out of the 1949 East-West All-Star Game, as was the Monarchs' Howard. Both players' owners already had suitors for their contracts and worried that putting them on the biggest stage possible ran the risk of souring any deals in the works.

Meanwhile, Artie Wilson, whom the Indians and Yankees had been fighting over earlier in the season, was now with neither team. Instead, he was in California, playing for the Oakland Oaks of the Pacific Coast League.[41] The dispute had been ugly and complicated, and Birmingham owner Tom Hayes came out of the experience embarrassed and irate with the Yankees brass. He vowed to never work with them again. In fact, if he had the opportunity to gain some revenge by refusing to sell them a highly prized prospect no matter what they offered and, even better, sending said prospect to another New York team out of spite, that was exactly the sort of thing he would do.

When summer ended, Mays returned to school and the baseball season concluded without a Negro League World Series. Again, Mays proved himself capable of playing with major-league stars in the barnstorming game against Robinson and Campanella, who called Branch Rickey after the game and urged him to send Dodgers scouts to assess Mays. He was told Wid Matthews, one of Rickey's most trusted scouts, already had and returned the verdict that Mays couldn't hit a curveball.[42] Matthews, who'd labeled Jackie Robinson a "hot dog" and expressed "reservations" about his on-field demeanor when he'd scouted him in 1946,[43] and who, as general manager of the Chicago Cubs, was accused of being slow to integrate the team, earned a reputation "that he didn't care for Black players."[44]

That winter and the subsequent spring were just a countdown to graduation. Davis left for spring training with the Red Sox. He wasn't allowed to dress and shower with the White players, instead using the visitors' locker room on practice days, and the umpires' on game days. He was assigned to their Double-A affiliate in Scranton, Pennsylvania – the team to which Boston hoped to send Mays – where he wasn't allowed to stay in the same hotels as his White teammates.

On May 15, a week and a half before Mays graduated, the Red Sox released Davis to avoid paying a bonus to Birmingham. Boston bought his contract for $7,500 with the agreement that Hayes would get another $7,500 if he remained with the franchise beyond the 15th. There was no guarantee that having the man who'd become like a second father to Mays on their payroll would have landed them the phenom, but cutting that man over a few thousand dollars and letting him return to Birmingham and tell the Black Barons of his treatment guaranteed that the dream outfield of Ted Williams and Willie Mays would never be.

Mays returned to the Black Barons as a full-time player, but everyone knew it would be for a limited time. "The big question on the club right now is can the Black Barons keep the youthful Willie Mays all summer?" wrote the *Birmingham News*.[45] "Mays may not be making many more appearances with the Black Barons, as it is known that several big league scouts are watching him closely. The Boston Braves and Chicago White Sox are reputed to have the inside track."[46]

Like the Red Sox, the Braves lost their chance to field a future Hall of Fame pairing in the outfield of Mays and Hank Aaron when the team refused to approve Maughn's request for $15,000 to purchase the contract from Hayes. The team was also considering Mays as a pitcher, which may have left him less inclined to sign.

On June 11, the Black Barons were on their annual East Coast road trip. Their bus entered the Holland Tunnel in New York City, but it didn't come back out. One by one, players began to smell smoke. The driver pulled over and everyone leapt out before flames consumed the vehicle that had shown Mays the world for two summers, along with their uniforms and equipment. When the team reached the ballpark, they were forced to borrow the Cubans' gray road uniforms and wear them inside out.

An obituary of Black Baron first baseman Alonzo Perry identified him "as the player the New York Giants came to scout and discovered Willie Mays." He related the story that "Carl Hubbell of the Giants began following me. He saw Willie and asked me who was the kid we had in centerfield. I told him 'Willie Mays.'"[47] This was a Giants' myth, repeated often enough to almost seem true. But the notion that Mays was "accidentally" scouted or that Hubbell was oblivious about one of the most coveted prospects in baseball is laughable.

Rather, the huge home-run hitter Perry provided cover for Hubbell, who'd been well aware of Mays for almost two years and had seen him play on multiple occasions. Hubbell worried about word spreading that the Giants were close to signing Mays, so instead muddied the waters by letting it get out that they were interested in Perry, giving a reason for their scouts' sudden interest in Black Barons games.

Ed Montague was one of several big-league scouts in Birmingham for a high-school all-star game on Friday, June 16. During the game, Maughn tipped him off to check out the Black Barons' center fielder the following day.

Montague had never seen Mays play before, and since there were no records of his being scouted because the Giants wanted to keep their interest in Mays a secret, the scout may have believed he'd discovered the future superstar. "I had no inkling of

Willie Mays," Montague later claimed, "but during batting and fielding practice, my eyes almost popped out of my head. … This was the greatest young ballplayer I had ever seen in my scouting career."[48]

Willie Mays played on Saturday, hitting a single and a double with four RBIs against the Cubans, unaware that he was playing his last Negro League game as his future was being negotiated while he was on the field. The Giants agreed to pay $15,000 – $10,000 to Hayes and $5,000 to Mays – to acquire the 19-year-old, reported as "a record price paid for a Negro player."[49] Montague approached a freshly showered Mays in the clubhouse, awed by the towel-clad player's physique, and asked if he would like to play in for the Giants.

The rest of the Black Barons found out the next day when their center fielder wasn't in the clubhouse to suit up for Sunday's doubleheader, and the newspapers reported later in the week that "the New York Giants have purchased the contract of Willie Mays, sensational Birmingham Black Barons centerfielder."[50]

Though he left the team and the league behind him, Mays would never leave the lessons he'd learned, and for more than two decades, he would show major-league fans and owners all that segregation had made them miss.

***Author's Note***

This has been the most frustrating, most interesting, and most fun project I have tackled for SABR to date. As with much Negro League-related research, records don't always exist and one is reliant on oral histories and imperfect memories. Timelines don't always match up, details change from one telling to another, statements can be misunderstood, and misstatements get repeated by others. For example, Mays tells a reporter he's been playing baseball professionally since he was 14, referring to the first time he was paid to play a game with the Industrial League, and the reporter assumes he means that he joined the Black Barons at 14, spreading the story that Birmingham had a 15-year-old center fielder in the 1948 World Series, which gets stated as a fact by Buck Leonard and others in later interviews and becomes a throwaway line in Ken Burns's *Baseball* documentary.

The epitome of this would be the tale Mays has often shared – and that some readers may have been upset to see excluded – of hitting a double in his first ever at-bat against Satchel Paige during a game against the Kansas City Monarchs in Memphis.

The story goes that after Mays slid into second, Paige asked his third baseman to let him know "when that little boy comes back up." When Mays later walked to the plate for his next at-bat, Paige informed him that he was "not going to trick you. I'm going throw you three fastballs and you're going to sit down."[51] He did exactly that, much to Willie's delight.

Unfortunately, it's unclear when – and if we're being honest, if – this showdown took place. Paige signed with the Cleveland Indians on July 7, 1948, three days after Mays made his Black Barons debut. Paige was also pitching for the Kansas City Stars, not the Monarchs, in 1948. This seems a minor detail, but it points to the larger problem of the story's evolution.

Sometimes the double comes off a fastball, sometimes a breaking ball. In an earlier autobiography, Mays implied he got his hit off Paige's "hesitation pitch" and that he struck out on three swings in each of his ensuing *three* at-bats, but "I never saw a fastball from him, only those crazy curves and other soft stuff."[52] Even earlier, in his 1972 autobiography, Mays says only, "I got to hit against Paige one game. I was one for two."[53]

It's possible Mays and Paige faced off, perhaps when Paige was barnstorming and Mays was playing for a community team or an Industrial League squad, but not as a Black Baron and a Monarch, respectively, and certainly not in the playoffs, as some versions of the story suggest. It seems likely that the retellings of the event were influenced by Buck O'Neil's story of Paige facing Josh Gibson in the 1942 Negro League World Series.

I've done my best to reconcile conflicting timelines and acknowledge some of the discrepancies in the endnotes.

## SOURCES

In addition to the sources cited in the Notes, the author accessed Baseball-Reference.com, Seamheads.com, and *The Sporting News* via Paper of Record, and consulted several other sources including:


Greene, Lee. *Willie Mays: A Baseball Life* (New York: Scholastic Book Services, 1972)

Holway, John. *Voices from the Great Black Baseball Leagues* (Mineola, New York: Dover Publications, 2010)

*Say Hey, Willie Mays!*, directed by Nelson George, HBO Sports/ Major League Baseball Productions/Company Name/Zipper Bros Films/Uninterrupted, 2022


## NOTES

1 Owen Caufield, "Mays Says Thanks to Black Leagues," *Hartford Courant*, June 25, 1981: D3.

2 James Hirsch, *Willie Mays: The Life, the Legend* (New York: Scribner, 2010), 46.

3 Hirsch, 30.

4 Hirsch, 30; Allen Barra, *Mickey and Willie: Mantle and Mays, the Parallel Lives of Baseball's Golden Age* (New York: Crown Archetype, 2013), 54.

5 Even as football and basketball began to integrate during Willie's high-school years – in 1946 and 1950, respectively – the decision to pursue a career in baseball remained paramount due to football or basketball requiring that Mays play in college first.

6 Willie Mays and John Shea, *24: Life Stories and Lessons from the Say Hey Kid* (New York: St. Martin's Press, 2020), 27.

7 Hirsch, 32.

8 Roger Shuler, "'Say Hey Kid' Has Little Good to Say about His Hometown," *Birmingham Post-Herald*, September 17, 1981: B6.

9 Mays and Shea, 23.

10 "Choo Choos Take Pair from Memphis Blue Sox," *Chattanooga Daily Times*, June 14, 1948: 10. The first record of Mays playing for Chattanooga appears roughly two months earlier in a recap of a game played in Macon, Georgia, between Chattanooga and the Newark Eagles: "Choo Choos, Champs in 12-Inning, 1-1 Tie," *Chattanooga Daily Times*, April 20, 1948: 13. This article, however, raises some questions. For starters, it identifies the Eagles as "champions of the [Negro] American League." The Eagles won the Negro League World Series in 1946, but moved from the American to the National League in 1947, where they finished second in the standings. Further, according to both Hirsch and Klima, Mays was not allowed to play for Chattanooga until after the school year ended, and April 19, 1948, was a Monday while school was in session. On pages 44-45 of *Willie's Boys*, Klima quotes former Black Barons second baseman Tommy Sampson as claiming he included Mays on a traveling team after the 1947 season, and that they played the Eagles in Macon, but then he lost Mays to Chattanooga. In the same paragraph, Klima indicates, however, that Mays has no recollection of ever playing for Sampson.

11 Hirsch, 33.

12 John Klima, *Willie's Boys: The 1948 Birmingham Black Barons, the Last Negro League World Series, and the Making of a Baseball Legend* (Hoboken, New Jersey: John Wiley & Sons Inc., 2008), 91.

13 Willie Mays and Lou Sahidi, *Say Hey: The Autobiography of Willie Mays* (New York: Pocket Books, 1988), 23; Hirsch, 43; Klima, 97. While Klima's book correctly identifies Memphis as the opponent, the others have Mays debuting against the Cleveland Buckeyes with starting pitcher Chet Brewer. That matchup didn't happen until a few weeks later.

14 "Black Barons Face Red Sox in Twin Bill," *Birmingham News*, July 4, 1948: 18.

15 Mays' contract is archived at the Memphis Public Library and Information Center. In 1972 Mays claimed these amounts were $70 per month with a $5 bonus every month he batted over .300. Willie Mays and Charles Einstein, *Willie Mays: My Life in and out of Baseball* (New York: E.P. Dutton, 1972), 69.

16 Klima, 105.

17 Klima, 99.

18 Klima, 152.

19 Joseph Durso, "A Legend Named Willie," *New York Times*, August 6, 1979: C6.

20 "Barons, First Half Negro Champions, Here Thursday," *Newark* (Ohio) *Advocate*, July 20, 1948: 9. This included both the National League and the American League.

21 Klima, 108.

22 Caufield, "Mays Says Thanks."

23 Hirsch, 46

24 When Mays relates this story, the plunking comes in his second at-bat as retaliation for a home run in his first at-bat. Mays' only official home run of the 1948 season was hit off Brewer, but it came in a later game.

25 This bit of racist rhetoric was rooted in the practice of selling slaves who acted disobediently or harbored any other trait a slaveowner might find objectionable to other plantations to the south, where treatment would be more harsh the farther south one went. This practice was the origin of the threat to "sell someone down the river," as Mississippi was commonly known to be the worst state for treatment of slaves. Years after emancipation, racists began positing that Blacks living in Deep South were less intelligent, less capable, less civilized, less whatever-nonsense-they-wanted-to-spout than their

Northern counterparts because they were descended from what they perceived as the worst stock of slaves.

26 Klima, 144.

27 The Washington Senators were the other team.

28 Though he wasn't eligible to play any longer, when the team would play out-of-state games against teams that wouldn't recognize him, Mays would sometimes put on a different jersey and use a fake name and throw a 50-yard touchdown or two.

29 Mays would win one of the other three.

30 Emory O. Jackson, "Hits and Bits," *Alabama Tribune* (Montgomery), December 31, 1948: 8.

31 "Black Barons Open Spring Drills March 21," *Birmingham News*, March 6, 1949: C-5.

32 "Black Barons and Buckeyes Collide Today," *Birmingham News*, May 22, 1949: C-6.

33 Or, more accurately, the teams that didn't.

34 "Powell's Seven Hit Pitching Wins for Barons," *Pittsburgh Courier*, May 14, 1949: 24; "Black Barons Lose, 6-2, 4-1," *Pittsburgh Courier*, May 14, 1949: 24.

35 "Black Barons and Buckeyes Collide Today," *Birmingham News*, May 22, 1949: C-6.

36 "Black Barons to Play Negro Hospital Benefit Contest," *Birmingham News*, May 24, 1949: 20. On a side note, the article mentions that "Jefferson County has no Negro hospital now. There are only 574 hospital beds for Negroes, of the county's 2,286, although Negroes make up 34.7 percent of the county population."

37 Klima, 195.

38 Klima, 199.

39 The signing may have also just been a publicity stunt. Since the color line had been broken, some teams were accused of having a quota for how many Black players they would sign, but Boston was beginning to attract attention for not signing any. The signing of Davis checked a box serving only to silence critics who "could no longer charge that the Red Sox organization had never signed an African American." Bill Nowlin, ed., *Pumpsie and Progress – The Red Sox, Race, and Redemption* (Burlington, Massachusetts: Rounder Books, 2010.)

40 "A Series with Barons," *Kansas City* (Missouri) *Star*, June 26, 1949: 3B.

41 The dispute over Wilson's contract had stemmed from a simple problem. The Yankees didn't want Wilson – or any other Black players, frankly – but they also didn't want talented players going to their competitors. When they got word that Cleveland was looking to buy Wilson, the Yankees claimed that Wilson and the Black Barons agreed to sell him to New York, which both the player and the owner denied. When the league awarded Wilson to New York, the Yankees turned around and sold him to Oakland. Cleveland had paid Hayes $15,000 for Wilson's contract. When Wilson was instead given to New York, Hayes was unable to pay back the money until the Yankees paid him, which wasn't for several months.

42 Campanella was frustrated by the shortsightedness of the scouting report. "Who ever heard of a 17-year-old hitting a curveball?" Bob Broeg, "Campy, a Man Paid to Play a Boy's Game," *The Sporting News*, July 24, 1971: 20.

43 Lee Lowenfish, *Branch Rickey: Baseball's Ferocious Gentleman* (Lincoln, Nebraska: University of Nebraska Press, 2007), 368.

44 Klima, 22.

45 "Black Barons Play Memphis Wednesday," *Birmingham News*, May 30, 1950: 23.

46 "Black Barons Battle Stars at Rickwood," *Birmingham News*, June 7, 1950: 34.

47 Bill Lumpkin, "Memories Abundant of 'El Gigante Azul,'" *Birmingham Post-Herald*, September 18, 1982: B3.

48 Joseph Durso, "A Shaking Rookie Who Became a Wonder," *New York Times*, September 21, 1973: 29.

49 "Mays, Black Baron Star, Is Going Up," *Birmingham News*, June 22, 1950: 18.

50 "Mays, Black Baron Star."

51 This quote can be found in a GQ interview and two biographies. Jason Gay, "Willie Mays Comes Home," *Gentleman's Quarterly*, February 1, 2010; Mays and Shea, 35; Hirsch, 47.

52 Mays and Sahidi, 20.

53 Mays and Einstein, 32.

# TRACKING DOWN WILLIE MAYS'S 1948 GAME LOG

BY TOM THRESS

**IN 2020, RETROSHEET** belatedly extended its work to include Negro League games and Negro League seasons. The first full season that Retrosheet attempted to compile was 1948, which also happened to be Willie Mays' rookie year.

The primary challenge for Retrosheet in putting together the 1948 Negro League season is that a full schedule of games was not compiled and reported at the time. To reconstruct the 1948 Negro League season required searching through old newspapers to compile games one at a time. In addition, while statistics were kept for league games in 1948, these statistics have not survived to the present day. And even if they had, official Negro National League and official Negro American League games represented only a fraction of the games played by these teams, even if one only considers games involving two Negro League teams.

To give something of an overview of the process, this article looks at Retrosheet's efforts to compile Willie Mays' statistics for his rookie year.

Mays began the 1948 season playing for a semipro team called the Chattanooga Choo-Choos. The earliest reference we can find for his playing against a major Negro League team was an exhibition game between the Choo-Choos and the Newark Eagles in Macon, Georgia, on April 19. The teams played to a 1-1 tie in 12 innings, and the *Chattanooga Daily Times* reported that "Willie Mays, 16-year-old centerfielder from Birmingham, was the hitting and fielding star for the Chattanooga team."[1] No more details are given. The article also fails to identify who pitched for Newark, which was still in spring training, so it is unclear whether Mays actually faced major-league pitching in this game.

Retrosheet has not attempted to compile game accounts for the 1948 Choo-Choos. But a newspaper search suggests that Mays was a star for the Choo-Choos. In a June 13 doubleheader against the Memphis Blue Sox of the Negro Southern League, he went 5-for-7 in a Chattanooga sweep and Mays' two-run home run in the sixth inning of the first game proved decisive in the Choo-Choos' 3-2 win.[2]

It was fairly soon after this game that Willie Mays was signed by the Birmingham Black Barons.

The first game for which Retrosheet has found definitive evidence of Mays playing for the Black Barons was the second game of a doubleheader in Birmingham (at Rickwood Field) on June 27, 1948, against the Indianapolis Clowns. The *Birmingham News* published box scores for both games of this doubleheader that show Mays did not play in game one but batted eighth and played left field in game two. He went 0-for-2 (probably with one walk) and had no putouts or assists.[3]

Interestingly, the Black Barons and Clowns had played in Chattanooga two nights earlier. The *Chattanooga Daily Times* ran a four-paragraph story and line score. The only Barons players mentioned by name were pitchers Nat Pollard and Jimmie Newberry, catcher Herman Bell, and third baseman John Britton, whose "[h]eavy hitting" was "a highlight of the game."[4]

Did Mays play in this game? Or did the Black Barons perhaps sign him at this time while they were in town? We don't know.

Overall, Retrosheet has found definitive evidence that Mays played in 27 games for the 1948 Black Barons. This total includes 10 playoff games.

Several accounts have suggested that Mays had two hits off Chet Brewer in his debut with the Black Barons, playing left field in the second game of a doubleheader at Rickwood Field. Based on Retrosheet's research, this appears to be an amalgamation of three separate games.

As best we can tell, Mays made his Black Barons' debut playing left field in game two of a doubleheader at Rickwood Field. Mays did have a two-hit game at Rickwood Field against the Cleveland Buckeyes (Chet Brewer's team) on August 12, 1948. But this was a single game (played on a Thursday night), and Sam Jones and John Brown pitched for the Buckeyes (Chet Brewer pinch-hit for Brown in the ninth inning).[5]

Mays did bat against Chet Brewer the night before, August 11, at Alberta Park in Tuscaloosa, Alabama. We have not found a box score for that game yet, but the game story we found did say that Mays hit a solo home run off Brewer in the bottom of the second inning to give Birmingham its first run in a game they won, 3-2.[6]

Mays' home run off Brewer was the first of two home runs he hit against Negro League competition that Retrosheet has found. Mays' second home run was a three-run first-inning home run off Raul Lopez of the New York Cubans at Blue Grass Field in Lexington, Kentucky, on August 27, 1948, in an 8-4 Black Barons win.[7] No box score has been found for this game either.

Overall, Retrosheet has found evidence of 17 regular-season games in which Mays played for Birmingham. In these games, Mays had at least 14 hits – including at least three multihit games: August 1 vs. the Kansas City Monarchs (three hits),[8] August 12 vs. the Cleveland Buckeyes, and August 15 vs. the New York Cubans.[9] Those 14 hits included at least three doubles, two triples, and two home runs. Retrosheet has found evidence of one regular-season stolen base by Mays – on August 1 vs. the Monarchs. In Mays' 17 known regular-season games, he scored at least nine runs and had at least 11 RBIs. Not bad numbers for someone who turned 17 years old less than two months before his debut.

The limitations of what we know about Mays' 1948 season are perhaps best illustrated by his postseason performance. The Black Barons won the first-half NAL title and played a best-of-seven series against the second-half winners, the Kansas City Monarchs. That series went eight games. (Game Five ended in a 3-3 tie.) Retrosheet has found box scores for seven of the eight games. Mays played center field and batted third or fourth in all seven of these games. He batted 7-for-25 (.280) with one double, four runs scored, and five RBIs.

We have been unable to find a box score for Game Three of this series, played at Martin's Park in Memphis on September 15. The Black Barons won that game, 4-3. All we know about the Barons' offense on that day is that left fielder Jim Zapp hit a home run.[10] Mays was not mentioned in any game articles that we have found.[11] He probably played in the game. But we cannot say that for certain, and if he did play, we have no idea what his stats were for the game.

The Black Barons won their playoff series against the Monarchs, earning the right to face the Homestead Grays in what would turn out to be the last Negro League World Series.

Retrosheet has found box scores for the first two games of this series.[12] In both of these games, Mays batted third and played center field. He went 1-for-7 with one run scored as the Grays jumped out to a 2-0 series lead.

Retrosheet has not found a box score for Game Three. However, we know that Mays played in this game, because he drove in the winning run in the bottom of the ninth inning with a single to center field.[13] That is all we know about Mays' performance in this game (a 4-3 Barons win), though.

There were two more games of the 1948 Negro League World Series, both of which were won handily by the Grays (14-1 and 10-6, although the latter game went 10 innings).[14] Retrosheet has not found box scores for either of these games. Nor have we found any reference to Mays playing in either game. It seems likely that he played center field and batted third in both of these games, but we cannot say for sure (yet).

Retrosheet continues to look for better accounts of Negro League games. In the meantime, what we know about Mays' rookie season is suggestive. Including the postseason, he played at least 27 games and had at least 23 hits, at least eight of which were for extra bases (four doubles, two triples, two home runs). In the games we know Mays played, he scored at least 14 runs and drove in at least 17, including the winning run in the only World Series game the Black Barons won. And he did all of that at the age of 17. Not bad at all.

## NOTES

1 "Choo Choos, Champs in 12-inning 1-1 Tie," *Chattanooga Daily Times*, April 20, 1948: 13.

2 "Choo Choos Take Pair from Memphis Blue Sox," *Chattanooga Daily Times*, June 14, 1948: 10.

3 "Black Barons Win Twin Bill," *Birmingham News*, June 28, 1948: 18.

4 "No Time for Clowning and Black Barons Win," *Chattanooga Daily Times*, June 26, 1948: 9.

5 "Black Barons Beat Buckeyes with Big Rally," *Birmingham News*, August 13, 1948: 36.

6 Rity Thompson, "Birmingham Black Barons Defeat Cleveland Buckeyes Before Large Crowd Here," *Alabama Citizen*, August 21, 1948: 2.

7 "Black Barons Whip N.Y. Cubans, 8-4, *Lexington Herald*, August 28, 1948: 10.

8 "Two for the Monarchs," *Kansas City Times*, August 2, 1948: 15.

9 "Black Barons Blast Cubans," *Birmingham News*, August 16, 1948: 17.

10 "Black Barons Win Again, 4-3," *Birmingham News*, September 16, 1948: 42.

11 In addition to the *Birmingham News* article cited in Note 10, see also "A Costly Monarch Error," *Kansas City Times*, September 16, 1948: 30; and "Black Barons Win Again," *Memphis Commercial Appeal*, September 16, 1948: 25.

12 Game One: "First Game to Grays, 3-2," *Kansas City Times*, September 27, 1948: 14. Game Two: "Homestead Grays Lead Black Barons 2-0 in World Series," *Memphis World*, October 5, 1948: 5.

13 "Grays Hold 3-1 Lead in Series," *Baltimore Afro-American*, October 9, 1948: 8.

14 Game Four: "Grays Overwhelm Black Barons, 14-1," *New Orleans Times-Picayune*, October 4, 1948: 26. Game Five: "Grays Blast Black Barons," *Birmingham News*, October 6, 1948: 27. Several additional sources have been found for both of these games, none of which mention Willie Mays.

# THE NEGRO LEAGUES BEYOND 1948, AND THE ADVENTURES OF A BOY NAMED WILLIE

BY ALAN COHEN

BY CONSENSUS, IT has been deemed that the Negro Leagues died in 1948. The last Negro League World Series was played that year. SABR's book on the 1948 Homestead Grays and Birmingham Black Barons was titled *A Bittersweet Goodbye*. Seamheads, an authority on Negro Leagues history, does not go beyond 1948. When Retrosheet began doing individual game records, it began with 1948 and went backward.

As we begin to look at the statistics of Black ballplayers who broke into the American and National Leagues and view their records on Baseball-Reference.com, there is a gap. With Willie Mays, we know his record with Birmingham in 1948, and we know his record with Trenton in 1950. What happened in between?

In these paragraphs, the story begins to unfold of the Negro Leagues beyond 1948 and some of Mays' early glories.

After 1948, two teams (the Homestead Grays and New York Black Yankees) left the Negro National League. To survive, the four remaining NNL teams combined with the six Negro American League teams to form a new league. The new 10-team league, called the Negro American League, had a limited schedule, with most games played on weekends. On August 14, 1949, the East-West All-Star Game was once again held at Comiskey Park and drew a good-sized crowd (31,097) to see the top players in the league. One player from that game, Jim Gilliam of the Baltimore Elite Giants, went on to have a great career with the Dodgers in Brooklyn and Los Angeles.

One Negro League player not in the game was Willie Mays of the Birmingham Black Barons. Why didn't he play? There have been reasons given but nothing conclusive. One explanation was that he was back in high school. Another was that his mentor and manager, Piper Davis, and Birmingham team owner Tom Hayes were hiding him, fearful that teams in the White major leagues would steal him away, offering little or nothing in the way of compensation.[1]

But the real reason seems to be that, at the time the team was chosen in early July, Mays was in a slump and the outfielders chosen were having better years. Houston's Johnny Davis was a top home run hitter in the league; Willard Brown of the Monarchs led the league in RBIs; Pedro Formental of Memphis led the league in triples; and Art Pennington of Chicago, who was replaced (after being sold to Portland of the Pacific Coast League) by teammate Lloyd Davenport, was among the league leaders in batting average.

How did Mays do in 1949?

The record is not yet complete; it looks as if he put his greatness on display almost from the start. Through June 5, he was batting .413.[2] The *Birmingham News*, a mainstream daily paper, gave ample coverage to the Black Barons and included many box scores. On a rainy Sunday, May 8, the Black Barons hosted the Chicago American Giants in a doubleheader at Rickwood Field. Mays had three total hits and sparkled in the abbreviated second game, ended by curfew after five innings. His fourth-inning single broke a 1-1 tie as the Black Barons won, 4-1. He also showed off his arm, gunning down Jesse Douglas at home plate after grabbing a fly ball hit by Lonnie Summers.[3]

On May 10, Mays hit his first homer of the season as Birmingham lost to the Louisville Buckeyes (formerly the Cleveland Buckeyes), 7-5.[4] The first game for which there is an available box score was played the next night; Mays doubled in a 4-3 win over the Chicago American Giants.[5] On May 13 Birmingham completed its homestand with a 5-3 win over the Kansas City Monarchs (featuring Curt Roberts, Gene Baker, and Elston Howard). Mays singled and scored.

Mays did not accompany his team on its first road trip. His high school would not allow it. When the Barons returned home for a doubleheader on May 22, he was in the lineup for each game. Birmingham won by scores of 14-2 and 18-8 against Louisville, and Mays went 3-for-7 in the two games. His hits included a double in the opener. One of the pitchers he victimized was future San Francisco Giants teammate Sam Jones. Mays had four RBIs and a stolen base in the 14-2 game. He had a stolen base in the nightcap.[6]

On May 25 Mays, who walked in a run and singled and scored in another plate appearance, got raves for his glovework. Running at full throttle, he made a barehanded catch of a ball by the outfield wall in the 6-3 win over Louisville.[7]

Two days later, his school year complete, Mays joined the Barons as they traveled to Louisville[8] before visiting New York. Birmingham faced the New York Cubans in a doubleheader at the Polo Grounds on May 29.

The *New York Sunday News* ran an article in late May 1949 reading: "The New York Cubans' '$100,000 Infield' will be scouted by aides of Carl Hubbell (of the New York Giants) when the Cubans oppose the Birmingham Black Barons in a twin bill which will open the local Negro American League season at the Polo Grounds today. Each of the infielders hit over .300 last season and led the league in fielding and in double plays."[9]

That small article, buried in the sports section of the top circulation newspaper in the country's largest city, gave notice that some extra sets of eyes would be in a position to take notice of Willie Mays' first visit to the spacious center field that would be his home playground early in his career with the New York Giants.

The *New York Age*, a weekly Black newspaper, gave the games good coverage. Each game resulted in an 8-4 score. Birmingham won the opener, and the Cubans won the second game. In the ninth inning of the second game, Willie Howard Mays Jr. hit his first Polo Grounds home run. It was an inside-the-park homer, but there was no report as to whether his cap came flying off as he rounded the bases. Earlier in the game, he had singled in a run.[10]

After a game in West Haven, Connecticut on May 30, Mays made his first Brooklyn appearance on June 1, but it was not at Ebbets Field. It was at Dexter Park (located in nearby Woodhaven in

Queens) against the Bushwicks, a popular semipro team that featured some veterans of the National and American Leagues. The Black Barons won, 7-4,[11] hopped back on the bus and headed, after a game with the Springfield (Queens, New York) Grays on June 2 toward Baltimore to face the Elite Giants in Baltimore on June 3, Wilmington, Delaware, on June 4, and back in Baltimore on June 5 for a doubleheader. Then it was on to Philadelphia's Shibe Park to face the Philadelphia Stars on June 6. The bus seemed to be always in motion. There were stops at Chester, Pennsylvania (June 7), Petersburg, Virginia (June 8), and Asheville, North Carolina (June 9-10), and finally, on June 11 and 12, the Black Barons were back in Birmingham to face the Cubans. No sooner had they gotten home than they and the Cubans were back on the bus. The teams played a doubleheader at Sportsman's Park in St. Louis on June 13 and were back in Birmingham two days later, after a scheduled game in Memphis on June 14 was rained out. On June 16, it was on to Tuscaloosa. Such was life in the Negro Leagues.[12]

Mays' next known home run came on June 19 at Birmingham's Rickwood Field in the first game of a doubleheader against the Indianapolis Clowns. He went 2-for-5 and, in addition to the homer, knocked a double in a 12-5 first-game win. In the second game, a 10-8 loss, he was 1-for-4 with an RBI and a stolen base.[13]

A long road trip in late June took the Black Barons to Kansas City and a game against the Monarchs. The teams took the show on the road for three stops in Nebraska.

Back at Rickwood on July 10, Mays had one of his best games with the Black Barons. He had five hits, including a double and the game-winning RBI, as Birmingham defeated the Philadelphia Stars, 13-12.[14] On July 27 he put on another show for the home folks with four hits, including a triple. His fourth hit, a game-winning RBI single in the bottom of the ninth, broke a 5-5 tie.[15]

On August 5 against Baltimore at Rickwood Field, he had one of his better innings. In the top of the third inning, he threw out a runner at home plate and in the bottom of the same inning, he walked, stole second base and scored the tying run on a single by Ed Steele. Unfortunately for his team, Baltimore scored in the following inning and won the game, 3-2.[16]

On August 24 at Montgomery, Alabama, the quintessential five-tool player showed off his arm in spectacular fashion. The game was a marathon affair that lasted 15 innings. In the seventh inning, Mays snuffed out a Kansas City rally by throwing from the 387-foot sign in left-center to third base and nailing an advancing runner. Birmingham won the contest, 3-2.[17] Mays hit his final home run of the season on September 23 as the Black Barons defeated the Buckeyes 7-1 at Rickwood Field. He also doubled in the game.[18]

By the time he hit that final homer of the 1949 season, Mays had gotten attention with a feature article in a predominant Black publication. On August 27, Russ Cowans acquainted his *Chicago Defender* readers with Mays, who was "coming up like a prairie fire."[19]

Another type of fire broke out on Saturday, June 10, 1950. Mays had graduated from high school on May 25 and was traveling with the Black Barons to New York. As it was about to enter the Holland Tunnel, the team's bus caught fire. The players escaped unharmed, but their equipment was consumed by the flames.[20] The team played a doubleheader at the Polo Grounds the next day.

Willie Mays remained with Birmingham until he was acquired by the Giants organization on June 21, 1950.[21] In his last game with Birmingham, on June 17, he doubled during a 7-1 win over the New York Cubans.[22] Reports of games were not as thorough in 1950 as they had been the prior year but during his last 20 games with Birmingham, from May 24 through June 17, Mays had four doubles and four home runs. Per an article in the *Chicago Defender*, his 22 RBIs placed him second in the league.[23]

After less than a year in the minor leagues, Mays joined the Giants in May 1951 and, on May 28,

1951, on the eve of the second anniversary of his first homer at the Polo Grounds, he hit the first of his 660 National League homers.

## SOURCES

Of the many biographies of Willie Mays, the following is particularly helpful in showing the development of Willie Mays with the Birmingham Black Barons from 1948 through 1950.

Klima, John. *Willie's Boys: The 1948 Birmingham Black Barons, the Last Negro League World Series, and the Making of a Baseball Legend* (Hoboken, New Jersey: John A. Wiley and Sons, 2009).

## NOTES

1 John Klima, *Willie's Boys: The 1948 Birmingham Black Barons, the Last Negro League World Series, and the Making of a Baseball Legend* (Hoboken, New Jersey: John A. Wiley and Sons, 2009), 215.

2 "Carl [*sic*] Mays Regains NAL Batting Lead with .413," *Chicago Defender*, June 18, 1949: 16.

3 "Black Barons Lose [*sic*], 6-2, 4-1," *Pittsburgh Courier*, May 14, 1949: 24; "Black Barons Cop Twin Bill," *Birmingham News*, May 9, 1949: 18.

4 "Buckeyes Break 5-Game Loss Streak," *Louisville Courier Journal*, May 12, 1949: 11.

5 "Black Barons Edge Chicago, 4-3" *Birmingham News*, May 12, 1949: 48.

6 "Black Barons Win Two, Play Wednesday," *Birmingham News*, May 23, 1949: 14.

7 "Black Barons Win Benefit Tussle, 6 to 3," *Birmingham News*, May 26, 1949: 49.

8 "Barons Blank Buckeyes 7-0," *Louisville Courier Journal*, May 28, 1949: Sports, 5.

9 "Spies to Eye Cubans," *New York Sunday News*, May 29, 1949: 33C.

10 "League-Leading Cubans Split 2 as Scantlebury Strikes Out 10," *New York Age*, June 4, 1949: 33.

11 "Bushwicks Drop Arc Light Opener," *Brooklyn Daily Eagle*, June 2, 1949: 21.

12 The itinerary for this road trip appeared in "Birmingham Black Barons to Play Normal Red Sox Here June 16," *Alabama Citizen* (Tuscaloosa, Alabama), June 4, 1949: 7.

13 "Black Barons Split Pair with Clowns," *Birmingham News*, June 21. 1949: 21.

14 "Mays' Single Gives Black Barons Win," *Birmingham News*, July 11, 1949: 18.

15 "Black Barons Nip Memphis Red Sox," *Birmingham News*, July 28, 1949: 42.

16 "Baltimore in 3 to 2 Victory Over Barons," *Atlanta Daily World*, August 9, 1949: 5.

17 Charles Littlejohn, "Black Barons Nip Kansas City, 3-2," *Montgomery Advertiser*, August 25, 1949: 16.

18 "Black Barons Defeat Buckeyes Easily, 7-1," *Birmingham News*, September 24, 1949: 9.

19 Russ J. Cowans, "Move Over, You Vets, Willie Mays is Coming Up Like a Prairie Fire," *Chicago Defender*, August 27, 1949: 14.

20 "Black Barons Lose Bus, Equipment but Win Two of Three," *Birmingham News*, June 13, 1950: 26.

21 "Giants Sign Black Barons' Willie Mays," *Birmingham Post-Herald*, June 22, 1950: 20; "Mays, Black Barons Star, Is Going Up," *Birmingham News*, June 22, 1950: 18.

22 "Mays Bats in Four/Black Barons Win, 7-1," *Birmingham News*, June 18, 1950: 44.

23 "Willie Mays Sparks Barons on Big Spree," *Chicago Defender*, June 24, 1950: 17.

# WILLIE MAYS IN TRENTON

BY STEVEN M. GLASSMAN

BIRMINGHAM BARONS CENTER fielder Willie Mays was not originally who scout Ed Montague was looking at for the New York Giants.[1] On Alex Pompez's recommendation to the Giants' director of minor league operations, Jack Schwartz, he was looking at Barons first baseman Alonzo Perry for the Sioux City (Iowa) Soos, the Giants' Class-A affiliate in the Western League.[2] John Saccoman wrote in Mays' SABR biography: "In a 1954 letter to Tim Cohane, the sports editor of *Look* magazine, Giants scout Eddie Montague stated that he was scouting the Black Barons first baseman, Alonzo Perry, for the Giants' Sioux City Class-A club, when Mays caught his eye. He said, '[T]his was the greatest young player I had ever seen in my life or my scouting career.'"[3]

Montague and another Giants scout, Bill Harris, went to see Mays at Rickwood Field in Birmingham. Leo Durocher wrote in his book *Nice Guys Finish Last* that Montague reported, "[T]hey got a kid playing center field practically barefooted that's the best ballplayer I ever looked at. You better send somebody down there with a barrelful of money and grab this kid."[4]

Multiple teams had their chances to sign Mays. In 1949 a Pittsburgh Pirates scout offered the Barons $2,000 to sign and convert Mays from an outfielder to a pitcher. The Boston Braves sent its scout Bill Maughn, and owner Lou Perini offered the Barons $7,500 for Mays in 1949, but there was a major-league rule that did not allow teams to sign players while they were still in high school. Mays graduated from Fairfield Industrial High School on May 31, 1950.

The Braves sent another scout, Hugh Wise. Wise watched Mays get one hit in a doubleheader on May 21 and said that one day was enough. The Braves did not make an offer because they had recently spent more than $100,000 to purchase outfielder Sam Jethroe from the Brooklyn Dodgers. Dodgers scout Wid Matthews said in 1949 that Mays could not hit curveballs. A second Dodgers scout, Ray Blades, was sent to see Mays in 1950. The Dodgers already had three established stars: Roy Campanella, Don Newcombe, and Jackie Robinson. The White Sox hired John Donaldson as their first African American full-time scout. He recommended Mays, but they did not listen to his recommendation to sign him. The Red Sox sent scouts Larry Woodall and George

Digby, but the Red Sox did not sign Mays because they signed the Barons' Piper Davis. The Yankees sent Bill McCorry and he had the same evaluation as the Dodgers' Matthews: that Mays could not hit a curve. Altogether, six teams had a chance to sign Mays before the Giants had their chance.

On June 22, 1951, "with an outlay of $15,000, of which the Birmingham Black Barons will receive $9,000 and the player $6,000, the New York Giants outbid five major league clubs."[5] According to an August 15, 1951, *Sporting News* article, "the Black Barons [were] temporarily low on ready cash because their bus had gone up in flames in the Holland Tunnel after a New York game."[6] Birmingham general manager Eddie Glennon thought Mays could be a pitcher because of his throwing arm. Barons manager Vic Harris wanted him in the outfield so he could play every day.

Mays was sent to the Trenton Giants of the Class-B Interstate League instead of Sioux City because of racial issues. He wrote in his autobiography, *Say Hey*: "But Sioux City was not the place for me at the moment. The city was in an uproar because they had buried an Indian in a whites-only cemetery only a few days before. The farm club refused to take me, fearing the consequences and 'bad' publicity. I was surprised, but I guess I should have been shocked. I had never heard of anything like that before. Then again, I had never played outside the Negro Leagues either."[7]

He wrote that his train ride from Birmingham to Hagerstown "seemed like an eternity that spring day in 1950. I kept fumbling with the bag of sandwiches that Aunt Sarah had made for me, but I was too nervous to eat. Look out the window, look at the bag, look at the hands. This ride was different. This was taking me to organized ball – the first big step in living out my boyhood dream of playing in the majors someday. … I had that chance now and I couldn't wait to play for Trenton – so much so that I even skipped my senior prom so I could there early."[8]

Mays was greeted by Trenton Giants radio broadcaster Bus Saidt at the Hagerstown train station. He met his manager, Chick Genovese, at Hagerstown Municipal Stadium. Mays wrote that Genovese was "someone who would be important to me in my first experience with so-called organized baseball. He greeted me warmly and made me feel comfortable."[9]

Mays was not in the Trenton starting lineup on June 23. Jason Arnoff wrote that "Len Matte also told Bill Klink about the time after Willie Mays first joined the team for a game in Hagerstown, Maryland. Before the game Matte was working with Trenton manager Chick Genovese, who was hitting fly balls to the new player Mays. Chick Genovese was hitting fly balls all over the outfield forcing Mays to run hither and yon to catch the balls. After watching Mays catch balls in far-flung parts of the outfield, Genovese turned to Matte and said, 'This guy has the kind of reflexes no one else has.'"[10] Tom McCarthy wrote in *Baseball in Trenton*, "there is no doubt that Mays refined his famous basket catch in the Negro Leagues and in the minor leagues, but some credit Matte for helping Mays with the basket catch."[11]

Mays also recalled his first professional weekend with Trenton in Hagerstown: "I was the first black in that particular league. And, we played in a town called Hagerstown, Maryland. I'll never forget this day, on a Friday. And, they call you all kind of names there, "n****r" this, and "n****r" that. I said to myself – and this is why Piper Davis came in – in my mind, "Hey, whatever they call you, they can't touch you. Don't talk back." Now this was on a Friday. And the Friday night I hit two doubles and a home run; they never clapped. The next day I hit the same thing. There was a house out there in the back there, I hit that twice. Now they started clapping a little bit. You know how that is, you know, they clapped a little bit. By Sunday there was a big headline in the paper: "Do Not Bother Mays." You understand what I'm saying? They call you all kinds of names. Now this is the first two games I played. By Sunday, I come to bat, they're all clapping. And I'm wondering, wait a minute, what happened to the Friday, what happened to the Saturday? This is running through my mind now."[12]

Mays added the following: "What I didn't get over was the long train ride that had brought me there. Although I did feel good during batting practice – I hit six or seven balls over the fence – in the game or for the rest of the four-game series. I started my organized baseball career oh-for-Maryland, and I in a segregated town, to boot. I wondered whether my showing confirmed some of those rednecks' feelings that I wouldn't do well in the big-time. What a way to start. And then after the game I found I couldn't stay with the team at their hotel. The club had already made arrangements for me to spend the weekend in a small hotel for blacks."[13]

He stayed at the Harmon Hotel in a segregated section of Hagerstown. James S. Hirsch wrote in his book, *Willie Mays: The Life, The Legend*: "Mays wasn't particular about hotels, but he had never been separated from his teammates before. He knew about segregation, but his segregation had always been collective – with friends, relatives, or teammates who derived strength and pride from their unity. Now he was segregated and alone."[14] Some of his teammates noticed this and sometime after midnight, there was a knocking on his window. Three of his teammates, including outfielder Bob Easterbrook, climbed the fire escape and were entering his room and checking in on him. The players stayed, slept on the floor in Mays' room, got up at 6 A.M., climbed out the window, and went to back to the Alexander Hotel. No one said anything about the late-night visit and no else had any knowledge. He slept soundly on his first night in the minors.

Mays reflected that "Chick Genovese took a special interest in me. I wouldn't have had a better manager for my first year in organized ball, and since he was a former outfielder, it made the whole thing that much better. … Chick quickly sized up my problem over the first few games: I was pressing. He made me aware of what I was doing, and told me just to relax and not over swing – the base hits would come."[15]

He later added in his autobiography that "Chick was my biggest rooter. He always watched over me. He knew about the effect that segregation was having on me, and he also knew there was nothing he could do about it. But there were things he could do in his own way. I didn't show it, and I never spoke about it, but maybe he could sense my loneliness and anxiety. There were times when he'd eat with me in a kitchen in a restaurant, either in Hagerstown or Wilmington, so I wouldn't be alone. Those were moments I still treasure. It was the first time I had been off by myself somewhere, for even when I was on the road with the Barons in a segregated situation, at least all of us were segregated at the same time in the same place."[16]

Mays made his Trenton debut vs. the York (Pennsylvania) Roses on June 26. He contributed two hits in the 4-3 win in front of 1,321 at Dunn Field. Defensively, "Three of his five putouts were remarkable catches, with throws to third base and home plate illustrating his exceptional throwing arm. In the third inning, he sped backward and leaped high enough to spear a long fly with his bare hand, much to the amazement of the onlookers. It was quickly realized that an unusually gifted player had joined the Trenton team."[17] Jason Arnoff writes that "Bill Klink, in The *Ol' Ball Game*, first quotes Eric Rodin, Trenton's right fielder that day. Rodin describes York's Bill Biddle hitting a ball to deep center field, a ball that would have carried over the fence. He assumed that Mays would not catch the ball. However, Mays did get to the ball, but as he reached up with his gloved hand, the ball went by his glove. Rodin continues, 'but his reflexes were such that he went up with his bare hand against the fence, caught the ball and came down.'"[18]

On June 28, Mays hit his first professional home run, a grand slam, in a 21-8 win on the road against the Sunbury Athletics.

Willie Mays and John Shea wrote in the book *24* that "Trenton second baseman Harry 'Ace' Bell said that Mays was a target of insults in other cities, including Sunbury, Pennsylvania, where the

Philadelphia A's had a farm team. Many of these fans around the league hadn't seen an African American play ball and were offended or even enraged by the notion of an integrated team. Mays turned heads with his elite performance and passion and began to soften some long-entrenched feelings of resistance and even hatred. Bell was impressed with how Willie rose above the abuse and focused on playing ball. 'Willie was such a nice kid,' Bell said. 'He was friendly with everybody, and he would praise everybody. He'd be your best fan. And you could tell right away he could hit. There wasn't anything that fooled Willie. I'm sure his Birmingham team had a better bunch of ballplayers than what Trenton had.'"[19] Mays and Shea added: "'We had guys looking out for him, making sure he had a room and transportation,' said Bell, who joined the team about the same time as Mays, after graduating college. 'A lot of places wouldn't accept a black person. Wilmington, Hagerstown. He had to go to a different part of the town. Three or four of the kids volunteered to find a place for him in those cities. They made sure he had a room. It was always in the black section. That's how Willie lived when we were on the road. That's the way it was at the time.'"[20]

Mays, according to *Say Hey,* "lived in a boarding house on Spring Street in Trenton, which was five blocks from Dunn Field. The room was fine. On the road, though, the Giants, thinking I was lonely by myself, sent Trenton a pitcher named Jose Fernandez. His father was the manager of the New York Cubans. They played their home games in the Polo Grounds. We didn't get along too well. He was a hot dog from New York and I was a country boy. One evening he didn't wake me up in time to make the team bus and Chick jumped all over him. Fernandez didn't last long. He was gone in a month. I was happy again."[21]

Traveling on the road on the team's bus, Genovese would try to have his players sing songs. Hirsch wrote that "Mays would start off with 'Clarence the Clocker,' and soon everyone would join in. In Mays' eyes, the bus rides were no different than those he had taken with the Black Barons, teeming with goodwill and camaraderie, young men who loved baseball and dreamed of making it to the big leagues. In 1950, white Americans across the country denied blacks equal treatment on buses, but on the Trenton Giant bus, Willie Mays received special treatment. In need of rest, he would pile the duffel bags in the back, lie down, and sleep."[22]

Saccoman wrote that "Mays also recalled a catch he made in Trenton in 1950. He said that Lou Heyman of Wilmington hit a ball 405 feet to dead center and he caught it barehanded, bounced off the wall, and threw the ball all the way home on the fly."[23] Mays added, "Nobody knew about it because it was just another game in a small town."[24]

Within a month, Hagerstown fans warmed up to Willie as well. On July 19, *Hagerstown Daily Mail* sports columnist Dick Kelly wrote that Willie Mays was now turning in "a very credible performance" and "making the grade in fine style with the Trenton Giants."[25]

Hirsch wrote that "Mays experimented on the field. During batting practice, he saw how close he could play in center while still being able to track down deep flies. On ground balls, he realized that if high grass or soft ground balls slowed the ball, he could reach hits in the gap while also snaring low line drives that would otherwise go for singles. For years, Mays would walk on the outfield grass before a game and throw a ball down to determine if the surface was fast or slow."[26] He added that "Mays thought he had already mastered baseball strategy, but Genovese, along with Trenton Giants general manager Bill McKechnie, expanded his education. Sitting on the bench before game or riding on the bus, the two men fired questions at Mays."[27]

Genovese would send the Giants reports on Mays' progress. For example: "He's a major league prospect. Possesses strong arms and wrist, runs good, has good baseball instinct. Wants to learn. Should play AAA ball next year."[28] Giants owner Horace Stoneham also noticed and would visit with some of his staff to Trenton more than once to see Mays.

Mays wrote about the origins of where "Say hey!" came from: "My teammates started to call me Junior, and I began to relax, even though I was only nineteen years old. I'd often shout back, 'Say hey!' whenever I wanted their attention. These were all new people to me and I didn't know their names. 'Say hey!' was guaranteed to get them to listen to me."[29]

As the season progressed after his first professional weekend in Hagerstown, Mays kept calm when opposing pitchers sometimes threw at his head. However, "this time I just glared back at the pitcher and he got my message that he couldn't intimidate me. As if that wasn't enough, Eric Rodin, the next batter, did something whose message couldn't be mistaken. After I made out, Rodin, a big rightfielder, laid down a bunt toward first base, attempting to run into the pitcher and knock him down when he tried to field it. Luckily the ball rolled foul. Who knows what would have happened? Here I was the first black ballplayer in the league's history, and my teammate was ready to start a fight with someone over me. Even though the ball was foul, both benches emptied onto the field. It was a show of strength and support for me by my teammates, and it cleared the air."[30]

Mays wrote in his autobiography: "I never believed in playing the game in a halfhearted way. And I suppose that because I put so much of myself into every at bat, every fly ball, every throw, every stolen base, that all these exertions took their toll. That first year I played hard, too. Near the end of the season, in fact, I collapsed from fatigue after playing a string of doubleheaders. One day I was so wiped out that they called for an ambulance. I'd go after every ball hit into the outfield – crashing into fences, falling on the ground, just running my head off – and think nothing of it. The other outfielders didn't mind it at all. In fact, Mo Cunningham, our left fielder, used to kid me. He'd yell, 'Plenty of room, Junior! We'll let you know where the fence is.'"[31]

In his autobiography, Mays noted the racist epithets and profanities directed at him. He wrote that "Len Matte, our catcher, told me that he'd take care of any trouble and that I shouldn't get involved. It was good advice. As the season wore on, there was less and less incidents and curses, until I didn't hear them anymore. I knew, anyway that I wouldn't be back in this league next year. I would be leaving Trenton for Minneapolis, the Class AAA in the American Association. Triple A ball was only one step from the majors."[32]

Trenton finished with a 73-65 record and in fourth place, nine games behind the Wilmington Blue Rocks (Philadelphia Phillies). The Giants were 42-36 after Mays' debut. The 42 wins after his debut were the fourth-best in the league. However, they lost 4-1 to Hagerstown in the postseason semifinals. In a February 24, 1954, *Sporting News* article, Genovese said, "Junior meant about three places in the standings for our club. Without him we'd finish seventh. With him we made fourth place."[33]

Mays hit over .400 for most of the Trenton season, but finished with a .353 batting average, a .510 slugging percentage, and a .438 on-base percentage in 81 games. Despite not making his debut until June 25, he was voted to the 1950 Interstate League postseason all-star team along with three teammates, first baseman Robert Myers, shortstop Tomas Korczowski, and pitcher Joseph Micciche.[34] Two of his teammates, right-handed pitcher Rinty Monahan (1953 Philadelphia Athletics) and outfielder Eric Rodin (1954 Giants), reached what was then termed the major leagues.[35] Defensively, he led the league with 17 outfield assists. He also boosted attendance at Trenton's Dunn Field, and whenever a runner took off from first base to second on a single, the crowd would rise in unison in expectation of a spectacular gun-down by Mays to third or home.[36]

"Chick's final words to me that season were, 'Willie, you're going to make a lot of money one day. I hope I helped you.'"[37]

Mays was invited to Giants spring training in 1951 and started the season for the Minneapolis Millers of the Triple-A American Association before making his National League debut on May 25, 1951, some 11 months after making his debut in Trenton.

Trenton moved to Sunbury, Pennsylvania, for the 1951 season. Minor-league baseball returned to Trenton in 1994, replacing London, Ontario, as a Detroit Tigers affiliate. Mays became the third player overall with Trenton ties and the first by the baseball writers' vote to be inducted into the National Baseball Hall of Fame.[38]

Mays returned to Hagerstown on August 9, 2004. The *Frederick News-Post*'s Joshua R. Smith wrote: "There was a large reception at the Clarion Hotel. When he was introduced by Suns General Manager Kurt Landes, a green curtain parted and Mays emerged, tipping his Giants cap before sitting down to hearty applause. Mays then spoke, telling the audience he was glad he returned, so he could see what the town was all about. 'Before I start crying,' he said, 'I better pass for a while,' motioning to Landes. Mays then lifted his glasses and dabbed tears as the fans rose again."[39]

Landes made two announcements before going to Hagerstown Municipal Stadium. Mays' Giants uniform number 24 would be retired and Memorial Boulevard would be renamed Willie Mays Way.[40] Smith wrote that "Mays arrived in a white Buick, and the anxious crowd cheered when he opened the door to step out. 'I didn't really think I would get the ovation I received today,' Mays said. 'It's wonderful.' Moments later, still wearing his suit jacket, Mays fired a strike for the game's ceremonial first pitch. Just inside the gate to the field, the mayor's wife, Gann Breichner, talked about how this was the best day of her husband's career. She said she knew Mays would return to Hagerstown if he was approached correctly. 'He's a man with a big heart,' she said."[41]

Allen Barra wrote in his book, *Mickey and Willie: Mantle and Mays, The Parallel Lives of Baseball's Golden Age*: "It was all the same to him where he played, but he had one objection to Trenton: the league was Class-B. No one could ever be certain how the Negro Leagues stacked up to the different levels of white minor leagues, but the Barons, Willie told Charlie Einstein, played better baseball than he saw at Trenton (and probably baseball as good as he later saw in Triple A). 'No one really got to know how good the players were in the Negro League since the press' – meaning, of course, the white press – 'never covered the games. But I knew I was so much richer from it. I didn't realize that my leaving was another nail in the coffin of all-black baseball.'"[42]

Genovese said after Mays played for him in 1950: "Junior is the best-looking young player I've seen in many a day. I played in Louisville when Duke Snider was at St. Paul and always thought Duke would become a tremendous hitter. Willie doesn't have Duke's power, but he can do everything else better. I believe he has the strongest, most accurate arm in baseball. I have not seen Carl Furillo, but I cannot believe any human can out-throw Mays. It's a low line strike every time, no matter how far out he may be. Mays in time will be an outstanding hitter. He hits straight away most of the time, and while you would not call him a real power hitter, he is always getting a piece of the ball, and sometimes will hit it a helluva ways. He hasn't seen any pitching yet, because he was too good for our league, but I predict wherever he goes he will, in a short while, learn to hit pitching."[43]

## SOURCES

In addition to the sources mentioned in the Notes, the author referred to https://www.baseball-reference.com/ and https://www.retrosheet.org/ for box scores, play-by-plays, and other pertinent information.

## NOTES

1 Montague was a Giants scout in 1942-1943 and 1946-1981.

2 Pompez previously recommended Monte Irvin and Hank Thompson to the Giants.

3 John Saccoman. "Willie Mays," SABR BioProject, https://sabr.org/bioproj/person/willie-mays/.

4 Saccoman.

5 "Giants Outbid Five Clubs for Mays, Negro Prospect," *The Sporting News*, July 5, 1951: 41.

6 Clay Felker, "Mays Dynamite at Bat, Magnet in Field," *The Sporting News*, August 15, 1951: 3.

7 Willie Mays with Lou Sahadi, *Say Hey: The Autobiography of Willie Mays* (New York: Pocket Books, 1988), 40.

8 Mays with Sahadi, 41.

9 Mays with Sahadi, 43.

10 Jason Aronoff, *Going, Going ... Caught!* (Jefferson, North Carolina: McFarland and Company, Inc., 2009), 152.

11 Tom McCarthy. *Baseball in Trenton* (Charleston, South Carolina: Arcadia Publishing, 2003), 31.

12 Academy of Achievement, "Willie Mays Biography – Academy of Achievement," accessed February 26, 2023. https://achievement.org/achiever/willie-mays/#interview.

13 Mays with Sahadi, 43.

14 James S. Hirsch, *Willie Mays: The Life, the Legend* (New York: Scribner, 2010), 66.

15 Mays with Sahadi, 43.

16 Mays with Sahadi, 44-45.

17 Randolph Linthurst, "Willie Mays' First Season,"https://sabr.org/journal/article/willie-mays-first-season/. This article was originally in SABR's *Baseball Research Journal* in 1974.

18 Aronoff.

19 Willie Mays and John Shea, *24* (New York: St. Martin's Press, 2020), 53.

20 Mays and Shea, 53.

21 Mays with Sahadi, 46. According to his *Sporting News* player contract card, Fernandez joined Trenton on June 29, 1950, went on the disabled list on July 20, was reinstated on July 31, and was released on September 18.

22 Hirsch, 68-69.

23 Saccoman.

24 Aronoff.

25 Jacob Kaplan, "'Oh-for-Maryland': When Willie Mays Said Hey to Hub City," *Boundary Stories*, June 22, 2017, https://boundarystones.weta.org/2017/06/22/oh-maryland-when-willie-mays-said-hey-hub-city.

26 Hirsch, 69.

27 Hirsch, 69.

28 Hirsch, 69.

29 Mays with Sahadi, 43-44.

30 Mays with Sahadi, 45-46.

31 Mays with Sahadi, 47.

32 Mays with Sahadi, 47.

33 Joe King, "New Spirit on Club as Mays Marches Back From Army," *The Sporting News*, February 24, 1954: 5.

34 Adam Hyzdu (1996), Dernell Stenson (1998), Raul Gonzalez (1999), Zoilo Almonte (2012), and Trey Amburgey (2018) are Trenton outfielders who were voted to the Eastern League Postseason All-Star team.

35 Rodin was in the same outfield with Mays, playing one inning with him on September 12, 1954, vs. the St. Louis Cardinals. He entered the game as a defensive replacement for Mays for the final three innings against the Brooklyn Dodgers at Ebbets Field on September 21, 1954. Rodin pinch-hit for Mays and remained in the game for the final six innings at the next day's game.

36 Mays with Sahadi, 47.

37 Mays with Sahadi, 47.

38 These are the Hall of Fame inductees who have a connection to Trenton: Bill McKechnie (1962 Veterans Committee) was the Trenton Giants general manager in 1950. Goose Goslin (1968 Veterans) was the player-manager of the Trenton Senators from 1939 through 1941. Walt Alston (1983 Veterans) was the player-manager of the Trenton Packers in 1944 and 1945. Frank Grant (2006 Veterans) played second base for the 1889 Cuban Giants of the independent Middle States League. Derek Jeter (2020 BBWAA) played five games for the Trenton Thunder (New York Yankees) as part of a rehabilitation assignment from July 7 to July 11, 2003, and two games from July 2 to July 3, 2011. Bus Saidt broadcast Trenton Giant games on WBUD from 1947 to 1950. He began working for the *Trentonian* in 1964 and then the *Trenton Times* in 1967. He was posthumously given the 1992 BBWAA Career Excellence Award.

39 Joshua R. Smith. "Willie Says Hey to Hagerstown," *Frederick* (Maryland) *News-Post*, August 10, 2004, https://www.fredericknewspost.com/archives/willie-says-hey-to-hagerstown/article_75611b9e-9ea3-5eae-86b8-8802d49cec91.html.

40 Mays wore uniform number 12 for Trenton. Jackie Robinson's uniform number 42 was universally retired in 1997. It not known if Hagerstown retired any more numbers after Mays' in 2004. The retired number is on the right-field wall.

41 Smith.

42 Allan Barra, *Mickey and Willie: Mantle and Mays, The Parallel Lives of Baseball's Golden Age* (New York: Crown Publishing Group, 2013), 112-113.

43 Joe King, "Willie Changes Giants' Gloom into Grins," *The Sporting News*, February 24, 1954: 5-6.

# WILLIE MAYS HAD A SPECTACULAR – BUT SHORT – STAY IN MINNEAPOLIS

BY STEW THORNLEY

THE NEW YORK Giants purchased the Minneapolis Millers in 1946. It took five years for Minneapolis fans to fully process the impact.

A charter member of the American Association in 1902, the Millers had a rich history that extended to the final decades of the nineteenth century. The locals had the chance to cheer on many players at cozy and quaint Nicollet Park who ended up in the Hall of Fame. Some were on their way up, such as Roger Bresnahan and Red Faber, although more were veterans who had already established their credentials in the majors, including Rube Waddell and Zack Wheat. Such was the nature of the minor leagues then, prospects combined with those hanging on as long as their talents could earn them a living.

However, the stalwarts were those who never reached such lofty levels but returned year after year – Henri Rondeau, Joe Hauser, Spencer Harris – and were familiar stars to loyalists.

Mike Kelley had operated the Millers since 1924[1] before being one of the last of the independent owners to turn his operation over to a major-league team. The Millers had had loose affiliations in the past, such as with the Boston Red Sox in 1937-38. However, the team was not fully stocked with players under the control of a parent team. The relationship did give Minneapolis fans the chance to see Ted Williams, who spent a season with the Millers in 1938 and won the league triple crown.

But the 1946 sale was a break toward the Millers being a team used for player development rather than an entity in their own right.[2] The fans got an inkling of what was to come with Harold "Tookie" Gilbert. After signing as a 17-year-old with the Giants, he was assigned to the Millers in 1947, too high a level as it turned out. Gilbert did better at lower levels and was back in Minneapolis in 1950. After only six games, the Giants brought him up to the majors, which again proved too much for him. Minneapolis writers used Gilbert as a cautionary tale against rushing a talented prospect too fast, and Gilbert also served as a warning to fans – even if they didn't yet realize it – that life as a farm team would be different.

Willie Mays, on the other hand, began playing professional baseball while still in high school. He was proving himself on the Birmingham Black

Barons of the Negro American League. After Mays graduated from Fairfield Industrial High School in 1950, the New York Giants signed him and sent the young star to Trenton, their farm team in the Class-B Interstate League, in 1950.[3] Clearly ready for more, New York placed him with Minneapolis, one of their top farm teams, in 1951.

The Giants had two Triple-A teams in 1951, the Millers and the Ottawa Giants in the International League. The Giants had abandoned Jersey City as a Triple-A team after the 1950 season and kept one of their farm teams in Ottawa in 1951. It was the last year the Giants had two Triple-A teams. SABR members Charlie Bevis and Mark Davis provided insight into why Mays went to Minneapolis rather than Ottawa – that the Giants lacked a commitment to the Ottawa team, having it play on a makeshift diamond within Lansdowne Park, which was the home of the Ottawa team in the Canadian Football League – and that Minneapolis seemed a natural pick over Ottawa for a prospect of Mays' stature.[4]

The Giants were committed to Mays, even keeping him from playing winter ball in Cuba.[5] Whether it was fear of injury or some other reason for keeping Mays out of winter ball,[6] the Giants clearly thought he was ready to perform at the highest level of the minor leagues.

It didn't take long for others to concur.

As their homestead was being pummeled by mid-March snowstorms,[7] the Millers gathered in sunny Sanford, Florida, and opened their exhibition season with a split of games with the Ottawa Giants. Mays homered in one of the games and knocked himself out crashing into the outfield fence in the other. The next day, Halsey Hall provided the first reports on Mays in the *Minneapolis Tribune:* "You watch him run and throw and hit and you are on his side in a minute, although nobody has thrown many curve balls at him yet and he's still a green pea in the organized realm. … Willie is lithe, beautifully muscled, just under six feet, weighs 170 pounds and doesn't vary five pounds in his weight off and in season. Righthanded all the way, he has great power to right center and here the dear old memory of Nicollet's fences in that direction come back."[8]

As the Millers won 13 of 19 spring-training games, Mays led the way with a .408 batting average, 5 home runs, and 29 runs batted in. Minneapolis opened the regular season with a circuit through Columbus, Toledo, Louisville, and Indianapolis. Mays hit .352 in those 13 games.

"Any worry about Willie Mays has just about evaporated," wrote Halsey Hall as the Millers prepared for their home opener. "He has made a swing through the East now, has faced all kinds of pitching, has been held hitless in only one game. … His throwing for power has lived up to reputation. … His throws are not 'arches.' Rather, they are power-laden, even when he throws to put the ball into the hands of a receiver on the ground.

"We think you'll like Willie."[9]

For a time, it had appeared that Minneapolis's Nicollet Park would be a relic of the past by 1951. It was still a relic – but one with a few years left in it.

In late 1948 the Minneapolis Baseball and Athletic Association (essentially the New York Giants) bought land just west of the Minneapolis city limits and announced plans for a new ballpark for the Millers. The Giants said they hoped to have an 18,000-seat stadium ready by 1950.[10] For some reason, a new ballpark on the site never happened. A common perception is that a moratorium on building sports facilities during the Korean War was the reason. However, it doesn't explain why construction (which likely would have been allowed to continue) hadn't started by the time the National Production Authority issued its moratorium nearly two years later.[11]

Whatever the reason, the Millers were still at Nicollet Park. Beyond the inviting nature of Nicollet's fences, referred to by Halsey Hall in a preceding paragraph, its location off Lake Street and Nicollet Avenue provided a convenient locale for Willie and other players to live.

Willie rented a room at 3616 4th Avenue, within walking distance of the ballpark. Across the street from Mays lived two other Black players on the Millers, Ray Dandridge and Dave Barnhill.[12] Andy Sturdevant, then a columnist for *MinnPost,* wrote that the players were "living in one of the centers of black life in the Twin Cities in the 1950s. The neighborhood's business and residential district was located around 38th Street and extended north and south several blocks. Forty-Second Street was the boundary '– the neighborhood to the north of 42nd Street had one of the highest percentages of black residents in the city,' according to one study by the city, with the neighborhood to the south almost entirely white. It was one of a few areas in the Twin Cities where African Americans owned their own houses in the postwar boom years, when the Twin Cities' black population grew by 60 percent. ... In the early 1950s, the neighborhood was home to a large number of black-owned shops, banks, groceries, community centers and churches."[13]

The weather in early May wasn't conducive to baseball, but nearly 6,500 fans showed up for the home opener, a Millers victory stopped by rain and poor field conditions in the last of the seventh. "Willie Mays said howdy do as bombastically as any newcomer in history," wrote Hall. "He got three hits, made a sparkling catch against the flagpole, unfurled a typical throw."[14]

A week later Mays made an incredible catch of a drive hit by Louisville's Taft Wright. "Willie Mays turned scoreboard boy," wrote Hall. "In the third inning the young genius looked like he was hanging up numbers as he leaped almost to the level of the big league board for a fly ball, banged into the wall and doubled a runner at second base. It will rank as one of the greatest catches you will ever see."[15]

Meanwhile, Wright put his head down and hustled into second base, assuming he had a stand-up double, and was incredulous when the umpire informed him he was out. Wright remained at second until manager Pinky Higgins came out and told him that Willie indeed had caught the ball.[16]

Not many people saw the catch by Mays; attendance for the game was 1,351. In the nearly three weeks the Millers were home, the average attendance was under 2,700. Unpleasant weather kept the crowds down, and many fans planned to see the new phenom when temperatures warmed up. They were in for a surprise.

Throughout the homestand, Mays thrilled those who braved the cold with his bat and his glove in addition to the excitement he generated on the basepaths. He kept it up when the Millers departed for games in Milwaukee and Kansas City. With another two hits on May 23, Mays had a batting average of .477 with 8 home runs, 38 runs, and 30 RBIs in 35 games. It was too much for the parent club to ignore.

The next day, the Giants decided it was time to promote Mays. The Millers were in Sioux City for an exhibition game when Willie got the word. Mays said that Giants manager Leo Durocher had seen him during spring training and told him he would be up later in the year. "I didn't expect to come up that quickly," Mays said, "and I didn't want to come up."[17]

Mays was comfortable with how he was playing with the Millers and fearful of how he would do in the majors. He started slowly with New York; he was hitless in his first three games before homering off Boston's Warren Spahn in the next one. Another drought followed, and his batting average slipped to .0476 (compared with .477 with the Millers), and dropped a bit more before he turned it around. He hit .274 with 68 RBIs in 121 major-league games. Mays received the National League Rookie of the Year Award in 1951 and played 23 seasons in the majors, the greatest baseball player ever in the opinion of many.

Mays wasn't the first, but to that point he was the most significant, player to be plucked in midseason by the parent club.[18] Giants President Horace Stoneham tried to mollify the Millers fans with a quarter-page letter – which appeared beneath ads for United Sewing Service, Farmer Jones Store, and Knaeble's Home Furnishers and Funeral Directors – in that Sunday's *Minneapolis Tribune.* "We appreciate his worth to the Millers, but in all fairness Mays himself must be a factor in these considerations. Merit must be recognized. ... Mays is entitled to his promotion, and the chance to prove that he can play major league baseball."[19]

Stoneham's message struck a positive chord with the *Tribune,* which printed an editorial three days later that read, in part, "... we have not witnessed such a tender observance of the amenities since Alphonse first bowed to Gaston in the comic strips. Stoneham thought that the Mays incident deserved an explanation, and so he explained it in poignant phrases calculated to thaw the coldest fury of the Miller baseball fan. ... Give credit to Horace Stoneham – he was gentleman enough to spread a little epistolary balm and ointment on the wounds opened up by Willie Mays' departure."[20]

Whatever balm the fans felt, it was not epistolary, and reporters shared the cynicism. After a call-up of another player (Hank Thompson) by the Giants later in the season, Halsey Hall wrote, "Let [Millers general manager] Rosy Ryan and [manager] Tommy Heath have the gold removed from their teeth and send it to the New York front office. They'll get it sooner or later anyway."[21]

Dick Cullum echoed Hall's sentiments and starkly spelled out what minor-league baseball had become:

"Baseball on the Triple-A farm is mere exhibition training and is not being conducted with an earnest effort to win games."[22]

Mays made a few more playing appearances in Minnesota, in exhibition games at Nicollet Park and Metropolitan Stadium, which became the Millers' home in 1956. He also played for the National League, in the 1965 All-Star Game. Mays returned for one last exhibition game, against the Twins in 1971, in which he played an inning in center field and one inning at each infield position.[23]

One of the largest crowds of the season came to the Met for that exhibition game. As a pair of 16-year-old cousins waited for the gates to open, one spotted an older man who appeared to have the same look of anticipation as the teenagers. One of the younger fans thought about asking the man if he had seen Willie play for the Millers. I'm still sorry I didn't.

*The author thanks Charlie Bevis, Mark Davis, Rod Nelson, Gary Fink, Richard Musterer, and Steve Gietschier among others for providing interesting and valuable information in response to the many queries I had on SABR-L, the SABR listserv.*

## NOTES

1 Kelley had been a player-manager with the St. Paul Saints in the early years of the American Association. He left St. Paul to become manager of the Minneapolis Millers in 1906 and was suspended by the league after twice attacking the integrity of umpires. He was eventually reinstated and spent many more years with St. Paul before returning to Minneapolis in 1924.

2 In a final act of independence (or perhaps defiance), Kelley acted on one final brainstorm that produced a record crowd for Nicollet Park. Moving up a game with the Saints from later in the season to create a Sunday doubleheader on April 28, 1946, Kelley then ordered the ushers not to close the gates and to let all who desired to see the game in. The result was a paid attendance of 15,761, with 5,000 of those fans on the field, some within 10 feet of the baselines. Special ground rules had to be implemented and all balls hit into the crowd were ruled doubles. The Millers and Saints ended up with 24 doubles in the twin bill as the Saints swept the doubleheader.

3 James S. Hirsch, *Willie Mays: The Life, the Legend* (New York: Scribner, 2010), 65. Hirsch said Mays went to Trenton in a Class-B league although the Giants would have preferred one of their Class-A affiliates. However, Hirsch says one of the affiliates was in the Southern Association, which included Birmingham. "The Giants weren't about to send their prize recruit into the heart of the Old Confederacy," Hirsch wrote. The other Class-A team was in Sioux City, Iowa, but "Racial tensions had been simmering there since an American Indian had been buried in a cemetery for whites, and the Giants feared the arrival of a black baseball player could plunge that town into turmoil." *Note:* The Giants did not have a farm team in the Southern Association in 1950; their other Class-A club was in Jacksonville, Florida, in the South Atlantic League. Both the South Atlantic League and Southern Association had a number of teams in the Deep South. Not only that, the South Atlantic League did not integrate until 1953, the Southern Association not until 1954 and then only briefly. For more, see John Thorn's Baseball Integration Timeline, https://ourgame.mlblogs.com/baseball-integration-timeline-b289bc04ca12.

4 Input from SABR members Charlie Bevis and Mark Davis provided insight on why the Giants sent Mays to Minneapolis rather than Ottawa. Email correspondence in July 2022.

5 "Willie Miranda, Nat Rookie, Sparkles in Cuban League," *The Sporting News,* February 14, 1951: 25. The Almendares club in the Cuban League had sought to sign Mays after losing another outfielder, Dick Williams, to the military, but the New York Giants refused.

6 After establishing himself with the Giants, Mays played in the Puerto Rican League, forming an eminent outfield with Roberto Clemente and Bob Thurman on a Santurce Cangrejeros team that won the Caribbean Series in 1954-1955.

7 A Minnesota adage was to not take off snow tires until after the boys' high-school basketball tournament, which seemed to be accompanied by heavy snow each year. In 1951 the storms hit before and after the tournament and even caused a sizable section of Williams Arena, site of the tournament, to collapse a few days before the tournament.

8 Halsey Hall, "19-Year-Old Miller in Fifth Year of Baseball," *Minneapolis Tribune,* March 20, 1951: 15.

9 Halsey Hall, "It's a Fact," *Minneapolis Tribune,* May 1, 1951: 18.

10 Halsey Hall, "New Ball Park Deal Closed," *Minneapolis Tribune,* December 13, 1948: 1.

11 The Minneapolis Park Board got permission to continue construction of football and baseball stadiums on the Parade Grounds on the edge of downtown Minneapolis despite the NPA moratorium, an indication that the Giants could have finished any baseball stadium it had started by that time. The Giants originally seemed intent on having a stadium finished by 1950 at the latest, and regular updates on the ballpark appeared in the St. Louis Park newspaper through 1949 before mysteriously disappearing in early 1950. The Giants, who had bought the land from a neighboring restaurant, held the property into the 1970s. The restaurant, which had reportedly sold the land at a discount, banking on a ballpark bringing in more customers, unsuccessfully sued the Giants based on an agreement the restaurant claimed it had with the Giants to be able to buy back the land if there was no ballpark on it within five years.

12 Rolf Felstad, "Such a One Is Willie," *Minneapolis Tribune,* Sunday, May 27, 1951: 3F.

13 Andy Sturdevant, "Willie Mays' South Minneapolis Neighborhood," *MinnPost,* October 12, 2016, https://www.minnpost.com/stroll/2016/10/willie-mays-south-minneapolis-neighborhood-just-two-months-1951.

14 Halsey Hall, "Millers 'Mudders' Overwhelm Columbus 11-0," *Minneapolis Tribune,* May 2, 1951: 19.

15 Halsey Hall, "Millers Beat Colonels 10-9," *Minneapolis Tribune,* May 8, 1951: 21.

16 Rob Tanenbaum, "Minneapolis Ignored Mays," *Minneapolis Star,* January 23, 1979: 3D.

17 Author interview with Willie Mays, July 9, 2002.

18 Ottawa fans were experiencing the same bruised feelings as those in Minneapolis. When the Giants called up Mays, they sent shortstop Artie Wilson, who had been a star with Birmingham in the Negro American League, to Ottawa. When the Millers had an injury to infielder Rudy Rufer, the Giants then transferred Wilson to the Millers to fill the gap. Joe Hendrickson, "Sports Views," *Minneapolis Tribune,* June 6, 1951: 20.

19 *Minneapolis Tribune,* May 27, 1951: 4E.

20 "That Stoneham Letter," *Minneapolis Tribune,* May 30, 1951: 6.

21 Halsey Hall, "It's a Fact," *Minneapolis Tribune,* August 31, 1951: 19.

22 Dick Cullum, "Cullum's Column," *Minneapolis Tribune,* August 30, 1951: 18.

23 For the Giants, Mays played in exhibition games in Minnesota against the Millers on August 11, 1954; June 23, 1955; June 7, 1956; June 17, 1957; and June 15, 1959. He played in an exhibition game against the Chicago White Sox on May 19, 1958, and against the Minnesota Twins on August 9, 1971. He also played for the National League in the All-Star Game in Minnesota on July 13, 1965. In eight games, he had a batting average of .455 with five home runs and seven runs batted in.

# WILLIE MAYS AT THE POLO GROUNDS

BY JOHN J. BURBRIDGE JR.

**CERTAIN BALLPARKS COMPLEMENT** the strengths of specific players. Yankee Stadium, which opened in 1923, was termed the House That Ruth Built. One reason for such a slogan was the short distance to the right-field stands, which seemed to cater to the powerful left-handed stroke of Babe Ruth.[1] While the benefits of Ruth playing in Yankee Stadium were immediate, it took many years for a player to take advantage of the vast center field at the Polo Grounds. That player was Willie Mays.

New York City was home to playing fields termed the Polo Grounds from 1876 through 1963. The first Polo Grounds, at 110th Street and Fifth Avenue in Manhattan, was used for polo. In 1880 the New York Metropolitans, owned by John B. Day, began playing baseball at the site. Day moved the Metropolitans to the American Association in 1883 while also taking control of a team from Troy, New York. That team was called the Gothams and played in the new National League. They became the Giants in 1885. Both teams played at the Polo Grounds after a second field was built on the site. The Metropolitans ceased operating after the 1887 season.

In 1889 New York City had plans for the 110th Street site and Day looked for a new home for the Giants. He settled on a field in Coogan's Hollow at 155th Street and Eighth Avenue in Manhattan for the new Polo Grounds. The Giants quickly got a neighbor, the New York team in the newly formed Players' League. They played their games at a field adjacent to the new Polo Grounds, Brotherhood Park. The Players' League folded after one year. The Giants decided Brotherhood Park was a better venue and made it their home field. It was also called the Polo Grounds.[2]

A fire just after the 1911 season began caused widespread damage to the wooden ballpark. The new ballpark, built with steel, concrete, and marble, was ready three months later.[3] This version of the Polo Grounds became the home of the Giants until they moved to San Francisco at the end of the 1957 season.

This last manifestation of the Polo Grounds was unique among ballparks. The right-field foul pole was just 258 feet from home plate while left field was 277 feet. However, both the right-field and left-field stands extended straight out, finally curving as they reached the center-field bleachers. The power alleys in both right and left were approximately 450 feet from home plate while center field was even more distant, 483 feet. A superb center fielder was required to cover this wide expanse of ground. Over the years, the Giants had good center fielders but it wasn't until 1951 that the team found a perfect fit in Willie Mays.

His journey to the Polo Grounds began in Birmingham, Alabama, where he joined the Black Barons of the Negro American League in 1948.

On a barnstorming trip to Birmingham, Roy Campanella became excited at seeing Mays patrol center field and throwing out the speedy Larry Doby at home plate.[4] He told the Brooklyn Dodgers they had to see this kid. They sent a scout, Wid Matthews, to look him over. Apparently, Mathews was not impressed, saying, "He could not hit a curve ball."[5] The Dodgers passed on Mays.

Another team that looked at Mays was the New York Giants. In a quirk of fortune, Giants scout Eddie Montague was looking at another Black Barons player when he spotted Mays. Montague said Mays was the greatest young player he had ever seen. The Giants quickly signed Mays in 1950 with a bonus of $4,000 and a salary of $250 per month.[6] Fate had intervened as Mays was destined for the Polo Grounds, not Ebbets Field, which was the Dodgers' home ballpark..

The Giants assigned Mays to the Trenton team in the Class-B Interstate League. After hitting .355 and playing a flawless center field at Trenton, he was invited to join the top farm team of the Giants, the Minneapolis Millers, for 1951 spring training. In a game with the parent club, Mays had a double and a home run and attracted the attention of Giants manager Leo Durocher. Durocher wanted Mays to play center field for the Giants in 1951. Horace Stoneham, the Giants owner, felt he needed more time in the minor leagues, given that he was only 19. Mays began the season with Minneapolis.

The Giants got off to a slow start while Mays was starring with the Millers. As the Giants struggled, Durocher kept lobbying Stoneham to bring Mays up to the majors. In late May Durocher finally got his wish and Mays became a Giant. He was no stranger to the Polo Grounds, having played several games there with the Black Barons.

Mays made his debut on May 25 in Philadelphia's Shibe Park. He went hitless and also struggled in the field. In the next two games in Philadelphia, he also went hitless. Returning to the Polo Grounds for a three-game series against the Boston Braves, Mays hit a home run over the left-field roof against future Hall of Famer Warren Spahn in the first inning. That was his only hit in the series. In the Giants' next game, against the Pittsburgh Pirates, he went 0-for-5. He was 1-for-26 in his first seven games.

After the game with the Pirates, Mays was found crying in the clubhouse. Coaches Herman Franks and Freddie Fitzsimmons called for Durocher. Mays told Durocher he couldn't hit big-league pitching and should be sent to the minors. Durocher responded, "As long as I'm the manager of the Giants, you are my center fielder. Tomorrow, next week, next month. You're here to stay. With your talent, you're going to get plenty of hits."[7]

Durocher also had some advice for Mays about his difficulties at the plate. He had noticed that Mays was turning over his right hand too quickly when swinging, leading to groundballs to the left side. He wanted Mays to take the ball to right field. Finally, he told Mays to pull up his pants as a way to raise his strike zone.[8]

Durocher also had the following guidance for Mays as he patrolled center field: "You have to catch balls line to line. The ball goes to the left, you gotta be over there. The ball goes to the right, you gotta be over there. Wherever the ball goes in the outfield, you gotta catch it."[9] Buck O'Neil summarized how well Mays pursued fly balls by stating, "While there are players faster than Mays, no one was faster while a fly ball was in the air."[10]

In the next game against the Pirates, on June 2, Mays was moved from third in the batting order to eighth. He responded by going 2-for-4 as the Giants won 14-3. Mays then went 13-for-33 in the final nine games of the homestand. There were no further concerns about him at the plate. In addition to his improved hitting, Mays was playing a flawless center field after some misfortune in that first game.

As the season progressed, the Dodgers surged and had a 13-game lead over the Giants on August 11. On the 14th the two teams began a three-game series at the Polo Grounds. The Giants won the first game, 4-2. The second game pitted Ralph Branca of the Dodgers against Jim Hearn of the Giants. With the two teams tied 1-1 after seven innings, Billy Cox led off the Dodgers' eighth with a single. Jackie Robinson pinch-hit for Wayne Terwilliger and flied out. Hearn committed a balk, moving Cox to second. Branca followed with a single, moving Cox to third and bringing up the dangerous Carl Furillo.

With runners on first and third, Furillo hit a fly ball to right-center field. Joseph Sheehan of the *New York Times* had the following description of what happened next: "It looked plenty deep enough to bring in Cox, especially since Mays had to run a long way to get the ball. But Willie, making a complete whirling pivot on the dead run, cut loose with a tremendous peg that boomed into [Wes] Westrum's mitt in perfect position for the catcher to tag the sliding Cox."[11] Eddie Brannick, the Giants road secretary since 1922, said, "I've seen [Tris] Speaker, [Joe] DiMaggio, [Terry] Moore, all of them, but I've never seen anything like that throw. This kid made the greatest throw I ever looked at."[12]

Both the Dodgers and Giants players were in disbelief. All the players and fans were certain the Dodgers were going to take the lead but the game remained tied after the inning-ending double play. Mays was first up in the bottom of the eighth and received a standing ovation. He singled to center field and scored on a two-run home run by Westrum. The Giants won, 3-1.

Whether this play or game proved to be the catalyst, the Giants went on a prolonged winning streak and tied the Dodgers for the National League lead during the last week of the season. They remained tied at the end of the season and a three-game playoff was needed to decide the pennant winner. That playoff ended with the Bobby Thomson home run that gave the Giants the pennant. Mays was on deck when Thomson hit the home run.

The 1951 season had to be considered a success for Mays. Durocher's contribution cannot be underestimated. Durocher was considered a tough taskmaster who demanded the utmost from his players. He also realized that not all players respond to such treatment. Durocher understood that Mays, a Black 20-year-old playing and living in a strange environment, had his confidence shaken in his first seven games in the major leagues. If Durocher employed those tough tactics with Mays, his performance may have suffered. Instead, Durocher softened his approach and reassured Mays that he belonged in the major leagues. Bill Rigney, who succeeded Durocher as Giants manager after the 1955 season, gave the former skipper a lot of credit for Mays' development.[13]

Monte Irvin also played a big part in helping Mays make the transition by ensuring that he did not develop any bad habits in New York City, the city that never sleeps. Mays said: "Monte taught me how to treat others and how to be treated. He played the game right and treated people right. He was a thinker. He made sure I didn't get into trouble."[14]

Another individual who had a major influence on Mays in 1951 was Frank Forbes, a Harlem boxing

*Alvin Dark, Monte Irvin, Wes Westrum, and Willie Mays, left to right, kept the Giants in the thick of many pennant races. SABR/The Rucker Archive.*

*Willie Mays batted .298 in 399 career games at the Polo Grounds and hit 98 home runs. Courtesy National Baseball Hall of Fame.*

promoter who was assigned by the Giants to be more or less Mays' guardian. Forbes wanted a good home environment for Mays and found a place on the first floor of a home owned by David and Ann Goosby at the corner of 155th Street and St. Nicholas Avenue, a short walk to the Polo Grounds. Mrs. Goosby prepared meals for Mays, washed his clothes, and provided sage advice. Mays also enjoyed playing stickball with the neighborhood kids. With Irvin, Forbes, and Mrs. Goosby, Mays would have a difficult time getting into trouble.

When Mays returned home to Alabama, he received his draft notice. The Korean War was still being fought and Congress had approved an expansion of the US military. Mays pursued a deferment given that his income was supporting his family. His deferment request was denied and he was told to report for duty on May 29, 1952. As a result, he went to spring training and began the 1952 season with the Giants before joining the Army.

At Fort Eustis, Virginia, Mays played a significant amount of baseball on the base team. While in the Army he perfected his trademark basket catch. He had seen Bill Rigney catch infield popups using that catch. Mays felt that making the catch close to his waist gave him a greater opportunity to retrieve the ball quickly and make any necessary throw. (Since Mays adopted such an approach, no other outfielder comes to mind who has made use of the basket catch.)

After the 1953 season, the Giants made a significant trade with the Milwaukee Braves. The Giants received left-handed pitchers Johnny Antonelli and Don Liddle and others for Bobby Thomson and Sam Calderone. Antonelli would have a big impact on the 1954 season.

Mays had a banner year with the Giants in 1954 as they won the pennant. He showed no rust after serving in the Army. In fact, it was somewhat obvious that playing Army baseball had enhanced his strength, maturity, and hitting skills. In his first 80 games, he hit 30 home runs. Sportswriters and fans were wondering if he was a threat to Babe Ruth's record of 60 home runs. However, Durocher had another idea. He suggested to Mays that rather than hit home runs, he should be hitting to all fields and pursuing the batting championship.

The strategy worked as Mays went into the final day of the season battling teammate Don Mueller and Dodgers star Duke Snider. Mays went 3-for-5 and won the title with an average of .345. He hit 41 home runs and had 110 RBIs. He was voted the league's Most Valuable Player.

The Cleveland Indians won 111 games as they easily captured the American League pennant. The first game of the World Series was played on September 29 with pitcher Sal Maglie starting for the Giants and Bob Lemon for the Indians. The Indians scored two runs in the top of the first but the Giants tied it in the bottom of the third. The game stayed tied as the two teams entered the top of the eighth inning.

Leading off for the Indians, Larry Doby drew a walk. Al Rosen's single put runners on first and second with no outs. Durocher replaced Maglie with Don Liddle. The first batter Liddle faced, Vic Wertz, already had three hits and two RBIs. With a 2-and-1 count, Liddle's next pitch was over the middle of the plate and Wertz hit a long fly, possibly 450 feet, to center field.

As soon as the ball was hit, Mays turned, ran with his back to the plate, and pounded his glove. The *New Yotk Time's* John Drebinger described what followed: "Traveling on the wings of the wind, Willie caught the ball directly in front of the green boarding facing the right-center bleachers and with his back still to the diamond."[15]

Once he caught the ball, Mays had the presence of mind to realize Doby would be tagging up at second base. If he didn't get the ball back quickly, Doby might even score. So after making the catch, Mays pivoted and unleashed a throw to second baseman Davey Williams, holding Doby at third. Even with Doby at third and only one out, the Indians failed to score.

The Giants ultimately won the game, 5-2, as Dusty Rhodes pinch-hit a three-run home run in the bottom of the 10th. While Rhodes became a hero, the game was really won in the top of the eighth with the catch and throw that Willie made. Whenever World Series highlights are shown, this play tends to be front and center. It has become known as "The Catch" and it only could have happened at the spacious Polo Grounds.

The Giants went on to win the next three games and sweep the Series. At the age of 23, Willie Mays had been in two World Series, won a batting title and an MVP, and made "The Catch."

Mays followed his 1954 performance with another excellent year in 1955. He hit 51 home runs as Durocher decided the Giants needed more power and asked Mays to hit for the fences. However, the year was bittersweet. During the last game of the season, Durocher pulled Mays aside and told him he would not be back in 1956. Tearfully, Mays responded, "But Mr. Leo, it's going to be different with you gone. You won't be here to help me."[16] Then Durocher told him, "Willie Mays doesn't need help from anyone."[17]

Rigney was named the next Giants manager. The former Millers skipper decided to establish a new culture and treat all the players equally. Rigney realized that there were some players who weren't happy with Durocher's treatment of Mays. Rigney publicly criticized Mays and even fined him for not running out a pop fly to the catcher. In addition to the tension between Rigney and Mays, the Giants were struggling to win games. As a result, Dark and Whitey Lockman were traded but the Giants still stumbled and finished sixth. Mays failed to bat .300, finishing at .296. He did become the first National League 30-30 player with 36 home runs and 40 stolen bases.

While the relationship between Rigney and Mays improved in 1957, the Giants still struggled. In addition, there was considerable speculation that the Giants would be moving after the season, The 1956 attendance showed a steep decline and 1957 was even worse. In addition, the ballpark was deteriorating. In an 8-to-1 vote, the Giants' board of directors made it official. They would be playing in San Francisco in 1958.

In the final game of the season at the Polo Grounds, Mays came up in the seventh inning with the Giants losing 7-1. He hit a groundball to third base but beat it out running full speed in a rather meaningless game, exciting the crowd. Mays came to bat once again in the bottom of the ninth. The small crowd of 11,606 greeted him with great applause. They recognized the excitement he had provided to all baseball fans and to New York City since 1951.

While it appeared that the Giants and Mays were never to play again in the Polo Grounds, they did return. The New York Mets began play as an expansion franchise in 1962. The Polo Grounds became their first home ballpark. On June 1the Giants and Mets began a four-game series there. Mays was greeted by the fans with "Say Hey Willie" signs and loud cheers. In the *New York Times* Arthur Daley wrote, "The center field turf at the Polo Grounds looks normal this weekend for the first time in five years. Willie has come home."[18] Mays did not disappoint as he hit three home runs in the four-game sweep.

While Willie Mays did return to New York to play for the Mets in 1972 and 1973, he was not the same player who roamed center field at the Polo Grounds in the 1950s. During those years, all baseball fans and especially Giants fans were thrilled by his performance. His fielding and "The Catch" facilitated by the spacious Polo Grounds outfield will be long remembered. As Donald Honig wrote, "Putting Mays in a small ballpark would have been like trimming a masterpiece to fit a frame."[19]

## NOTES

1 Chris Landers, "Yankee Stadium's Short Porch in Right Field Is Responsible for Some of Baseball's Biggest Moments," January 29, 2019, https://www.mlb.com/cut4/why-does-yankee-stadium-have-a-short-porch-in-right-field-c303279930.

2 Stew Thornley, "Polo Grounds (New York)," SABR BioProject, https://sabr.org/bioproj/park/polo-grounds-new-york/.

3 Thornley.

4 John Saccoman, "Willie Mays," SABR BioProject, Willie Mays – Society for American Baseball Research (sabr.org).

5 Saccoman.

6 Saccoman.

7 James S. Hirsch, *Willie Mays The Life The Legend* (New York: Scribner, 2010), 103.

8 Hirsch, 104.

9 Willie Mays and John Shea, *24: Life Stories and Lessons from the Say Hey Kid* (New York: St. Martin's Press, 2020), 65.

10 Hirsch, 102.

11 Joseph M. Sheehan, "Mays Helps Hearn Topple Brooks, 3-1," *New York Times,* August 16, 1951: 38.

12 Jason Aronoff, *Going, Going ... Caught! Baseball's Great Outfield Catches as Described by Those Who Saw Them, 1887-1964* (Jefferson, North Carolina: McFarland & Company, 2009), 155.

13 Mays and Shea, 61.

14 Mays and Shea, 63.

15 John Drebinger, "Giants Win in 10th From Indians, 5-2, on Rhodes' Homer," *New York Times,* September 30, 1954: 1.

16 Hirsch, 244.

17 Hirsch, 245.

18 Hirsch, 352.

19 Hirsch, 104.

# WILLIE MAYS – ALL-TIME ALL-STAR

BY JASON HOROWITZ

*"They invented the All-Star Game for Willie Mays."*

–Ted Williams[1]

**IT STARTS WITH** the numbers, but certainly doesn't end there. The stats show that Willie Mays is the greatest performer in the history of the All-Star Game. He leads or shares the lead in All-Star games played (24), plate appearances (82), at-bats (75), runs (20), hits (23), total bases (40), triples (3), stolen bases (6), and singles (15).

Mays played in 24 All-Star games over 20 years, starting in 1954 and ending in 1973. Some of his counting stats are high because for four years (1959-62) the leagues played two All-Star Games per season. Though the sample size of All-Star plate appearances is small, rate metrics show that Mays' All-Star Game play compares favorably to his regular-season performance even though he was hitting against the best arms the American League had to offer. In All-Star Games, Mays had a slash line of .307/.366/.533 (for an OPS of .899), which is close to his career marks of .301/.384/.557 (OPS .940).[2]

A review of the context for these performances tells us even more about their significance. Mays led a resurgence in the fortunes of the National League All-Star teams.[3] Before his first All-Star Game appearance, the American League led the series (which started in 1933), 12 wins to 8. After his final appearance, in the 1973 midsummer classic, the NL led the AL 25-18. During his career, played entirely in the National League, the NL went 17-6-1.

One of the main reasons for the NL's midcentury dominance was the senior circuit's greater propensity to sign and retain African American and Black Latino players.[4] Willie Mays was a link between the "color-line" pioneers (his first ASG was Jackie Robinson's last one, and Mays substituted for Robinson in that game) and the generation of Black players who dominated the game in the late 1950s and the '60s (including his Giants and NL teammates Orlando Cepeda and Willie McCovey).

Another factor that made Mays' All-Star Game performances stand out was the relative (compared to now) importance of the midsummer game in the sports media landscape of the 1950s and '60s. Most regular-season games were not on local TV – for the Giants this was particularly true after the move to San Francisco[5] – and national games were restricted to a "game of the week," the All-Star Game, and the World Series. There was no regular-season interleague play during Mays' career, so only fans in National League cities saw him play in person.

In this environment, a star like Mays could be legendary due to his statistics and performance highlights (such as "the Vic Wertz catch" in the 1954 World Series). He was also visible via advertisements, endorsements, and promotional appearances. Still, fans only had limited opportunities to see him play. All-Star Games presented one of the main chances, and Mays made the most of them. Over the first 15 years or so years of his career, almost every All-Star Game included performances that made Willie Mays' All-Star Game legend. Here are the highlights.

**1954** – One couldn't script a better changing-of-the-guard moment. In his first All-Star Game appearance, Mays substituted for the great Jackie Robinson in the home half of the fourth inning. Mays took his place in center field and Duke Snider, who had started there, slid over to Robinson's position in left. It was Robinson's final All-Star appearance. In the game, played in Cleveland, Mays singled in his second at-bat, in the eighth inning, and scored the tying run on a home run by Gus Bell. But the AL scored three times in the bottom of the eighth to win, 11-9.

**1955** – Mays again came off the bench, this time playing a pivotal role in a 6-5 NL extra-inning victory in Milwaukee. After replacing Snider in center field in the top of the sixth, Mays singled twice and scored two runs. But his most remarked-upon play in the 1955 classic came on defense. In the top of the seventh, with the AL still up 5-0, two outs, and a runner on first, Ted Williams hit a long drive to the wall in right-center. Mays sprinted toward the ball, leapt above the wall and caught it in his glove for the final out of the inning.[6] Years later, Mays cited this as his personal favorite catch over and above the more celebrated one from the 1954 World Series.[7]

*Willie Mays played in a record 24 All-Star games. Here, he talks with, left to right, Charlie Neal, Henry Aaron, Ted Williams, and Stan Musial before the second game of 1959. Courtesy National Baseball Hall of Fame.*

**1956** – Mays was once again the backup center fielder as ballot stuffing in Cincinnati led to the selection of Gus Bell as the starter at the position. Mays pinch-hit for Bell in the top of the fourth and hit his first All-Star Game home run, a two-run shot that put the NL up 3-0. He scored again after walking in the top of the seventh inning. The NL won the game, played at Washington's Griffith Stadium, by a 7-3 score.

**1957** – Mays got his first start as the NL center fielder in St. Louis, but only after Commissioner Ford Frick countermanded the Cincinnati fans' vote for Bell. From 1958 to 1969, All-Star Game starters were picked by a vote of players, managers, and coaches to prevent ballot stuffing. Mays singled and tripled (scoring two runs) in his final All-Star Game appearance as a New York Giant.

**1958** – Mays started in center field and led off (unusual for him in normal play, but something fans would see often over the next decade of midsummer classics). This year, in a game the AL won 5-4 in Baltimore, Mays scored two runs, the second of which came after he stole second and reached third on a catcher throwing error.[8]

**1959** – This was the first of four consecutive years with two All-Star Games. The additional game was added to benefit the players' pension fund. It's worth noting that in six of the eight games in these years, Mays played all nine innings. This reflected the seriousness with which the leagues and players approached the contests as well as Mays' preeminence among NL outfielders.

In the first 1959 game, played at Pittsburgh's Forbes Field, Mays tripled in the bottom of the eighth, driving in Henry Aaron and giving the NL its final 5-4 margin. The second game that year was played in Los Angeles at the Memorial Coliseum, and Mays uncharacteristically went 0-for-4 at the plate.

**1960** – At age 29, Mays had his best year as an All-Star, going 6-for-8 across two games with a home run, a triple, a double, two runs scored, and an RBI. He also stole a base and had nine putouts in center field, the most of any year in his career.

In the year's first All-Star Game, played at Kansas City, Mays singled, doubled, and tripled. In his final at-bat, in the top of the sixth, he flied out to right, missing the opportunity to hit for the cycle. Vada Pinson replaced him in the field for the bottom of the sixth with the NL ahead 5-0. (They held on to win 5-3.)

In the second 1960 game, played at Yankee Stadium, Mays delighted the New York crowd with two singles and a home run, the second of his three round-trippers in All-Star play, to lead the NL to a 6-0 win. In the first inning, he stole third base, but was later picked off and caught trying to steal home.

**1961** – The first All-Star Game took place at Candlestick Park in San Francisco, the only time Mays played in an All-Star game in his home ballpark. He had "only" two hits in five at-bats, scoring two runs (including the game-winner in the bottom of the 10th inning) and driving in another. Besides showcasing Mays' skills, this game helped cement Candlestick's national reputation as a blustery arena. Giants reliever Stu Miller was blown off the mound in the top of the ninth and called for a balk, sending the game to extra innings after the NL had gone into the ninth leading 3-1.[9] The second 1961 game, at Fenway Park in Boston, ended in a 1-1 tie when rain ended play after nine innings. Mays went 1-for-3 with a walk.

**1962** – This was the final year with two All-Star Games. In the first one, at the new DC Stadium in Washington with President John F. Kennedy in attendance, Mays went hitless, but still managed to impress *The Sporting News* writer Fredrick Lieb:

> Willie Mays, who came into this first 1962 game with a batting average of .425 for his previous 11 All-Star games, drew only one walk in four trips to the plate, but he made one spectacular steal of third base, and was a tower of strength in center field. . . .
>
> When the American League cause was nearly dead with two out in the ninth, and two on, Looie [*sic*] Aparicio, who had been tagging the ball well all day, sent a drive to right-center that looked as though it might duplicate Luis' earlier triple. But, Mays sprinted for it, made another fine catch, and ran grinning for the exit gate.[10]

In 1962's second game, held at Chicago's Wrigley Field, Mays went 2-for-2, but didn't score any runs.

He was replaced in the field by Henry Aaron in the top of the fourth.

**1963** – The 1963 All-Star Game was the first for which Mays was designated Most Valuable Player. (The award had been introduced only the previous year.) Batting cleanup, he hit 1-for-3 with two runs, two RBIs, and two stolen bases. Again, his most noted play came in the field: With two out in the AL eighth, he made a running catch of a Joe Pepitone drive near the center-field fence. After he made the catch, his spikes got caught in Cleveland Stadium's chain-link fence and he was replaced in the field for the ninth by Roberto Clemente.[11]

**1964** – The All-Star Game was played at Shea Stadium in front of Mays' original New York City fan base. It was a relatively quiet game for the superstar with no base hits in three official at-bats. Still, in the narrative of *The Sporting News's* Carl Lundquist, Mays sparked the winning rally and scored the tying run:

> Here's how it all developed in that nerve-nipping ninth. It was altogether fitting and proper that wondrous Willie Mays, still an authentic hero to New York fandom, should be the instigator. He drew a walk off reliever Dick Radatz, the generally peerless Red Sox bull-pen star. Then, after an approving glance from National League Manager Walter Alston, who assured him he was on his own as he strolled to first, Willie stole second with the easy nonchalance of a fellow walking his dog.
>
> That put the next move up to Giant teammate Orlando Cepeda and he blooped a Texas League single behind first base. Mays, now accelerating to the point where he was almost airborne as they say at nearby LaGuardia Airport, needed no second invitation to soar home as Yankee first baseman Joe Pepitone threw badly for an error and Cepeda took second.[12]

**1965** – Batting first for the visiting National Leaguers in Minnesota, Mays led off the game with a home run, his third and, it turned out, final one in All-Star play. The National League raced out to a 5-0 lead in the first two frames, but the AL came back and tied it in the fifth inning. In the top of the seventh, Mays walked, advanced to third on a single by Henry Aaron, and scored the winning run on Ron Santo's base hit. In the AL eighth, with the NL leading by one and AL runners on second and third, Mays made a leaping backhand catch to rob reserve center fielder Jimmie Hall of a base hit and the AL of a late lead. The NL won, 6-5.

**1966** – As the 1960s continued, the major leagues entered an era of dominant pitching, reflected in the next few All-Star Game scores. The 1966 midsummer classic played at brand-new Busch Stadium in St. Louis started with three perfect innings pitched by Detroit's 22-year-old Denny McLain. Mays contributed to his team's victory, singling and coming around to score in the bottom of the fourth. The 35-year-old Mays played all 10 innings as the NL edged the AL, 2-1.

**1967** – Slowed by injuries, Mays was an All-Star reserve for the first time in more than a decade but still got four at-bats as a substitute for starter Lou Brock. The dominant-pitching theme continued as the NL again won 2-1, this time in 15 innings. The game featured 30 strikeouts and only two walks by both teams.

**1968** – The first All-Star Game played indoors and at night was held in Houston's Astrodome on July 9, 1968. Mays led off and played the entire game in center field. He also scored the game's only run in the bottom of the first – singling, advancing to second on an errant pickoff throw by Cleveland's Luis Tiant, going to third on a wild pitch, and scoring on a double play by his Giants teammate, Willie McCovey. It was the only run in the NL's 1-0 victory and, for his effort, Mays was rewarded with his second All-Star Game MVP award.

The hit in the 1968 game was Mays' last in any midsummer classic. At the conclusion of that game, Mays' All-Star slash line stood at .348/.411/.606 (OPS 1.017). It's fair to assess his ASG play over the 15 seasons from 1954 to 1968 as one of the most sustained bursts of excellence in the history of the game.

Mays subsequently played in five more All-Star Games, including starting in 1970-72 after the selection of the starting lineup was returned to a fan vote. By then, during his age 38-42 seasons, Mays was in the twilight of his long career, and the fan votes in those years can be interpreted as appreciation for achievements across his long career.

One way to understand the impact of Willie Mays' All-Star Game performances is to look at his peers. In his early games, he played against Ted Williams, whose ASG appearances went back to 1940, and alongside Stan Musial, who debuted in the 1943 game. In 1972-73, he played against Carlton Fisk, who played in his final All-Star Game in 1991. The years 1940-1991 constitute an awesome half-century of baseball history to consider. Mays played in All-Star Games with pioneers of integrated baseball, including Jackie Robinson, Roy Campanella, and Don Newcombe. He also played alongside the next generation of Black and Latino all-stars, including Roberto Clemente, Orlando Cepeda, Maury Wills, Bob Gibson, Frank Robinson, and Curt Flood. Later in his career, he played with and competed against yet another generation of all-time greats including Tom Seaver, Pete Rose, Joe Morgan, and Reggie Jackson.

Another (perhaps, the best) way to appreciate Mays' All-Star Game achievement is on YouTube. Highlight reels are available for most of his All-Star appearances and an interested viewer can find many of the plays mentioned here. To spend a half-hour viewing these clips is to appreciate Mays's speed and power, his joy and grace – in other words the charisma and the mastery that made Willie Mays the greatest of baseball players and a superstar among All-Stars.

## SOURCES

In addition to the sources cited in the Notes, the author consulted Baseball-Reference.com and Retrosheet.org. The box scores and play-by-play game accounts at Retrosheet.org were particularly invaluable in writing this account.

Several of the themes discussed here were suggested by SABR's John Fredland.

## NOTES

1 This quote is used widely, including on the National Baseball Hall of Fame website, but the author has been unable to locate the original source.

2 To be fair, Mays' All-Star BABIP (Batting Average on Balls in Play) of .345 suggests that his ASG totals include a few lucky hits. (His career BABIP of .298 is close to the league average of .300.)

3 Mays spoke about the importance of the All-Star Game to him personally and to the National League in this era in his book *24: Life Stories and Lessons from the Say Hey Kid* (New York: Macmillan, 2020), written with sportswriter John Shea. See excerpts at https://www.newsweek.com/2020/06/26/willie-mays-explains-why-baseballs-all-star-game-meant-so-much-his-generation-1508994.html.

4 The competitive advantage gained by the NL during the era of integration is discussed in many places. Andy McCue, *Stumbling Around The Bases: The American League's Mismanagement in the Expansion Era* (Lincoln: University of Nebraska Press, 2022) touches on integration as part of a very thorough examination of the business of baseball in this period.

5 Steve Treder, *Forty Years a Giant: The Life of Horace Stoneham* (Lincoln: University of Nebraska Press, 2021), covers the Giants television contracts and coverage in New York, on pp. 161-4, and in San Francisco, on p. 243.

6 See the game account by Nelson "Chip" Greene, "July 12, 1955: Stan Musial seals Milwaukee's first baseball All-Star celebration," published in *From the Braves to the Brewers: Great Games and Exciting History at Milwaukee's County Stadium* (Phoenix: SABR 2016). On the web at https://sabr.org/gamesproj/game/july-12-1955-stan-musial-seals-milwaukees-first-baseball-all-star-celebration/.

7 See Mays' biography on the American Academy of Achievement website, https://achievement.org/achiever/willie-mays/.

8 The catcher was Baltimore's Gus Triandos.

9 The balk is recorded in the Retrosheet box score and game account, but Treder in *Forty Years a Giant* gives a slightly

different and more colorful version of what happened, on page 243.

10 Frederick G. Lieb, "President Kennedy Among 45,480 at D.C. Spectacle," *The Sporting News,* July 21, 1962: 7.

11 Bob Broeg, "N.L.'s Swifties Scamper Past A.L. All-Stars: Mays Steals Twice – Bats In Two Runs," *The Sporting News,* July 20, 1963: 5.

12 Carl Lundquist, "N.L. Pens New Fairy Tale – Callison Wonderland," *The Sporting News,* July 18, 1964: 5.

# WILLIE MAYS AND TED WILLIAMS FACE OFF

BY BILL NOWLIN

THERE WERE THE All-Star Games, of course, and the two faced each other once in each of the years from 1954 through 1960. Williams was at the end of his career and Mays starting his. The first game in which Mays played was 1954. Williams, back from missing most of two years in Korea, resumed his own All-Star Game career that same year. Over the nine games, Williams was 3-for-19 with four runs scored and two RBIS (both in 1956), while Mays was 9-for-23, with nine runs scored and four RBIs.

All told, in 19 All-Star Games, Williams hit .304, with 10 runs scored, four homers, and 12 RBIs (four in 1941 and five in 1946). Mays played in 24 All-Star Games, with a .307 batting average, 20 runs scored, with three homers and nine RBIs.

Williams holds the record for most RBIs in All-Star Game history, with 12. (He also holds the records for bases on balls, with 11.) Mays holds the record for the most base hits in All-Star Game history, with 23. He also holds record for the most extra-base hits (8), most triples (3), most total bases (40), most stolen bases (6), and most runs scored (20).[1]

There were two games in which they each played with their own teams – the Red Sox for Williams and the Giants for Mays – in head-to-head competition. They were exhibition games in June 1951. The first was on June 11 at the Polo Grounds in New York, a benefit game for the National Amputation Foundation. Roger Bowman pitched for the Giants, giving up a run in the second on hits by Williams and Bobby Doerr. Mays homered off Red Sox starter Paul Hinrichs in the bottom of the second, helping the Giants build a 3-1 lead. Boston took a 4-3 lead in the eighth, Buddy Rosar's two-run pinch-hit single giving them the lead. They added a fifth run in the ninth when Johnny Pesky singled, Clyde Vollmer walked, and Williams singled off the right-field wall. The final was 5-3, Red Sox.

The second matchup was two weeks later on June 25 at Boston's Fenway Park, and the Giants turned the tide, beating the home team Red Sox, 5-4, in a benefit for the New England Hospitalized Veterans Fund. Monte Irvin homered after Mays had singled, for two runs in the second. Bobb Thompson twice singled in a run. Williams had won a home-run-hitting contest before the game, beating out teammates Doerr, Vollmer, and Vern Stephens, and Giants Irvin, Mays, and Henry Thompson. (Doerr had won the contest in the Polo Grounds.) Williams batted just once in the game, 1-for-1 with a single. Mays was 2-for-2 with the single and a later double.

## SOURCES

*Boston Herald, New York Times, Springfield Union,* and baseball-almanac.com.

## NOTES

1 Mays is tied with Stan Musial for the most extra-base hits and most total bases, and tied with Brooks Robinson for most triples.

# MANTLE VS. MAYS

BY DAVID KAISER

**WILLIE MAYS AND** Mickey Mantle were both born in 1931 and reached the majors almost simultaneously in 1951, competing against each other as rookies in the World Series. Together with Duke Snider, they appeared in 11 World Series between 1951 and 1956, and arguments about their relative ability raged throughout the city of New York and beyond. The older Snider faded from the National League's leaderboards after that, but Mantle and Mays continued to dominate their leagues and start every All-Star Game in center field well into the 1960s. Until Henry Aaron's successful pursuit of Babe Ruth's all-time home-run record captured the nation's imagination, they remained unquestionably the most famous and the highest-praised players of their generation.

Who was better – and in particular, who was the better player at his peak? In his first *Historical Baseball Abstract* in 1988, Bill James, the founder of modern sabermetrics, argued very strongly for Mantle. "Mickey Mantle was, at his peak in 1956-57 and again in 1961-62, clearly a greater player than Willie Mays – and it is not a close or difficult decision," James wrote. Identifying Mantle's three best seasons as 1957, 1958, and 1961, and Mays' as 1954, 1955, and 1958, he used his runs created formula to measure offensive performance, and claimed that Mantle had created about 35 more runs per season in his best years than Mays had in his.

Turning to baserunning, which was not part of the runs created formula, James pointed out that Mickey's stolen-base percentage (although not his stolen-base total) was higher than Willie's, and that he grounded into far fewer double plays (obviously because he batted left-handed for the great majority of his at-bats). Then, without using any statistical method, James argued that while Mays was probably the greater center fielder, Mantle was "a *very good* center fielder," and that the difference between them in the field could not possibly make up for Mantle's superiority at the plate.[1] By the time he brought out a revised edition of the *Abstract* in 2001, James had developed Win Shares, his single measurement of a player's offensive and defensive value. Based on win shares, he now identified Mantle's best seasons as 1957-58 and 1961 and Mays' best as 1965. He did not assert Mantle's superiority so dramatically, but he still claimed that those three seasons of Mantle's were all better than Mays' 1965 season.[2] He also acknowledged that Mays had been by far the better player over the course of their entire careers.

In 2011 Michael Humphreys published *Wizardry*, a new study of fielding statistics, which longtime sabermetrician Richard Cramer has described as "the greatest single intellectual accomplishment in the history of sabermetrics."[3] Humphreys used a new method, Defensive Regression Analysis or DRA, to measure the fielding ability of a player at any position against the league average at that position. By his measurements, Humphreys ranked Mays as the second-best defensive center fielder of all time (between Andruw Jones, first, and Tris Speaker, third), and wrote that Mantle's defensive performance was only significantly above average in two of his 14 seasons in center field –1952 and 1959 – and was -41 runs worse than average over his whole career.[4] Those numbers led me to reevaluate the question of whether Mantle's best seasons really were significantly better than Mays' based on the method I developed for my own book, *Baseball Greatness*.[5]

That method combines offensive data from the website baseball-reference.com with Humphreys' fielding data to compute a single number for Wins Above Average. As I explained in this book, I used Wins Above Average (WAA) rather than Wins Above Replacement (WAR) because average performance can be computed much more accurately than replacement performance, and because WAA gives a much clearer indication of a player's value to his team.[6] I eventually defined a superstar season as 4 WAA or more and found 1,803 such player seasons in the major leagues from 1901 through 2019. We shall see in a moment that Mays' and Mantle's best seasons were more than twice as good as that.

My calculations showed that Mantle's best seasons (in order of highest WAA) were 1957, 1956, and 1961, while Mays had four seasons at a comparable level, 1954, 1958, 1964, and 1965. Rbat represents runs above average generated by hitting, Rbaser is baserunning runs, Rdp represents runs gained or lost via frequency of grounding into double plays, and Rfield is runs saved in the field according to DRA.

| Player | Year | **WAA** | Rbat | Rbaser | Rdp | Rfield |
|---|---|---|---|---|---|---|
| Mantle | 1957 | **9.4** | 84 | 6 | 1 | 1 |
| Mantle | 1956 | **8.8** | 84 | 6 | 2 | 5 |
| Mantle | 1961 | **8.8** | 80 | 6 | 2 | 1 |
| | | | | | | |
| Mays | 1954 | **9.2** | 61 | 3 | 0 | 30 |
| Mays | 1958 | **8.2** | 54 | 8 | 0 | 18 |
| Mays | 1964 | **8.1** | 53 | 7 | 0 | 12 |
| Mays | 1965 | **8.0** | 62 | 4 | -1 | 8 |

Before going any further, we must understand exactly how extraordinary these seasons were. Each man had one season with more than 9 WAA – and in the whole history of baseball there have been only 39 seasons that good. They also had five of the 59 seasons between 8.0 and 8.9 WAA. This table confirms that Mantle's best offensive seasons were indeed superior to Mays', mainly because Mantle walked so much more frequently. His batting runs above average (Rbat) substantially exceed Mays' in every one of these years. In addition, Mantle was indeed very marginally superior as a baserunner because he grounded into fewer double plays, although Willie earned an extra run or two on the bases in other ways. Above all, however, Humphreys' fielding data shows that Mantle, in two of these three seasons, was essentially average, while Mays ranged from significantly above average to the fielding stratosphere in 1954. And that is why, in place of the substantial overall superiority that James ascribed to Mantle, we find that he had only a marginal superiority comparing their best three seasons, and that only Mantle's best season was superior to Mays' best, which turns out to be 1954 because of his fielding. Mantle's superiority in peak value earned the Yankees less than one extra win per season.

*Baseball fans liked to debate who was the better center fielder, Mickey Mantle or Willie Mays. SABR/The Rucker Archive.*

We must also look at one other adjustment. WAA measures an individual's performance against league average performance, and by the mid-1960s the National League was significantly stronger than the American League because it was more integrated and included far more outstanding Black players. Comparing Willie's and Mickey's best seasons, we find that Black players earned only 60 WAA in the 1957 American League, while earning 143 WAA in the 1954 National League. Black players in the AL in 1956 and 1961 – Mickey's two other best seasons – earned 99 and 138 WAA, whereas in the NL in 1958, 1964, and 1965 – Willie's other greatest seasons – they earned 251, 560, and 645 WAA. Using a rough calculation, I attempted to estimate how much the additional Black players in the National League added to league average performance by "replacing" them, theoretically, with average players. The results of the adjustment are shown below.

| Player | Year | WAA |
|---|---|---|
| Mantle | 1957 | 9.4 |
| Mantle | 1956 | 8.8 |
| Mantle | 1961 | 8.8 |
| | | |
| Mays | 1954 | 9.3 |
| Mays | 1958 | 8.4 |
| Mays | 1964 | 8.6 |
| Mays | 1965 | 8.7 |

Yankee fans, take heart. Mantle's three best seasons are still superior to Willie's – by the microscopic total of 0.1 WAA, equivalent to about one run created per season. While Mantle's offensive contribution was bigger, Mays balanced that out with his almost unparalleled work in center field. Meanwhile, their joint dominance of their leagues for a 13-year period was extraordinary. Mantle led all American League hitters (and usually all AL players) in WAA six times: in 1955, 1956, 1957, 1959, 1961, and 1962. Mays led all NL hitters (and usually all NL players) 10 times, in 1954-58, 1960 (when he tied with Henry Aaron), 1962, and 1964-66. While Mantle won three MVP Awards and Mays two, both of them arguably deserved a lot more. And at their peaks they performed at an extraordinarily similar level.

## NOTES

1 Bill James, *The Bill James Historical Baseball Abstract* (New York: Villard Books, 1988), 403-406.

2 Bill James, *The New Bill James Historical Abstract* (New York: The Free Press, 2001), 728. James has never explained exactly how he incorporated fielding measurements into Win Shares.

3 Richard D. Cramer, *When Big Data Was Small* (Lincoln: University of Nebraska Press, 2019), 54.

4 Michael Humphreys, *Wizardry* (New York: Oxford University Press, 2011), 286, 308-13.

5 David Kaiser, *Baseball Greatness: The Best Players and Teams According to Wins Above Average* (Jefferson, North Carolina: McFarland, 2017).

6 I also dropped baseball-reference.com's practice of adding points for players at more demanding defensive positions and taking points away from those at easier positions, for reasons that I explained therein.

# WILLIE RETURNS TO NEW YORK

BY ROBERT F. GARRATT

**AFTER ALMOST 20** years as a Giant, Willie Mays was traded from San Francisco to the New York Mets in May 1972. It was a shock to the baseball world, since Horace Stoneham, old-fashioned owner of the Giants, had said on numerous occasions that he would never trade Mays, that Mays was both the face and the heart of the Giants franchise, and that the Giants boss regarded Mays almost as family. His affection for the Giants superstar went back to the spring of 1951, when Stoneham brought Mays up to the New York Giants from Triple-A Minneapolis; it remained strong during all of Mays' years as a Giant, both in New York and San Francisco. Stoneham was adamant that he wanted Mays to finish his career in baseball as a San Francisco Giant. But in the spring of 1972, Stoneham's finances were such that he let Mays go, trading him to the New York Mets.

A closer look at the history of the Mays trade reveals a different timetable. Stoneham's financial difficulties actually took root five years earlier despite his remarks to the contrary. In the spring of 1967, Charles O. Finley, the maverick owner of the Kansas City Athletics, persuaded his American League fellow owners that the Bay Area was a great place to put an American League club to share the riches that the Giants had been raking in since their move in 1958 from New York City to San Francisco.[1] So, at the end of the '67 season, Finley packed up his team and moved west, to Oakland. The Oakland A's began the 1968 season nine miles across the bridge from San Francisco.

Finley's move dealt a severe blow to Stoneham's finances and signaled the beginning of the end for his time as Giants owner. Sensing the restrictions that the Athletics would put on his potential revenue, the Giants boss was outspoken about sharing the Bay Area market. While others in baseball praised the move and thought of it as growth for baseball, Stoneham was uncharacteristically blunt in his opposition. "Certainly the move will hurt us," he said. "It is simply a question of how much and if both of us can survive. I don't think the area at the present time will take care of both of us as much as [the Athletics] think it will."[2]

Stoneham was prescient. After only one season, the pattern was clear: the A's cut the Giants attendance in half, with huge consequences for the remainder of Stoneham's ownership, the end of the

1975 season. Baseball's days of television contracts, merchandising, and playoff revenue-sharing lay in the future; in the late 1960s and early 1970s, the gate was still the primary source of income for ballclubs. Once the A's came to Oakland, the Giants saw a huge drop-off in their gate receipts; attendance fell to about half of what they were drawing in the early 1960s. The interesting thing about the A's coming to the Bay Area was the regularity of the attendance figures. A new American League franchise in the Bay Area did not attract or generate more fans. Rather it split the existing yearly totals of fans coming to baseball games. Through the 1960s the Giants had been drawing consistently about 1.5 million every year. From 1968 on (with the arrival of the A's), both teams essentially split the annual draw the Giants had maintained earlier in the decade.[3] This result was rather surprising, given the great baseball Oakland was playing in the early 1970s, winning three consecutive World Series from 1972 through 1974.

This loss of annual revenue hurt the Giants' ability to put a competitive team onto the field and dictated that Stoneham would have to limit his expenses, greatly affecting the success his teams would have in the standings. One way to reduce costs was to sign younger, less expensive ballplayers; the other was to jettison the established, and better players, those with high-end contracts. Stoneham was forced to do both, a painful necessity for a player-friendly owner. By the end of 1973, most all were gone, those players who contributed to the glory years of the 1960s. Orlando Cepeda was dealt in 1966 to the St. Louis Cardinals, before the fiscal difficulties were apparent. Cy Young winner Mike McCormick was traded to the Baltimore Orioles in 1970; Gaylord Perry was dealt to Cleveland before the 1972 season (where he was a Cy Young Award winner the next year). Shortstop Hal Lanier was sold to the Yankees in 1971 for cash and All-Star catcher Dick Dietz was claimed by the Dodgers off waivers in early 1972. Slugging third baseman Jim Ray Hart was sold to the Yankees in April 1973. Willie McCovey was sent to San Diego in the fall of 1973, and Juan Marichal was sold to the Boston Red Sox that December.[4]

But no one trade or player sale brought with it the agony Stoneham felt when he realized he would have to part with Willie Mays. In 1971 Mays turned 40 and everyone knew that his best playing days were behind him. Still, Stoneham had such deep affection for Mays that he wanted him to retire as a Giant – the only team he had played for in his entire 20-year career. The Giants' finances, however, no longer resembled the profitable early years in San Francisco, due primarily to the arrival of the A's; simply put, Stoneham was running out of money. The blunt reality came off the bottom line: The Giants could not afford to keep Mays, at least in the manner that Stoneham intended. Once the two-year salary was cobbled together for his star center fielder – $165,000 for the 1972 and 1973 seasons – Stoneham knew he would have to find Mays a new home, a place where he would be happy, where he could be guaranteed this two-year salary (something the Giants could not do), and where his future might be secure, possibly as a coach or even a manager. With his ballclub's revenue fading fast, Stoneham put all of his efforts into getting Mays settled. The Giants boss decided to look in the one obvious place for Mays' comfort and well-being.

In the spring of 1972, Stoneham entered into secret negotiations with Mets owner Joan Whitney Payson, and chairman of the board M. Donald Grant to trade Mays to the New York team. They were the only club Stoneham contacted because, in a clearly nostalgic move, he felt that Mays should be back where he began his career, had so many wonderful years and was a legend, still, in the city. A crucial part of the trade details for Stoneham involved assurances from Payson and Grant that Mays would be given some kind of extended contract with the ballclub once his playing days were over.

As is the case with an old-fashioned and well-intended player-first owner, Stoneham felt the need for secrecy in the event the deal with the Mets fell through and that Mays' pride would be hurt, the result of feeling discard by a cash-poor owner.[5] The attempts at secrecy failed, however, as newspapers on both coasts caught wind of the story. Immediately, columnists in San Francisco and New York began speculating about the results. A surprised and somewhat annoyed Mays learned third-hand about the trade when the Giants were visiting Montreal in early May, wondering why the organization for which he had played his entire career would not inform him of such a possibility, and maybe even involve him in the talks. Briefly, he thought about retiring from the game.[6]

On May 11, 1972, the finalized negotiations became official news. Willie Mays was traded to the Mets for a minor-league pitcher named Charlie Williams; there was also a hint of an additional unspecified amount of cash from the Mets, rumored to be between $50,000 and $200,000.[7] In a gesture that conveyed the highest form of respect (and an attempt to mollify the player), Stoneham brought Mays in on the final hours of deliberation with Payson and Grant and then ushered him in to the hastily organized press conference at the Mayfair Hotel announcing the trade.[8]

*The great player's skills had diminished by time the Mets traded for him in May 1972. SABR/The Rucker Archive.*

In his remarks, the Giants owner tried to put on a brave face for the situation but could hardly hide his disappointment, nor conceal his dire economic circumstances. "I never thought I would trade Willie, but with two teams in the Bay Area, our financial situation is such that we cannot afford to keep Willie and his big salary as well as the Mets can."[9] Grant followed with some perfunctory remarks, saying that the Mets planned to keep Mays around for a long time, securing his future in baseball. The player himself spoke briefly, and diplomatically, saying that he was happy to be back in New York, was looking forward to playing for the Mets, and that he was grateful to Stoneham and the Giants for all that they had given him.[10] The press conference ended and with it one of the most fabled chapters in Giants history.

In a bizarre twist, Mays' start in a Mets uniform would be against his former team, which traveled to New York after its series with Montreal. As if to underscore his legendary status in Gotham, Mays homered to break a 4-4 tie, leading his new team to a 5-4 victory. During the Mets series in New York, Stoneham, who had stayed on in New York after the press conference, asked to see Mays after one of the games. The two stayed up late into the night in the owner's hotel suite, Stoneham drinking and talking emotionally and regretfully about the trade, and Mays quietly listening. Looking back on that night more than 40 years later, Mays reflected on Stoneham's genuine concern "for my welfare, not only for my salary but that I would be taken care of in the future. I realized then how much he cared for me and how hard the trade was for him to make."[11]

The press's reaction to Mays' return to New York reflected the changing tides of two cities' connections to their baseball teams. In New York, Mays was treated as an Odyssean hero, finally home after years of wandering exile. "WILLIE COMES HOME" read one East Coast headline for the Alabama-born ballplayer's trade to the Mets.[12] Much of this welcome was for the player himself, his prominence, and his reputation as the greatest player of his generation. Nor did his age bother some writers. Dick Young of the *New York Daily News* wrote that even a 40-year-old Mays was better than many players in the game.[13] But others saw in Mays' return a chance to rewind the clock and bask in nostalgia. *New York Times* columnist Red Smith reminded his readers of a young Mays, roaming the outfield at the Polo Grounds during the golden age of New York center fielders: DiMaggio, Snider, Mantle, and Mays.[14] In another article, headlined "Moments to Remember," Arthur Daley interpreted Mays' return as cathartic, healing the old wounds left by the painful memories of the Giants leaving New York after the 1957 season, taking with them the young superstar who had dazzled Polo Grounds fans with his amazing exploits. Daley reverently recited the famous New York moments in Mays' career, including the "impossible" throw to nail the Dodgers' Billy Cox at home during the 1951 pennant race and the astounding catch of Vic Wertz's fly ball in the 1954 World Series.[15]

*Financial difficulties forced Giants owner Horace Stoneham to trade Willie Mays. SABR/The Rucker Archive.*

On the other coast, reporting of the Mays trade also revealed an emotional edge, but unlike New York's in every respect. The tone was negative, and pointedly critical toward the Giants and Stoneham. Bucky Walters of the *San Francisco Examiner* wrote that it was too little, too late. With a rebuke for Stoneham and the front office, Walters complained that instead of the no-name rookie pitcher Charlie Williams, "it would have been possible for the Giants to have gotten several established players for Mays a couple of years back when his market value was still high."[16] Other San Francisco sports journalists joined in with the criticism. Most took note of Mays' reduced productivity and took it as a sign of decline in quality. And his departure was one more example of the good old days that are gone forever. The commentary was less concerned about losing Mays and more about the sagging state of Giants baseball. A few hundred miles to the south of San Francisco, Jim Murray of the *Los Angeles Times* used the Mays trade to sling a few barbs north. Picking up on the rumor that there was some cash involved in the Mays trade, Murray scolded Stoneham for selling one of baseball's gods for "30 pieces of silver," and, using the Mays trade as a ruse, the writer shifted his target to the city he loved to hate.

> San Francisco has an abhorrence of strangers and Willie was a 14-year stranger – in San Francisco but not OF it – and the townspeople kept looking at each other with a "Who invited him?" look. San Francisco frowns on enthusiasm, anyway, preferring a bored acceptance. It is not a town, it's a cocktail

> party. Willie must have felt like a guy who showed up wearing brown shoes with his tux."[17]

Murray's snide allusion to Stoneham's betrayal of Mays for a handful of silver set off others in the press, some of whom castigated the Giants owner for his plantation boss's attitude (a gross inversion of Stoneham's actual concern for and connection to his players), especially the ones with whom Stoneham had developed long-term relationships, like Mays. Initially, an emotional Stoneham didn't respond to criticism, preferring instead a difficult – and what must have been an especially painful – silence. Years later, however, he corrected the record in an interview with Mays biographer Charles Einstein. When Einstein got around to asking Stoneham exactly how much money he actually got in the Mays trade, the answer was surprising.

> [Stoneham] said, "There was no money."
>
> "None?"
>
> "None. Do you think I was going to give him up for money?"
>
> The only element involving money, Stoneham said, was what the Mets pay Mays over the next few years that Stoneham couldn't.[18]

For the two principal actors in the Mays trade, things wound down rather quickly, so that both would be out of baseball in the next few years. After the trade, things hardly improved for Stoneham. His teams finished well off the pace in the post-Mays years, and he lost at the gate as well. In 1974 and 1975, the Giants' home attendance was the lowest of any season since the team moved west, barely clearing the 500,000 mark for each year. There were some games in 1974 and 1975 when the attendance was below 1,000. Indeed, the Giants' attendance was so low in those years that it prompted *San Francisco Chronicle* columnist Herb Caen to write, "[T]he Giants' 'Fan Appreciation Day' is coming up soon and I can't wait to see what Horace Stoneham gives him."[19] As a result the Giants' financial situation was dire. In the spring of 1975, Stoneham approached his fellow National League owners with grim news; he had enough money to meet only two months of payroll and would need a loan to finish the season. At the same time, he announced his intention to sell the team, hoping to find a local buyer to keep the Giants in San Francisco. After some complicated and dramatic turn of events, Stoneham did just that; he sold the ballclub to San Franciscan Bob Lurie in February of 1976 and, after more than 50 years in baseball, retired to Scottsdale, Arizona.

The trajectory for Mays was a bit different and slightly longer. Initially, he enjoyed some real success as a New York Met, although he was no longer an everyday player. Nonetheless, his presence on the Mets roster and the likelihood that he would play energized New York City fandom. As it turned out, by midseason the 1972 Mets were beset with crucial injuries and Mays had to be called upon to play more than he wanted or could with full energy. But he still drew plenty of fans, both at home and on the road. One memorable away game was his return to Candlestick Park on July 21, where he dressed for the first time in the visitors clubhouse. At every at-bat, he received a standing ovation from the home crowd and the fans were particularly roused when he hit a two-run homer in the fifth inning. The Mets finished third in 1972 and Mays' first season as a Met was substandard for him – 69 games played, a .267 batting average, but with a .402 on-base percentage that led the team and a .466 slugging percentage that was second on the team.

The real measure of his success, however, came from the steady adulation of New York baseball fans, who were delighted to have a living legend back in their midst, even if their hero was in the sunset of his playing days. One writer claimed that Mays' return rejuvenated a troubled city. "Willie Mays is reminding New York of our best moments. … The city is an unhappy land that needs a hero, but we are less unhappy now that Willie Mays is back where he belongs."[20]

After the 1972 season, things turned a little sour for Mays in New York. He had had some difficulties with Mets manager Yogi Berra over his playing time and his role as a leader in the clubhouse. He wanted his time in the lineup to be parceled out to include rest days, so he could maximize his energy in the field and at the plate. Berra wanted to control when Mays would play and how much (usually more than Mays wanted). The younger players looked up to Mays but also could sense his frustrations over declining abilities. Nonetheless, they saw him as a true leader. Tom Seaver recalled that Mays approached him before a game to find out how he would pitch to everyone in the opposing lineup in order that Mays could position himself in the outfield. Seaver was quoted as saying that no other position player had ever asked him how he was going to pitch to hitters: "Nobody ever did that to me ... Nobody."[21]

During the winter of 1972-73, Mays sensed that his playing days were coming to an end. He made up his mind that 1973 would be his last year.[22] Injuries were mounting and it became obvious, especially to him, that he could no longer perform even at the level of his last few years in San Francisco. By midseason in 1973, playing sparsely, he was hitting .214. On more than one occasion in the outfield, he dropped a fly ball, or had to underhand a toss to another outfielder to get the ball back into the infield. It was painful for everyone to see, all the more because of who it was in the field or at the plate. Fans may have recognized it, but for the most part overlooked it, in admiration of the legend behind the man. But the sportswriters saw it, and, with a certain amount of anguish and pathos, began to reflect on Mays' changes in their columns. In what was the characteristic tenor of the New York writers, Roger Angell wrote, "His failings now are so cruel that I am relieved when he is not in the lineup. It is hard for rest of us to fall apart quite on our own; heroes should depart."[23]

The San Francisco columnist Wells Twombley thought Mays' decision to keep playing was tragic.[24] Players, however, were more sympathetic, even though they were aware of the diminishing powers. Teammate Tug McGraw saw the anguish in Mays' situation. "Willie was forty-two and was hurt a lot. ... [H]e wanted to help the club and also not embarrass himself. Sometimes he forced himself to play, and then he'd hurt himself again while trying to do it." Tom Seaver remarked that they were going to have to tear the uniform off him, "It is sad to see, but it's a beautiful thing too, because of the love he had for what he had done for some twenty-odd years."[25]

In early August of 1973, the Mets announced plans for a Willie Mays Night to be held at Shea Stadium on September 25. That event signaled that 1973 would be Mays' last year (even though he had not officially announced retirement, rumors circulated) and the National League began saying goodbye during the remainder of the season: Mays drew standing ovations on the road, playing for the last time in each city. Then, with the season almost over, the official announcement came. On September 20, on the NBC *Today* show, Willie made it official by announcing the end of his playing career once the 1973 season was over. Later that afternoon at Shea Stadium's Diamond Club, he held a press conference for the organization and spoke candidly about his feelings. "When you're forty-two and hitting .211, it's no fun. ... I just feel that the people of America shouldn't have to see a guy play who can't produce."[26]

A few days later, he was honored at the Willie Mays Night festivities, attended by former greats including Joe DiMaggio, Stan Musial, and Duke Snider, New York Mayor John Lindsay, local celebrities, and Willie's family; the event was emceed by sports announcer Lindsey Nelson. A number of former Giants were in attendance as well, including Bobby Thomson, a 1951 teammate. Gifts poured in from various sources, including corporations, local stores, and a number of individuals. There were coats, food items, plaques, even an honorary degree from Mills College. Mays and his wife received a his-and-her pair of Chrysler automobiles; Horace Stoneham sent a congratulatory card and a Mercedes-Benz car as a gift. The teetotaler Mays received a case of scotch and a case of champagne. In a strange twist that has never been fully explained, the Mets gave Mays nothing, not a card, nor a single gift.[27]

But Mays' playing career did not end with the final regular game of the 1973 season. The Mets went on to win the National League pennant and faced the Oakland A's in the World Series. The A's won the Series in seven games and Mays played sparingly, appearing in three games, with two hits in seven at-bats and just one RBI; he committed one error.

Nonetheless, it was a fitting bookend for Mays in baseball. He broke into the National League in 1951 and played in a World Series his rookie year with the New York Giants; he was ending his playing career with a World Series appearance in 1973 with another New York team.

He remained a few more years with the Mets as a bench coach, but it was an uneasy fit for him. The adjustment to not playing, but nonetheless being at the ballpark every day took its toll, emotionally and psychologically. In the late fall of 1979, Mays accepted an offer from Bally Casino Resort to work in public relations, mainly playing golf and hosting dignitaries. The salary of $100,000 per year gave him much more financial security than the coaching position with the Mets. But the position with Bally, a gambling organization, did not sit well with baseball. Commissioner Bowie Kuhn took exception to Mays' position, with its proximity and connection to organized betting, and suspended him from baseball. Mays complained but did not challenge Kuhn's authority.[28]

Six years later, a new commissioner, Peter Ueberroth, reinstated Mays. By this time Mays was living in the Bay Area and it wasn't long before the San Francisco Giants, with new owner Peter Magowan, offered him a lifetime contract to be the ballclub's ambassador to the general public. It appears that you can go home again, which is what the Bay Area had become for the Giants star. In a gesture of supreme appreciation, the Giants and the city of San Francisco would underscore the tie that Mays had with the Bay Area by proclaiming the address of the Giants' new ballpark as 24 Willie Mays Plaza.

The Mets honored Willie Mays on August 27, 2022, in ceremonies at Citi Field. Joan Whitney Payson was said to have promised Mays that he would be the last Mets player to wear uniform number 24. As Anthony DiComo wrote for MLB.com, "Acquiring Mays was important to Payson, who had built the Mets into the hollow space vacated by the Giants – the team for which Mays would always be best-known."[29] His son Michael Mays represented his father at the pregame ceremonies, which included 65 former Mets players and four former managers. Mets President Sandy Alderson said, "There has been a 50-year gap, if you will, between a promise made and a promise kept. We felt that on this occasion today, in light of all the players we had here, all the generations, that this was the time to keep that promise."[30]

## NOTES

1 Finley was keen on promotions, stunts, giveaways and entertainment exhibitions. He paraded around the ballpark before games with his mule named Charlie O. He advocated for zany uniforms, argued for colored baseballs at night games, promoted the designated-hitter rule and pushed, unsuccessfully, for a designated runner to be used with free substitutions. His reputation among fellow owners was poor; he was regarded as petulant, boorish, and bullheaded.

2 "Stoneham's View: 'Move Will Hurt Giants'," *San Francisco Chronicle*, October 16, 1967: 47.

3 The A's drew around 1 million during their great 1972-1974 World Series championship years, when the Giants fell off to just over 500,000. See baseball-reference.com for attendance figures.

4 The source for these transactions is baseball-reference.com.

5 Charles Einstein, *Willie's Times: Baseball's Golden Age* (Carbondale: Southern Illinois University Press, 2004), 329.

6 Willie Mays, interview with the author, October 29, 2014.

7 "Mays for Charlie Williams," *San Francisco Chronicle*, May 12, 1972: 53.

8 Associated Press, "Willie Arrives in New York for Owners' Meeting," *Los Angeles Times*, May 11, 1972: G1.

9 Jack Lang, "Willie Warms Up for Second New York Run," *The Sporting News*, May 20, 1972: 16.

10 James S. Hirsch, *Willie Mays: The Life, the Legend* (New York: Scribner, 2010), 508.

11 Willie Mays, interview with the author, October 29, 2014.

12 United Press International, "Giants Trade Willie Mays to Mets," *Boston Globe*, May 11, 1972: 53.

13 Dick Young, "Young Ideas," *New York Daily News*, May 14, 1972: 122.

14 Red Smith, "Strawberries in the Wintertime," *New York Times*, May 12, 1972: 33.

15 Arthur Daley, "Moments to Remember," *New York Times*, May 14, 1972: S2.

16 Quoted in Joe Eszterhas, "A Town Without Willie," *Newsday* (Long Island, New York), June 11, 1972.

17 Jim Murray, "Willie Mays Didn't Leave HIS Heart in San Francisco," *Los Angeles Times*, May 16, 1972: E1.

18 Einstein, *Willie's Times*, 331.

19 "Caen on the Cob," *San Francisco Chronicle*, August 11, 1974: 107.

20 Jeff Greenfield, *Sport*, October 1972, quoted in Hirsch, *Willie Mays: The Life, the Legend*, 519.

21 Hirsch, *Willie Mays: The Life, the Legend*, 513.

22 Allen Barra, *Mickey and Willie* (New York: Three Rivers Press, 2013), 388-390.

23 Einstein, *Willie's Times*, 334.

24 Wells Twombley, "Tragic Ego Trip of Willie Mays," *San Francisco Examiner*, May 11, 1973.

25 Hirsch, *Willie Mays: The Life, the Legend*, 520.

26 "'Maybe I'll Cry Tomorrow,' Says Mays," *New York Times*, September 21, 1973: 27.

27 Alan Barra, *Mickey and* Willie, 392. One writer speculates that by the middle of 1973 Donald Grant and the Mets front office had soured on Mays and wanted him gone. An ailing Joan Whitney Payson, who favored Mays, had lost her authority in the ownership and could not advocate for Willie, even though she never lost her affection for him. See Hirsch, *Willie Mays: The Life, the Legend*, 520. Honors came from other sources as well. The San Francisco Giants hosted Mays on Willie Mays Day at the ballpark in celebration of his 80th birthday. Steve Kroner, "Willie Mays Celebrates 80th Birthday," *San Francisco Chronicle*, May 8, 2011, sfgate.com; President Barack Obama awarded May the Presidential Medal of Freedom at the White House on November 24, 2016, www.nbcsports.com/bayarea/giants/willie-mays-receive-presidential-medal-freedom.

28 Had he done so, he might have pointed out to the commissioner that he had nothing to do with the gambling side of the casino and indeed was prohibited as an employee from betting. Moreover, owners like George Steinbrenner (Yankees) and the Galbraith family (Pirates) owned racehorses., but they faced no action from the Office of the Commissioner.

29 Anthony DiComo, "Mets Retire Willie Mays' No. 24 During Old Timers' Day," MLB.com, August 27, 2022. https://www.mlb.com/news/mets-retire-willie-mays-no-24. Accessed December 21, 2022.

30 DiComo.

# WILLIE MAYS NIGHT AT SHEA STADIUM

BY THOMAS J. BROWN JR.

WILLIE MAYS RETURNED to New York in a trade on May 11, 1972.[1] "It's a wonderful feeling to be coming back here," said the longtime Giants superstar, who left with the team for California after after the 1957 season. "I've always loved New York and I liked San Francisco, but this is like coming back to Paradise."[2] Mays played in 69 games with the Mets that season, batting .267 and hitting eight home runs.

Mays suffered several injuries early in the 1973 season, telling him that it was time to finally step away from the diamond.[3] On September 9 Mays cracked two ribs while chasing a foul ball in a game in Montreal. When the Mets took the field in Philadelphia on September 11, Mays was not there and members of the press had started to criticize him. The criticism bothered him, his friend and agent Sam Sirkis said, and "finally he had enough. He wanted to announce his retirement."[4]

The skills that led Mays to the pinnacle of baseball over the previous 20 years were diminishing. But this was perhaps the most difficult decision he would make in his career. "Baseball is my life. It's not something that you can just walk away from and say good-bye to," he told his teammates.[5]

Mays announced his retirement on September 20 when he appeared on the *Today* show. That same afternoon, he held a press conference at Shea Stadium. "I thought I'd be crying by now," Mays said. "But I see so many people here who are my friends." He said he was hanging up his uniform "because when you're forty-two and hitting .211, it's no fun. I just feel that the people of America shouldn't have to see a guy play who can't produce."[6]

Mays also told the reporters that he played in 1973 only because he was in New York. "New York fans love me," he said. "They showed me that. You know New York – when they love you, they love you. I never considered myself a superstar. I considered myself a complete player."[7]

With the Mets in a pennant race, Mays was not contributing to their success. Mets manager Yogi Berra was struggling to find a role for Mays on the team. "It appears that when Willie, who admittedly is aging and hurting and without his old skills, retired, it took a load off Yogi and the team," said Joe

Black, a former teammate of Mays, after hearing the announcement.[8]

"Look at it. It was Willie largely who brought the Giants out of the doldrums and now it's Willie's inspiration – in another way – that I think will carry the Mets to the National League championship and maybe their second World Series title," said Black, reflecting on Mays' impact on New York baseball.[9]

After September 25 was announced as Willie Mays Night, Mays was left to organize the festivities with Sirkis. The two planned the event in a room at the Roosevelt Hotel with the room expenses covered by Colgate. Mays wanted to present his wife, Mae, with a fur coat. When he met with the owner of the American Fur Industry, he selected a coat that turned into a gift from owner Irwin Katz, who told Mays, "This is my personal gift to you for all the joy that you have given me."[10]

The Mets were on a roll by the time Willie Mays Night arrived. They had won 17 of 25 games in September to move from fifth place to first. The official attendance was listed at 43,085 but at least one report wrote that more than 53,000 fans showed up to honor Mays.[11] New York Mayor John V. Lindsay had earlier declared the day to be Willie Mays Day.

"A GIANT AMONG METS" [said] the banner in right field. None of the 53,603 at Shea Stadium had to ask who it was. … Willie Mays is so much a part of New York that the fans who gathered to shower him with gifts and hear his farewell speech on Willie Mays Night don't think of him as a Giant any more," wrote Don Drumm of the *White Plains Journal News*.[12]

Mets broadcaster Lindsey Nelson was as the emcee for the evening's event. The celebration started at 8 P.M. when Mays came out of the Mets dugout and walked to home plate. The crowd rose to its feet and applauded him for six minutes as the Mets scoreboard lit up with SO LONG, YES; GOODBYE, NEVER.

Then Mays was presented with numerous gifts. The bounty included several cars, golf clubs, his and hers snowmobiles, lifetime supplies of records, scotch and champagne, two trips, and enough clothing for him and Mae to fill up several closets.[13]

"Old teammates, old rivals, friends, and the hierarchy of sports and politics turned out to pay tribute to the weary, ailing old warrior," said one account.[14] Pee Wee Reese and Duke Snider were there. Bobby Thomson and Dusty Rhodes showed up. Larry Doby and Black, who had barnstormed with him early in his career, were there. Joe DiMaggio and Stan Musial stood among the baseball luminaries at home plate.

Several players shared stories with the crowd. "All I can say [is] I hated to see him come to bat, I hated to see him get on base and it was a tragedy when we hit one to him," said Snider.[15] Reese told this story: "I'll never forget the time there were runners on second and third, first base was open and Willie was at the plate. [Dixie] Howell was catching because Roy Campanella was injured. [Howell] had suggested to Walt Alston [the Dodgers manager] that we pitch to Mays. Before Walt got back to the dugout, Willie had hit the ball out of the ballpark."[16]

After others had showered him with praise, it was time for Mays to address the crowd. First he apologized to the players and fans for delaying the game. Then he told them "This is a very sad night for me. I may not look it but in my heart I'm sad because I hear you cheering for me and I am unable to do anything for you."[17]

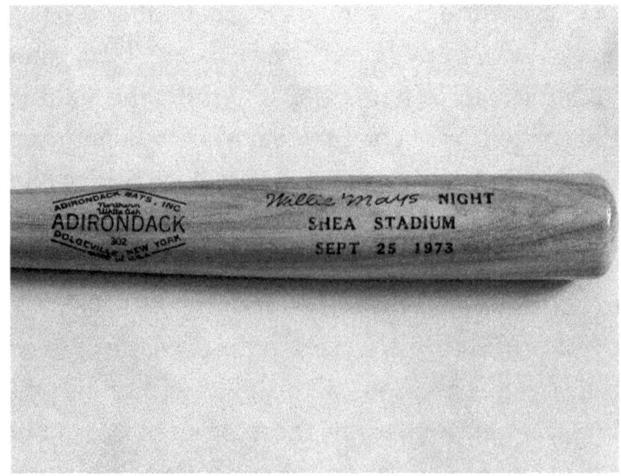


*This is a souvenir bat from Willie Mays Night at Shea Stadium in 1973. Courtesy Les Masterson.*

He closed by saying, "I look at the kids over here and they are playing and they are fighting for themselves tells me one thing: Willie, say goodbye to America."[18] In one final gesture, Mays held his hand high in the air and waved his cap at the crowd. "Yea, Willie," came the roar from the kids. The parents couldn't applaud for crying."[19]

Mays hugged Mae and his son Michael. He raised his cap and saluted the fans as they shouted back their admiration. As he slowly walked back to the dugout the Shea Stadium, organist Jane Jarvis played "Auld Lang Syne."

Mets left fielder Cleon Jones, who was also from Alabama, was watching in the dugout. "I felt I wanted to cry," he said later. "I know how Willie must have felt to say he can't perform anymore. It got next to me. I think I might have dropped one or two tears. It was one of those times when you cry inside."[20]

The Mets took the field at 8:35 to face the Montreal Expos. Left-hander Jerry Koosman started for New York. Koosman had a 12-15 record but had gone 4-1 with a 2.83 ERA in September. Montreal got two hits through the first four innings, a walk in the second and a double in the third, but couldn't score. The Expos had two singles against Koosman in the fifth but they were unable to get a runner to cross the plate.

Rookie right-hander Steve Rogers started for the Expos. He entered the game with a 9-4 record and a 1.32 ERA.[21] Rogers matched Koosman and kept the Mets from scoring through the first four innings despite allowing runners to reach base in the first, second, and fourth.

The Mets grabbed the lead, 1-0, in the fifth. Bud Harrelson led off with single. Koosman's sacrifice moved him to second. Wayne Garrett singled to put runners at the corners. Felix Millan's fly ball to left plated Harrelson.

Montreal tied the score in the sixth. Ron Woods singled with one out and stole second. Koosman walked Bob Bailey. Bailey was thrown out at second when the Expos tried a double steal. With Woods on third, Garrett threw wildly to first on Hal Breeden's grounder. Breeden reached second on the error as Woods crossed the plate, tying the game 1-1.

The Mets reclaimed the lead in the bottom of the inning on Jones's one-out home run. Jones later said that Mays was one of his childhood heroes while growing up in Mobile and he was pleased that he could provide the winning hit.

"When you played as a kid, did you pretend that you were Willie Mays?" Jones was asked. He said he followed fellow Mobile native Hank Aaron more closely but "it depended if I got to the ballgame early or late. If I got there late, somebody else was Willie Mays and I had to be somebody else."[22]

Koosman got in trouble in the seventh. After a pair of two-out singles put the tying run in scoring position, Mets manager Berra called on Tug McGraw. The first batter he faced was Felipe Alou, who hit a long fly ball to left-center.

Jones got a good jump and caught the ball while running at full speed with his arm fully extended. "I know Alou hits a lot to left-center and right-center, so I cheated a little to make sure I could get to one in the gap," Jones said. "I didn't think I'd get it when it was first hit but I just kept running and saw the ball was hanging. I got to the right spot at the right time."[23]

Mike Marshall, making his 88th appearance of 1973, relieved Rogers in the seventh.[24] He walked McGraw and gave up a single to Garrett that put McGraw on second. But Millan hit into a double play to end the inning without the Mets scoring.

Hanging on to a one-run lead, McGraw got into an eighth-inning jam. He gave up a leadoff single to Wood and walked Bailey. Breeden hit a grounder to McGraw who threw out Woods at third. The lefty reliever ended the threat by getting out the next two Expos.

The Mets had another chance to score in the bottom of the eighth. Jones walked with two outs. Don Hahn doubled but Jones was thrown out trying to score.

McGraw retired the Expos in order in the ninth, notching his ninth save of the month as he helped Koosman earn his 13th win of the season.

The Mets now had a seven-game winning streak, giving them a 1½-game lead over the Pittsburgh Pirates. Mays watched the game from the dugout. With the pregame ceremony, he felt he was retired from baseball. He hadn't played since September 9. Mays spoke to Mets owner Joan Payson after the game and told her he was planning to return home. "She urged him to reconsider. 'You can't go home now,' she said. So he stayed."[25]

When he heard about Mays' announcement, Tom Seaver said, "There are individuals you know you're going to have to tear the uniform off of. It's like a battlefield and you're in the trench, and the mentality is exactly the same with baseball. You're going to fight and play until they tear the uniform off. And you got that sense with Willie – they were going to have to tear the uniform off him. It's sad to see, but it's a beautiful thing to, because of the love he had for what he had done for some twenty-odd years."[26]

Mays did not play in another regular-season game. He did get into one game and drove in a run in the National League Championship Series against the Cincinnati Reds as the Mets won the series in five games. Mays played three games and drove in another run in the World Series as New York lost to the Oakland Athletics in seven games.[27]

The Mets honored Mays again on August 27, 2022. The team retired his number 24 when it held its first Old-Timer's Day in 28 years. When Joan Payson, the Mets' first owner, recruited Mays to come back to New York in 1972, she promised him that the team would retire his number.

Payson died before she could honor that promise and future owners failed to carry it out. "A promise was made," said Mets team President Sandy Alderson. "It needs to be fulfilled." Cleon Jones said Mays deserved the honor. "He was a difference-maker in the ballpark and a difference-maker in the clubhouse," said Jones. "He made the atmosphere in the clubhouse conducive to winning."[28]

Mays, then 91 years old, did not attend after undergoing hip surgery, but he sent a statement that was read by his son Michael. "I can never forget the way it felt to return to New York to play for all the loyal Mets fans. I'm tremendously proud I ended my career in Queens with the Mets during the '73 World Series. It's an honor to have my number retired in my two favorite cities – New York and San Francisco. New York was a magical place to play baseball."[29]

## SOURCES

In addition to the sources cited in the Notes, the author used the Baseball-Reference.com and Retrosheet.org websites for box-score, player, team, and season pages, pitching and batting logs, and other pertinent material. The author also viewed Mays' farewell speech on MLB.com, which can be accessed at https://www.mlb.com/video/mays-speaks-on-his-night-in-1973.

https://www.baseball-reference.com/boxes/NYN/NYN197309250.shtml

https://www.retrosheet.org/boxesetc/1973/B09250NYN1973.htm

## NOTES

1 The San Francisco Giants traded Mays to the New York Mets for Charlie Williams and $50,000. "We're hopeful that Willie will help us this year and maybe next," said Mets President M. Donald Grant. "... I personally hope he's here for the rest of his baseball life." Red Foley, "Mets Deal Brings Willie 'Back to Paradise,'" *New York Daily News*, May 12, 1972: 95.

2 Foley.

3 The Mets medical staff had to frequently drain fluid from Mays' knees. He had hurt his left knee playing in the outfield. When he favored the right one, it eventually caused him daily pain. Mays also injured his right shoulder when he misjudged a leap against the outfield wall. He was so hurt that he played only three games in September.

4 James Hirsch, *Willie Mays: The Life, The Legend* (New York: Scribner, 2010), 519.

5 Hirsch, 520.

6 Hirsch, 521.

7 Hirsch, 521.

8 Will Grimsley, "World of Baseball Bids Good-bye to One of Greatest Performers," *Selma* (Alabama) *Times-Journal*, September 26, 1973: 11.

9 Grimsley.

10 Hirsch, 520.

11 Don Drumm, "Fans Say So Long," *White Plains* (New York) *Journal-News*, September 26, 1973: D1.

12 Drumm

13 Newspapers reported on the many gifts Mays received. Other gifts that were mentioned: two limousines, a Mercedes Benz, 100 record albums, a lifetime supply of Atlantic Records recordings, lifetime supplies of Teachers scotch and Moët champagne, a set of luggage, a Fisher console stereo system, a private telephone system, a collection of Willie Mays dolls and games, bedsheets, towels and bedspreads, numerous clothing outfits, a silver tray, a trip around the world, a trip to Mexico, a typewriter, a mink coat and watch for his wife, Mae, an honorary doctorate from Miles College in Fairfield, Alabama.

14 Grimsley.

15 Frank Dolson, "Thousands Cheer Mays in His Last Hurrah," *Philadelphia Inquirer*, September 26, 1973: C1.

16 Sam Goldaper, "Baseball Says Good-bye to Willie Mays and Era," *New York Times*, September 26, 1973: 29.

17 Ron Drago, "We Love You Willie," *Hackensack Record*, September 26, 1973: D1.

18 "Mays Speaks on His Night in 1973," MLB.com. https://www.mlb.com/video/mays-speaks-on-his-night-in-1973.

19 Grimsley.

20 Hirsch, 524.

21 Rogers eventually finished second in the Rookie of the Year voting to Gary Matthews.

22 Drumm, "Fans Say So Long."

23 Ron Drago, "Cleon Contributes Special Gift to Mays," *Hackensack Record*, September 26, 1973: D1.

24 Marshall made 92 appearances in 1973 to lead the league for the second time in two years. Marshall set the major-league record for relief appearances (106) in 1974, when he played for the Dodgers.

25 Hirsch, 524.

26 Hirsch, 520.

27 Perhaps even more significant than his play on the field was the role Mays played in third game of the series. Cincinnati's Pete Rose tried to break up a double play in the fifth inning with a hard slide into second. He knocked down New York shortstop Bud Harrelson, who jumped up and charged Rose. Both benches emptied and the two teams brawled for over five minutes before the umpires separated the players. When Rose took the field in the sixth, Mets fans pelted him with all sorts of items. After he was almost hit with a bottle, Rose walked off the field. Cincinnati manager Sparky Anderson said he wouldn't continue the game until his players were safe. When the Mets' public-address announcer asked the fans to stop, they ignored him with a chorus of boos. National League President Chub Feeney consulted with umpires and asked Mets manager Berra to send out a player to calm the crowd. Berra chose Mays and when Mays left the dugout the fans cheered him. He gave the peace sign to the fans and pointed to the scoreboard, reminding them that the team was ahead 9-2. Then he went down the foul line along with Staub, Seaver, and Jones. Mays shouted to the fans, "We're ahead! Let 'em play the game." Hirsch, 525.

28 "Mets Retire Willie Mays' No. 24 in Surprise Moment at Old Timers' Day," The Athletic.com, August 27, 2022. https://theathletic.com/3543073/2022/08/27/willie-mays-mets-number-retirement/.

29 Associated Press, "New York Mets Retire Willie Mays' No. 24 Jersey in Old-Timers' Day Surprise," ESPN.com, August 27, 2022. https://www.espn.com/mlb/story/_/id/34473093/new-york-mets-retire-willie-mays-no-24-jersey-old-rs-day-surprise.

# THE DEFENSIVE EXCELLENCE OF WILLIE MAYS

BY MARK SIMON

ONE OF THE game's greatest players of all time was also one of the greatest *defensive* players of all time.

Willie Mays set a standard of excellence for outfielders that is virtually unmatched. As Dodgers executive Fresco Thompson said, Mays' glove was "where triples go to die."[1]

Mays is the leader in games played as a center fielder (2,829) and putouts as both a center fielder (7,024) and outfielder (7,112) since 1901. He ranks seventh in assists as a center fielder (188) and third in double plays (59).

For the modern stat, Total Zone Runs, an estimate of runs saved based on available defensive data dating back to 1953, Mays ranks second among center fielders behind only Andruw Jones.

Mays' 12 Gold Glove Awards are tied with Roberto Clemente for the most for an outfielder since the award was first given out in 1957.

Mays was the only unanimous choice for the inaugural Gold Gloves, which were selected by a panel of writers organized by *The Sporting News*.[2]

"You can't have all of it like Willie did, but he did," said Hall of Fame catcher Johnny Bench, who presented Mays with the Lifetime Achievement Award at the Gold Glove Awards ceremony in 2013, describing Mays' defensive work. "He possessed a gift that very few people will ever have, and anybody will ever have. He played the game the way we all wanted to."[3]

He also played in a way that was distinct at the time and is still so now. Mays' signature play was the basket catch, a play he worked on while serving in the US Army in 1952 and 1953, inspired by teammates Chic Genovese[4] and Bill Rigney.[5] Though Mays understood the showy nature of the way he caught balls, there was a practical aspect to it, particularly when there were men on base.

"If you catch it down here, at the middle of your body, you'll get rid of it more quickly," Mays said.[6]

But it was considerably more than the basket catch that made Mays memorable. His speed allowed him to reach balls that others couldn't. Mays often played a shallow center field but was able to track balls to the extent that he knew exactly where he needed to go to make the catch.[7]

The many newspaper accounts of great plays by Mays almost all describe a sprint, gallop, or dash of varying lengths. The ball rarely beat him to the spot. And his throwing arm was elite. As is noted below, the way he threw a baseball was often compared to those competing in Olympic throwing events.

Mays knew how important his defense was. He often said that defense was the key to playing baseball. He used mostly MacGregor gloves, though his most famous catch was made with a Rawlings. Mays would make a 12-inch glove 14 inches by pulling his palm out of his glove to allow greater extension.[8]

Here is a summary of 24 great plays made by Mays. They begin when he was a 17-year-old in the Negro Leagues and conclude at age 50 in an Old-Timers Day game. It's far from an all-encompassing list, but these plays will give you a sense of how Mays amazed everyone who watched him, not just at bat, but also in the field.

### 1) September 30, 1948

Mays' defensive origin story began in his brief time as a 17-year-old with the Birmingham Black Barons, most notably in Game Three of the Negro World Series against the Homestead Grays.

First, he made a running catch near the center-field fence in the third inning. Then he threw out future Hall of Famer Buck Leonard, who was trying to go from first to third on a single Mays fielded in the sixth inning. And for good measure, Mays' walk-off hit won the game in the ninth.[9]

### 2) July 23, 1950

A 19-year-old Mays played 81 games with the Trenton Giants in the Interstate League and wowed his teammates with one amazing play after another.

One example: Chasing down a fly ball while crashing into and then toppling over the left-center-field temporary wire fence to end a bases-loaded threat in the fifth inning of a game at Memorial Stadium in York, Pennsylvania.

"I thought he was going to catch the ball," said left fielder Maurice Cunningham. "It was just a matter of whether he was going to hold it when he started going over the fence."[10]

He did. Of course, he did. People learned early on not to doubt Mays' defense.

### 3) July 25, 1951

It took only a few months into Mays' major-league career before he began making catches that had few precedents, like one against Rocky Nelson in the first inning of a 5-4 loss to the Pirates.

As described by the *New York Daily News*:

"The Giants center fielder, after a long gallop, caught up with the ball about 400 feet from the plate and made a bare-hand catch on the dead run."[11]

Said Branch Rickey, then the Pirates' GM: "That was the finest catch I have ever seen and the finest catch I ever expect to see."[12]

It wasn't the first time Mays made a barehand catch either. He made one in his Trenton Giants home debut a year earlier, then telling his teammates that the reason he went with the barehand was that "I couldn't get my glove up in time."[13]

Thirty-eight years later, another Giant would become famous for making a barehand catch, when left fielder Kevin Mitchell made one against Cardinals shortstop Ozzie Smith.

### 4) August 15, 1951

It is amusing in hindsight that the lede of the *New York Daily News* game story for this contest between the Giants and Dodgers was "Now that it doesn't matter too much anymore, the Giants have discovered that they can beat the Dodgers if they make an all-out try."[14]

In this case, that meant a running catch by Mays and a throw home to nail Billy Cox of the Dodgers trying to score in the top of the eighth inning. Catcher Wes Westrum tagged Cox for the final out of the frame, keeping the score tied, 1-1.

Wrote Jim McCulley: "It looked as though Cox would easily make the plate after the catch. But

Mays, after making the nab, made a complete turn like a discus heaver, and fired a strike to Westrum."[15]

Mays and Westrum teamed up again in the bottom of the eighth. After Mays singled, Westrum hit a two-run home run that gave the Giants a 3-1 win. It was the fifth win in a 16-game winning streak that helped the Giants overtake the Dodgers for the NL pennant.[16]

## 5) April 18, 1952

One can read a lot of accounts saying that this catch or that catch was judged by someone to be Mays' greatest. The catch made on this day is the one that Mays himself called the best one.

In the seventh inning of a game against the Dodgers, Mays caught pinch-hitter Bobby Morgan's bid for an extra-base hit with a dive and a slide near the fence in left-center field.

"I didn't think I had a chance at all to get it," Mays told reporters.[17] "It was sinking fast and seemed to be curving away. But I stayed with it and got it on the dive – with both hands together."

Mays noted later that he hit the wall and briefly knocked himself out. "When I came to, I can see Leo [Durocher] and Jackie [Robinson]. Leo wanted to see how I was doing, and Jackie wanted to see if I caught the ball."[18]

## 6) June 18, 1953

While serving in the Army, Mays played for the Fort Eustis (Virginia) baseball team and regularly wowed his fellow soldiers.

Jim Shoop told of a play Mays made against him when Shoop, playing for the Patuxent River Naval Air Station, tried to go from first to third on a single.

"Mays had darted to his left, completely eliminating the gap. He snared the liner on one hop, pivoted smartly and unleashed a bullet of a throw to third base," wrote Jim's son, Tom Shoop. "As Dad chugged along, the third baseman caught Mays' perfect throw and waited patiently for him to arrive. Dad executed a textbook slide – right into the tag."[19]

## 7) August 15, 1954

Six weeks before the famous play in Game One of the 1954 World Series against Vic Wertz, there was one against Duke Snider, a reaching, leaping catch in the seventh inning, just in front of the part of the Ebbets Field fence that contained a garage door.[20]

The Dodgers defeated the Giants, 9-4, that day, though Mays extended his hitting streak to 17 games with a home run. Sportswriter Dick Young overheard an unimpressed Dodgers fan wonder about the defensive play.

"How come he didn't catch it at his belt?"[21]

## 8) September 29, 1954

"I had it all the way," Mays said of his catch on the 450-foot fly ball hit by Indians slugger Wertz.

Never mind that Mays ran "for about five minutes" in his initial chase in the eighth inning, per *Daily News* writer Dick Young, than for "another couple of minutes" when he realized he hadn't quite reached the ball's landing point yet.[22]

"I remember him busting for the ball and tapping his glove, which means he's got it," said Joe Amalfitano, then a rookie catcher who was in the Giants' bullpen ready to warm up potential relief pitchers. "Then he started to slow down. I knew he had the ball tracked."[23]

After making the catch, Mays made an incredible throw back into the infield, as Larry Doby tagged and went from second to third. Mays took pride in telling people about the importance of that heave.

"The throw is the key to that play," Mays has repeatedly said.[24]

Wrote Arnold Hano in *A Day in the Bleachers,* "Mays caught the ball and then whirled and threw, like some olden statue of a Greek javelin hurler, his head twisted away to the left as his right arm swept up and around."[25]

Sometimes forgotten is the context in which this catch was made. Had the ball fallen, two runs would have scored, putting the Indians up 4-2. Instead, Mays caught the ball and the game remained tied as the Giants escaped the inning, then won it in the 10th on a walk-off home run by Dusty Rhodes.

The other thing forgotten is that Wertz was in the middle of his greatest World Series game. A hit would have been his fourth in four at-bats, and he'd have had driven in all four Indians runs.

Instead, he's "the other guy" in the story of one of the most memorable catches in baseball history.

## 9) July 12, 1955

Forty-seven years before Torii Hunter robbed Barry Bonds in Milwaukee in 2002, Mays stole a potential home run from Ted Williams in the All-Star Game at County Stadium in Milwaukee.

With the AL leading 5-0, Williams hit a drive to deep right-center field, one that looked as if it would add two runs to the lead. But Mays "drifted to the seven-foot-high screen, waited to time his leap, then sprang as high as possible and came down with the ball. The crowd swooned."[26]

Said Mays, "I guess I made a real good jump."[27]

The catch was a turning point. Mays singled twice and scored two runs as the NL rallied for a 6-5 win on Stan Musial's home run in the 12th inning.

## 10) March 29, 1956

About a year and a half after making the catch against Wertz in the World Series, Mays did it again to Wertz in the fifth inning of an exhibition game between the Giants and Indians in Tucson, Arizona.

"It didn't mean as much, but Willie ran after it just the same," wrote McCulley for the *Daily News*. "He kept running and running and snagged it with one hand, 400 feet in right-center and used the other hand to back himself away from the wall."[28]

## 11) July 31, 1956

In this part of his career, Mays was frequently topping himself, at least in the eyes of those who saw him regularly. A case in point was this catch

*One baseball executive said Willie Mays' glove was "where triples go to die." SABR/The Rucker Archive.*

in the eighth inning of a 5-1 win in the first game of a doubleheader against the Reds.

"... Mays made one of his all-time best catches to rob [Wally] Post of at least three bases," wrote McCulley. "Willie, after a long, speedy gallop, and a last-second leap[,] nabbed Wally's blow in the left field bullpen for the second out."[29]

## 12) June 3, 1957

This was another one for the top-all lists. Here's what some observers said of Willie's "60-yard dash" to catch Roberto Clemente's 440-foot drive to the left-center gap, opposite where Mays was playing.

"That ball is uncatchable" – Giants manager Bill Rigney.

"This is an impossible thing" – Giants coach Tommy Henrich.

"He's the only ballplayer that ever played baseball that could have caught the ball" – Pirates manager Bobby Bragan.[30]

## 13) June 10, 1957

Another Wally, this time Cardinals slugger Wally Moon, did his best Wertz impersonation, hitting a ball to dead center field at the Polo Grounds in the fourth inning. The *Daily News* estimated that Mays was 450 feet from home plate when he made the catch.[31] The Associated Press put it at 470 feet away[32] and the AP photo of the play makes it appear that he's just a step from the 480-foot mark.[33]

This one didn't get quite the writeup of some of the others, maybe because Mays lost a ball in the sun earlier in the game, the first of a doubleheader in which the Giants were swept.

## 14) July 7, 1957

This one was another of the drives to deep center field that would have been at least 40 feet over the fence in any modern ballpark. But Dick Rand's line drive to straightaway center field at the Polo Grounds, only two innings after a home run, was just another ball that Mays made like Superman to catch up to.

"Mays took off as though jet propelled and this looked too hard to handle," wrote *Pittsburgh Press* columnist Les Biederman. "This one was a line drive, not a towering fly, and for an instant it appeared the ball would beat Mays to the spot in front of the clubhouse. But somehow Mays reached the warning track about 450 feet from the plate and took the ball over his left shoulder. The wonder of it was how he made it look so routine."[34]

## 15) September 16, 1959

The 1959 pennant race was one in which the Giants clung to the divisional lead with six games remaining but were overtaken by the eventual World Series-winning Dodgers.

Mays did all he could in the field to keep the Giants in front, hitting .488 in the last 12 games of the season. He did his best on defense, too, making a leaping catch at home against the right-center-field fence on Milwaukee Braves third baseman Eddie Mathews in the fifth inning of what would be a 2-0 loss.

"Willie came down in a heap, clutching his sore shoulder," wrote Curley Grieve in the *San Francisco Examiner*. "But after resting on his knees momentarily, he got up and trotted to the dugout."[35]

*Willie Mays' 12 Gold Gloves tie him with Roberto Clemente for the most among outfielders since the award was first given out in 1957. Courtesy National Baseball Hall of Fame.*

The AP photo of the catch captures Mays in mid-jump. The photo caption provided by the AP editors invites us to take note of a boy in the picture who was "more interested in his bag of peanuts than in the play."[36]

Mays did this just three days after bruising his thigh chasing (and missing) a ninth-inning fly ball hit by Harry Anderson of the Phillies. He recovered to make a great running catch later that inning (preserving a 1-0 win)[37] and then this one against Mathews.

## 16) May 17, 1961

Only 17 days after hitting four home runs in a game, Mays had another top-all moment, an all-timer of a catch against Dick Bertell of the Cubs. This was another over-the-shoulder snag of a line drive near the 410-foot mark in center field at Candlestick Park.

*San Francisco Examiner* writer Grieve and other writers polled those with the Giants who were there for both this catch and Mays' catch on Wertz in the 1954 World Series. Then-manager Alvin Dark said it was better than the Wertz catch. Coach Wes Westrum agreed. Whitey Lockman disagreed.

This was Dark's take: "This one, he turned his back and raced for it. It had to be perfect judgment. He caught it like a football."

Mays chose not to weigh in, saying he had a hard enough time remembering the Wertz catch.[38]

The *Sacramento Bee* offered a neutral take, saying the catch on Bertell "had just a mite more of greatness attached to it."[39]

## 17) June 22, 1963

A pair of photos, one from the Associated Press and one from United Press International that ran in the *San Francisco Examiner*, commemorate this catch by Willie Mays against Joe Torre in the third inning of a 3-0 shutout of the Milwaukee Braves at County Stadium.

The first photo shows Mays leaping and making a one-handed catch just in front of the fence. The second shows the aftermath, Mays tumbling over as if doing a headstand, the ball visible in his glove.[40]

## 18) July 9, 1963

"I play to win," Mays told reporters at the 1963 All-Star Game at Cleveland Stadium.

That's why Mays had no concern for injury in making a running catch of Joe Pepitone's eighth-inning fly ball. Mays won the game MVP for that play, as well as his two hits and two runs scored. A stubbed toe, which got caught underneath the chain-link fence after Mays made the grab, was of little consequence.[41]

Mays' toe injury did nothing to impede his season. He hit .376 with 16 home runs in the first 46 games after the All-Star break.

## 19) August 22, 1963

Mays took a lot of bumps and bruises in that 1963 season. Six weeks after the All-Star Game, he went hard after a line drive to right-center by Lee Maye in the third inning of an 8-6 win against Milwaukee. The *Oakland Tribune* referred to it as "an impossible-except-for-Willie catch."

Mays banged his right wrist on the grass when he dove to snag the ball.

"It wasn't hurt, it was numb, like when you whack your funny bone," Mays told reporters.[42]

Again, Mays healed up. He walked in his last two plate appearances in this game, then had multiple hits in each of his next five games.

## 20) May 17, 1966

Mays remembered this day well enough to talk about it in his book with John Shea more than 50 years later. He had three outfield assists in a game for the only time in his career in a 2-1 13-inning loss to the Dodgers. That was short of the major-league record of four, last done by Wally Berger of the Braves in 1931.[43]

The first throw nailed Willie Davis trying to go from first to third on a single. The second was described as a fake-out, with Mays conning Don

*Willie Mays led the NL in assists three times and putouts twice. Courtesy National Baseball Hall of Fame.*

Drysdale into thinking he wouldn't catch the ball, then doubling him off first base.

The last was described as "an amazing heave" that needed a relay from Willie McCovey against the Dodgers' fastest runner, Maury Wills, who was trying to score on Jim Gilliam's double. It kept the game tied temporarily in the 11th inning.[44]

"I had another guy at second but (Tito) dropped the ball," Mays said, referring to a potential fourth assist to second baseman Tito Fuentes. "He felt bad about it, but I told him don't worry, that's baseball."[45]

## 21) April 11, 1970

Thirty-nine-year-old Willie Mays still had the aggressive instincts of his younger days, even if it came at the detriment of his teammates.

In the third inning of NBC's *Game of the Week* between the Reds and Giants, Bobby Tolan hit a fly ball to right center that looked as though it was going to be a home run. Tolan had already been denied a hit by Mays when leading off the game. He was about to be thwarted again.

"The only question was how I would catch the ball," Mays said.[46]

Mays and right fielder Bobby Bonds both came hard toward the ball, and it was Mays who reached well over the fence with his glove to pull the ball back. He did so as he crashed hard into Bonds, with Bonds' left shoulder going directly into Mays' chest. Mays then fell on top of Bonds on the way down, this time taking a shot from Bonds' knee.

Mays held on to the ball even as he was knocked out for a few seconds. After a five-minute delay to allow Bonds and Mays to recuperate, both players were able to finish the game.[47]

"I don't like you," Barry Bonds remembers telling his father. "You hurt Willie."[48] Mays was his favorite player (and godfather).

## 22) June 19, 1972

The great defensive plays were fewer for the 41-year-old Mays, but they didn't completely disappear. In a 3-0 loss to the Astros in which the Mets were one-hit by Larry Dierker, Mays made two standouts.

The first was a diving catch against Bob Watson that left two runners on base in the fifth inning. One writer noted that Mays was "sliding 10 to 20 yards across the AstroTurf" after making the catch. Mays also chased down a double by Larry Howard and got the relay to shortstop Bud Harrelson quickly enough to throw out Tommy Helms at the plate.[49]

## 23) July 8, 1973

The narrative of Willie Mays falling over himself in the outfield in his final days as a major leaguer is a pervasive one but doesn't tell the complete story. Mays was still capable of making a great play.

Darrell Evans of the Atlanta Braves learned that the hard way. Evans thought he homered in the eighth inning. But his 410-foot fly ball to center field didn't quite carry far enough. Mays jumped at the fence to make the catch and denied Evans a chance to circle the bases.[50]

## 24) October 3, 1981

On the 30th anniversary of Bobby Thomson's "Shot Heard 'Round the World," the Mets staged an Old-Timers Day Game at Shea Stadium and

Mays flashed back to his 20-year-old days for a few glorious seconds.

The now 50-year-old Mays made a running catch on the warning track in left-center field to take an extra-base-hit away from Ron Swoboda.

"It was a play many modern major leaguers half his age would not make," wrote *New York Daily News* writer Jack Lang.[51]

Mays at any age was simply a marvel. He came to the major leagues making plays that no seasoned veteran could make. And he ended his playing days in much the same way.

***Acknowledgments***

Special thanks to Willie Mays biographer John Shea, Eduardo Pérez, Gary Mintz and the members of the New York Giants Preservation Society, and Bill Klink for their assistance.

## SOURCES

In addition to the sources cited in the Notes, the author consulted the following:

http://Baseball-Reference.com

http://Newspapers.com

## NOTES

1 Jim Murray, "Willie Gets a Roasting," *Los Angeles Times*, December 3, 1971: 18.

2 Associated Press, "Mays Heads Fielding Stars," *Poughkeepsie* (New York) *Journal*, December 15, 1957: 2B.

3 Author telephone interview with Johnny Bench, October 7, 2022.

4 Randolph Linthurst, "Willie Mays First Season," SABR *Baseball Research Journal 1974*, https://sabr.org/journal/article/willie-mays-first-season/.

5 John Shea, *24, Life Stories and Lessons from the Say Hey Kid* (New York: St. Martin's Publishing Group, 2020), 74.

6 Shea, 72.

7 Shea, 241.

8 Shea, 241.

9 John Klima, *Willie's Boys* (Hoboken, New Jersey: John Wiley & Sons. 2009), 181-183.

10 Bill Klink, "Willie's Wonder Years," *Sports History*. March 1989: 45-46.

11 "Diamond Dust: Feller, Reynolds to Duel Today," *New York Daily News*, July 26, 1951: 69.

12 Gary Livacari, https://www.baseballhistorycomesalive.com/willie-mays-makes-an-incredible-catch/

13 Klink, "Willie's Wonder Years."

14 Jim McCulley, "Giants Do It Again! Flock Victims, 3-1," *New York Daily News*, August 16, 1951: C20.

15 McCulley.

16 Dan Fields, "August 15, 1951: Willie Mays Defensive Gem Caps Giants Victory," SABR Games Project: https://sabr.org/gamesproj/game/august-15-1951-willie-mays-defensive-gem-caps-giants-victory/.

17 Dana Mozley, "Mays Catch Greatest, Giants, Dodgers Agree," *New York Daily News*, April 19, 1952: C16.

18 Shea, 90.

19 Tom Shoop, "The Day Private Willie Mays Threw Out My Dad," February 21, 2021. https://www.defenseone.com/ideas/2021/02/day-private-willie-mays-threw-out-my-dad/172187/.

20 Charles Hoff, "Out for a Sunday Drive" photo in the *New York Daily News*, August 16, 1954: 44.

21 Dick Young, "Walt: We're Still 2nd; Leo: 40 games left to Play," *New York Daily News*, August 16, 1954: C20.

22 Dick Young, "Dusty's HR in 10th Wins Opener," *New York Daily News*, September 30, 1954: C24.

23 Interview of Joe Amalfitano by John Shea, November 30, 2022.

24 Shea, 86.

25 Arnold Hano *A Day in the Bleachers*, (New York: Crowell, 1955), 23

26 "Musial HR in 12th Beats AL, 6-5," *New York Daily News*, July 13, 1955: 64.

27 "Musial HR in 12th Beats AL, 6-5."

28 Jim McCulley, "Mays Magnificent in Vain, 10-5," *New York Daily News*, March 30, 1956: 46.

29 Jim McCulley, "Giants Win, 5-1; Then Bow, 7-3," *New York Daily News*, August 1, 1956: 65.

30 George Kiseda, "Willie's Catch Greatest," *Pittsburgh Sun-Telegraph*, June 4, 1957: 22.

31 Dana Mozley, "Cards Trounce Giants, 2-1, 10-7; 3½ Off Pace," *New York Daily News*, June 10, 1957: 58.

32 "6-Run Sixth Gives Cards Sweep Over NY, 2-1, 10-7," *Elmira* (New York) *Advertiser*, June 10, 1957: 7.

33 Jack Harris, "Willie Amazes 'Em," photo in *Asbury Park* (New Jersey) *Press*, June 10, 1957: 14.

34 Les Biederman, "Les Biederman's Scoreboard: Willie Mays Pulls Another Robbery," *Pittsburgh Press*, July 8, 1957: 19.

35 Curley Grieve, "Jones: Bush Hits Beat Me," *San Francisco Examiner*, September 17, 1959: 3, 3.

36 Ernest K. Bennett, "Play of the Day," *Daily Independent Journal* (San Rafael, California), September 17, 1959: 14.

37 Curley Grieve, "Defense Finally Has Its Day in the Sun," *San Francisco Examiner,* September 14, 1959: 43

38 Curley Grieve, "Mays, Alou Fielding Gems Save the Day for Giants," *San Francisco Examiner*, May 18, 1961: 53.

39 "Mays Catch of Long Bertell Drive Is Called Greatest," *Sacramento Bee*, May 18, 1961: D1.

40 "Unscheduled Tumbling Act by Giant Star in Milwaukee Backfield," *San Francisco Examiner*, June 23, 1963: 55.

41 Mike Rathet (Associated Press), "Mays Flamboyant, Modest, Breaks All-Star Records," *Chillicothe* (Ohio) *Gazette*, July 10, 1963: 18.

42 George Ross, "Juan Halts Skid With His 19th Win," *Oakland Tribune,* August 23, 1963: 43.

43 https://www.baseball-almanac.com/rb_ofas.shtml.

44 Harry Jupiter, "Desperation Peg Loses in L.A., 2-1." *San Francisco Examiner.* May 18, 1966: 66.

45 Shea, 240.

46 Shea, 93.

47 Jim McGee, "Ron Hunt Hero of Giants Win," *San Francisco Examiner,* April 12, 1970: C3.

48 Nelson George, *Say Hey, Willie Mays!* Documentary. HBO Sports, 2022.

49 Sam Fields, "Houston Fields Strong Astros," *Concordia* (Texas) *Sentinel*, June 28, 1972: 6A.

50 Red Foley, "Hank Hits Pair, Trails Babe by 18; Mets Clipped, 4-2," *New York Daily News*, July 9, 1973: C22.

51 Jack Lang, "Mays at 51, Still Gloved Bandit," *New York Daily News*, October 4, 1981: 77.

# "NOW PLAYING IN…" – WILLIE MAYS' OTHER POSITIONS

BY STEVEN M. GLASSMAN

WILLIE MAYS PLAYED in more regular-season games in center field than anyone else in major-league baseball history (2,832). He also played 83 games at first base, 12 in right field, 2 in left field, 2 at shortstop, and 1 at third base. This article presents the positions in order by when Mays made his first regular-season appearance at each position.

## Shortstop (2)

Mays made his first appearance at a position other than center field when he made his major-league shortstop debut on August 13, 1963, vs. the Cincinnati Reds at Crosley Field. It was his 1,651st career game, and he was filling in for Ernie Bowman. Manager Alvin Dark simply ran out of manpower, what with injuries and a suspension of Willie McCovey.[1] Mays laughed and said, "Man, that's too close to the hitter."[2] At the next locker, Norm Larker said, "If you think that's too close, Willie, have you ever tried to hold a guy on at first base with McCovey hitting?"[3] He made his other shortstop appearance in the second game of a doubleheader against the New York Mets at Shea Stadium on May 31, 1964. In the 23-inning game, Mays moved from center field to shortstop in the 10th inning, replacing Jim Davenport, and Matty Alou replaced Mays in center. Mays went back to center in the 13th and finished the game there.

## First Base (83)

Mays made his first-base debut on May 1, 1964, vs. the Los Angeles Dodgers at Dodger Stadium. He started the game in center but was limping after a fly ball and was not running full speed after reaching on a single in his first plate appearance. In the second inning, Dark changed the outfield alignment. Mays was moved to first base, Jesus Alou went from right to center, McCovey moved from first to left, and Duke Snider went from left to right. "A man doesn't have to move around too much at first base," explained Dark, "and Willie wasn't hurting so bad he had to leave the game. I wanted his bat in there. And besides, almost every day and night, Willie works out a little at first base. I knew he was a little familiar with the position."[4] In Mays' first inning as a first baseman, he ran out to right field and retrieved an errant Jack

Sanford pickoff throw attempt on John Roseboro. In the third, he tagged Willie Davis on another Sanford pickoff attempt. Mays got his first assist and double play when Ron Fairly's groundball went to second baseman Chuck Hiller. Hiller threw to Mays for the first out, and Mays threw to shortstop Jose Pagan to complete the double play. He repeated what he said when he played shortstop in 1963 and added: "It was fun playing there. I'm always talkin' to people and at first base there are more players around to talk to. In center field, you're lonely."[5]

Mays again played first base on July 21, 1968, in the second game of a doubleheader vs. the Houston Astros at Candlestick Park. McCovey, hampered by fluid on his right knee, sat out the game.[6] Mays next played at first on June 15, 1969, in the second game of a home doubleheader vs. the Montreal Expos to again give McCovey a rest. Mays also filled in at first for McCovey in 1970 for five games. For example, he played the first two games of a Giants-Dodgers road series in May because "McCovey was idled by his shoulder bruise."[7] On July 29, 1970, Mays played first vs. the Mets because McCovey "had to sit out the final game of the three in New York because of the pain."[8]

Mays played a career-high 48 games at first base in 1971 because of McCovey's various injuries. When Mays was acquired by the Mets on May 11, 1972, manager Yogi Berra told him that he would be used almost exclusively against left-handers at first base and some in the outfield to give Tommie Agee "occasional rest."[9] In seven of his nine starts at first base for the Mets, the opposing pitcher was left-handed.[10] On August 3, 1973, Mays announced that he could no longer play in center because of his sore shoulder. "I can catch the fly balls and I can run," he told writers. "But I can't throw. I can throw, but I can't throw hard."[11] Mays played 15 of his final 17 regular-season games in the field at first base with his last one on September 9 vs. the Expos at Jarry Park in Montreal. On September 20 Mays, "sidelined with two cracked ribs,"[12] announced his retirement.

### Third Base (1)

Mays made his only third-base appearance on August 26, 1964, vs. the Dodgers at Dodger Stadium. He started the game in center field, but moved to third base in the bottom of the second inning "when rookie third baseman Jim Ray Hart was skulled by Dodger shortstop Maury Wills while trying to break up a double play at second base."[13] Mays was replaced in center by Matty Alou. In the seventh, Mays went back to center, Alou went back to right, and Jim Davenport replaced Mays at third. In the ninth, Mays went back to third, Alou went back to right, and Davenport went back to shortstop. The Dodgers won in the bottom of the ninth, 2-1, on Doug Camilli's two-out walk-off single to left. Altogether, Mays played six innings in his only major-league career appearance at third base.

### Right Field (12)

Mays made his first appearance in right field on July 30, 1956, in the All-Star Game at Griffith Stadium in Washington. He remained in the game in center field in the fourth after pinch-hitting for the Cincinnati Reds' Gus Bell. Mays was then moved from center to right in the fifth when the St. Louis Cardinals' Stan Musial was moved right to left and Brooklyn Dodgers star Duke Snider was moved from left to center. Mays finished the game in right.

After 1,887 regular-season games in center field, Mays played right field on June 30, 1965, vs. the Astros in the Houston Astrodome. His first experience playing an outfield position other than center field was a painful one. Late in the game, he "pulled a muscle in his thigh, near the groin."[14] The Giants tied the game, 4-4, with a two-out, three-run rally in the eighth off starter Turk Farrell and reliever Claude Raymond. Mays began the rally with a single to left off Farrell, took third on McCovey's single to right, and scored on Jim Ray Hart's single to third baseman Ken Aspromonte. According to a San Francisco sportswriter, Mays "ran like crazy on Hart's hit, and pulled up limping after crossing the plate."[15] Mays, who had been at his usual spot in center, was moved to right in the bottom of the eighth. He went on to play 11 more games (all starts) in right from 1965 into 1969. Mays played his last two games in right in 1969, the first one on August 6 at Connie Mack Stadium in Philadelphia. Mays will remain in right field until his left knee, injured in a collision at the plate with catcher Randy Hundley, Chicago Cub catcher is completely sound, [Giants manager Clyde] King said.[16] He started his final game in right field on August 8 against the St. Louis Cardinals in Candlestick Park. Mays did not finish the contest because he "left the game after six innings when his sore left knee began to bother him."[17] He returned to center on August 15 vs. the Chicago Cubs in Candlestick Park and played the remainder of the 1969 season there.

### Left Field (2)

After 1,886 regular-season starts in center field, Mays started his first game other than in center on July 4, 1965, vs. the Cubs at Wrigley Field. He "had been slowed by a pulled groin muscle."[18] Mays "played there to cut down the running area because of a pulled muscle in the left groin, suffered in Houston [on June 30]"[19] Matty Alou started in center. Herman Franks put the captain in left because he figured there would be less business than in center or right.[20] Mays made six putouts in the 7-4 win.[21] He made his other left-field appearance on September 7, 1966, vs. the Dodgers at Dodger Stadium. Mays once again "was aching with a painfully pulled groin muscle."[22] Before Willie Davis led off the eighth inning with a triple to center, Franks had rearranged his outfield. Ken Henderson came in to play center field, Ollie Brown moved from center field to right field, and Mays moved from right field to left field, replacing Jesus Alou. Pinch-hitter Tommy Davis lined out to Mays, scoring Willie Davis with game-tying run. Mitch Chortkoff wrote in the *San Francisco Examiner* that "It wasn't just that Willie made a sparkling catch of Tommy Davis's shot, but that he then fired the ball all in one motion directly to the plate. The throw wasn't in time, but that didn't detract from the effort."[23] Franks reshuffled the outfield again in the ninth and Mays moved back to and finished the game in right.

As a center fielder, Mays took part in 59 double plays and had an overall .981 fielding percentage. Playing first base in 83 games, he logged 61 double plays and played the position almost as well as he had in center – with a .979 fielding percentage. At the other positions, he played fewer games – handling just one chance at third base and none in his brief time at shortstop. His fielding percentage was 1.000 in left field and .958 in right.

## SOURCES

In addition to the sources mentioned in the Notes, the author referred to https://www.baseball-reference.com/ and https://www.retrosheet.org/ for box scores, play-by-plays, and other pertinent information. The following websites were also consulted: https://www.newspapers.com/ and https://sabr.org/.

## NOTES

1 Bob Stevens, "Giants Put 'Handyman' Mays at Short in Manpower Crisis," *The Sporting News*, August 24, 1963: 9. McCovey was suspended two games and fined $50 for how he reacted to home-plate umpire Ed Vargo's called third strike vs. the Phillies on August 11.

2 "Giants Put 'Handyman' Mays at Short in Manpower Crisis."

3 "Giants Put 'Handyman' Mays at Short in Manpower Crisis."

4 Bob Stevens, "Willie Makes Gateway Bow; 'It's Fun, So Chatty,' He Says," *The Sporting News*, May 16, 1964: 25.

5 "Willie Makes Gateway Bow."

6 Harry Jupiter, "Mays Switched to Gateway So McCovey Could Rest," *The Sporting News*, August 3, 1968: 7.

7 Pat Frizzell, "Stretch Swings a Sizzling Home Run, RBI Stick," *The Sporting News*, May 30, 1970: 15.

8 Pat Frizzell, "Juan Reels In and Starts Over After Seeing Old Movie," *The Sporting News*, August 15, 1970: 18. The author also wrote that McCovey was "missing several games with his arthritic right knee and hamstring injury in his right leg."

9 Jack Lang, "Mets Guarantee Lifetime Security for Mays," *The Sporting News*, May 27, 1972: 24. He would platoon with Ed Kranepool at first base.

10 Mays' first start at first base vs. a right-handed pitcher was against the Atlanta Braves' Phil Niekro on June 2, 1972, at Shea Stadium. The other was vs. the Chicago Cubs' Burt Hooton on September 16, 1972, at Wrigley Field.

11 Jack Lang, "Career in Center Field May Be Over for Mays," *The Sporting News*, August 18, 1973: 26.

12 Jack Lang, "Mays Ends 'a 22-Year Love Affair,'" *The Sporting News*, October 6, 1973: 3.

13 Bob Stevens, "Giants Look to Japan for Mound Help," *The Sporting News*, September 12, 1964: 19.

14 Harry Jupiter, "Astros 'Wynn' 6-4," *San Francisco Examiner*, July 1, 1965: 61.

15 "Astros 'Wynn' 6-4."

16 James K. McKee, "Marichal Is Giants' No. 1 Worry," *San Francisco Examiner*, August 7, 1969: 54.

17 James K. McKee, "Slider Fools Giants," *San Francisco Examiner*, August 9, 1969: 29.

18 "Mays Starts in Left Field for First Time in Majors," *The Sporting News*, July 17, 1965: 42.

19 Edward Prell, "Giants' Rally Defeats Cubs," *Chicago Tribune*, July 5, 1965: Section 3, 2.

20 Harry Jupiter, "J. Alou Sparks 7-4 Victory Over Cubs," *San Francisco Examiner*, July 5, 1965: 55.

21 Two of the Cubs' seven hits were hit in Mays' direction. Glenn Beckert's first-inning leadoff double went to left-center and Don Landrum followed with a home run to left-center off Ron Herbel. Matty Alou had three putouts in center, and three of the Cubs' hits were hit in his direction. Jesus Alou had four putouts and six of the Cubs' hits were hit in his direction.

22 Harry Jupiter, "How Mays Fooled L.A.," *San Francisco Examiner*, September 8, 1966: 53.

23 Mitch Chortkoff, "Roseboro's Explanation," *San Francisco Examiner*, September 8, 1966: 53.

# WILLIE MAYS – THE LEADER IN EXTRA-INNING HOME RUNS

BY BILL NOWLIN

WILLIE MAYS HIT 22 home runs in extra innings, tops among all major leaguers, and four more than the second batter on the list.

When you rank in the top 10 home-run hitters of all time, it's not surprising that you would also rank high among those who hit home runs in extra innings. As of the 2022 season, Willie Mays ranks number 6 on the list of career homer hitters with 660. With 22 homers hit in extra innings, he ranks number 1.

**Some extra-inning batting statistics:**

| Extra-inning HR | | AB | R | H | 2B | 3B | RBI | AVG | SLG |
|---|---|---|---|---|---|---|---|---|---|
| 22 | Willie Mays | 292 | 57 | 87 | 11 | 6 | 45 | .298 | .603 |
| 18 | Jack Clark | 179 | 41 | 58 | 5 | 2 | 41 | .324 | .676 |
| 16 | Frank Robinson | 250 | 45 | 76 | 7 | 1 | 44 | .304 | .532 |
| 15 | Albert Pujols | 155 | 27 | 47 | 9 | 1 | 37 | .303 | .665 |
| 14 | Mickey Mantle | 122 | 39 | 44 | 8 | 1 | 28 | .361 | .787 |
| 14 | Hank Aaron | 254 | 38 | 76 | 13 | 4 | 38 | .299 | .547 |
| 13 | Ted Williams | 129 | 29 | 47 | 9 | 0 | 32 | .364 | .736 |
| 12 | Willie Stargell | 188 | 23 | 53 | 7 | 2 | 32 | .282 | .532 |
| 12 | Mark McGwire | 110 | 21 | 30 | 2 | 1 | 30 | .273 | .636 |
| 12 | Rafael Palmeiro | 178 | 36 | 58 | 10 | 0 | 37 | .326 | .584 |
| 12 | Jim Thome | 153 | 29 | 37 | 8 | 0 | 26 | .242 | .529 |
| 12 | David Ortiz | 139 | 17 | 36 | 9 | 0 | 26 | .259 | .583 |

Having had the most at-bats in extra innings certainly provides more opportunities.

Of the top 10 home-run hitters, half don't make the list of those with a dozen or more homers in regular-season extra-inning games. Missing are Barry Bonds, Babe Ruth, Alex Rodriguez, Ken Griffey Jr., and Sammy Sosa.

Players hitting a higher number of extra-inning homers who don't crack the top 10 for overall quantity are Jack Clark (who ranks number 103 in the number of total homers hit), Mickey Mantle, Ted Williams, Willie Stargell, Mark McGwire, Rafael Palmeiro, and David Ortiz.[1]

Let's look briefly at each of the 22 extra-inning Willie Mays home runs.

**June 22, 1951:** Playing at Wrigley Field in his 29th big-league game, Mays saw the Cubs' Hal Jeffcoat hit a two-run homer in the bottom of the ninth, tying the game, 6-6, and sending it to extra innings. Mays had a single in the sixth but had struck out in the second, the fourth, and the eighth. In the top of the 10th, with one out and runners on first and second, Mays swung at Cubs reliever Emil "Dutch" Leonard's first pitch and hit a three-run homer to deep left off "the wall beyond the left field catwalk."[2] The 9-6 score held, and the Giants won. It was the 10th win in a row for the Giants at Wrigley. The homer was the fifth of Mays' career.

**July 3, 1951:** Nine games later, Mays hit another extra-inning homer, this one at the Polo Grounds against the visiting Phillies. The score was 5-5 after nine. Both teams scored one run in the 10th. Neither team scored in the 11th, but both scored once in the 12th. The Phillies took an 8-7 lead in the top of the 13th. With one out in the bottom of the 13th, Mays homered (off Jocko Thompson) "into the left-field stands" to – once again – tie the score.[3] Wes Westrum walked. Monte Irvin singled a pinch-runner to second, and Whitey Lockman hit "one of the longest singles in Polo Grounds history," to center, winning the game.[4] The ball had gone well over the center fielder's head and "struck the bleacher wall, some 450 feet distant, on one hop."[5]

**July 7, 1951:** Just four days later, the Boston Braves were in New York. Three times the Braves took the lead and three times a Giants home run retied the game. The score was 4-4 after the first nine innings; a two-run homer by Bobby Thomson in the bottom of the eighth had evened the score. The Braves scored, bizarrely, in the top of the 10th. Boston's Roy Hartsfield singled. Sam Jethroe's drive struck Hartsfield and so the baserunner was out. Jethroe stole second and catcher Sal Yvars's errant throw went wild, allowing Jethroe to take third. (Yvars had just entered the game.) Second baseman Eddie Stanky retrieved the throw and, in turn, threw wildly to third base, Jethroe scoring. With one out in the bottom of the 10th, Mays homered to left field off George Estock, "off the left field façade, where it read 414 feet."[6] The *Times* described his homer as one that "hit the cigarette pack in deep left field."[7] The game, tied again, went to 11. The Braves scored once to take a 6-5 lead. Yvars led off in the bottom of the 11th and atoned for his miscue by hitting the third Giants home run of the day that tied the score. With one out, Stanky tripled off reliever Warren Spahn. He tagged and scored on Al Dark's fly ball to left.

**April 30, 1954:** Returning to baseball after missing most of 1952 and all of 1953 due to military service, Mays was back at Wrigley Field on the last day of April. He broke up a 2-2 tie in the top of the 14th inning. With one out, Mays homered "into the left center field seats" off Warren Hacker's first pitch.[8] It was the game-winner, though a subsequent walk, single, and Monte Irvin's sacrifice fly gave the Giants an insurance run.

**May 13, 1955:** On a Friday afternoon at Busch Stadium, Mays had a 3-for-4 day. Al Dark singled and so did Mays in the top of the first. Monte Irvin doubled them both home. Stan Musial doubled home two in the bottom of the second to tie the score. Each team scored once in the third. It was still 3-3 after nine innings, and Cardinals starter Harvey Haddix was still in the game. The first batter in the 10th was Willie Mays. Haddix's first pitch to Mays "almost removed the button from Willie's cap."[9] The *New York Times* said Mays was visibly angry. The *St. Louis Globe-Democrat* wrote, "Mays then got up and hit the ball off the premises"[10] – he homered into the bleachers in left field. The 4-3 lead held.

**June 4, 1955:** It was Cubs vs. Giants again, but this time at the Polo Grounds. Mays was struggling against Chicago; his home run in the fourth inning into the upper tier in left field was his first homer hit in 30 at-bats against Cubs pitching in 1955. The Giants led 7-2, but with three runs in the seventh and two in the eighth, the Cubs came from behind and tied it 7-7. In the top of the 12th, Ernie Banks singled and drove in two runs for Chicago. Mays led off the bottom of the 12th. Pitching for the Cubs was, again, Warren Hacker. Mays homered "onto the left field upper story roof,"[11] bringing the Giants to within one. A single, a wild pitch, and a walk followed, but the Giants were unable to score and lost despite two Mays home runs.

**June 30, 1955:** The Brooklyn Dodgers won the game, hosting the Giants at Ebbets Field. In the bottom of the ninth, they scored one run to tie the game, 3-3, and send it into extra innings. Ed Roebuck took over pitching duties for Brooklyn in the 10th. Dark led off with a single. Lockman forced him at second, but Mays hit a two-run homer into the upper deck in center field, giving the Giants a 5-3 lead.[12] Marv Grissom had taken over to pitch the seventh; in the 10th, Jim Gilliam singled and Duke Snider tripled. Hoyt Wilhelm was brought in to pitch to Jackie Robinson, who bunted. Second baseman Wayne Terwilliger could not handle Wilhelm's throw to first, and Snider took advantage by sprinting safely home. Tied again, the Dodgers won in the 11th. Ramon Monzant walked Carl Furillo, who took second on Dixie Howell's sacrifice, and scored on George Shuba's pinch single.

**July 4, 1955 (second game):** On a bases-loaded walk in the bottom of the ninth at Pittsburgh's Forbes Field, the Pirates won the first game, 4-3, for their hometown fans. Mays – who had homered once in the first game – doubled and scored in the first inning of the second game. Pittsburgh scored one run in the second. The Giants took a 2-1 lead in the third and added a third run in the fourth on a balk. That balk call had almost resulted in a forfeit after incensed Pirates fans showered the field with bottles and cans. One can reportedly landed rather close to Mays; the game resumed after 15 minutes. The Pirates scored twice in the seventh. The 3-3 game went into extras. Reliever Lino Donoso pitched a scoreless 10th but gave up a single to Al Dark with two outs in the 11th and a two-run homer to Mays hit over the Forbes Field left-field wall.[13] Pittsburgh failed to score, and the Giants celebrated a 5-3 win.

**July 14, 1957:** His eighth extra-inning home run was his first that was a walk-off. The Giants were hosting the Cubs on a Sunday afternoon. The first six runs (two by the Giants and four by the Cubs) all scored on homers, and the Cubs led 4-2 through 3½. The Giants tied it, saw the Cubs go up 6-4 in the seventh, and then tied it again, 6-6, in the bottom of the ninth on a two-out, two-run homer by Whitey Lockman. Marv Grissom – working his fifth inning of relief – saw the Cubs load the bases with one out in the top of the 12th but escaped damage. With two outs in the bottom of the 12th, Johnny Antonelli walked and Mays homered off Jim Brosnan to deep left field to win the game. **Walk-off.**

**August 4, 1957 (first game):** Mays' solo home run at Crosley Field in the top of the eighth cut Cincinnati's lead to 4-2. The Giants tied it in the ninth. Mays tripled and scored to start the 10th, but the Redlegs responded and tied the score again. Mays was first up again in the 12th and homered to right-center, once again giving his team the lead in extra innings. But Ed Bailey hit a solo homer for Cincy, and the game was tied yet again. The Giants went ahead for good in the 14th by scoring on – of all things – a bases-loaded, inning-ending double play. The bases were loaded on three walks. With one out, pinch-hitter Ray Katt hit for reliever Marv Grissom. It was a sacrifice fly to left, scoring one runner with the go-ahead run but a 7-5-3 double play followed when Ozzie Virgil didn't get back to first quickly enough. Grissom got another win.

**May 21, 1958:** Once again on the road in Cincinnati, the (now San Francisco) Giants scored twice in the top of the first but had fallen behind 4-2 by the sixth. Lockman singled in a third run for New York in the seventh, and Mays followed with a game-tying sacrifice fly off Hal Jeffcoat. Still tied after nine, Mays led off the 10th with a home run into the right-field bleachers off Jeffcoat.[14] The score held and for the third time in a row Grissom got the win on a Willie Mays extra-inning home run.

**June 29, 1959:** Two former New York teams squared off as the Los Angeles Dodgers hosted the San Francisco Giants on a Monday night at Los Angeles Memorial Coliseum. The score was tied 3-3 after three. Neither team scored again until the ninth inning, when each put across one run. After 12 innings, it was still 4-4. Roger Craig had started for the Dodgers, with Sandy Koufax pitching three innings in relief before being removed for a pinch-hitter, fellow pitcher Don Drysdale. Stan Williams took over for the 13th and was greeted by solo home runs by leadoff batter Jim Davenport and then Willie Mays, both into the left-field seats. Mike McCormick got the win in the 6-4 game. It was the first extra-inning game the Dodgers ever lost at the Coliseum.

**July 10, 1959:** Back at Crosley Field, Orlando Cepeda hit a three-run homer in the top of the first to give the Giants a 3-0 head start. Though it was 4-0, then 5-1, Ed Bailey hit a pair of solo home runs for the Reds and the scoring ran to 6-4 until Frank Robinson tied it with a two-run homer in the bottom of the seventh. In the top of the 11th, Orlando Pena pitching, Felipe Alou doubled for the Giants and was sacrificed to third. Willie Kirkland's sacrifice fly scored him. Mays then hit a homer into deep left-center for an insurance run. The final score was 6-4.

**June 29, 1961 (first game):** The Giants won the first game of two at Philadelphia's Connie Mack Stadium, 8-7, with Mays driving in five runs. He hit a two-run homer in the top of the first off Dallas Green and a solo homer in the third (also off Green), but the scoring was even at the end of nine, 7-7. Frank Sullivan was starting his fifth inning in relief for the Phillies when Mays homered into the "left-field corner of the second deck" leading off the top of the 10th.[15] Juan Marichal earned the win in relief.

**May 26, 1962:** The New York Mets were visiting Candlestick Park on a Saturday afternoon in San Francisco. Mays had been given a day off on Wednesday, then hit five home runs in the three games that followed, including the two in this game. Each team scored in four different innings, with Mays homering in the bottom of the eighth to tie the score at 5-5. In the top of the 10th, the Mets' Felix Mantilla homered off San Francisco's Don Larsen for a 6-5 lead. Mets starter Jay Hook was still pitching and gave up a leadoff single to Harvey Kuenn in the bottom of the 10th. Chuck Hiller attempted a sacrifice, but it led to a force out at second base. With Hiller on first, Mays swung on a 3-and-0 count and homered "far over the left-centerfield screen" and won the game, 7-6.[16] It was just his second extra-inning walk-off home run. **Walk-off.**

**June 13, 1963:** The Cubs were at Candlestick when Mays did it again on a Thursday afternoon. The scoring was sparse. Both starters went all the way – Dick Ellsworth for the Cubs and Billy O'Dell for the Giants. Mays had saved O'Dell a run in the second inning with a throw some 300 feet in the air from the warning track to Joey Amalfitano at second base, for a double play. In the top of the fifth, after a double, a walk, and another double play, the Cubs had a man on third. Pitcher Ellsworth singled off O'Dell and Chicago took a 1-0 lead. Felipe Alou homered for the Giants, leading off the bottom of the seventh. O'Dell retired each of the final 13 batters he faced, through the top of the 10th. First up in the bottom of the 10th was Willie McCovey, who flied out to center. Second up was Willie Mays, who homered "over the center-field screen at the 400-foot mark" and won the game, his third extra-inning walk-off.[17] **Walk-off.**

**July 2, 1963:** This game was the famous scoreless pitching duel between Juan Marichal of the Giants and Warren Spahn of the Milwaukee Braves, which went on and on for 15 full innings without a run for either team. There were a few threats here and there through the first seven innings. (Among them, Mays had thrown a runner out at the plate in the fourth inning and McCovey had hit an apparent game-winning homer in the bottom of the ninth, only to have it ruled foul by the first-base umpire.) But from the eighth through the 13th only once did a team (the Braves) get a runner as far as second. In the bottom of the 14th, Kuenn led off with a double and Mays was intentionally walked. The Giants loaded the bases but could not score. Heading into the bottom of the 15th, each pitcher had given up eight base hits. Hank Aaron – described by the *Milwaukee Journal* as "the Braves' best bet to break up a deadlock" – was 0-for-6. With one out in the bottom of the 16th, Mays connected off the first pitch he saw from Spahn for a game-winning home run "far over the left-field fence."[18] **Walk-off.**

**August 4, 1963:** Just over a month later, the Giants were at Wrigley Field. It was another low-scoring game. In the top of the fourth, Orlando Cepeda reached safely and took second on a throwing error. He scored on Ed Bailey's single. The Cubs got a run in the top of the eighth when Ron Santo led off with a solo home run off starter Billy O'Dell. The Cubs loaded the bases but couldn't score in the bottom of the ninth. The second Giants batter in the top of the 10th was Willie Mays, who hit a solo home run "which barely cleared the left field bleacher wall" off Lindy McDaniel.[19] Or perhaps landed higher; the *Chicago Tribune* said it was on a 2-and-0 count and went "halfway up the seats in the left field bleachers."[20] Wherever it landed, it did the trick. Reliever Don Larsen, who had shut down the threat in the ninth, retired the Cubs in order in the 10th.

**June 13, 1967:** It was almost four years before Mays hit another homer in extra innings, though he had hit 154 other homers in the interim and led the league with 47 in 1964 and both leagues with 52 in 1965. On June 13, 1967, he played indoors – at the Astrodome in Houston. The Giants scored once in the top of the second; Astros pitcher Dave Giusti homered for two runs in the bottom of the inning. Mays entered the game in the top of the sixth, pinch-hitting, and grounded into a double play. In the top of the eighth, left fielder Jim Ray Hart tied it, 2-2, with a solo home run. In the top of the 10th, Giusti gave up a one-out walk and a single, and was relieved by Barry Latman, who struck out Hart. Latman walked Jim Davenport, loading the bases. Mays was up and ready to do damage. First-pitch swinging, he "drove it so far from the plate a $5 stamp wouldn't have been enough postage to get it back."[21] It was a grand slam that "landed 10 rows deep into the second deck of the left centerfield seats."[22] The Astros went down in order in the bottom of the 10th.

**September 27, 1968:** The Giants were in second place, nine games behind St. Louis. The host Reds were in third place but had no hope of reaching second with only three games to play. The small Crosley Field crowd saw Mays go 4-for-7. San Francisco scored once in the second, Cincinnati scored twice in the sixth, and the Giants tied it, 2-2, in the top of the seventh. After 14 innings, it was still 2-2. The third Reds pitcher of the game was Ted Abernathy, who came in to pitch the 15th. It was three minutes before midnight, and apparently the crowd had dwindled to something like 1,500. The first batter Abernathy faced was Mays, who homered to deep right field. Mike McCormick got the win in relief for San Francisco.

**April 15, 1969:** The score was 5-5 after seven innings in Cincinnati, after a 30-minute rain delay in the sixth. In the top of the ninth, the Giants scored three runs to take an 8-5 lead – but the Reds matched that in the bottom of the inning. In the top of the 10th, pitcher Mike McCormick led off with a home run to right field. Mays (batting leadoff) followed that with a homer to left field. Why was a power hitter like Mays hitting in the leadoff slot?

Giants manager Clyde King explained, a tribute to the slugger a few weeks from turning 38: "Because he is the fastest man getting from first to third on a single."[23] The Reds tied it, though, with two runs of their own. In the bottom of the 12th, with Gaylord Perry pitching for San Francisco, Alex Johnson led off with a triple. Perry then gave intentional walks to the next two batters. Johnny Bench singled to right-center and won the game. It was the fourth extra-inning homer Mays had hit in Cincinnati.

**June 6, 1971 (second game):** The Phillies won the first game of two in San Francisco, 1-0. Mays had been 0-for-3 with two strikeouts. His first three times up in the second game he grounded out, flied out to second base, and hit into an inning-ending double play. The Phillies took a 2-0 lead and were still ahead 3-1 heading into the bottom of the ninth, when the Giants tied it, perhaps inspired by a leadoff Mays double. Ken Henderson singled, driving in Mays. A sacrifice sent him to second base. Henderson scored the tying run on a Bobby Bonds single. In the 10th, the Phillies' Jim Bunning gave up two one-out singles (one to Mays) and – after an intentional walk – escaped a loss on a force play at the plate followed by a groundout to first unassisted. In the 12th, the score still 3-3 and Joe Hoerner pitching for Philadelphia, the 40-year-old Willie Mays came up again, with one out, and "smashed a cloud-dusting 12th-inning home run" that "reached the seats deep behind the left-field screen."[24] **Walk-off.**

After a May 11, 1972, trade to the New York Mets, Mays homered eight times the rest of the season and six times in 1973 but none of his home runs were in extra innings. One provided the winning runs in a game during the fifth inning of the July 21, 1972, game against the Giants in San Francisco. On August 12, 1972, his sixth-inning homer provided the run that sent a 1-1 game into extras; the Mets beat the Cubs in 10, on Tommie Agee's home run. On June 9, 1973, his third-inning homer gave the Mets a 3-2 lead in a game they won, 4-2, against the Dodgers at Shea Stadium. The final home run of his career was in the third inning of a game at Shea against Cincinnati on August 17. It was a solo home run off Don Gullett. The Reds tied it 1-1 in the ninth, and won 2-1 in the 10th.

Extra-inning home runs in road games: 14
Extra-inning home runs in home games: 8
Extra-inning HRs that were walk-offs: 5.
Extra-inning home runs that were game-winners (provided the final go-ahead run): 14, 9 of which were on the road
Extra-inning home runs in losses: 3, one at home and two on the road
Extra inning homers by inning:
10th: 11 (June 22, 1951; July 7, 1951; May 13, 1955; June 30, 1955; May 21, 1958; June 29, 1961; May 26, 1962; June 13, 1963; August 4, 1963; June 13, 1967; April 15, 1969.
11th: 2 (July 4, 1955; July 10, 1959)
12th: 4 (June 4, 1955; July 14, 1957; August 4, 1957; June 6, 1971)
13th: 2 (July 3, 1951; June 29, 1959)
14th: 1 (April 30, 1954)
15th: 1 (September 27, 1968)
16th: 1 (July 2, 1963)

Through 2019, Mays is the only batter to have hit at least one career home run in each of these seven extra innings, the 10th through the 16th. No other batter has homered in the 10th through the 15th. Eight have homered in the 10th through the 14th innings – in alphabetical order: Dante Bichette, Jack Clark, Jason Giambi, Howard Johnson, Graig Nettles, Andy Pafko, Albert Pujols, and Carl Yastrzemski.

## SOURCES

In addition to the sources cited in the Notes, the author consulted Baseball-Reference.com and Retrosheet.org.

Thanks to Tom Ruane of Retrosheet for providing information regarding rankings and to Trent McCotter and Lyle Spatz.

**A bit of a personal postscript**

Reflecting a personal interest in Ted Williams, I could not help but notice how Ted Williams stands out on the list for the fewest number of strikeouts in extra innings among the top homer hitters.

| HR Player | AB | SO |
|---|---|---|
| 22 Willie Mays | 292 | 40 |
| 18 Jack Clark | 179 | 41 |
| 16 Frank Robinson | 250 | 49 |
| 15 Albert Pujols | 155 | 14 |
| 14 Mickey Mantle | 122 | 19 |
| 14 Hank Aaron | 254 | 29 |
| 13 Ted Williams | 129 | 7 |
| 12 Willie Stargell | 188 | 65 |
| 12 Mark McGwire | 110 | 30 |
| 12 Rafael Palmeiro | 178 | 18 |
| 12 Jim Thome | 153 | 56 |
| 12 David Ortiz | 139 | 23 |

The next-closest had twice as many strikeouts. Frank Robinson had seven times as many as Williams (albeit in twice as many at-bats), and both Thome and Stargell had more than that.

## NOTES

1 Joey Votto surpassed Clark during the 2022 season, claiming the number-102 position.

2 Edward Burns, "Giants Defeat Cubs in 10th, 9-6," *Chicago Tribune*, June 23, 1951: B1. The *New York Times* said the Mays home run had gone "high into the seats in left." Louis Effrat, "Mays' 3-Run Homer in 10th Halts Chicago for Polo Grounders, 9-6," *New York Times*, June 23, 1951: Sports 10.

3 Associated Press, "Giants Top Phillies in 13th to Gain on Beaten Dodgers," *Hartford Courant*, July 4, 1951: 14.

4 Joseph M. Sheehan, "Giants Defeat Phils with Two Runs in 13th," *New York Times*, July 4, 1951: Sports 21.

5 Sheehan, "Giants Defeat Phils with Two Runs in 13th."

6 Jack Barry, "Giants Rally 3 Times with Homers, Tops B's in 11th, 7-6," *Boston Globe*, July 8, 1951: C42.

7 Joseph M. Sheehan, "Giants Defeat Braves, 7-6, with Two Runs in Eleventh," *New York Times*, July 8, 1951: Sports 1.

8 Edward Prell, "Cubs Lose, 4-2, in 14th," *Chicago Tribune*, May 1, 1954: 1.

9 John Drebinger, "Mays' Hit in 10th Tops St. Louis, 4-3," *New York Times*, May 14, 1955: 14.

10 Jack Herman, "Mays' Home Run in Tenth Beats Cardinals, 4-3," *St. Louis Globe-Democrat*, May 14, 1955: 14.

11 Edward Prell, "Banks' Single Beats Giants After Miksis' Homer Ties 'Em," *Chicago Tribune*, June 5, 1955: B1.

12 The home run gave Mays 10 RBIs in the three games against the Dodgers. He had stayed in the game despite being thrown out at the plate in the eighth, the collision sending catcher Rube Walker to the hospital with a left shoulder injury. John Drebinger, "Dodgers Rally to Down Giants in Eleventh Inning on Pinch Single by George Shuba," *New York Times*, July 1, 1955: 15.

13 Lester J. Biederman, "Pirates Finally Get That Relief," *Pittsburgh Press*, July 5, 1955: 24.

14 Associated Press, "Giants Win in Tenth on Mays' Homer," *Washington Post*, May 22, 1958: D1.

15 Bob Stevens, "Mays' Spree Caps 8-7, 4-1 Wins," *San Francisco Chronicle*, June 30, 1961: 39.

16 Rob Stevens, "Mays' Two HRs Edge Mets, 7-6," *San Francisco Chronicle*, May 27, 1962: 37, 39.

17 Bob Stevens, "Mays Beats Cubs, 2-1, on 400-Foot Homer in 10th," *San Francisco Chronicle*, June 14, 1963: 53.

18 Bob Wolf, "Spahn Loses Shutout on Homer by Mays," *Milwaukee Journal*, July 3, 1963: Part 2: 9. The actual headline was a line score comprising 31 zeroes and the number "1" in the bottom of the 16th.

19 "Mays Homer Beats Cubs, 2-1," *Chicago Daily Defender*, August 5, 1963: 24. The *Defender* suggested that Mays was getting revenge for being thrown out on an attempted steal of third base in the top of the eighth.

20 Richard Dozer, "Cubs Lose in 10th," *Chicago Tribune*, August 5, 1963: Section 3: 5.

21 Bob Stevens, "Giants Win on Mays' Slam," *San Francisco Chronicle*, June 14, 1967: 53.

22 United Press International, "Mays 'Slam' in 10th Wins," *San Diego Union*, June 14, 1963: C2.

23 Associated Press, "Johnson Finds 'Right Movement,'" *Columbus* (Ohio) *Dispatch*, April 16, 1969: 37B.

24 Bob Stevens, "Mays' Homer Gives Giants Split," *San Francisco Chronicle*, June 7, 1971: 47.

# ROOMIE: THE RELATIONSHIP WILLIE MAYS AND MONTE IRVIN SHARED

BY DUKE GOLDMAN

*Roomie – that's Monte Irvin. He and I room together when the ball club's on the road. Many's the time I've hollered for him to get me out of what I'm in. Like the time we were posing for the team picture and a guy came up to me and said "Willie, I'm Jumble from the Daily Mumble," and wanted me to predict the outcome of the world series. ...*
*"Well," Mr. Jumble from the Daily Mumble said, haven't you any idea how the series is going to go?*
*"Yes," I said. "I got an idea. First two games be played at the Polo Grounds. Then we go to Cleveland." ...*
*"All right," he said, "then how would you compare your outfield with theirs?*
*"Roomie!" I yelled out. "Come over and take care of this man!"*[1]

WILLIE MAYS AND Monte Irvin were lifelong friends. Although they likely first met as opposing players on a Southern baseball diamond, their first significant encounter was as roommates with the 1951 New York Giants. Irvin was Mays' only road roommate in National League baseball, with the possible exception of early 1952, when Irvin was recovering from a broken ankle suffered in spring training and Mays played less than a quarter of the season prior to his Army induction.

Irvin played a significant part in the development of Mays' character, both on and off the field. In turn, Mays was a galvanizing force in the life and livelihood of Irvin and on the Giants team, helping them overcome a 13½-game Dodgers lead in the 1951 pennant race and becoming the linchpin of a successful Giant demolition of the 1954 American League champion Cleveland Indians, winners of 111 games.

By 1955, Irvin's career was beginning to wind down, while the 24-year-old Mays was still in the early stages of a 22-season National League career as arguably the best all-around position player in baseball history. Irvin played his last games for the Giants in June 1955 and retired early in the 1957 season after a final season with the 1956 Chicago Cubs, where he mentored another young Black superstar, Ernie Banks. Between Mays' debut in May 1951 and June 1955, Irvin's mentoring of Mays was comparable to the constant support and encouragement Mays received from Giants manager Leo Durocher. Reflecting back on his life, Mays titled the fifth of 24 chapters in his 2020 memoir, *24*, "Honor Your Mentors: The Story of Leo Durocher and Monte Irvin."[2]

*Monte Irvin offered the younger Willie Mays both advice and friendship. SABR/The Rucker Archive.*

## Initial Encounters

Mays and Irvin were both born in Alabama, but Irvin's family moved to New Jersey in 1927, four years before Mays was born.[3] Mays and Irvin's first recorded encounter likely occurred in Macon, Georgia, on April 19, 1948. The 16-year-old Mays briefly suited up for the Negro Southern League's Chattanooga Choo Choos, who were playing Irvin's Newark Eagles in Macon. Mays was cited as the "hitting and fielding star for the Chattanooga team."[4] Although this author has found no lineups or box scores to show whether Irvin played in this preseason exhibition game, it seems certain that he did, or at least that he became aware of the 16-year-old phenom, who was also the son of a semipro Black baseball player, William Howard "Kitty Kat" Mays.[5]

If Irvin did not notice Mays when their respective teams played against each other in Macon, he certainly should have become aware of him two months later, on Saturday, July 25, 1948, when the Eagles defeated the Birmingham Black Barons, 14-4, before 7,273 fans at Birmingham's Rickwood Field. Now 17 years old, Mays played left field and batted third in the Black Barons' lineup, and went 1-for-4 with two RBIs, while Irvin batted cleanup and played left field, going 4-for-5 with three RBIs for the victorious Eagles.[6] According to several sources, Irvin and Mays played with each other on barnstorming teams as well.[7]

As recounted in Irvin's 2007 book *Few And Chosen*, despite these earlier encounters, he and Mays really became acquainted when Mays joined the New York Giants in 1951.[8] They first saw each other at a Philadelphia hotel on May 25, 1951, the day after Mays was summoned to New York from Minneapolis after a torrid .477 start to his 1951 Triple-A season, not unlike Irvin's .510 start to his 1950 Triple-A season for the Jersey City Giants, the Giants' other Triple-A affiliate. Mays had arrived in New York on a flight from Minneapolis, met Giants owner Horace Stoneham and signed his contract at the midtown office of the Giants. He took a train down to Philadelphia, passing through Trenton, where he tore up the Class-B Interstate League in 1950, hitting .353.[9]

On May 25 Willie went 0-for-5 in his first game as a Giant and nearly collided with Irvin, who was playing right field alongside center fielder Mays, as the Giants won 8-5.[10] According to some accounts, this is what led Durocher to tell Irvin and whoever else was playing right field to let Mays catch any ball he could reach.[11] As is well-known, Mays started out his career 0-for-12 before hitting a home run off Warren Spahn, and was 1-for-26, an .038 batting average, before he really got going. Famously, Mays asked Durocher to send him down to the minor leagues, but Durocher said that as long as he managed the Giants, Willie would be his center fielder, adding that Mays was "the best center fielder I've ever looked at."[12] Mays followed his slump with a 9-for-24 tear and helped New York on an epic pennant drive. In some sources, Mays came first to Irvin for solace when he started so glacially, and Irvin both encouraged and advised him – either way, between Durocher and Irvin, Mays was given sufficient support and encouragement.[13]

When Mays joined the Giants in 1951, the team was 17-19 and in fifth place, a vast improvement from its start of 2-12, the last 11 of which were losses, but still well behind the front-running Dodgers. As Mays grew comfortable, the rest of the team became more comfortable around him. Irvin had started the season playing first base, and when Mays arrived, Irvin was moved to the outfield, starting in right field and ending up primarily in left, switching with Whitey Lockman, while Mays largely replaced Bobby Thomson, who settled in at third base.[14] According to Irvin, "Willie joined the club in 1951 and it was instantly improved at four positions."[15]

In later years, Irvin consistently stated that Mays was the team's galvanizing force, the glue that brought the Giants together.[16] In Irvin's autobiography *Nice Guys Finish First,* he said that "when Willie Mays arrived, everybody saw right away what a sensational young budding star he was, and that really helped the racial situation all around."[17] Upon Mays' arrival, the Giants had four Black players – Irvin, Mays, outfielder-third baseman Henry "Hank" Thompson, and Cuban catcher Rafael "Ray" Noble.[18] And on June 3, 1951, Irvin, Mays, and Thompson were all on base at the same time, the first time that happened with three Black teammates. Later, in the World Series, Thompson, Irvin, and Mays replicated this notable event in the outfield.[19]

Irvin stated that the Dodgers were a clearly superior team, but that the Giants were able to play together as a team and support one another, which enabled them to come roaring back from a 13½-game deficit.[20] After all, Irvin and Mays were the only two Giants to be inducted into the National Baseball Hall of Fame, and Irvin was elected as much for his Negro League play as for his play in the National League. In contrast, five players in the 1951 Dodgers starting lineup – catcher Roy Campanella, first baseman Gil Hodges, second baseman Jackie Robinson, shortstop Pee Wee Reese, and center fielder Duke Snider – are Hall of Famers. While Campanella, like Irvin, had a substantial Negro League career, his Hall of Fame-worthy production occurred primarily in the National League, unlike that of Irvin. Meanwhile, both Robinson and Mays had only limited Negro League experience.

Mays' 20 home runs, 68 RBIs, and .274 batting average, along with his already-stellar outfield play, certainly contributed a great deal to the Giants' 1951 pennant drive. Informed commentators, however, generally have acknowledged that the Giants' 1951 MVP was Irvin, with 24 home runs, a league-leading 121 RBIs, and a .312 batting average. For the season, Irvin was number one in WAR (wins above replacement) among Giants position players with 6.9, followed by Al Dark, Eddie Stanky, Thomson, and then Mays with 3.9.[21]

During the Giants' season-ending 39-8 run, which included a three-game playoff win against the Dodgers, Irvin's starring role contrasted with Mays' late-season slump. He still won the Rookie of the Year Award. Starting on August 11, when the Giants began a long homestand, Irvin batted .322

with 10 home runs and 38 runs batted in, while Mays batted only .247 with 3 home runs and 16 runs batted in.[22] Already, Mays had made several astonishing plays in the outfield, ones that Irvin, among others who played with Mays, rated more highly than his most famous outfield play, "The Catch," in Game One of the 1954 World Series. Whether or not Mays was starring offensively, he was certainly leading the team in exuberance. On the last play of the 154-game regular season, Sid Gordon hit a routine fly ball to Monte Irvin, which would clinch a win for the Giants and at least a playoff with the Dodgers. According to Mays, "I went over from center as fast as my legs could go. ... Monte was there, waiting. I shouted at him. He patted his glove a couple of times. I shouted some more. Then Monte made the catch. I jumped on him out of just plain joy."[23]

## October 3, 1951, and the 1951 World Series

The climax of the 1951 season was the three-game playoff series between the Giants and the Dodgers. Never before, and never again, would the 154-game regular season end with three New York teams all in first place, albeit the Giants and Dodgers tied for that position (those same three teams would be in the same exact position – the Yankees winning the AL and the Dodgers and Giants tied for first, albeit after a 162-game regular season – eight years later. Once again, the Giants came from behind in the ninth inning to win the third game of the championship playoff – but by then, of course, the two NL teams were in San Francisco and Los Angeles). After splitting the first two games, the Giants trailed 4-1 in the ninth inning of Game Three. In what was later called the "Miracle of Coogan's Bluff," the Giants punctuated their amazing season-end comeback from a 13½-game deficit with a miracle rally culminating in Bobby Thomson's game-winning homer off Ralph Branca. Where were Irvin and Mays during this rally? Irvin made the only out, a foul popup against Dodger starter Don Newcombe with two men on base, while Mays knelt on deck as Thomson ended the game. Irvin later related that Mays was glad to have avoided being in a game-ending situation by virtue of Thomson's "shot heard 'round the world, as "his knees had been knocking so badly that he wasn't at all sure whether he could have made it up to the plate.[24] In the clubhouse celebration after the Giants' dramatic win, Mays drank champagne, and was overwhelmed by its effects. As Irvin could attest, when Mays went out, he drank Cokes.

The World Series between the Giants and the Yankees started the next day, October 4. In Game One, the Giants started Irvin in left field, Mays in center field, and Hank Thompson in right field – the first time three Black players appeared as a complete outfield in what was then considered "major-league" baseball. This milestone happened because Don Mueller, the Giants' regular right fielder, broke his ankle the previous day after sliding into third base on a single to right immediately after Irvin's popout and before Thomson's blast. Not only did the Giants bring down a racial barrier by virtue of their all-Black outfield, they did it in Yankee Stadium, against a home team that did not integrate until four years later with Elston Howard in 1955.

For Willie Mays, the 1951 Series was the second of five World Series he played in. His offensive performance in those World Series included no home runs and a .230 batting average.[25] The Giants took a 1951 Series lead of two games to one, but the Yankees swept the last three contests to take the Series, four games to two, the third in a five-year World Series-winning streak that was unprecedented in major-league history and, to date, has never been repeated. But for Monte Irvin, the Series was a standout performance, as he batted .458 with 11 hits in 24 at-bats, including a spectacular catch, and a steal of home in the first inning of Game One of the World Series. Despite the disappointing ending, it was a great season for the Giants and a magical beginning to the career of Willie Mays.

## 1952 – Willie joins the Army; Monte breaks his ankle

In spring training of 1952, the Giants seemed poised to potentially repeat their 1951 triumph over the Dodgers. Mays would be starting his first full season as Giants center fielder, with Monte Irvin now ensconced in left field beside him. Unfortunately for the Giants, neither Mays nor Irvin would play a full season for the Giants in 1952. Willie Mays had a date with the military, after playing the first quarter of the season. The Giants started 1952 with a won-lost record of 26-8, thereby following up their end of 1951 stretch run of 39-8 – meaning that for roughly half a season, the Giants were 65-16! For the season's start, Mays had not played stellar baseball, hitting a mere .236 with four home runs – but even more surprising given the Giants' smashing start was that Monte Irvin, fresh off his third-place finish in the 1951 MVP voting, was out of commission with a broken ankle suffered in an April 2 exhibition game against the Cleveland Indians.

In that fateful exhibition game, Irvin was perched on first base with a walk when Mays drove his own hit to right field. Irvin started to slide into third base but, realizing that there was no chance of being thrown out, abruptly stopped his slide – a big mistake. When Willie Mays and other Giants players came over to where Monte Irvin lay in the dirt near third base, they saw a grotesque sight – Irvin's ankle was gruesomely sticking out and he had to be carried off the field. Mays' response was to start crying – and sources have differed as to the reason for his crying. Irvin, in his autobiography, claimed that Mays cried because he saw the chances of the Giants winning the pennant again flying out the window, along with a substantial postseason check.[26] Most other sources say that Mays was distraught over his roomie's horrible injury – and let us remember that Willie Mays was still only 20 years old![27] Furthermore, Mays already knew that he was going to the Army pretty early in the 1952 season, which bolsters the explanation that Mays' crying had more to do with sadness over his buddy's terrible injury than with the likely loss of the 1952 pennant, a pennant he would not be around to see to its completion.

Monte Irvin did return to the Giants in August 1952, and hit .310 but with only four home runs, tying Willie Mays in that slugging category. With the Giants missing a total of 36 home runs and 145 RBIs combined from Mays and Irvin (20 home runs and 100 RBIs less from Irvin, 16 home runs and 45 RBIs less from Mays), it is surprising that the Giants still came in second, only 4½ games behind the Dodgers. At various times, both Mays and Irvin extolled the managerial acumen of Leo Durocher; perhaps his best performance as skipper was in 1952, when two of his top stars, Mays and Irvin, missed most of the season.

## 1954 – WS Sweep and "The Catch"

Mays remained in the military for the rest of the 1952 season and all of 1953, although Monte Irvin played with Willie Mays on Roy Campanella's barnstorming team before the 1953 season and observed that Mays was still in top form.[28]

Irvin himself returned strongly in 1953, hitting .329 (a career high) with 21 home runs and 97 RBIs despite reinjuring his ankle on August 9 in a home-plate collision with Del Rice of the Cardinals and missing most of August and part of September.[29] Despite Irvin's comeback year, the Giants, without Mays and with lackluster pitching, dropped to fifth place in the standings. Despite this poor showing, the Giants were looking forward to 1954 – when Mays would return and hopefully join with Irvin and a surging Hank Thompson (24 home runs, 74 RBIs, and a .302 batting average with a .967 OPS in 1953 while playing roughly two-thirds of the time) to bring the Giants back into contention.

In spring training of 1954, the Giants squad could hardly contain themselves, showing tremendous enthusiasm for Mays' return. Perhaps manager Durocher, feeling the heat for 1953's weak showing, was the most excited for Mays to rejoin the team, as Irvin indicated that "Willie Mays, of course was Leo's favorite. He was the only one who received special handling from Durocher. Leo's relationship with other players, even those he liked was different from the one he enjoyed with Willie."[30] In a foreshadowing of the 1954 postseason, the Giants and the Cleveland Indians played during spring training, as they both trained in Phoenix and barnstormed home together before the start of the 1954 season.

In the early going, both Mays and Irvin were struggling to establish themselves – but Mays quickly went on a tear and for the first time, showed himself to be a true superstar. Irvin, in contrast, showed that he was now on the downside of his career, with occasional key hits but a demonstrably declining overall performance. Although Bobby Thomson had been traded away to the Milwaukee Braves, the acquisition of Johnny Antonelli in return bolstered the Giants' pitching staff, as Antonelli had his first big season, winning 21 games, losing only 7, with a league-leading 2.30 ERA. Mays dominated National League pitchers, with 41 home runs, 110 RBIs, and a league-leading .345 batting average, beating out on the season's last day teammate Don Mueller's .342 in the batting race. Not surprisingly, Mays won the 1954 National League MVP for his stellar performance. Meanwhile, Hank Thompson contributed 26 home runs and 86 RBIs, so that Monte Irvin's 19 home runs and 64 RBIs with a measly .262 batting average, by far his worst Giants season so far, was good enough. It is also helped that James "Dusty" Rhodes, playing part-time in left field and increasingly spelling Irvin in the late going along with regular pinch-hitting duties, contributed 15 home runs, 50 RBIs, and a 1.105 OPS (slightly better than that of Willie Mays, whose OPS was 1.078 albeit in 401 more at-bats than Rhodes had).

For the only time in five seasons (1952-1956), the Giants beat out the Brooklyn Dodgers in the NL pennant race, winning 97 games to the Dodgers' 92. Though the Giants were therefore five games better than the Dodgers, over in the AL, the Cleveland Indians posted 111 wins, 14 more than the NL Giants. Based on regular-season performance, the Indians appeared to have a decided advantage in the 1954 Series – but thanks especially to one unbelievable and now-legendary play by Willie Mays, and an outstanding performance by Dusty Rhodes, who pinch-hit for Monte Irvin on three occasions, the Giants turned the tables on the Indians with a four-game World Series sweep.

As Arnold Hano described so beautifully in his book *A Day in the Bleachers*, the catch that Willie Mays made on a 430-plus-foot drive off the bat of dangerous Vic Wertz in the eighth inning of a 2-2 tie in World Series Game One at the Polo Grounds was an amazing over-the-shoulder-grab, followed by a pirouetting, dead-on-accurate throw by Mays to not only stop an immediate tiebreaking score by Larry Doby as well as a likely triple or even inside-the-park home run by Wertz, but also to keep Doby from advancing beyond third base, as he potentially could have scored from second base on the catch itself.[31] As in many instances of Willie Mays' early career, Monte Irvin was at hand, playing left field next to Mays. In later years, Irvin depicted the catch itself as "something special"[32] and he described Mays' saying that "I had it all the way" as they both returned to the dugout at the end of the inning with the score still knotted at 2-2.[33] Willie Mays also made a great defensive play on Wertz in the 10th inning, keeping the game tied so that Dusty Rhodes could come up in the bottom of the 10th and hit a 250-foot dying quail just over the left-field fence for a three-run, game-winning home run.[34] Twice more, Dusty Rhodes would come up to pinch-hit for Monte Irvin – and he delivered, to the tune of two home runs, a run-scoring single, and seven RBIs in the Series, which became a rout of the Indians. Monte Irvin was finally left in the game to hit for himself and delivered a two-run single, driving in Don Mueller and Willie Mays, in the Game Four triumph that clinched the Series sweep for the Giants.

Without Mays' amazing catch and throw off Wertz's eighth-inning drive, the Giants would likely have lost Game One of the Series, and perhaps the whole Series would have turned out differently.

As Monte Irvin and others have described about Mays, he could defeat you in so many ways – so even though he batted only .286 with four hits in that Series, one could argue that he rivaled Rhodes as the Series MVP, at a time when there was no such award.

Despite the greatness of Mays' play on Wertz, others, including Monte Irvin, always maintained that Mays made better plays, even if this one was the most important, given its placement at a crucial juncture of the one World Series that Mays – and for that matter, Irvin and manager Durocher as well – would win in their Giants careers (and in Durocher's case, in his entire career as a manager – though Durocher played on the World Series-winning 1934 Gas House Gang Cardinals). For Irvin, the best catch Mays made was in the summer of 1951 in Pittsburgh's Forbes Field. Pirates first baseman Rocky Nelson hit the ball, and as Irvin described it:

> Rocky hit the ball directly over Willie's head in center field. At the crack of the bat, Willie turned and ran. When he turned and got ready to make the catch, the wind had taken the ball over to his right. He saw that he didn't have time to bring his glove hand over to make the catch, so at the last minute he caught the ball in his bare hand on a dead run for out number three.[35]

## Roommates No More

In 1955 the Giants, coming off their first World Series triumph in 21 seasons, were led by 23-year-old Mays and were hoping for a comeback season from the 36-year-old Irvin. Mays delivered on his part of the bargain, crashing 51 home runs, the first of two 50-homer seasons in his career, with 127 RBIs, a .319 batting average, and a 1.059 OPS, the second straight league-leading OPS for Mays. For Irvin, though, it was another story. After a lackluster start to 1955, with a .253 average and only one home run in 51 games, he was sent down to Minneapolis of the American Association. Although Irvin revived in Minneapolis and helped lead the Millers to a Junior World Series triumph under the managerial leadership of soon-to-be-Giants skipper Bill Rigney, Irvin's Giants career – and his rooming with Willie Mays – was over. The Giants finished in a distant third place, 18½ games behind the eventual World Series champion Brooklyn Dodgers, who started the season with a 22-2 record and were never headed. Irvin would go on to have a decent comeback season with the 1956 Chicago Cubs, where he helped mentor a young Ernie Banks, but his playing career ended after four games with the 1957 Hollywood Stars, a Brooklyn Dodgers affiliate, when his back acted up. Mays no longer had either of his two main mentors – manager Durocher had been let go at the end of the 1955 Giants season – but the Say Hey Kid was by 1956 a fixture in the Giants lineup for many more seasons.

By 1956, Mays was mentoring others, notably Giants rookie first baseman Bill White, and winning the first of four straight National League stolen-base titles and putting together two straight "30-30" (30 home runs, 30 stolen bases) seasons in 1956 and 1957. No major leaguer had posted a 30-30 campaign since Ken Williams did it for the St. Louis Browns in 1922.

## The Relationship Between Willie Mays and Monte Irvin

Irvin and Mays had a mutually supportive relationship. When Mays arrived in New York, Irvin "took him under his wing" – and it is unquestioned that no teammate was more important and influential in the development of Mays, on and off the field, in his formative major-league years.[36]

In the first Willie Mays/Charles Einstein collaboration, *Born to Play Ball,* which was released in 1955, Mays credited Irvin with teaching him a great deal about outfield play, as well as how to steal home, which Irvin did five times during the 1951 season and in the first inning of Game One of the World Series against the New York Yankees.[37] As Mays described, Irvin taught Mays how to aim his cutoff throws at the cutoff man rather than all the way home, with the result being Mays' amazing throw to nail Billy Cox at the plate in a 1951 game against the Dodgers. According to Mays, "I came out of a turn and saw Whitey Lockman and threw at him. Lockman was the cutoff man. He just stepped to one side, let the ball ride through to the plate, and we had Cox."[38] Yet another conversation between Mays and Irvin involved the older, more experienced Irvin imparting surprising advice – that it was sometimes easier to steal home when a left-handed hitter was at-bat, even though a right-handed batter blocks the catcher's view. According to Irvin, if a left-handed pull hitter was at bat, the third baseman would play wide of the bag, allowing him to take a bigger lead off third base.[39] "From the outset, Mays was a willing student, asking Monte Irvin for the tendencies of each hitter and seeking guidance in the outfield on positioning.[40] Although Mays had a long way to go before establishing himself as the premier offensive and defensive center fielder in major-league baseball, the seeds were planted. As for hitting, Mays told *Sporting News* correspondent Joe King that "(W)hen I first came up, I didn't hit well and I didn't know too much about the league and Monty [*sic*] would always sit beside me and tell me things."[41]

From the beginning of their time together, the teammates had a supportive, friendly, and at times even playful interaction. Upon beginning his major-league tenure in a big slump, Mays knew that Irvin would know how to counsel him and that Durocher wanted Mays to stay no matter what he hit. Mays knew that Irvin would "run interference" for him wherever they went, as Irvin "preached to Mays the virtues of handling himself with class and dignity on and off the field."[42] At the same time, Irvin recognized that Mays was a sensitive young man and would not criticize him but rather suggest "If it were me … I'd do it this way" when Irvin thought Mays had done something wrong.[43]

At home in New York in 1951, Mays lived with David and Ann Goosby near the Polo Grounds, where he was under the watchful eye of boxing promoter and former Negro League official Frank Forbes.[44] Even there, Irvin was still a significant influence, vetting Mays' activities, including after-hours bar-hopping and dating. Mays' many autobiographies as well as his comments when Irvin died in 2016 suggested that Irvin had taken care of him and made sure he did not make serious mistakes in his day-to-day life. Mays described how Irvin would invite him to his New Jersey home, and how the two would take walks together. "We'd walk through a park near his home in New Jersey talking about baseball and life. He made sure that I didn't go into the wrong crowd. You don't know as much as you think you know when you're young, and he was my mentor and made me aware of what I could and couldn't do.[45] Irvin related going to Toots Shor's, a favorite "watering hole" where athletes, especially baseball players, were alternatively insulted and protected by owner and New York Giants fan Shor. According to Irvin, he and Mays were welcomed there in those early integration days but knew they were seated on the periphery. "Now it wasn't exactly balanced there. Willie Mays and I rarely sat all that close to Joe DiMaggio's or Mickey Mantle's table over at Toots' place but we were there."[46] In contrast, Mays and Irvin often went together to Harlem nightspots like Small's Paradise and Red Rooster, where, according to Mays, Irvin "called ahead to restaurants and told them so that when I got there … they had a Coke with a cherry waiting for me. They said, 'No drinking.' Monte had told them."[47]

But there was a lighthearted side to their relationship as well. In a September 1954 article, Mays told sportswriter Milton Richman about games that he and Irvin would play with each other. In "distance," whoever hit the farthest in batting practice "wins all the pop he can drink in the clubhouse. Loser pays for the pop. We got one rule, though. A man must drink his winnings the same day. Else he don't get 'em."[48] On the road, they would play "Captain of the Room," in which the player who got the most hits in the game that day has to take care of bags, get newspapers, and turn on the radio.[49] As related by Irv Goodman in *Sport* magazine, Irvin, "his closest friend on the team, grabbed Willie in the shower room and scrubbed his butt with a coarse-haired floor brush. Willie roared with laughter throughout the ordeal, and the rest of the team, witnessing the byplay, ate it up."[50] What did Mays do to earn this treatment from his roomie? He made a game-saving catch.

As described by biographer James Hirsch, Mays had a "catalytic effect" on Irvin.[51] If Irvin was in a bad mood, Mays would dispel it with music, whether sung by him or put on his portable phonograph, or suggest games or other diversions for Irvin. Mays' presence would lift Irvin's mood, as Irvin stated: "Willie gave me a lift. ...You always knew when he was around, because the love of life just flowed out of him, and it got to the point where it was a pleasure to come to the ballpark every day."[52] Later in Mays' career, after Irvin had been retired for 11 years and was just starting his stint as an assistant director of promotion and public relations to soon-to-be-former Baseball Commissioner William "Spike" Eckert, he reminisced about his career in an interview with *New York Times* Pulitzer Prize-winning sportswriter Arthur Daley. After relating Mays' devastated reaction to Irvin's broken ankle, Irvin said that "[T]he two greatest guys I ever met in baseball are Willie Mays and Ernie Banks. They are joys to be with."[53]

Most importantly, when Mays faced racial prejudice as a young Giant, Irvin was there – to counsel him, and to defuse the situation. Author Roger Kahn told the story of Mays watching a dice table in a Las Vegas casino that the Giants visited during spring training in 1954. According to Kahn, he was told by a casino security chief to get Mays away from the tables because of his race, with the chief using the ugliest of racist epithets. Kahn reacted with outrage and brought Irvin into the situation. Not only did Irvin get Mays out of the casino, but he also prevailed upon Kahn not to tell this story for many years. In Irvin's view, the publicity could only cause more trouble for Mays, as "[W]illie is only twenty-three. If you write what happened at the hotel, you could put Willie in the middle of a huge racial storm. I think it would be too much for the kid."[54]

In 1954 Mays and Irvin went into business together, purchasing a liquor store in Brooklyn that they called Willmont Liquors. Surprisingly, Irvin and Mays went to Howard Cosell, who was practicing law before embarking on his broadcast career, for advice. Along with being a self-aggrandizing storyteller, embellishing his role in the transaction – from helping to arrange the transfer of the store to Harlem (which required a more expensive liquor license) to involvement in the store purchase itself – Cosell was viewed by both Mays and Irvin as an annoying person.[55] The liquor store was short-lived, as Mays and Irvin sold it the next year.

Irvin enjoyed a notable post-playing career and remained one of Mays' close friends. At many events where Mays was honored, Irvin was there – for Willie Mays Day at the Polo Grounds on May 3, 1963, for an August 1979 event at the Polo Grounds houses on 155th Street, and for Mays' Hall of Fame induction on August 5, 1979.[56] Both Irvin and Mays were in the initial group of 38 inductees for the National Black Sports Hall of Fame in 1973,[57] and on October 14, 1973, Irvin was present for the last hit of Mays' major-league career, in Game Two of the 1973 World Series, with Irvin now an assistant to Commissioner Bowie Kuhn and Mays finishing up with the Mets. In a column by Arthur Daley, Irvin was quoted as follows: "I saw you make your first hit ... and I've seen you make your last one. Confidentially, Willie, the last one was easier to follow."[58] As Mays' first hit was a "titanic blast over the Polo Grounds roof" and his last was a "splash up the middle for a run-scoring single," Irvin's wry assessment was spot-on.[59]

## An Assessment

In a documentary film about Mays released in 2022, the role of Durocher in Mays' development was prominently featured but no mention was made of Irvin. This runs counter to Mays' frequent commentary of the important role Irvin played in his early development and to the comments of Bobby Thomson and others. According to Thomson, "[T]hey always gave Leo credit for putting his arm around Willie and bringing him along. From what I saw, it seemed to me that Willie had an awful lot of respect for Monte. Monte was like a father to him."[60] Similarly, 1954 World Series hero Dusty Rhodes said that "[M]onte roomed with Willie and had a lot of influence on him. Monte was like an old professor. When he talked, you listened. He helped Willie get straightened out.[61]

While Durocher was undoubtedly an important influence on Mays, the skipper also had a downside. He was a well-known lady's man, agitator, and "man about town" who ran with a "fast crowd." Irvin's reputation was always stellar – as a ballplayer and as an individual. Most recently, Mays said that "Monte taught me how to treat others and how to be treated. He played the game right and treated people right. He was a thinker. Everyone respected him. He made sure I didn't get into trouble."[62] And listen to Durocher himself, a man known to be a self-promoter, speaking at an event that Irvin also attended: "Monte Irvin has as much to do with Willie's success as I did."[63]

Neither Irvin nor Mays was known to be confrontational about issues of civil rights. When Jackie Robinson wrote the book *Baseball Has Done It* in 1964, he interviewed Irvin as one of several key figures in baseball's integration. Irvin stated that "I can't for the life of me understand why I and the others, *including Willie*, didn't protest more than we did" about incidents when they were segregated from their teams (emphasis added).[64] Irvin went on to say that "[b]aseball has done more to move America in the right direction than all the professional patriots with their billions of cheap words. Baseball has proved that it can be done."[65]

Mays declined to be interviewed for Robinson's book. According to Robinson, "Willie didn't exactly refuse to speak. He said that he didn't know what to say."[66] Robinson editorialized that Mays and Maury Wills, another nonparticipant in the book, "did not wish to stir things up."[67] As with the racial incident in Las Vegas, both Mays and Irvin were more likely to speak with their activities as participants than with their voices as protesters. As he reflected on that incident, Kahn characterized Irvin thusly: "[I]t was his way to avoid confrontations and to strive for civil-rights progress by diplomacy, so to speak."[68] When Kahn spoke to Mays after Kahn had revealed the incident in Las Vegas years later, Mays asked that he not be associated with the reaction its revelation might cause, saying, "I wasn't much for controversy. Not then. Not now, either. I guess not ever."[69]

When Irvin died in 2016, Mays did not show up at his memorial. But it was not because he was otherwise busy or because he deemed it unimportant. Rather, it was because he was too choked up to be there. He sent in his commentary, as follows:

> Your [*sic*] all going to hear a lot of things about Monte Irvin today. There is much to be said. He was a good man, a good father, a good baseball player and a great friend. …
>
> Monte taught me without directly teaching me. He taught me without preaching or lecturing or even without me knowing that I was learning. …
>
> Monte was wise and generous and tough as they come. He was all the things that you've heard, and he was more. There will never be another Monte Irvin.[70]

The same, for somewhat different reasons, could be said of Mays – as an all-around player, as a center fielder, as the quintessential five-tool-player, there will never be another Willie Mays.

***Acknowledgments***

The author wishes to acknowledge the friendship and support of late SABR member Alan Kaufmann, who was planning to contribute to volumes like these until his sudden passing.

## NOTES

1 Willie Mays, as Told to Charles Einstein, *Born to Play Ball* (New York: G.P. Putnam's Sons,1955), 6-7.

2 Willie Mays and John Shea, *24* (New York: St. Martin's Press, 2020), 59.

3 Monte Irvin with James A. Riley, *Nice Guys Finish First* (New York: Carroll &Graf Publishers, Inc., 1996), 14.

4 *Chattanooga Daily News*, April 20, 1948: 13, cited in Rocco Constantino, *Beyond Baseball's Color Barrier* (Lanham, Maryland: Rowman & Littlefield, 2021), 80.

5 John Saccoman, "Willie Mays,' in *The Team That Time Won't Forget* (Phoenix: Society for American Baseball Research, 2015), 124.

6 http://www.retrosheet.org. Negro League Seasons accessed 12/21/22.

7 See, e.g., *Born to Play Ball*, 43 (Willie Mays: "I got to play against and with some pretty fair ballplayers, not only while I was with the Barons, but a year or so later on, when Roy Campanella took me on for his barnstorming team during the winter months. I met Monte Irvin that way. ..."); James S. Hirsch, *Willie Mays* (New York: Scribner, 2010), 70 (After the 1950 season, Piper Davis "rounded up some players to compete against major leaguers on a barnstorming tour. The games allowed Mays to meet two black players with the New York Giants, Monte Irvin and Hank Thompson.")

8 Monte Irvin with Phil Pepe, *Few And Chosen* (Chicago: Triumph Books, 2007), 93: "The first time I ever set eyes on Willie Mays was when he joined the New York Giants in May 1951, but I had heard a lot about him by then." (bold in original). Perhaps at age 88, Irvin did not remember the earlier encounters he had with Willie Mays.

9 Hirsch, 92-93.

10 Some sources, including a contemporary newspaper account, state that Mays and Irvin did collide in the outfield, but the game accounts of the *New York Times* and *The Sporting News* clearly indicate that they did not. See W. Rollo Wilson, "'Sorta Scared' He Says," *Pittsburgh Courier*, June 2, 1951: 15 ("He made several nice catches and in his zeal to make good had a collision with right fielder Monte Irvin in the ninth inning. ..."); Charles Einstein, *Willie's Time* (New York: J.P. Lippincott Company 1979), 41 ("Against the Phillies in his first game as a Giant ... he ran into teammate Monte Irvin. ...); John Drebinger, "Polo Grounders Trip Phils 8-5, With 5-Run Splurge in Eighth," *New York Times*, May 26, 1951: 24 ("In the ninth, however, Mays had a close call when his great speed almost brought him into collision with Monty [*sic*] Irvin on Waitkus' smash into right center); "Arrival of Mays Starts Thomson on Batting Spree," *The Sporting News*, June 6, 1951: 11. See also Ray Robinson, *The Home Run Heard 'Round The World*, (New York: HarperCollins Publishers 1991),122 (describing the May 25, 1951, game, states that "on one play [Mays] ran right up Irvin's back as he went for Eddie Waitkus' liner.")

11 Robinson, 123. "After the [May 25] game, Leo told Irvin and Thomson that in the future they should let Mays take everything that came near him in center field. He's got the range, said Durocher, you guys just guard the lines."

12 Paul Dickson, *Leo Durocher* (New York: Bloomsbury 2017), 206; Hirsch, 103.

13 According to Hirsch, 95, Mays was sulking on the way home from Philadelphia after his 0-12 start and "Irvin tried to relax him. 'Listen man,' he said. 'We won three in a row without you hitting. Now figure it out. As long as we hit, we don't win. Only trouble'll be if you get a hit." In Mays' 1966 autobiography, he says that Irvin suggested that Mays guess fastball and swing at the first pitch against Spahn, the result being Mays' first hit and home run. Willie Mays as told to Charles Einstein, *Willie Mays* (New York: E.P. Dutton & Co., Inc. 1966), 94.

14 Irvin was moved to left field for the first time on May 21, 1951, with Whitey Lockman simultaneously moving to first base. On May 25, Mays was put in center field, with Bobby Thomson switched to left field and Irvin to right field. Irvin played both right and left field between Mays' debut and late July, at which point he played left field for the entire 1951 pennant stretch drive. Baseball-Reference.com Game Logs for Monte Irvin 1951.

15 "Mets Plan Sentimental Party for Mays," *Chicago Defender*, September 15, 1973: 28.

16 See, for example, Joe King, "Giants Bolstered, but Rise Depends on Irvin's Ankle," *The Sporting News*, February 17, 1954: 17. Monte Irvin quoted as follows: "Willie gives us a lift. ... I don't only mean those impossible catches he makes. I mean the way he can get everybody loose in the clubhouse and make us laugh and work up a spirit.

17 Irvin, 129.

18 To make room for Willie Mays, the Giants sent down Black shortstop and former Black Barons teammate Artie Wilson. Irvin stated that there was an "unwritten quota system that limited the number of black ballplayers on a ballclub." Irvin, 142. According to Hirsch, 79, Wilson later said that he had "urged Durocher to call up Mays and that he would rather play in the Pacific Coast League than sit on the bench in the majors." Wilson played through 1957 primarily in the PCL but never returned to the major leagues, finishing his New York Giants career with four hits in 22 at-bats.

19 Hirsch, 137.

20 Arthur Daley, "Another Pioneer," *New York Times*, September 1, 1968: S2. Quoting Irvin: "[W]e never had the slightest idea when our drive started that we could catch the Dodgers. They had the equivalent of an all-star team, and we were merely trying to make it close." See also "The World of Sports," *Alabama Tribune*, October 12, 1951: 7. "The Giants are the Cinderellas of baseball, but they became so because they were united in purpose, well-balanced and daringly managed."

21 Baseball-Reference.com 1951 New York Giants Statistics. Pitchers Sal Maglie with a 6.6 WAR and Larry Jansen with a 5.5 WAR were also ahead of Mays, leaving him seventh in WAR among all 1951 Giants players.

22 Stan Jacoby, "The Numbers Say It Ain't So, Bobby: Did '51 Giants Steal the Pennant?" *New York Times,* March 4, 2001: SP 11.

23 *Born to Play Ball*, 69.

24 Irvin, 159.

25 Baseball Reference.com Postseason Game Logs for Willie Mays. Note that Mays' World Series totals now include 3 at-bats in the 1948 Negro World Series for the Birmingham Black Barons.

26 Irvin, 171.

27 Hirsch, 148. A photograph of the play shows Mays walking off the field with Indian Harry "Suitcase" Simpson's arm around him, both of them tearing up. "Willie Mays never made it to second base. When he saw and heard the calamity at third, he collapsed to the ground, pounded on the dirt, and began to cry." It certainly appears that Mays was upset over the horrible injury his roomie had just sustained as well as perhaps his role in it.

28 Hirsch, 159.

29 Arch Murray, "Monte's Exploits in Orient Cheered at Polo Grounds," *The Sporting News*, November 18, 1953: 18.

30 Irvin, 155.

31 Arnold Hano, *A Day in the Bleachers* (New York: Da Capo Paperback edition 1982), 116-125.

32 Irvin as told to Pepe, 98.

33 Irvin, 181.

34 Hano, 141-142.

35 Irvin, 182. In Willie Mays and John Shea, *92*, coauthor Shea states that Irvin considered a catch by Mays off the bat of Dodger Bobby Morgan in 1952 to be Mays' best catch. Irvin does describe that catch in his autobiography, but says it was made in 1954, and makes it sound as if he was there. Irvin, 183. According to Hirsch, 149-150, Irvin was in his hospital bed when Mays made his play on Morgan on April 18, 1952, barely over two weeks after Irvin broke his ankle. Based on this evidence, the author concludes that the catch off the bat of Rocky Nelson was the best catch Willie Mays made in Monte Irvin's presence.

36 Mays and Shea, 61-63.

37 *Born to Play Baseball*, 21-22, 48-49.

38 *Born to Play Baseball*, 22.

39 *Born to Play Baseball*, 49 (stealing home normally against right-hand hitter); Hirsch, 107 (easier to steal when lefty pull hitter at the plate).

40 Hirsch, 107.

41 Joe King, "Should Be Better Fielder Insists Glove Whiz Willie," *The Sporting News* January 19, 1955: 9.

42 King, "Should Be Better Fielder Insists Glove Whiz Willie."

43 Hirsch, 120.

44 Hirsch, 114-115.

45 Mays and Shea, 63.

46 Roberta Newman and Joel Rosen, *Black Baseball, Black Business* (Jackson: University Press of Mississippi 2014), *ix-x*.

47 Mays and Shea, 63.

48 Willie Mays as told to Milton Richman, "I'd Play for Nothing," *This Week Magazine* September 12, 1954: 16. Clipping in Willie Mays Cooperstown File 1951-1965.

49 Mays as told to Milton Richman, "I'd Play for Nothing."

50 Irv Goodman, "Is There a Willie Mays?" *Sport Magazine,* October 1954: 69. Clipping in Willie Mays player file at the National Baseball Hall of Fame, 1951-1965.

51 Hirsch, 122.

52 Hirsch, 122.

53 Arthur Daley, "Another Pioneer," *New York Times*, September 1, 1968: S2.

54 Roger Kahn, *Memories of Summer* (New York: Hyperion, 1997), 258-261. The story is rendered there in complete detail; Willie Mays was not yet 23 when the incident happened in late March of 1954.

55 *See* "J.G.T. Spink, "Personal Counsel to Players," *The Sporting News* August 10, 1955: 6. Cosell not only claimed falsely that he helped Irvin and Mays with the purchase of the liquor store, but he also suggested that he played against Irvin in high school. The reader can draw their own conclusions. Mark Ribowsky, *Howard Cosell* (New York: W.W. Norton & Company), 71-73 (quoting Irvin saying "[H]e was the only person I ever met during my career that I disliked. I mean really disliked."

56 Monte Irvin, "Batting The Ball," *New Pittsburgh Courier* May 11, 1963: 8. (Irvin describes attending Willie Mays Day); Michael Givens, "Say Hey! ... Willie!" *New York Amsterdam News* August 11, 1979: 53 (Irvin attending event honoring Mays at the Polo Grounds Houses).

57 "38 Athletes Named to Black Hall of Fame," *New York Times* June 29, 1973: 33.

58 Arthur Daley, "Twilight of the Gods," *New York Times* November 4, 1973: S2.

59 Daley, "Twilight of the Gods."

60 Irvin, 131.

61 Irvin, 131.

62 Mays and Shea, 63.

63 Durocher quoted in "Willie Mays Returns to Harlem," *Columbus (Georgia) Times*, August 31, 1979: 24.

64 Jackie Robinson, *Baseball Has Done It* (Brooklyn: Ig Publishing, paperback edition 2005), 100.

65 Robinson, *Baseball Has Done It*, 101.

66 Robinson, *Baseball Has Done It*, 209.

67 Robinson, *Baseball Has Done It*, 208.

68 Kahn, 259-260.

69 Kahn, 261-262.

70 John Shea, "Willie Mays' Heartfelt Words for Mentor Monte Irvin," SFGate.com, May 2, 2016 SFGate. https://www.sfgate.com/giants/article/Willie-Mays-heartfelt-words-for-mentor-Monte-7388040.php Accessed February 3, 2022.

# FRIGHTENING PITCHERS WITH GIANT WILLIES: THE SLUGGING DUO OF WILLIE MAYS AND WILLIE MCCOVEY

BY GORDON GATTIE

WILLIE MAYS AND Willie McCovey formed one of the greatest one-two power combinations in baseball history. The pair were teammates on the San Francisco Giants from 1959 to 1972. During that stretch, they won the 1962 National League pennant and 1971 NL West Division title, while finishing second for five consecutive years: in the NL from 1965 to 1968 and the NL West Division during 1969. Although the pair never won a World Series together, this potent duo – the right-handed batting, right-handed throwing outfielder Mays and the left-handed batting, left-handed throwing first baseman McCovey – were the heart and soul of the Giants lineup throughout the 1960s and into the early 1970s. While these two historic greats shared the same uniform for over a decade, their relationship was complex. A 1978 *Sports Illustrated* article noted, "The premier ballplayer of his generation, Mays was never as fully accepted by San Francisco fans as [Orlando] Cepeda and McCovey were. There was too much of New York about him, and while the younger players appeared publicly about town, Mays was virtually invisible away from the park."[1]

As prolific home-run hitters, the Mays-McCovey partnership combined to hit 801 home runs while wearing Giants uniforms, the third-most career home runs as teammates in baseball history, trailing only Hank Aaron/Eddie Mathews (863) and Lou Gehrig/Babe Ruth (859).[2] During their 13 full seasons together, both Mays and McCovey hit at least 30 home runs seven times, with one or the other leading the NL in home runs six times. Mays topped the NL in 1962, 1964, and 1965. McCovey led the league in 1963 (tied with Aaron), 1968, and 1969. In four other seasons, either Mays or McCovey finished no lower than fourth.[3] From 1954 through 1970, except for 1961, either slugger led the Giants in home runs.

Mays was an established veteran when McCovey joined the Giants. Mays had completed five-plus seasons in New York (1951-1952, 1954-1957), two years in the US Army during the Korean War (1952-1954), and two years in San Francisco (1957-1958) by the time McCovey arrived in the majors. Mays helped the Giants transition from New York City to San Francisco, while McCovey was a local fan favorite upon his debut, from winning the Rookie of the Year Award in 1959 to his celebrated return in 1977.

McCovey played first base throughout his minor-league career, and the Giants already had two first basemen when he went to his first major-league spring-training camp in 1959: veteran Bill White and the 1958 Rookie of the Year Cepeda.[4] Mays was impressed with McCovey, and while there wasn't room for another first baseman, Mays recalled, "It was one of those situations, though, that you knew if we got into a pennant race, he'd be called up to give us an extra bat."[5] McCovey was recalled to the Giants in late July, and stayed with them for the rest of the season, playing first base while White and Cepeda shifted roles. While Mays appreciated McCovey's talents, he considered McCovey more of a satellite than a protégé. Although McCovey played some outfield, he knew that "I wouldn't be a Willie Mays and anybody who saw me play there [outfield] could tell that right away."[6] McCovey played in a part-time role, splitting time between outfield and first base until 1963, and eventually became the Giants' full-time first baseman in 1965. During McCovey's struggles learning to play the outfield, Mays complimented his teammate: "I've been taking care of Stretch [McCovey] in the outfield. I tell him where to play and try to keep boostin' his confidence. He's done real nice. There are a lot of outfielders in the league that ain't as good as Stretch."[7]

The transition of the Giants from New York to San Francisco mirrored McCovey's development and arguably ended on June 1, 1962, when the Giants played the first-year expansion New York Mets at the Polo Grounds in New York City. This game marked the first time the Giants played in New York since leaving the Big Apple after the 1957 season. McCovey started the scoring with a first-inning home run. He homered again in the third inning. Mays homered two innings later. The Giants won 9-6.[8]

The pair came closest to winning a World Series in 1962. The Giants won the NL pennant after defeating their longtime rival Los Angeles Dodgers in a best-of-three playoff series. The two teams finished the regular season deadlocked with identical 101-61 records. During the first playoff game, Mays' two homers helped San Francisco win 8-0. The Dodgers won Game Two on a game-ending sacrifice fly. Mays and McCovey contributed to the historic Game Three rally. San Francisco was trailing 4-2 in the top of the ninth inning when McCovey drew a one-out walk. Mays singled two batters later. McCovey was replaced with a pinch-runner. Both runners eventually scored as the Giants shocked the Dodgers with a four-run rally at Dodger Stadium.[9]

The 1962 World Series between the San Francisco Giants and New York Yankees featured Mays and McCovey playing critical roles, espe-

*Willie Mays and Willie McCovey, along with Ron Santo and Cleon Jones, pitched Adirondack bats. SABR/The Rucker Archive.*

cially during the final game. The teams were tied at three games apiece. During Game Seven with the Yankees leading 1-0, Mays lined to left field, but an out-of-position left fielder caught the ball, preventing Mays from reaching base.[10] McCovey, the next batter, tripled but was stranded at third base. Heading into the bottom of the ninth, San Francisco still trailed 1-0. Giants leadoff hitter Matty Alou singled. The next two hitters struck out. Mays doubled into right field, but the ball was slowed down by the wet ground. Combined with a perfect relay from right fielder Roger Maris to second baseman Bobby Richardson, the ball was returned to the infield quickly enough to prevent Alou from scoring the tying run.[11]

With Alou on third and Mays representing the Series-winning run on second, McCovey hit a screaming line drive directly at Richardson to dramatically end the Series. According to one newspaper account, "Richardson couldn't have made the catch had McCovey's smash been an inch or two higher or so much as a finger length to either side."[12] Both Mays and McCovey struggled throughout the Series. Mays hit .250 with no homers and one RBI but played well in the field. McCovey played in

*Willie Mays and Willie McCovey played together for 14 seasons, including in McCovey's 1969 MVP campaign. SABR/The Rucker Archive.*

only four games and hit .200 with one homer and one RBI. Mays returned to the World Series with the 1973 New York Mets, but McCovey never did.

The superstars occasionally roomed together. McCovey commented, "He'd even take me along on dates with him. He'd drag me everywhere. I looked up to him. All of us did. He was such a great player."[13] McCovey joined Mays for Mays' first date with his second wife, Mae Louis Allen.[14] The pair were depicted together on several baseball cards throughout the 1960s as league leaders (e.g., 1965 Topps Home Run Leaders) and featured on 1967 Topps Baseball Card #423 titled "Fence Busters," where they struck a conversational pose.

The 1971 season was a challenging one for the aging Giants, who went 1-11 from September 5 to 16 and saw their West Division lead over the Dodgers plunge from eight games on September 5 to a single game. The 33-year-old McCovey played in only 105 games at first base that season due to lingering knee issues while Mays, who also battled injuries all season long, played in 136 games, including 48 games at first to replace McCovey. Upon winning the division title, McCovey complimented his longtime friend: "You know who I'm happiest for? Willie. He played too much. He played when I couldn't because one of us had to be in there."[15]

Change appeared on the horizon as the 1972 season started. The players strike caused the season to start later than normal. Mays wanted a long-term contract and McCovey was injured in the season's fourth game. San Francisco was struggling in the standings and at the gate. On May 11 Mays was traded to the Mets for a minor-league pitcher and cash.[16]

Both players were voted into the National Baseball Hall of Fame on their first appearance on the ballot. Mays was inducted in 1979, receiving 94.7 percent of the writers' vote. McCovey was inducted in 1986, receiving 81.4 percent.

Both Mays and McCovey worked in the Giants' front office after their playing days, making public appearances on behalf of the club and offering expertise to players. Mays joined the front office in 1993 when former Giants president Peter Magowan signed him to a lifetime contract. McCovey formally joined the front office in 2000[17] and remained with them until his death in 2018. The two often appeared together at Giants games; they also shared a farewell to Candlestick Park during the NFL San Francisco 49ers' final regular home game in 2013.

Mays and McCovey shared characteristics and noteworthy records. Both Hall of Famers were born in Alabama: Mays in Westfield and McCovey in Mobile. Each slugger delivered 30 or more home runs for six consecutive years: Mays from 1961 to 1966 and McCovey from 1965 to 1970. Both hit at least three homers in a game three different times, with Mays clouting four on April 30, 1961.[18] The evening before Mays clobbered four home runs, the pair ate ribs from a nearby take-out restaurant. That night, Mays fell ill, waking up at 3 A.M., vomiting, collapsing, and passing out. McCovey immediately called team physician Doc Bowman, recalling, "I was really scared. I was pleading not to let him die."[19] Mays prepared for an offday. However, during batting practice, he blasted a dozen home-run balls into the bleachers and insisted he remain in the lineup. When he returned to the dugout after hitting his fourth homer, McCovey asked him, "How 'bout some more ribs?"[20]

The similarities aren't limited to their numerous home runs. Mays and McCovey, along with catcher Buster Posey, are the only Giants in franchise history to win both the Rookie of the Year Award and a Most Valuable Player Award. Mays and McCovey, along with Pablo Sandoval, are the only three San Francisco Giants to have two separate 20-plus-game hit streaks.[21]

The pair rank first and second in multiple categories among San Francisco Giants all-time hitting records, including games played (McCovey, 2,256; Mays, 2,095); at-bats (Mays, 7,578; McCovey, 7,214); hits (Mays, 2,284; McCovey, 1,974); and triples (Mays, 76; McCovey, 45). McCovey and Mays also rank second and third, respectively, on the all-time San Francisco Giants home-run list (McCovey, 469; Mays, 459).[22] They are also tied for the most sacrifice flies playing for the San Francisco Giants (67).[23] From a fielding perspective, Mays played the most games as an outfielder in the history of the New York Gothams/New York Giants/San Francisco Giants from 1883 to 2021 (2,749 games), and McCovey holds the similar record for first basemen (1,775).[24] Both have 15 starts on Opening Day wearing a San Francisco Giants uniform.[25] As a further testament to their longevity, both hit at least one round-tripper in 22 National League seasons.

Toward the end of his career, McCovey reflected on his relationship with Mays, "I guess I was as close to him as anyone can be, but I don't think anyone can get real close to him. We're neighbors now. I live in Woodside and he lives in Atherton, but we hardly ever see each other."[26]

Their legacies in San Francisco well established, both have their uniform numbers retired by the Giants (Mays, 24; McCovey, 44) and nine-foot-tall bronze statues erected outside Oracle Park.

***Acknowledgments***

The author thanks Carl Riechers for his fact-checking, Bill Nowlin and Glen Sparks for their editing, and Lisa Gattie for her meaningful input.

## SOURCES

Besides the sources cited in the Notes, the author consulted AABaseball.com, Baseball-Reference.com, Retrosheet.org, TheBaseballCube.com, and the following:

Khalid, Sunni. The "other Willie" and the early San Francisco Giants. https://andscape.com/features/willie-mccovey-and-the-early-san-francisco-giants/. Accessed December 2, 2022.

Mays, Willie, as told to Charles Einstein. *Willie Mays: My Life in and Out of Baseball* (New York: E.P. Dutton & Co., Inc., 1966).

Shea, John. Blowing Out the Candle, SFGate, April 4, 1999. https://www.sfgate.com/sports/shea/article/Blowing-ou-the-candle-3089625.php. Accessed December 15, 2022.

Vecsey, George. "McCovey's Toughest Opponent," *New York Times*, January 10, 1986: A19.

## NOTES

1 Ron Fimrite, "The Cable Cars, the Fog – and Willie," *Sports Illustrated*, April 17, 1978: 41.

2 Don Schlossberg, "McCovey and Mays Gave Foes of Giants 'The Willies,'" *Fortune*, November 1, 2018.

3 In 1961 Mays finished second in home runs among NL players. In 1966 Mays finished third and McCovey fourth. In 1967, McCovey finished third. In 1970 McCovey finished fourth.

4 Mark Armour, "Willie McCovey," Society for American Baseball Research BioProject. https://sabr.org/bioproj/person/willie-mccovey/. Accessed December 1, 2022.

5 Willie Mays and Lou Sahadi, *Say Hey: The Autobiography of Willie Mays* (New York: Simon & Schuster, 1988), 153.

6 Fimrite.

7 James S. Hirsch, *Wille Mays: The Life, the Legend* (New York: Simon & Schuster, 2011), 359.

8 Alan Cohen, "June 1, 1962: Willie Mays, Giants return to New York for first time, beat the Mets," SABR Games Project. https://sabr.org/gamesproj/game/june-1-1962-willie-mays-giants-return-to-new-york-for-first-time-beat-the-mets/. Accessed December 1, 2022.

9 Tim Otto, "October 3, 1962: The Giants Win the Pennant, Part Two!," SABR Games Project. https://sabr.org/gamesproj/game/october-3-1962-the-giants-win-the-pennant-part-two/. Accessed December 1, 2022.

10 Willie Mays, "'Yankees' Mistake Cost Me a Double," *San Francisco Examiner*, October 17, 1962: 54.

11 John Carmichael, "Series Left a Big Question Mark: Could Matty Alou Have Scored? *Buffalo Evening News*, October 17, 1962: 71.

12 Prescott Sullivan, "They Couldn't Have Sliced It Thinner," *San Francisco Examiner*, October 17, 1962: 53.

13 Fimrite, "The Cable Cars, the Fog – and Willie."

14 Hirsch, *Wille Mays: The Life, the Legend*, 453.

15 Hirsch, 500.

16 "Mays to Mets for Cash, Pitcher," *San Francisco Examiner*, May 11, 1972: 57.

17 Matt Chisholm, Liam Connolly, Megan Brown, Maria Jacinto, Erwin Higueros, Allison Mast, and Nancy Donati, *San Francisco Giants 2018 Media Guide* (San Francisco: San Francisco Giants Creative Services Department, 2022), 19.

18 Mike Passanisi, Megan Brow, Maria Jacinto, Erwin Higueros, Mariana De Paula, and Matt Chisholm, *San Francisco Giants 2022 Media Guide* (San Francisco: San Francisco Giants Creative Services Department, 2022), 447.

19 Hirsch, 340.

20 Mays and Sahadi, *Say Hey: The Autobiography of Willie Mays*, 168. There's a second Mays-McCovey connection with Mays' four-home-run game. After the game, Ed Sullivan invited him to appear on his television show in New York City. After Mays' television appearance, he went to a Harlem nightclub where Wilt Chamberlain gave Mays Mae's phone number and suggested she call him. McCovey.

21 *San Francisco Giants 2022 Media Guide*, 450.

22 *San Francisco Giants 2022 Media Guide*, 404.

23 *San Francisco Giants 2022 Media Guide*, 399.

24 *San Francisco Giants 2022 Media Guide*, 415.

25 *San Francisco Giants 2022 Media Guide*, 435.

26 Fimrite, "The Cable Cars, the Fog – and Willie."

# FATHERLY WILLIE MAYS TOOK BOBBY AND BARRY BONDS UNDER HIS WING

BY RICHARD CUICCHI

SAN FRANCISCO GIANTS Hall of Famer Willie Mays influenced the lives of two other Giants, Bobby and Barry Bonds, both of whom who had significant careers of their own. He was Bobby's teammate with the Giants, while taking on the role of godfather for Barry as a youngster. When Barry later became a Giant, Mays continued their close relationship.

Mays was inextricably linked to the father/son duo, both on and off the field. He was a factor in their on-field performance, serving as a motivator, mentor, and coach. During the course of their personal relationships, he was their confidant, at times helping them with teammate and media issues, as well as the demons affecting their personal lives.

Mays grew up in Fairfield, Alabama, near Birmingham, in the segregated Deep South of the 1930s and '40s. He learned the game from his father, who played in Black semipro leagues. Willie eventually played alongside his father, who encouraged him to pursue a professional career after Jackie Robinson broke the color barrier in major-league baseball in 1947. He played with the Birmingham Barons in the Negro Leagues for parts of the 1948 and 1949 seasons,[1] where manager Piper Davis was instrumental in honing his skills.[2] Mays signed with the New York Giants for a $5,000 bonus in 1950 as a 19-year-old.[3]

Mays was batting an amazing .477 with Triple-A Minneapolis before being called up to the Giants in late May of 1951. There was considerable anticipation about the 20-year-old's hitting ability, and he didn't disappoint the Giants as he contributed 20 home runs and 68 RBIs to their pennant-winning cause. He was named the National League Rookie of the Year.

After missing most of the 1952 season and all of 1953 while serving in the US Army, the 23-year-old Mays remarkably earned the National League MVP Award in 1954, based on his 41 home runs, 110 RBIs, and his league-leading .345 batting average, .667 slugging percentage, and 1.078 OPS. He was on his way to becoming arguably the best center fielder in baseball history.

Mays combined power and speed in becoming a perennial All-Star from 1954 through the remainder of career. When he retired after the 1973 season, he was the National League career leader in home runs with 660. He led the league in stolen bases four times and was a 12-time Gold Glove winner. Mays earned his second MVP Award in 1965 and was a first-ballot Hall of Famer in 1979.

Bobby Bonds grew up in Riverside, California, where future major-league player and manager Dusty Baker was his childhood friend. Bobby's father, Robert, had a drinking problem, which often made home life unpleasant. Bobby resented his father and developed a closer relationship with his mother. But then he followed his father's path and also became an alcoholic. As early as his sophomore year in high school, Bobby was bringing bottles of wine and cans of beer to his athletic competitions.[4]

However, his drinking habits did little to affect his performance as an amateur. Bobby was a well-known track and field star in the Los Angeles area. In 1964 he won the state long-jump championship, with a jump only 15 inches shorter than the national record. He once ran the 100-yard dash in 9.8 seconds while wearing baseball shoes.[5]

Bobby also excelled in baseball, where his speed was a significant part of his game. By his senior season in high school, San Francisco Giants scout Evo Pusich was regularly following him. After graduating from high school, the Giants offered him an $8,000 signing bonus and a guaranteed $500 monthly salary. Pusich told Bobby at his signing, "By the time you get to the big team, Willie Mays will have two or three years left. He'll be your teacher."[6]

Pusich's sales pitch with Bonds turned out to be true. Bobby broke in with the San Francisco Giants in late June 1968, in Mays' 17th big-league season, and immediately became a regular starter in right field. The 37-year-old Mays, took him under his wing and oriented Bobby to the life of a major leaguer. Bobby learned how to play the outfield from Mays, who had been a perennial Gold Glove winner. With Mays' tutoring, Bobby developed into a solid outfielder and won three Gold Gloves of his own.

Like Mays, speed and power became Bobby's game. He tied Pete Rose to lead the league with 120 runs scored in 1969 and stole 45 bases for third place. He added 32 home runs and 90 RBIs and began drawing comparisons to Mays. He was being touted as Mays' replacement.

The media began to label Bobby the "next Willie Mays," a moniker Mays didn't like for Bobby or himself. This put undue pressure and elevated expectations on Bobby. Mays sought to protect Bobby from resulting distractions, including taking him to dinners and movies. Aware of Bobby's struggles with alcohol, Mays urged him to focus on the game.[7]

Bobby had grown up in a racially diverse neighborhood in California, but his time spent as a minor leaguer in Lexington, North Carolina, was filled with hardship due to racial hostility. At one point, he was ready to quit baseball.[8] After Bobby arrived in the majors, Mays was able to draw on his own experience of growing up in the South to help Bobby deal with lingering prejudices of teammates, the media, and the front office.

Bobby learned from Mays that being a superstar meant having the persona of a superstar. For Bobby, it translated into having a bit of swagger, becoming difficult at times with the media, and keeping certain teammates at a distance.[9]

Bobby had been married before he finished high school, with son Barry being born in 1964. When Barry was 4 years old, he began going to Candlestick Park with his father in a child-sized Giants uniform. He liked going to Mays' locker and trying to play pranks on him. Mays took to the youngster and often entertained him with playful antics. Mays would take him out to the field to play catch and shag balls.[10] Eventually, Bobby's wife, Pat, asked Mays to become Barry's godfather, a role he graciously accepted.[11] Mays' personal relationship with Barry continued well into Barry's adulthood.

By 1971, Bobby had become a legitimate star in his own right. He finished fourth in the voting for MVP, earned his first All-Star selection and captured his first Gold Glove. When Mays was traded to the New York Mets on May 11, 1972, Bobby's production regressed during the balance of the season. Mays had become an idol for Bobby, who said, "When Willie left, half of me left. I just went through the motions after that. I had no desire, no determination." He lamented, "It was one of the worst things I could have done – allowing myself to feel that way."[12]

The Giants brass had convinced themselves that Bobby was the solution to the aging Mays. Bobby took his place in center field. He was unusual for the time – a power hitter leading off. Even though he averaged 31 homers and 41 stolen bases from 1969 to 1973, it became apparent that Bonds wasn't going to become another Mays. For that matter, how many players could ever be another Mays? Even Bobby acknowledged the gap. "I never thought of myself as another Mays," he said. "There was only one of him."[13]

Those unrealistic expectations were made worse by his continuing reliance on alcohol, which became public knowledge after his arrest in 1973 for drunk driving and resisting arrest. Perhaps caused by his alcoholism, Bobby developed a persona that revealed itself through moody periods and aloofness. The Giants traded Bobby to the Yankees for Bobby Murcer in October 1974 after Bobby's lowest home-run and RBI output since his rookie season.[14]

Barry's opportunity to hang around Mays at the ballpark ended at age 10 once Bobby was dealt to the Yankees. Barry grew up in predominantly White San Carlos, a suburb of San Francisco, not far from Candlestick Park. He demonstrated a passion for baseball, which pleased his father. Barry would later say Bobby pushed him into a baseball career. A growing tension developed between the two because of frequent separations of Bobby from the family. Years later, Barry said that as a boy he hadn't liked his father because of the way Bobby treated him and his mother in the home. Barry complained that his father hadn't paid attention to his athletic and scholastic achievements.[15]

Barry was a product of his father's athletic genes and baseball acuity. He learned the game from both his father and godfather. The only Black player on his team, he was a standout for Junipero Serra High School in San Mateo, California. The Giants drafted him out high school in the second round in 1982, offering a $70,000 bonus. On the advice of his father and Mays, he instead chose to play baseball at Arizona State University.[16]

After his junior season with the Sun Devils in 1985, the Pittsburgh Pirates drafted Barry in the first round as the sixth overall pick. He earned his first MVP Award in 1990. He finished second in the voting in 1991 and followed with another first-place finish in 1992.

After the 1992 season, Barry he became a free agent. Only the Yankees and Giants made serious offers to him, and the Yankees withdrew from the pursuit after he turned down a five-year, $36 million proposal. Supermarket industry tycoon Peter McGowan had just purchased the Giants franchise, keeping it from being relocated to Tampa-St. Petersburg by previous owner Bob Lurie. McGowan hoped to revitalize the team, and he set his sights on attracting Barry back to the San Francisco area.[17]

The Giants' prior connection to his father and Mays appealed to Barry. He recalled a childhood dream of playing in the same outfield with them.[18] He returned to his baseball roots with the Giants when he signed in December 1992, with the largest contract in baseball – six years guaranteed at $43.7 million, with two option years as well.

The deal was popular in the Bay Area because Barry offered the Giants an opportunity to return to the days when Mays wore the orange and black. Dusty Baker, his father's childhood friend, was hired as the manager and brought on Bobby as hitting coach. The move united Bobby and Barry from 1993 to 1996.

Upon his signing, there was controversy over which uniform number Barry would take. He had worn number 24 with Pittsburgh in honor of his godfather. It was reported that Mays offered to take the number out of retirement so Barry could wear it. Barry wound up taking his father's number 25.[19]

Mays remained a factor in Barry's life. During their quiet times together, among the topics they discussed were how to be a good teammate and how to deal with the front office and the press. Like his father, these were issues Barry grappled with throughout his Giants career. Barry and Willie's conversations were a form of "schooling" that Barry never received from his father or his coaches.

When Bobby was cancer-stricken and near death in August 2003, Mays visited him in the hospital. Bonds told him, "Willie, you've got to take care of Barry. He's not going to listen to other people like he does you and me."[20] Barry took his father's death hard. Bobby's stint as Giants hitting coach had drawn Barry closer to him. Despite his taking time off to manage his father's personal affairs, his performance didn't suffer. He earned his third straight MVP Award and sixth of his career. Upon receiving the award, he said, "This is more special to me than any award I've ever received because it's dedicated to my father."[21]

Mays heeded Bobby's request and made himself available to then 39-year-old Barry during the offseason after Bobby's death. Mays was a source of comfort that Barry valued. "Just being with my godfather trying to go through the healing process without my father, just through our conversations and support of me in the wintertime has changed my outlook on a lot of things," Barry said. "[Bobby has] been my coach my whole life. The best thing is, Willie has taken that role for me now and he's been working out with me three days a week in the wintertime and easing the pain for me to go through the process without my father."[22]

Barry was called to testify before a grand jury in December 2003 during the BALCO steroids case. When spring-training camps opened in 2004, the investigation results were on everyone's mind. While Barry was not indicted, his association with BALCO officials was well-known. Early in March 2004, the *San Francisco Chronicle* reported that Barry was one of the players to receive steroids from BALCO, which was at the center of the major leagues' PED scandal.[23]

Mays continued to support Barry with frequent visits to the Giants clubhouse during the season. While Mays was publicly silent on the allegations, he remained Barry's confidant during the challenging time. Dusty Baker realized Mays was a reassuring influence with Barry and deferred to Mays for heart-to-heart discussions with the embattled player. Baker said, "What Willie was telling him superseded and was more important than what I could've told him. He was coming in with a different level of respect. It was almost like the Lord talking to him. I wasn't the Lord, not even close. But Willie was Willie Mays, man."[24]

With the start of the 2004 season, Barry was apprehensive about passing his hero's 660 career home runs. He said, "I never wanted to pass him. Willie's my idol. But he's the one who encouraged me to go after it all. My dad always did, and I listened to my dad, but like I said, Willie put the period after the sentence."[25]

Barry tied his godfather in the Giants' home opener at SBC Park on April 12, 2004, with a three-run homer into McCovey Cove. After Barry rounded the bases, Mays emerged from the Giants' dugout with a diamond-encrusted souvenir Olympic torch that he presented to Barry with a fond embrace. It served as a symbol of "passing the torch" to the 39-year-old slugger.[26] After the game, Barry said, "My father was supposed to be the next Willie Mays. I kind of kept the tradition in my family. It feels great."[27]

Barry passed Mays the next day, leaving only Henry Aaron and Babe Ruth ahead of him. Even with Mays in the stands, there wasn't as much ceremony and fanfare around this homer as there was the previous day. Barry admitted that 660 was more special because of his relationship with Mays. He said, "Six-sixty was the one. That's the one that will be on my desk forever. I don't feel I'm ahead of Willie because Willie is my mentor. He always will be. I still feel he's the greatest player of all time. That hasn't changed."[28]

If Barry was bothered by all the negative press from BALCO, he didn't show it on the field. Incredibly, he was able to record the best batting line of his career – .362/.609/.812 – and his seventh MVP Award.

Three years later, 42-year-old Barry finished his career with 762 home runs, the most in baseball history. As late as 2022 he was on the all-time Top 10 list for on-base percentage, slugging average, OPS, and OPS+. One of the most feared hitters in the game, he is the all-time leader in walks and intentional walks. His seven MVP awards are the most in history for one player. These were numbers that certainly should have earned him a plaque in Cooperstown.

Yet, when Barry became eligible for election to the National Baseball Hall of Fame in 2013, the specter of his alleged use of performance enhancing drugs hung over his head. He received only 36.2 percent of the vote, well short of the 75 percent minimum required to be elected. Barry became one of the poster boys of annual campaigns by many baseball writers to refuse votes for players associated, real or perceived, with PEDs. While some of the living Hall of Famers, like Joe Morgan, publicly spoke out against the players' election,[29] Mays became a vocal supporter of Barry. (Bobby Bonds spent 11 years on the Hall of Fame ballot and topped out at 10.6 percent in 1993.)

While not having the same consequence to his career as Barry, Mays had experienced his own banishment of sorts. In 1983 Commissioner Bowie Kuhn prohibited Mays and Mickey Mantle, both then retired, from associating with major-league clubs while they were working for an Atlantic City casino as goodwill ambassadors. Mays was bitter about the situation and later felt it had tarnished his image.[30] In a way, he could relate to Barry's being blocked by Hall of Fame voters.[31]

At the Giants' ceremony to retire Barry's jersey number 25 in August 2018, Mays called for baseball writers to vote his godson into the Hall of Fame.[32] Mays urged, "You go by the numbers, he should be in. When I was on the ballot in '79, twenty-three writers didn't vote for me. You never know. I just think he should have the honor."[33]

Mays was in the minority, though, as most of the baseball writers continued to pass over Bonds on their ballots. When he received 60.7 percent of the vote in 2020, it appeared he might be on the verge of overcoming the PED bias. But in his last year on the ballot, 2022, he finished with only 66 percent.

Bobby never met the expectations of being "the next Mays" and his productive career is largely underappreciated. Mays was the standard to which Barry aspired. Barry wound up rivaling the Hall of Famer as one of the best hitters of all time, although his career remains tainted by the BALCO case.

Willie, Bobby, and Barry share one set of milestone statistics involving their patented combination of speed and power. They are three of only eight players (as of 2022) to hit 300 home runs and steal 300 bases. Bobby and Barry are the only players to hit more than 300 home runs and steal more than 400 bases.

## SOURCES

In addition to the sources cited in the Notes, the author consulted Baseball-Reference.com.

## NOTES

1 Neither Seamheads.com nor Baseball-Reference.com shows any statistics for Mays with Birmingham in the 1949 season. His biography in *Willie Mays, A Biography* says that he was with the team in 1949.

2 Mary Kay Linge, *Willie Mays, A Biography* (Westport, Connecticut: Greenwood Press, 2005), 17.

3 Linge, 19.

4 Jeff Pearlman, *Love Me, Hate Me: Barry Bonds and the Making of an Antihero* (New York: HarperCollins Publishers, 2006), 17.

5 Pearlman, 19.

6 Pearlman, 21.

7 Pearlman, 26.

8 Pearlman, 21.

9 Pearlman, 33.

10 Steven Travers, *Barry Bonds: Baseball's Superman* (Champaign, Illinois: Sports Publishing, 2002), 35.

11 Linge, 149.

12 Ron Fimrite, "Getting It All Together," *Sports Illustrated*, April 8, 1974. https://www.si.com/vault/1974/04/08/628485/getting-it-all-together. Accessed September 12, 2022.

13 Fimrite.

14 Mark Fainaru-Wada and Lance Williams, *Game of Shadows* (New York: Gotham Books, 2006), 25.

15 Fainaru-Wada and Williams, 26.

16 Fainaru-Wada and Williams, 28.

17 Pearlman, 138.

18 Linge, 175.

19 David Bush, "Bonds Will Wear No. 25," *San Francisco Chronicle*, December 11, 1992: E1.

20 Willie Mays and John Shea, *24: Life Stories and Lessons From the Say Hey Kid* (New York: St. Martin's Press, 2020), 275.

21 Guy Curtright, "Emotions Strong for MVP Bonds," *Atlanta Journal-Constitution*, November 19, 2003: 3D.

22 Henry Schulman, "'The New Say Hey Kid': With Mays in Support, Bonds Set to Embark on His Toughest Season," *San Francisco Chronicle*, February 24, 2001: C1.

23 Lance Williams and Mark Fainaru-Wada, "Bonds Got Steroids, Feds Were Told," *San Francisco Chronicle*, March 2, 2004: A5.

24 Mays and Shea, *24, Life Stories*, 285.

25 Mays and Shea.

26 Gwen Knapp, "660: Bonds Ties Mays," *San Francisco Chronicle*, April 13, 2004: A1.

27 Henry Schulman, "Bonds Equals His Godfather When Blast Counts Most," *San Francisco Chronicle*, May 13, 2004: D1.

28 Ray Ratto, "Bonds' HR One-Ups Mays," *San Francisco Chronicle*, May 14, 2004: D1.

29 Joe Posnanski, "Joe Morgan's Letter," Joe Posnanski Blog, November. 21, 2017. https://medium.com/joeblogs/joe-morgans-letter-9e1138815983d. Accessed September 26, 2022.

30 Linge, 173.

31 One of new Commissioner Peter Ueberroth's first actions in March 1985 was the reinstatement of Mantle and Mays.

32 Mark Townsend, "Willie Mays Says Barry Bonds Belongs in Hall of Fame as Giants Retire No. 25," Yahoo Sports, August 11, 2008. https://www.yahoo.com/video/barry-bonds-honored-giants-willie-mays-emotional-jersey-retirement-ceremony-012435543.html. Accessed October 2, 2022.

33 Mays and Shea, 289.

# WILLIE MAYS AND HIS MANAGERS

BY MARK S. STERNMAN

**THE TIES LINKING** superstars and managers follow patterns often beginning as mentee-mentor before changing into relationships of equals, then deference to the player based on his status, and, finally, awkwardness as the star's skills (but not his ego) deteriorate with age. On the one hand, Willie Mays and his managers followed this typical arc; on the other hand, Mays faced challenges as one of the first Black greats in the National League who had to play for a racist. Personal ups and downs notwithstanding, the records of the 11 men who managed the future Hall of Famer in professional baseball show how pronounced an impact Mays had on the teams for which he played.

Piper Davis: 1948 Birmingham Black Barons

- Pre-Mays: n/a
- With Mays: 51-27 (.654)[1]
- Post-Mays: n/a

Mays had the good fortune as a teenager to debut under the friendly but firm Piper Davis in the Negro American League. As Mays recounted 40 years later, "Piper was the most important person in my early baseball years. I learned one thing about him very quickly. He told you something only once, and he expected you to go from there. That's a big reason why I matured so quickly. …"[2]

The lessons Mays picked up from his skipper, who also hit .393 that year for Birmingham, would serve Mays well when he faced pitchers like Don Drysdale and Bob Gibson who thrived on making batters uncomfortable at the plate. After getting hit by Chet Brewer, Mays admitted, "I'm on the ground crying. … Piper comes out, kicks me, and says, 'There ain't no damn crying in this game. … What you do now, you steal second, you steal third.' So I steal second and third, and I score. … Piper comes over to me … and says, 'Now that's the way you play baseball.'"[3]

Mays played just 13 games with the Black Barons in 1948. He stayed with the team in 1949, playing 75 games,[4] but that season in the Negro American League has not been elevated to major-league status.[5]

Mays played another quarter-century but never again played for a Black manager.

Chick Genovese: 1950 Trenton Giants

- Pre-Mays: 72-73 (.497)

- With Mays: 73-65 (.529)
- Post-Mays: 333-387 (.463)

In his final teenage season, Mays played one campaign in the Class-B Interstate League, where he first demonstrated his star potential over the course of 81 games. In a pattern that recurred in his early years, Mays seemed slow to recognize his own skills. Accordingly, Genovese had to instill confidence in his young player, not too difficult a task given that he called Mays "the best-looking young player I've seen in many a day," and added, "I played with Louisville when Duke Snider was at St. Paul and always thought Duke would become a tremendous hitter. Willie doesn't have Duke's power, but he could do everything else better."[6] Genovese "made it his mission to get the young center fielder all the way to the majors. He identified Mays' problem in those first few games – he was pressing, overeager to make a good first impression."[7]

Having raised his batting average from .233 in Birmingham to .353 in Trenton, Mays, with the help of Genovese, clearly gained the confidence he needed to advance one step closer to the National League.

Tommy Heath: 1951 Minneapolis Millers
- Pre-Mays: 335-249 (.574)
- With Mays: 77-75 (.507)
- Post-Mays: 974-1096 (.471)

Amazingly, Mays had an even greater jump in batting average when he advanced to Minneapolis, where he hit an astounding .477 with 30 RBIs in 35 games. Heath "knew he would not have Mays for long. One morning, Heath called him into his office and said, 'Willie, we're taking you ... to Minneapolis, but I ... have the feeling that you're not going to spend the whole summer with us. I think it's only a matter of time before the Giants call you up."[8]

Despite his prowess, Mays did not want to leave Heath and the Millers to go to New York, but he reluctantly went.

Leo Durocher: 1951-1955 New York Giants
- Pre-Mays: 955-771 (.566)
- With Mays: 350-233 (.600)
- Post-Mays: 703-705 (.499)[9]

Mays had another model player-manager relationship with Durocher, who could straight-talk his center fielder while simultaneously supporting him. The Giants promoted Mays from the minor leagues on May 25, 1951, and batted him third in the order even after he went hitless in his first 12 at-bats before homering off Warren Spahn. While Durocher later moved Mays throughout the lineup over the course of the famed 1951 campaign, the manager always kept faith with his prized rookie.

As recounted by Paul Dickson in his Durocher biography, "Mays said he just couldn't hit big league pitching. Durocher replied, 'As long as I'm the manager of the Giants, you are my center fielder. ... You are the best center fielder I've ever looked at.' Then he told Mays to hitch up his pants to give himself a more favorable strike zone."[10]

Mays and Durocher went to two World Series in their five years together. As Mays became one of the best players in the game, Durocher understandably treated him differently from the other Giants. "'Leo had all these friends in the clothes and jewelry business,' [fellow New York outfielder

*Whitey Lockman and Willie Mays made Leo Durocher a happy man. Courtesy National Baseball Hall of Fame.*

Monte] Irvin said, 'and Willie's locker was just full of stuff Leo got from them – shirts, ties, watches. ... Leo did all these things for Willie and forgot about the rest of us.'"[11]

Bill Rigney: 1956-1957 New York Giants and 1958-1960 San Francisco Giants

- Pre-Mays: n/a
- With Mays: 332-342 (.493)
- Post-Mays: 907-979 (.481)

Starting with Rigney, Mays never again played for a Giants skipper with prior major-league managerial experience. The front office seemed to think novices could guide a team led by a player as great as Mays. Perhaps as a result, Mays went to only one more World Series with the Giants in his many remaining years with the team.

Maybe Mays should have no longer needed a boost from his manager and teammate during the 1951 and 1952 seasons, but he "suffered badly from the departure of [Durocher]. In the words of one long-time Giant, 'Rigney was out to prove that Willie was just one of twenty-five men. You could see Willie looking ... for a couple of kind words, but Rig never ... had a smile for him.'"[12]

Of all the managers who had Mays for at least one full season, only Rigney posted a losing record. Rigney strangely failed to appreciate one of the strongest aspects of the game of the slugger and his best player (Mays led the Giants in WAR every season from 1954 to 1965): "It is Rigney's belief that if Mays will forget about home runs and consistently punch the outside pitch into right field, he can hit .380," according to sportswriter Ed Linn.[13]

Tom Sheehan: 1960 San Francisco Giants

- Pre-Mays: n/a
- With Mays: 46-50 (.479)
- Post-Mays: n/a

Mays experienced his first in-season managerial change in 1960 when the senior citizen Sheehan had his first and only managerial job. Sheehan turned an underachieving winning team into a losing one, but initially understood his good fortune in getting the surprising opportunity to manage Mays.

*Manager Yogi Berra and Willie Mays sometimes clashed during Mays' time with the Mets. SABR/The Rucker Archive.*

Under Sheehan, Mays "went on a 19-game tear during which he hit .494. ... [H]e made a leaping catch ... to rob Gil Hodges of a homer, and the normally hostile Coliseum fans ... burst into cheers. 'He's the greatest centerfielder I ever saw,' [said] Sheehan, 'and I saw [Tris] Speaker and [Joe] DiMaggio. I don't know how they could be better.'"[14]

Sheehan's superlatives notwithstanding, the two clashed near the end of the manager's brief tenure. In the waning weeks of the 1960 season, Mays twice sought leave to take care of personal matters in New York. Sheehan gave him permission the first time, but not the second, threatening him with a fine if he did not show up for a game in Philadelphia. Mays, maybe with his pocketbook in mind, relented.[15]

Alvin Dark: 1961-1964 San Francisco Giants

- Pre-Mays: n/a
- With Mays: 366-277 (.569)
- Post-Mays: 628-677 (.481)

Dark had the best regular-season winning percentage of all the Giants managers who had Willie

*"If somebody came up and hit .450, stole 100 bases, and performed a miracle in the field every day, I'd still look you right in the eye and tell you Willie was better." — Leo Durocher. SABR/The Rucker Archive.*

*Willie Mays worried that he could not hit big-league pitching. Leo Durocher told his young ballplayer not to worry. Courtesy National Baseball Hall of Fame.*

on the team, but Dark's bigotry rightly damaged his reputation.

Dark, another former teammate of Mays, certainly appreciated his superstar and "often said Mays was the greatest player he had ever seen."[16] Early in the 1964 season, Dark appointed Mays captain, saying, "Mays is a leader, without even opening his mouth."[17]

This praise notwithstanding, Dark singled out Black players for criticism, comments that irreparably harmed his legacy.[18]

Mays did not share this perspective. After Dark died, Mays observed, "It's a sad day for me with all the help he gave me. He was such a mentor to me."[19]

Herman Franks: 1965-1968 San Francisco Giants

- Pre-Mays: n/a
- With Mays: 367-280 (.567)
- Post-Mays: 238-241 (.497)

Even before he managed his first game, Franks understood where he stood vis-à-vis his star player: "When you've got Mays on your side, you're starting out ahead. No team can win with just one man, but Willie is a winning force. He gives the team everything he's got. Managers don't win pennants; it's the horses."[20]

Mays appreciated how Franks asked for his input in contrast to "when [Dark] first named me captain, it was pretty much an empty honor outside of taking lineup cards to the plate before each game. Now it's different. [Franks] talks to me about many subjects involving the players."[21]

In a sign of their strong relationship, Mays stayed in touch with Franks even after the latter had lost his managerial position. As quoted in the *New York Daily News*, Franks said, "Willie and I talked about his playing out the string in New York. So, we have done some thinking about it together."[22]

Clyde King: 1969-1970 San Francisco Giants

- Pre-Mays: n/a
- With Mays: 109-95 (.534)
- Post-Mays: 125-134 (.483)

Mays appreciated how Franks "gave me more rest ... than any manager I've ever had. That's because the rest spells came at the right time. My other managers took me out when they thought I was tired. The trouble with this is that they didn't really know. I'm the only one who knows that."[23] Mays lacked that same rapport with Franks' successor, Clyde King.

Before a game in June of King's first year at the helm, he noticed that Willie was not on the bench to bring the lineup card to home plate, and angrily scratched Mays' name from it. ... Mays arrived in the dugout seconds later, and ... was furious."[24]

King learned that although he may have had the top title, he did not have the most power and apologized for the snafu: "Hereafter, I will check with Mays daily. ... I made it clear to him that I won't push him when he feels tired and unable to play." Mays' comment: "It wasn't much of an argument," commented Willie, who said he was a "lover" and not a "fighter" and that the manager's version was accurate.[25]

Charlie Fox: 1970-1972 San Francisco Giants

- Pre-Mays: n/a
- With Mays: 165-141 (.539)
- Post-Mays: 212-230 (.480)

Remarkably, Mays played under his sixth consecutive rookie manager when Fox replaced King during the 1970 campaign. Fox treated the veteran Mays with deference. After he "delegated coaching of the outfield to Mays," Bobby Bonds and Ken Henderson played better in the field. "Willie and I have a great rapport going," Fox said. "I ... let him play a week or 10 days, and then give him a day or two off."[26]

Yogi Berra: 1972-1973 New York Mets

- Pre-Mays: 113-70 (.617)
- With Mays: 152-146 (.510)
- Post-Mays: 220-229 (.490)

The deference days did not carry over when Mays returned to New York to play for the Mets in May 1972. The pairing of Mays and Yogi Berra, which in the 1950s or early 1960s would have worked out well for both men, worked out for neither in the early 1970s. As we have seen from his last San Francisco experience, "With the Giants, Mays had been allowed the privilege often given to longtime aging superstars to dictate when he would play. ... But Yogi had been criticized in 1964 for losing control of his Yankee ball club, and he adamantly refused to let Mays dictate anything."[27]

Mays "was a huge pain in the ass [to Berra]. By the final month of the [1972] season, with the Mets playing well but out of the pennant race, Mays was openly criticizing Yogi for playing him too much – a strange complaint, as Mays batted just 195 times during the season"[28] in 69 games.

As Berra said before the start of the 1973 season, "I appreciate that Willie isn't 18 years old –he's 42. But you can't have two sets of rules."[29]

The 1973 Mets amazingly made the World Series, but more despite the aged Mays than because of him, a sharp contrast to the starring role Mays had played for so long with the Giants.

Totals:

- With Mays: 2088-1731 (.547)
- Without Mays: 5815-5991 (.493)

The 11 men managed 11,806 games for teams that did not have Mays on the roster; in those contests, they lost 176 games more than they won. With Mays on the team, however, the managers had a great deal more success, finishing 357 games over .500. Mays overcame the challenges of playing for so many average managers and led his teams to steady on-field success.

## NOTES

1 Neither Baseball Reference nor Seamheads has game-by-game results for the teams Mays played for before joining the Giants, and the "With Mays" records for Birmingham, Trenton, and Minneapolis all reflect the full 1948, 1950, and 1951 seasons, respectively, rather than for the particular games Mays did and did not play in for those teams.

2 Willie Mays with Lou Sahadi, *Say Hey: The Autobiography of Willie Mays* (New York: Simon & Schuster, 1988), 40.

3 Willie Mays and John Shea, *24: Life Stories and Lessons from the Say Hey Kid* (New York: St. Martin's Press, 2020), 33-34.

4 John Saccoman, "Willie Mays," sabr.org/bioproj/person/Willie-Mays/ (accessed October 28, 2022).

5 "MLB officially designates the Negro Leagues as 'Major League,'" https://www.mlb.com/press-release/press-release-

mlb-officially-designates-the-negro-leagues-as-major-league (accessed November 1, 2022).

6 Joe King, "Willie Changes Giants' Gloom Into Grins," *The Sporting News*, February 24, 1954: 5.

7 Mary Kay Linge, *Willie Mays: A Biography* (Westport, Connecticut: Greenwood Press, 2005), 24.

8 James S. Hirsch, *Willie Mays: The Life, the Legend* (New York: Scribner, 2010), 73.

9 Mays was in the U.S. Army in 1953 and did not play for the Giants that season, but Durocher's post-Mays record includes the 1953 New York season.

10 Paul Dickson, *Leo Durocher: Baseball's Prodigal Son* (New York: Bloomsbury USA, 2017), 206.

11 Bill Madden, *1954: The Year Willie Mays and the First Generation of Black Superstars Changed Major League Baseball Forever* (Boston: Da Capo Press, 2014), 47.

12 Ed Linn, "The Woes of Willie Mays," *Saturday Evening Post*, April 13, 1957: 105.

13 Linn, 106.

14 Robert H. Boyle, "The Sad, Bad Giants," *Sports Illustrated*, July 18, 1960: 15.

15 Bob Stevens, "Mays Plays After Threat of Big Fine," *The Sporting News*, September 21, 1960: 13.

16 Matt Schudel, "Alvin Dark, Baseball Player and Manager Who Led Oakland A's to 1974 Title, Dies at 92," *Washington Post*, November 13, 2014.

17 Jack McDonald, "Herbel Quits Tacoma Shuttle to Clang Giant Victory Bell," *The Sporting News*, June 6, 1964: 5.

18 Leonard Koppett, "The Dark Controversy," *New York Times*, August 4, 1964: 23.

19 John Shea, "Alvin Dark, Giants, A's World Series Manager, Dies at 92," *San Francisco Chronicle*, November 14, 2014, www.sfgate.com/news/article/Alvin-Dark-All-Star-shortstop-and-Giants-A-s-5891185.php (accessed October 28, 2022).

20 "'Willie Gives Pilot Big Edge at Very Start,' Says Franks," *The Sporting News*, January 30, 1965: 5.

21 James Enright, "Willie Fights 'Delayed Fatigue' by Passing Up Swatting Drills," *The Sporting News*, October 9, 1965: 34.

22 David Krell, "'It's Like Coming Back to Paradise': Willie Mays and the Mets," Spring 2022 *Baseball Research Journal*, quoting "With Friend Like Franks, Mays Needn't Worry," *New York Daily News*, May 14, 1972: 123.

23 Jack McDonald, "Golf Bug Bites Mays – 18 Holes Per Day," *The Sporting News*, January 8, 1966: 4.

24 Mark Mulvoy, "The Pursuit of Willie and Clyde," *Sports Illustrated*, September 15, 1969.

25 United Press International, "Mays Close to Punching In for Work," *New York Times*, June 26, 1969: 48.

26 Bill Becker, "Giants Aim to Go All the Way in Marking 'Year of the Fox,'" *New York Times*, May 30, 1971: S2.

27 Peter Golenbock, *Amazin'* (New York: St. Martin's Press, 2002), 293.

28 Allen Barra, *Yogi Berra: Eternal Yankee* (New York: W.W. Norton & Company, 2009), 331-332.

29 Joseph Durso, "Mays Has His Way, and Yogi Has His Way" *New York Times*, March 2, 1973: 25.

# WILLIE AND THE GIANTS: WHY THE GREATEST PLAYER WON ONLY THREE PENNANTS

BY DAVID KAISER

FROM 1954 THROUGH 1966, Willie Mays dominated the National League. While he won the MVP Award only twice, in 1954 and 1965, he led it in Wins Above Average (whose derivation I shall explain below) nine times, in 1954-58, 1962, and 1964-66, and finished among the leaders in all the other years in that span. From 1962 through 1966, his teammates included four other Hall of Famers: Orlando Cepeda, Willie McCovey, Juan Marichal, and Gaylord Perry. Yet despite this extraordinary constellation of talent, the Giants won only two pennants, in 1954 and 1962. Essentially, they failed to take advantage of Willie and their other extraordinary assets because they balanced their superstars with a long list of dreadful players, dragging down the team's won-lost record and losing two very close races to Dodgers teams whose top talent was far below theirs.

To show how this happened, I shall use the methodology I developed and explained at length in my book *Baseball Greatness*.[1] Although Wins Above Replacement (WAR) has generally become the statistic of choice among sabermetricians, I used Wins Above Average (WAA) for two reasons. First, while the value of a replacement player is inevitably something of a guess, we can measure the value of an average player very accurately, making WAA a much more precise measurement. Second, WAA makes it much easier to understand the value of any individual player to his team. A team of perfectly average players could be expected to win 77 games before expansion, or 81 games after it. A post-expansion team of average players and Willie Mays in one of his greatest seasons, in which he earned 8 WAA, could be expected to win 89 games, and another superstar (defined as 4 WAA or more per season) would get that team within pennant-winning range. Unfortunately, a player with -3 WAA would negate a substantial portion of Mays' value – and we shall find that the Giants' lineup in many critical years included far too many such people. That, ultimately, is why he played in only three World Series, winning just one.

My calculations of WAA for position players like Mays use raw offensive data from baseball-reference.com, but they differ from that publication in two ways. First, I use Michael Humphreys's fielding data, based on his Defensive Regression Analysis (DRA), in place of the methods used by baseball-reference because I am convinced that DRA is by far the most accurate historical fielding measurement.[2] Second, for reasons explained in *Baseball Greatness,* I do not adjust players' value up or down based upon the defensive position they played, which baseball-reference.com does for both WAR and WAA.

The Giants won their first pennant with Willie in his rookie year, 1951, and that team was an excellent example of a balanced pennant winner. Monte Irvin, with 6.1 WAA, was their only superstar, but Willie and Bobby Thomson added 2.9 WAA each, Alvin Dark and Eddie Stanky combined for an additional 4.8 WAA, and no Giants regular was below average. Altogether their lineup earned +13 WAA and their pitching staff +2, keeping them close enough to a Dodgers team with a superior lineup and slightly weaker pitching to tie them at 96 wins and win the three-game playoff. After Mays missed nearly all of 1952 and 1953 while in the US Army, the Giants won the pennant in 1954 thanks largely to his greatest season, in which great hitting and fantastic fielding earned him an extraordinary total of 9 WAA. Only two of his teammates in the lineup, Monte Irvin and Hank Thompson, were above average, and the whole lineup without Mays was dead average. Giants pitching was outstanding, earning 11 WAA, and the Giants won 97 games. Then, a long drought began.

In 1955 Mays hit 51 home runs and finished the season with 7.1 WAA, but Hank Thompson was the only other above-average player in the lineup and Don Mueller, Alvin Dark, and Davey Williams had terrible seasons. The pitching staff also slumped badly and the Giants won just 80 games. In 1956 Mays led the league for the third consecutive year with 5.8 WAA, but rookie first baseman Bill White was the only other above-average player in the lineup. Dreadful performances by the aging Mueller and Dusty Rhodes and others left the lineup as a whole -13 WAA and the team went 67-87. Mays improved to 6.6 WAA in 1957 but White went into the Army and the Giants' record improved by only two games in their last year in New York. Things improved in San Francisco in 1958 when the Giants added Orlando Cepeda (2.1 WAA) and above-average outfielders Leon Wagner and Felipe Alou, but Mays' remarkable 8.2 WAA – his second-best season to date – was three wins better than that of the team as a whole, which finished 80-74. In 1959 Mays, Cepeda, and rookie sensation Willie McCovey combined for 11.6 WAA, but the rest of the lineup was -2.6 WAA and the pitching barely above average, and the Giants won just 83 games. Mays, Cepeda, and McCovey remained the only above-average players in the lineup in 1960 with 10.2 WAA between them, while the pitching staff declined to below average and the team won 79 games. The National League had now reached a generally mediocre level. The Giants actually had the best run differential in the league in 1961 and projected to win 91 games, but they missed that projection by four wins while the Reds exceeded their projected record by 10 wins and took the pennant.

The 1962 Giants finally found the right formula and emerged as the strongest team Willie Mays ever played on, winning 101 regular-season games and again defeating the Dodgers in a three-game playoff. Mays was the team's only superstar, with a tremendous 7.3 WAA – his highest total since 1957 – but outfielder Felipe Alou (2.8 WAA), third baseman Jim Davenport (2.5), McCovey (1.9), and Cepeda (1.8) added 9 WAA between them, and the only below-average player in the lineup was shortstop Jose Pagan (-2.6 WAA.) A fine pitching staff added 6.1 WAA to the lineup's 12.4. The 1963 team, however, established the disastrous pattern of the next four years. They were one of only two National League teams since 1901 to include four superstar players with 4 WAA or more: Mays (7 WAA), Cepeda (4.4), McCovey (4.1), and pitcher Juan Marichal (5.2).[3] The rest of the Giants' pitchers were slightly above average, but the rest of the lineup included five infielders totaling -8.9 WAA. The lineup as a whole earned just 2 WAA, despite three superstars' total of 15.5. The team won just 88 games and finished third. In 1964 McCovey had a terrible season, falling below average, but Mays (a great 8.1 WAA) and Cepeda (2.5) were joined by a new find, third baseman Jim Ray Hart (an excellent 3.2 WAA.) Felipe Alou, however, had been traded, the infield was as bad as ever, and the whole line up earned -3.8 WAA. The pitching, led by Marichal, was outstanding, with 12.4 WAA, but the team finished fourth with 90 wins.

The Giants in 1965 and 1966 lost very close pennant races to the Los Angeles Dodgers on the last weekend of the season – and the Dodgers provided a fascinating contrast to the chronically unbalanced Giants. The Dodgers (because of Sandy Koufax and Don Drysdale) had a reputedly great pitching staff while the Giants, with Mays and McCovey, were known for their power. Sandy Koufax, however, was the only great pitcher on the Dodgers in that era, while the rest of the staff benefited from pitcher-friendly Dodger Stadium.[4] The Giants staff, led by Marichal, was actually superior in 1965, earning 15.8 WAA to the Dodgers' 6.[5] And as for their lineups, while the Giants' three best players – Mays (8.5 WAA thanks in part to 52 home runs), McCovey (3.1), and Hart (2.1) – earned 13.7 WAA among them, the Dodgers' best three, shortstop Maury Wills (2.5), second baseman Jim Lefebvre (2.4), and left fielder Lou Johnson (1.6), totaled 6.5. Catcher John Roseboro (-1.9 WAA) was, however, the only below-average player in the Dodgers lineup, while the Giants lineup included Matty Alou (-2.2), Davenport (-2.5), Dick Schofield (-2.6), and Hal Lanier (-3.7). Overall, the Giants lineup earned -5.8 WAA despite Mays, McCovey, and Hart, while the Dodgers lineup earned 4.8. LA won the World Series that year against the Minnesota Twins. In 1966 Mays (who led the National League for the last time with 7.7 WAA), McCovey (4.8), and Hart (3.7) were the only above-average players in the Giants lineup, whose outfield now featured Jesus Alou (-2.8), Ollie Brown (-1.8), and Cap Peterson (-1.4), along with the usual dreadful infielders. Lefebvre and first baseman Wes Parker led the Dodgers lineup with 3.4 and 3.2 WAA, and the lineup as a whole finished with 4 WAA to the Giants' 2. The Dodgers pitching staff also improved to 10.5 WAA while the Giants' declined to just 3.1. The Giants were very lucky to finish just two games behind.

The two Willies performed at a superstar level in 1967-8, but the rest of the team remained too weak to challenge the St. Louis Cardinals in those years. Mays finally fell below the superstar level in 1969, but he regained that level for the last time at age 40 in 1971 with 4.8 WAA, when the Giants won the NL Western Division championship with just 90 wins. They lost the LCS in four games to the Pirates.

Led by their owner, Horace Stoneham, the Giants seemed to believe that just about anyone could fill in the rest of the lineup as long as they had a few big stars. Writing *Baseball Greatness*, I discovered that other clubs have shown the unfortunate tendency to believe that with two great players in the lineup, they need not worry too much about other positions. The New York Giants in the late 1920s and early 1930s had three of the greatest players in the National League, Mel Ott, Bill Terry, and Carl Hubbell, yet won only one pennant because of a terrible supporting cast. Between 2008 and 2013, I found three AL Eastern Division rivals – the Yankees, Red Sox, and Rays – that competed on pretty equal terms, with the Yankees averaging 94 wins, the Rays 92, and the Red Sox 89. During that period, Red Sox players posted 13 superstar seasons, the Yankees six, and the Rays only four. The Rays, however, almost never had a below-average player in their lineup, while the two richer clubs had many. There's no substitute for having Willie Mays or his contemporary counterpart Mike Trout on your club, but it's a lot easier to improve your club by finding an average player to replace a man earning -3 WAA a year than it is to find the new Willie Mays. Sadly, the Giants failed that test for much of his career.

## NOTES

1 David Kaiser, *Baseball Greatness: Top Players and Teams According to Wins Above Average, 1901-2017* (Jefferson, North Carolina: McFarland, 2018), esp. pp. 1-22.

2 See Michael Humphreys, *Wizardry: Baseball's All-Time Greatest Fielders Revealed* (New York: Oxford University Press, 2011).

3 The other such National League team was the 1972 Reds, with Johnny Bench, Pete Rose, Joe Morgan, and Tony Perez. Five American League teams have accomplished this feat.

4 Don Drysdale's great seasons were behind him by 1965. He was average in 1965-66 and only 1-2 WAA above average in 1967-68.

5 This was partly because Dodgers fielding was very good, while Giants fielding was dreadful.

# THAT ONE TIME WHEN WILLIE MAYS WASN'T PERFECT

By Rob Neyer

**IF WE DIDN'T** have proof, we probably wouldn't believe it. If there hadn't been hundreds of magazines published in the 1960s about baseball, a large percentage of them containing articles and essays about Willie Mays and his San Francisco Giants, we probably wouldn't believe that during the 1960s, there was a cottage industry seemingly devoted to blaming Willie Mays, arguably the greatest player ever, for the Giants' failure to reach more than one World Series during Mays' many years in San Francisco.

Because they had Willie Mays – along with stars like Orlando Cepeda, Willie McCovey, and Juan Marichal – the 1960s Giants were simply expected to win, or at least be tremendously competitive, every single year. Which they hadn't been, early on. In their first three seasons in San Francisco, the Giants finished third, third, and (in 1960) fifth.

In 1961 Fawcett Publications published (at least) two preseason magazines, and *both* included stories (by different writers) headlined "What's Wrong With the Giants?" Despite a new manager (Alvin Dark), the '61 Giants finished third again, and afterward another Fawcett magazine included the story "The Truth About the Giant Troublemakers" (among them Willie Mays, but hardly anyone of note escaped suspicion).[1]

*What's wrong with the Giants?*

As it turned out, nothing at all. At least not in 1962, when the Giants won 103 regular-season games (including two in a pennant playoff against the Dodgers) and missed winning the World Series by just a few inches (which broke Charlie Brown's heart, among others).

They never returned to the World Series, though. Every fall for the rest of the decade, it was instead the Dodgers or the Cardinals or (just that once) the Mets. The Giants dropped back to third place in '63 and fourth in '64 (despite solid records that granted were inflated by expansion), then finished second in five straight seasons (1965-1969). They never came close to a losing record. In those seven post-Series years, the Giants won more regular-season games than any other National League team: Giants 635, Cardinals 634 (and Dodgers just 605, in case you're wondering).

So were there "What's wrong with the Cardinals?" stories when St. Louis didn't win? No, not really. There were a few Dodgers stories like that in the late

'60s when they suffered two straight losing seasons. But even then, the stories were about the *Dodgers* ... and not Don Drysdale or Walter Alston or Willie Davis. Whom I mention because in the wake of 1963's third-place finish, a significant percentage of that early-'60s "What's wrong" energy turned into "What's Wrong with Willie Mays" energy.

Which in retrospect seems ... crazy, right? Over the seven seasons from 1963 through 1969, Mays ranked third in the National League in home runs, fourth in runs scored, fifth in RBIs, and – not that we knew this until recently – first in Wins Above Replacement. In that latter category, Mays's advantage is slight over Henry Aaron, Ron Santo, and Roberto Clemente. But you can at least make a reasonable argument that Mays was, during that stretch, the most valuable player in the National League despite being the oldest of those players by a fair piece. (He had three years on Aaron, more on the others.)

In 1964 the June issue of *Sport World* magazine included a Paul Donley-penned story, "Is Willie really worth $105,000?"[2]

That season he wound up leading the National League with 47 home runs, earned his eighth straight Gold Glove, and finished sixth in MVP balloting. But Mays *did* struggle during the summer, after a tremendously hot start, and finished with a .296 batting average, which set off alarm bells (note to younger readers: Baseball writers used to be utterly obsessed with batting averages, and specifically the value and meaning of .300-plus batting averages).

The next year, he hit a career-high 52 homers and won his second Most Valuable Player Award (and another Gold Glove). The Giants finished second.

Skipping ahead a few years, for just a moment ... In 1971, an issue of *Sport Scene* magazine included an article, "Willie Mays Is Hurting the Giants!"[3]

How exactly was he doing this? "Usually no man wins or loses a pennant by himself," the story read, "but an overreliance on Mays may very well have cost the Giants one or more flags."[4]

Let's assume for the moment that Willie Mays was the greatest player of the 1960s (practically inarguable), if not the greatest player ever (arguable, with Babe Ruth and Mays' godson Barry Bonds having vastly different arguments). Why, year after year, would the writers of the time look toward *him* for explanations of the Giants' supposed failures?

Bill James observed, a few decades ago and not really so long after Mays' career ended, that the media often focuses on a team's *best* player to explain its failures. He wasn't writing specifically about Willie Mays and I don't know if James read those magazines in the 1960s. But I doubt if you could find a better exemplar of Bill's theory.

Mays was a target for the writers mostly because he was the *biggest, easiest* target. He was the Giants' best player, obviously, and also their longest-serving; he was there before Marichal and McCovey showed up, and he was there well after Cepeda left. Mays

*Some sportswriters in the 1960s worried that Willie Mays was actually hurting the Giants. One magazine headline asked, "Is Willie really worth $105,000?" SABR/The Rucker Archive.*

played (in San Francisco) for managers Bill Rigney, Tom Sheehan, Alvin Dark, Herman Franks, Clyde King, and Charlie Fox.

In fairness to the writers (and editors), Mays *was* more than just his tremendous statistics. During the 1964 season, manager Alvin Dark named Mays the first Black team captain in American League or National League history, and Mays would later write about taking charge of positioning not only the outfielders who flanked him, but also the *infielders*.[5]

It's not clear that Mays was emotionally suited to that role, though; it seems he already had more than enough on his mind.

In 1964, the *San Francisco Chronicle*'s Bob Stevens wrote of Mays (in yet another preseason magazine): "Willie plays the game too hard to last fantastically long. He never relaxes. On defense he literally plays three fields; on offense he hits with the best of them, better than most; on the bases he runs with more electrifying derring-do than any of them and he directs traffic, too. And he has collapsed twice from sheer exhaustion, once in '62 and once in '63."[6]

It was probably more than twice. In both 1957 and '58, Mays spent two or three days in the hospital. There were references to viruses, exhaustion, various other maladies, but Mays might have best explained his various hospitalizations, usually (but not always) in the middle of seasons. There were hospital stints in later seasons, too.

In 1958 he told reporters, "I need help like anybody else. I try not to worry too much, but I'm human too."[7]

In 1959 Mays was quoted in *Sport* magazine: "When I'm in a slump, people ask me so many questions that I go into the hospital and have nobody bothering me. If I could get the same privacy somewhere else, just a complete rest, I wouldn't go to the hospital."[8]

In 1967 he told *Sports Illustrated*, "Some guys can go 0 for 4 the way I have and lose the way the Giants have and then go home and sleep. Not me. I worry. They pay me to win and when I don't win, I worry and don't sleep."[9]

Oh, those famous (at the time) slumps. In a 1962 issue of *Inside Sports, featuring Mickey Mantle's Baseball Magazine*, Ed Stacy wrote, "For all his abundant talents, the 'Say Hey Kid' himself has suffered, from time to time, the agonies of a batting slump. Warren Spahn of the Braves explained this once by saying, 'Willie, despite his greatness, makes more mistakes at bat than any good hitter in baseball.'"[10]

Sounds like a weakness that Spahn, among the greatest pitchers of the era, could have taken good advantage of, no?

In fact, Mays faced Hall of Famers Spahn and Don Drysdale far more times than anyone else; he batted .305/.368/.587 against Spahn, and .330/.374/.604 against Drysdale. In 24 All-Star Games over the course of 20 years, Mays batted .307/.366/.533 against the best pitchers American League managers could throw at him.

The notion that Mays was particularly slump-prone showed up again and again, though; the 1963 *True's Baseball Yearbook* – yet another Fawcett publication – mentioned in passing "his periodic hitting slumps," and this came up again and again in contemporary stories about Mays.[11] Of course nobody actually *checked* to see if Mays was any streakier than other superstars who played nearly every game. But if he *was* streaky, his insistence on playing through a multitude of minor injuries might well have led to the occasional slump, which (since it was *Willie Mays*) everyone noticed. And asked him about.

He never really slumped in 1962, but he did collapse in September and spent a few days in a Cincinnati hospital. "His sudden collapse late in the season," *True's Baseball Yearbook* wrote, "was attributed by doctors to Willie's turbulent personal emotional life. He had recently gone through a divorce from his wife, Margheurite, and the strain of keeping his private tensions locked up inside while he carried the pressures of being a super-ballplayer simply was too much for him, or any human being, to bear."[12]

After the Giants finished fourth in 1964 – a season in which Alvin Dark created an ethnically charged situation that ultimately led to his firing – *Dell Sports* magazine wrote of Dark's replacement,

> Herman Franks has inherited the massive headache. He is a manager in the Durocher tradition: bold, aggressive, fearless, and talkative. He also has one other Durocher characteristic, which could serve him better than all others in this particular situation: he knows how to blow smoke up Willie Mays' nostrils.
>
> Al Dark couldn't do that, and if he could, he wouldn't. Al Dark figured Willie Mays was a great ballplayer without having to be told it every day, so Al Dark didn't tell it to Willie Mays every day. To Willie Mays, this was a clear indication that Alvin Dark didn't like him, so Willie Mays batted less than .300 for the first time in eight years, and there were days, during the pennant drive, that Willie Mays was too tired to play at all.
>
> Willie Mays is a great ballplayer, and if he requires a daily confidence-builder, he can paste this on his wall and read it daily:
>
> **WILLIE MAYS, YOU ARE GREAT**
>
> Still, Herman Franks has a plan to work with Willie. "I will give him occasional rests during the middle part of the season," says the new manager, "so he won't get in the state he was in during September of this past season."
>
> It must go a bit beyond that. Franks, or someone, just convince Mays that when a man reaches 34, which Willie does in May, certain muscles and glands require more care and more rest.
>
> "You cannot dance all day," observed a critical Giant teammate, "and play ball at night."[13]

Read that once or twice extra, and you might guess that entire observation is one long euphemism. To which we might respond, good luck with that, buddy.

A few months later, the cover of *Official Sports Magazine (Baseball '65)* included a banner across the top: SPECIAL – HOW WILLIE HAS FAILED THE GIANTS. Inside, writer John Bergen identified *six* "major raps" against, you know, the greatest baseball player on the planet at that moment: "1) His withdrawal from teammates; 2) His unorthodox relationship with his managers; 3) His sensitivity to criticism; 4) His strained relationships with the press; 5) His annual exhaustion; 6) His curious brand of leadership." Next come approximately 3,000 words explicating all these deficiencies, whether perceived or real.[14]

Also in the middle of the 1965 season, the first (and only?) issue of *Baseball in Action* magazine ranked Mays as the National League's top center fielder, naturally. But every player in the positional rankings did get assigned one weakness. Mays'? "Puts forth such a total effort that he runs risk of physical exhaustion during course of a season."[15]

It wasn't that all these magazines, which presumably inflated claims and arguments in the interest of selling more magazines, were always (or usually) *right*. Earlier in '65, one of the preview magazines opined, in somewhat blaring font size, that the Phillies "can't lose, now that Belinsky's here."[16] But they did reflect, at least to some degree, the opinions of the men who wrote them, and we must assume they helped form popular opinion of baseball's teams and players. And all the above is just a sampling. Other examples from the era:

*Willie Mays is Headed for Disaster* (1962)
*How Trouble Has Changed Mays and Mantle* (1963)
*What's Left for Willie Mays?* (1964)
*How Sick Is Willie Mays? A Penetrating Analysis* (1964)
*The Brass Has Put Too Much Pressure on Mays* (1966)
*They're Asking the Impossible of Willie* (1966)

Again, just a sample! (I've got a whole bunch of those 1960s magazines, but hardly all of them.)

You've heard the old joke about the job interview? Interviewer asks that ridiculous question – "What's your biggest weakness?" – and instead of answering honestly – "I get raging drunk every night, I always wind up hating my boss within two weeks," whatever – you say something like "I guess I just care too much about doing a good job."

If Willie Mays had a weakness, it might have been that he cared just a little too much. "Filled with nervous energy," biographer James Hirsch wrote, "Mays seemed incapable of relaxing in between the white lines."[17] If he'd cared just a little less, if he'd been able to relax some, he might have been a little healthier, a little happier. If he were playing today, he'd get a day off every few weeks; he'd have someone to talk to about his worries and his troubles.

But instead he played more often than he should have, and he kept things bottled up. Still, for a lotta years nobody played better, and the San Francisco Giants were exceptionally fortunate to have him. Second place, and magazine writers, be damned.

## NOTES

1 Bruce Lee, "The Truth About the Giant Troublemakers," *Official Baseball Annual*, 1962.

2 Paul Denley, "Is Willie Really Worth $105,000?," *Sport World*, June 1964.

3 James S. Hirsch, *Willie Mays: The Life, the Legend* (New York: Scribner Books, 2010), 498-499.

4 Hirsch, 498-499.

5 Willie Mays and Lou Sahadi, *Say Hey: The Autobiography of Willie Mays* (New York: Simon & Schuster, 1988), 158-159.

6 Bob Stevens, "National League All Stars," *Sports All Stars 1964 Baseball*, 1964.

7 "Big Man of the Giants," *Baseball's Best*, 1960.

8 Dick Young, "What About Those Willie Mays Rumors?," *Sport*, May 1959.

9 Mark Mulvoy, "Say Hey No More," *Sports Illustrated*, August 7, 1967.

10 Ed Stacy, "The Stars Tell How They Break 'The Slump Barrier,'" *Inside Sports, Featuring Mickey Mantle's Baseball Magazine*, June 1962.

11 "8 of the Best: A Color Portrait Gallery," *True's Baseball Yearbook*, 1963.

12 "8 of the Best: A Color Portrait Gallery."

13 Dick Young, "Dick Young's National League Outlook for 1965," *Dell Sports*, March 1965.

14 John Bergen, "How Willie Mays Has Failed the Giants," *Official Sports Magazine (Baseball '65)*, October 1965.

15 Joe Reichler, "The Best in the Business," *Baseball in Action*, July 1965.

16 *Official Sports Magazine (Baseball '65)*, June 1965.

17 Hirsch, 357.

# THE UNLIKELY CELEBRITY: THE "SAY HEY KID" IN SONG AND ON SCREEN

BY BOB LEMOINE

JAMES S. HIRSCH, a biographer of Willie Mays, wrote that even before his Rookie of the Year Award, his MVPs, batting title, numerous Gold Glove Awards, All-Star Game appearances, his 660 home runs, and his amazing play called simply "The Catch," Willie Mays was already a star. "By the time he retired," Hirsch wrote, "he was an American icon whose athletic brilliance and stylistic bravado contributed to the assimilation of blacks during the turbulent civil rights era, a distinctive figure of ambition, sacrifice, and triumph who became a lasting cultural touchstone for a nation in search of heroes. Mays represented the quintessential American dream."[1]

Many aspects of Mays, the baseball and American legend, can be and have been explored over his long lifetime. The "Say Hey Kid" can also be examined for his impact on popular culture. Mays was not one to seek the limelight. Hirsch explains: "Mays was an unlikely celebrity, but he flourished in an increasingly intense media culture. He appeared on television variety shows, talk shows, sitcoms, and in documentaries – timid, to be sure, but also handsome, respectful, and self-deprecating. Magazines splashed him on their covers while recording artists celebrated him in song, screenwriters immortalized him in films, and cartoonists grandly etched him in print."[2]

How many celebrities have been interviewed by both Ed Sullivan and Jon Stewart? Probably very few, but Willie Mays is one such person, an example of his longtime stardom. When Sullivan first interviewed Mays, the TV show was called *Toast of the Town* and not yet the legendary *Ed Sullivan Show*.[3] Television was in its black-and-white rabbit-eared infancy. When he was interviewed by Stewart over 50 years later, it was on a cable channel devoted solely to comedy and could be streamed and watched anytime on a device you held in your hand. While Mays' achievements on the field are a source of amazement, so are the people he met off the field. He has been celebrated in song and his mere presence on screen lit up the room.

Here are some of the songs celebrating Mays and some of his notable television appearances.

## Songs

### *"Say Hey (The Willie Mays Song)" by the Treniers (1954)*

Willie Mays had returned from military service in Korea, and New York public-relations agent Ted Worner thought a new song honoring the "Giant kid" would be a huge success. Worner had promoted the postseason barnstorming tours of the Jackie Robinson All-Stars, and pitched the idea to two important people: syndicated columnist Dick Kleiner and musical performer Jane Douglass. Kleiner wrote "The Marquee" column, which covered the Broadway theater world. His career, stretching through the 1980s, would take him to Hollywood, where he interviewed an estimated 8,000 movie and television stars. Douglass was a Women's Army Corps captain and musician during World War II.[4]

Kleiner wrote the lyrics over one weekend, and the following weekend Douglass set the words to music. Worner and his friend, music publisher Jack Spina, spent months trying to interest record companies in the song. Marv Holtzman of Epic Records, an affiliate of Columbia Records, took notice. He said Epic would sign a deal for the song if they could get Mays on the recording. The song was performed by The Treniers with speaking parts by Mays.[5]

The Treniers – twin brothers Claude and Cliff – were a Las Vegas lounge act who began performing at Alabama State College in the late 1930s and took their show on the road. They became one of the first Black musical groups to perform on the Las Vegas Strip. The Trenier Twins made their first recordings for Mercury Records in 1947, joined by Don Hill on the saxophone and Gene Gilbeaux on the piano. They frequently performed with legends Nat King Cole, Sammy Davis Jr., and Louis Armstrong at casinos where they could not stay the night because of segregation. Their brothers, Milt and Buddy Trenier, joined the group by 1951. The Treniers appeared in several rock 'n' roll movies, including *Don't Knock the Rock* and *The Girl Can't Help It.*[6]

The song was recorded on a 45 RPM record with "Out of the Bushes" on the opposite side. Quincy Jones conducted the orchestra. This tribute to Mays has stood the test of time, often serving as the soundtrack for his highlight reels.

***Lyrics:***

Fan 1: Go get it Willie, say hey Willie, go get it.
Fan 2: Whatta' ya mean go get it? Man, that ball is way in left field.
Fan 1: I don't care what field it's in, Willie plays all fields.
Fan 2: Every time we come to the game you talkin' about Willie plays in all the fields.
Fan 1: That's right he plays …
Fan 2: Let's call Willie and ask him. Call em.'
Fan 1: OK. Hey Willie!
Mays: Yes.
Fan 1: Are you Willie Mays?
Mays: Yes.
Fan 1: Whose ball was that?
Mays: Where was it?
Fan 1: In left field.
Mays: Well, that's Irvin's ball.
Fan 1: I told you that, every time we come to the game. We gotta talk about. The next time I'm goin' to sit in the grandstands
Mays: Say Hey Fellas, what's your name?
*Chorus:*
(Say who?)
Say Willie. Say hey!
(Say who?)
Swinging at the plate. Say hey!
(Say who?)
Say Willie. That Giants kid is great.

When he hits the ball it's long gone, man,
Hits it farther than Campy can.
Swings the bat like a little lead pipe,
When they reach the ball it's overripe.

*Chorus repeats*

He runs the bases like a choo-choo train,
Swings around second like an aeroplane.
His cap flies off when he passes third,
And he heads home like an eagle bird.

*Chorus repeats*

Yes, he covers center like he had jet shoes,
The other batters get the Willie blues.
Anything hit his way is out,
Man, it just don't pay those guys to clout!

*Chorus repeats*
When Willie served his Uncle Sam,
He left the Giants in an awful jam.
But now he's back and he's Leo's joy,
And Willie's still a growing boy!

*Chorus repeats*
That Giants kid is great.
Say Willie, Whatcha' ya gonna say?
Mays: Say Hey!

The New York Giants granted exclusive rights to Epic Records to create this Mays song.[7] Other record companies also profited on Mays' popularity.

### *"Amazin' Willie Mays" by the King Odom Quartet (1954)*

The King Odom Quartet was composed of David "King" Odom, David "Boots" Bowers, Isaiah Bing, and Cleveland Bing. The group received a contract from Musicraft in 1949 and joined the NBC radio show *Swingtime*. The group dissolved in 1952. David Odom assembled some (apparently unknown) singers for this Mays song for Perspective Records before calling it quits.[8] The song was produced on a 78 RPM record with "Basin Street Blues" on the opposite side of the disk.[9]

***Lyrics:***
Take me out to the ballgame, cause I want to see amazin' Willie Mays!
*Verse 1*
Who got a solid hit,
Just when we needed it?
Amazin' Willie Mays.
Who raced to catch the ball,
Way out against the wall?
Amazin' Willie Mays.
Who has a step and style,
Who has a winning smile?
Who hits the ball a mile?
Who makes the plays?
Who threw the runner out?
Who made the people shout?
Amazin' Willie Mays.
*Chorus*
Say hey, say hey, say hey kid,
Let's see you make another catch the way you did.
Say hey, say hey, say hey, boy,
You're making all the Giant rooters jump for joy.
*Verse 2*
Who has a super arm?
Who has a special charm?
Amazin' Willie Mays.
Who scored the winning run?
And did it just for fun?
Amazin' Willie Mays.
Who has that extra spark?
Who makes the game a lark?
Who brings me to the park?
Who makes the plays?
Who hit a hefty clout?
Who made the people shout?
Amazin' Willie Mays.
*Chorus repeats*
*Verse 1 repeats*
What a player!
Amazin' Willie Mays.
Say hey.
Amazin' Willie Mays.

***"Say Hey Willie Mays" by the Singing Wanderers (1954)***

Jay Warner, in his book *American Singing Groups: A History From 1940s to Today*, described the Wanderers as a "pop-jazz group" who "were probably too pop for the rock and roll era and too jazzy for success as rhythm and blue artists."[10] The band consisted of Ray Pollard, Frank Joyner, Robert Yarborough, and Shephard Grant. In 1953 the group recorded "We could Find Happiness" for Savoy Records. The following year, they were rebranded the "Singing Wanderers" and recorded two discs for Decca Records, with "Say Hey" being one of those. The Wanderers appeared in the 1955 Fritz Pollard film, *Rockin' the Blues*.[11]

***Lyrics:***

There's a new thriller diller on Coogan's Bluff,
A horsehide killer that's rough and tough.
Fans by the millions are singin' His praise,
Say hey! Willie Mays!
Got an arm like DiMaggio, runs like Cobb,
Could this be Speaker back on the job?
Makes lippy dippy with His magical plays,
Say hey, Willie Mays!
In New York town, believe it or not, when the pennant flag is raisin',
The Duke will crown him Prince of Swat, if Willie keeps on amazin';
I'm not a prophet or a prophet's son,
But he'll be the daddy when the Duke is done.
So put all your money on the Birmingham blaze,
Say hey, Willie Mays!
He runs like a rabbit, sly as a fox,
Got home run habits in the batter's box.
He belts that ball and say,
"Hey, it's over that fence and far away!"
Got eyes like an eagle, watchin' the skies,
It just ain't legal how he snags a fly.
The minute they hit it he's comin' on,
To grab that ball when it's almost gone.
Say hey, hey, Willie Mays, say hey. (repeats)
He belts that ball so far away. (repeats)
Hey Willie, there's a story told that we believe is true,
The Lord made you and lost the mold so there's only one of you.
For a place in the Baseball Hall of Fame,
Scribes are writing down Willie's name.
For he is a credit to our national game,
Glory to his name!
Say Hey! Say Hey! Say Hey! Willie, Willie Mays!
Say Hey, Willie, Willie Mays! (repeats)

***"Say Hey (A Tribute to Willie Mays)" by the Nite Riders (1954)***

The Nite Riders were an ensemble in the 1940s-1950s led by James "Doc" Starkes and included Harry Crafton, Melvin Smith, Jimmy Johnson, and Joe Sewell. Early in their tenure, Smith was the sole vocalist behind the instrumentation of the group. The group did more harmonizing in the 1950s.[12]

The song was produced on a 45 RPM disc by Apollo Records, with "Women and Cadillacs" on the opposite side.

***The opening lyrics:***

There is a kid from Alabama,
You gotta dig his southern manner.
He is a wizard on the field,
But dig his main spiel:
Say Hey (repeated).
His name is Willie Mays.
How he feels everyone, when he hits a home run,
Man at third tries to steal, threw him out from centerfield,
There goes a long fly ball headin' over to the wall,
Don't worry 'bout that ball, he got it that's all.
Say Hey! (repeats)
His name is Willie Mays.

***"Say Hey, Willie Mays" by Johnny Long and his Orchestra (1954).***

Johnny A. Long was a major orchestra leader and violinist in the 1930s and '40s. He was best known for his dance music, but his band also played nearly every type of music. After his passing in 1972, the *Charlotte News* wrote, "From the time of his graduation from Duke University in 1935 to 1958 he and his band were starred at every major college and university in the country, playing proms in all 48 states."[13] Probably the high point of Long's career was performing at President Franklin D. Roosevelt's birthday ball in 1941.[14]

Long's piece on Willie Mays was adapted from the Wanderers' version and written by Willard Robinson. It was recorded for Coral Records on a 78 RPM record with "Pussy-Footin' (Back to Me)" on the opposite side. Lem Johnson accompanied Long on this recording. The *Montgomery Advertiser* noted that Long's version of "Say Hey, Willie Mays" gained "a measure of popularity in the waning days of [the] baseball season."[15]

*This is the musical score to one of the songs devoted to Mays in 1954, written by Willard Robinson and performed by Johnny Long and His Orchestra. Used with permission from KeyMan Collectibles (keymancollectibles.com).*

### *"Say Hey" by Ray Anthony and his Orchestra (1954)*

Ray Anthony received a trumpet from his father for his fifth birthday in 1927. In 2022 that trumpet still sat by his bedside as Anthony celebrated his 100th birthday and a life "hooked on the horn," in the words of *Los Angeles Times* columnist Sean J. O'Connell.[16] It had been 65 years since Anthony was immortalized among the first 1,500 on Hollywood's Walk of Fame. The teenage Anthony joined the famed Glenn Miller Orchestra and was called upon to entertain the troops as a Navy officer in World War II. He formed his own orchestra after the war and by the 1950s he and his 18-member band had produced many dance singles, including a rendition of "The Hokey Pokey" that seemed to get the whole country swaying. Anthony may be best remembered for a 1952 release party of their new single, "Marilyn," written for rising star Marilyn Monroe. Her arrival at Anthony's house party overshadowed the presence of other legendary celebrities, such as Mickey Rooney and Sammy Davis Jr. Anthony made television appearances in eight straight decades.

"Say Hey" was recorded for Capitol Records on a 78 RPM record, with instrumental music of the South African song "Skokiaan" on the flip side. "Say Hey" is mainly instrumental music with the words "Say Hey" intermixed several times. "Willie Mays has made 'Say Hey' a trademark for the New York Giants," William Laffler wrote in his "Platter Chatter" column in the *Pasadena Independent*, "and Ray Anthony's is the latest orchestra (Capitol) to pay its respects to Willie. You're familiar with the tune by now through the courtesy of your disc-jockey, but Anthony has made it a danceable number."[17]

### *Notable Television Appearances*

The Internet Movie Database (IMDB) lists 99 appearances by Mays on screen, but this is likely incomplete, given the lack of information available.[18] His appearance on the June 27, 1954, episode of CBS's *Toast of the Town* (*The Ed Sullivan Show*) is not listed on IMDB, for instance. "Frank, and flashing that broad smile, supported by a perfect set of white ivories," wrote the *Detroit Tribune* of Mays' appearance. "He is a natural."[19]

The 1954 season was a busy one. On July 11 Mays appeared on an episode of the quiz show *What's My Line?* hosted by John Daly. The popular quiz show ran on CBS from 1950 to 1967 (and until 1975 in syndication) and involved the hilarious interactions between celebrity panelists attempting to guess the occupation of the contestant by asking "yes" or "no" questions. The program included a segment with a famous mystery guest appearing while the panelists were blindfolded. The celebrity panelists included Bennett Cerf, co-founder of Random House publishing; actress Arlene Francis; journalist and columnist Dorothy Kilgallen; and future host of the *Today Show* Jack Paar. Mays used a high-pitched voice to disguise himself. Francis quickly caught on, asking if Mays was part of the sports world, involved in baseball, part of the National League, a member of "my ball team, part of the Giants team," and finally if he had hit his 31st home run that day. "Do you play center field? Are you 'Say Hey' Willie Mays?" she asked to the applause of the audience. Mays explained that "Say Hey" originated as his greeting when he first came to the Giants because he didn't know anyone's name. Mays departed by shaking hands with the panelists, and a beaming Francis said, "Boy, you're just the greatest!"[20]

On August 22, Mays performed a version of "Say Hey" (Treniers version) on an episode of NBC's *Colgate Comedy Hour*, hosted by Dean Martin and Jerry Lewis.[21]

After the Giants' regular-season finale on September 26, Mays appeared on both *Toast of the Town* and the *Colgate Comedy Hour*. The fact that both programs aired live at the same time on Sunday night did not hinder the "Say Hey Kid." When Mays and an agent arrived at the Ed Sullivan studio at 7:25 P.M., they realized his Giants uniform had been sent to the Colgate studio. They took a cab from 57th Street and 8th Avenue to 53rd and Broadway to retrieve his uniform and race back to Sullivan. Mays was on stage with Sullivan from 8:10 to 8:20, nabbed a cab and made it to NBC by 8:35.[22]

The next morning, Mays appeared on the *Today Show* with its first host, Dave Garroway. That night, Mays appeared on the inaugural episode of the new NBC show *The Tonight Show*, hosted by Steve Allen.[23]

Mays appeared on *The Merv Griffin Show* nine times, according to IMDB.[24] One episode aired on February 1, 1966, when Mays joined actress Tallulah Bankhead and actor/singer David Burns. Griffin asked Mays if he was the only player to use the basket catch method on fly balls. "I have to do something to make a living," Mays joked. Mays and Griffin took turns batting balls into the audience. When asked who would win the pennant that year, Mays answered "We're going to play 162 games and at the end we'll probably know."[25]

Also in 1966, Mays had a cameo appearance on ABC's fantasy comedy sitcom *Bewitched*, starring Elizabeth Montgomery and Dick York. Montgomery portrayed a witch who married a mortal (York) and sought to live as a normal housewife. In Season Three's Halloween episode entitled "Twitch or Treat" (aired October 27, 1966), Mays appears at a Halloween party. "Say hey, Willie!" Montgomery greets him. A befuddled York suddenly realizes Mays must be a warlock. "The way he hits home runs,"

*The fashionable outfielder pitched dress socks and other items. SABR/The Rucker Archive.*

*Willie Mays appeared on magazine covers as well as TV shows such as What's My Line?, The Donna Reed Show, and Bewitched. SABR/The Rucker Archive.*

Montgomery explains, "what else?" Mays realizes it's time to get to the ballpark and promptly vanishes.[26]

In 1971 Mays was again on the *Merv Griffin Show*. "Baseball is not working," Mays said in reference to Griffin's question of the pressure he faces in the game. "Baseball is fun. It's a fun game. When you stop having fun in baseball, as far as I am concerned, then it's time to get out." He was joined by actors James Brolin and Dennis Hopper and actress Diane Baker.[27]

In 1989 Mays appeared on the ABC sitcom *Mr. Belvedere*, starring Bob Uecker. The comedy centered on the adventures of Belvedere, an English housekeeper (Christopher Hewett), working for George Adams (Uecker) and his American family. The episode "The Field" was the first episode of Season Six and aired on September 16, 1989. Belvedere decides to help George fulfill a lifelong fantasy to play baseball with some of the all-time greats. Mays, Hank Aaron, Johnny Bench, and others arrive.[28]

In 2010 Mays was interviewed by Jon Stewart of *The Daily Show* on Comedy Central to discuss the new biography written by Hirsch, *Willie Mays: The Life, the Legend*. Stewart asked Mays if he could have hit 800 home runs had he not missed time for military service or played so many of his home games at Candlestick Park. Mays didn't believe he could have done so, since he opposed so many great pitchers of his day: Bob Gibson, Sandy Koufax, and Don Drysdale.

"I'm just lucky to have what I have, man" Mays said.[29]

We are the lucky ones, experiencing the "Say Hey Kid" for over eight decades.

## SOURCES

In addition to the sources cited in the Notes, the author consulted:

Lent, Cassidy, Giamatti Research Center, National Baseball Hall of Fame, Cooperstown, New York.

"Disc & Data by Fred Arthur-Gene Robbins," *Casper* (Wyoming) *Morning Star*, July 24, 1954: 10.

Roberts, Jay, "Say Hey in Song" in *Jaybird's Jottings* blog. September 15, 2006. Retrieved August 20, 2022. https://jay.typepad.com/william_jay/2006/09/say_hey_in_song.html

"Speaking of Records," *Raleigh News and Observer*, September 5, 1954: 7.

**Selected Recordings**

"8 MLB Hall of Famers vs Little Leaguers." YouTube. Retrieved November 20, 2022. https://www.youtube.com/watch?v=S_urw9771ZY

"Amazin' Willie Mays," by the King Odom Quartet (1954). YouTube. Retrieved November 1, 2022. https://www.youtube.com/watch?v=xAPwJ8V4geI

"Say Hey," by the Nite Riders (1954). YouTube. Retrieved November 1, 2022. https://www.youtube.com/watch?v=mvorvNmlK_Y

"Say Hey," by Ray Anthony and His Orchestra (1954). Internet Archive. Retrieved November 1, 2022. https://archive.org/details/78_say-hey_ray-anthony-and-his-orchestra-ray-anthony_gbia0012319a/

Say+Hey+-+Ray+Anthony+and+His+Orchestra+-+Ray+Anthony.flac

"Say Hey (The Willie Mays Song) by the Treniers. YouTube recording. Retrieved November 1, 2022. https://www.youtube.com/watch?v=ngrhKECHDLo

"Say Hey, Willie Mays," by Johnny Long and His Orchestra (1954). Internet Archive. Retrieved November 1, 2022. https://archive.org/details/78_say-hey-willie-mays_johnny-long-and-his-orchestra-lem-johnson-willard-robinson_gbia0448694a/SAY+HEY%2C+WILLIE+MAYS+-+JOHNNY+LONG+And+His+Orchestra.flac

## NOTES

1 James S. Hirsch, *Willie Mays: The Life, the Legend* (New York: Scribner, 2010), 4.

2 Hirsch, 5.

3 The *Ed Sullivan Show* was a staple variety show on CBS on Sunday nights from 1948 to 1971.

4 "How Willie Got to Say, 'Say, Hey' on a Platter," *Fort Lauderdale News*, August 8, 1954: 2-C; "Dick Kleiner," *Washington Post*, March 1, 2002: B8.

5 "How Willie Got to Say…"

6 Associated Press, "Claude Trenier, 84, a Member of Family's Las Vegas Ensemble," *New York Times*, November 22, 2003: B7.

7 "Willie Mays Goes on Wax," *Pittsburgh Courier*, July 24, 1954: 14.

8 Mitch Rosalsky, *Encyclopedia of Rhythm & Blues and Doo-Wop Vocal Groups* (Lanham, Maryland: Scarecrow Press, 2008), 346; Marv Goldberg, "The King Odom Quartet." Marv Goldberg's Yesterday's Memories Rhythm & Blues Party. Retrieved November 1, 2022. https://www.uncamarvy.com/KingOdomQuartet/kingodomquartet.html

9 From the Discogs website. Retrieved November 1, 2022. https://www.discogs.com/release/14293423-The-King-Odom-Quartette-Amazin-Willie-Mays-Basin-Street-Blues.

10 Jay Warner, "The Wanderers," in *American Singing Groups: A History From 1940s to Today* (Milwaukee: Hal Leondard Corp., 2006), 311.

11 Rosalsky, 519.

12 Rosalsky, 413.

13 "Ex-Band Leader Johnny Long Dies," *Charlotte* (North Carolina) *News*, November 1, 1972: 7.

14 Christopher Popa, "Johnny Long." Big Band Library, November 2008. Retrieved November 13, 2022. bigbandlibrary.com/johnnylong.html.

15 Doug Donehue, "'Shanty' Still Bread, Butter for Long After Many Playings," *Montgomery* (Alabama) *Advertiser*, October 26, 1954: 10.

16 Sean J. O'Connell, "Life by the Horns," *Los Angeles Times*, January 25, 2022: E1.

17 William Laffler, "Platter Chatter," *Pasadena Independent*, August 24, 1954: 12.

18 "Willie Mays," Internet Movie Database. Retrieved November 1, 2022. https://www.imdb.com/name/nm0563092/

19 "'Amazing Mays' Mobs Pitchers in Senior Loop," *Detroit Tribune*, July 3, 1954: 6.

20 "What's My Line: Willie Mays," Internet Movie Database. Retrieved November 22, 2022. https://www.imdb.com/title/tt0746427/?ref_=nm_flmg_eps_tt_1; Dialogue taken from a YouTube upload of the episode, retrieved November 22, 2022. https://www.youtube.com/watch?v=XoQOIf7utlY

21 "The Colgate Summer Comedy Hour," *La Crosse* (Wisconsin) *Tribune*, August 22, 1954: 13.

22 Hirsch, 189.

23 Hirsch, 189.

24 "Willie Mays," Internet Movie Database. Retrieved November 22, 2022. https://www.imdb.com/name/nm0563092/?ref_=nm_rvi_nm_t_1.

25 Dialogue taken from a recording of the episode on Tubi TV. "The Merv Griffin Show," Tubi TV. Retrieved November 22, 2022. https://tubitv.com/tv-shows/501209/s01-e06-episode-6?start=true Note: Tubi TV and IMDB give different dates for this episode.

26 "Bewitched: Twitch or Treat," Internet Movie Database. Retrieved November 20, 2022. https://www.imdb.com/title/tt0523274/?ref_=nm_flmg_eps_tt_1; Dialogue taken from Mays' cameo available on YouTube, "New York Baseball Great Willie Mays in 'Bewitched' Television Series Halloween Episode | 1966." Retrieved November 20, 2022. https://www.youtube.com/watch?v=_BopU2frrJk.

27 "The Merv Griffin Show: Willie Mays, Dennis Hopper, Diane Baker," Internet Movie Database. Retrieved November 22, 2022. https://www.imdb.com/title/tt0646852/?ref_=nm_flmg_eps_tt_1; Dialogue taken from a recording of the episode on the Roku Channel. Retrieved November 22, 2022. https://therokuchannel.roku.com/watch/59fd2dbe42d6edc9f0c148d1204f0a4d.

28 "Mr. Belvedere: The Field," Internet Movie Database. Retrieved November 20, 2022. https://www.imdb.com/title/tt0651936/?ref_=nm_flmg_eps_tt_1.

29 Transcript taken from a recording of the episode on Comedy Central. "Willie Mays," February 10, 2010. Retrieved November 22, 2022. https://www.cc.com/video/ipyqsz/the-daily-show-with-jon-stewart-willie-mays.

# SAY HEY FOREVER

BY BRENT KALLESTAD

My lifelong adoration of Willie Mays began quite accidentally in the summer of 1954 when as an 8-year-old I was just starting to learn the game playing catch with a friend, Carl Sisk, who lived right across the street from me and was two years older.

We were polishing our skills playing softball on a vacant lot just north of our home in Miller, South Dakota, and even let a girl or two play to even out the teams.

At some point that summer I'd heard a lot of this guy Mickey Mantle and decided that's who I'd pretend to be, but Carl also wanted to be Mickey and we actually had a fight over who'd get to be him. Well, a bit older and a lot quicker, Carl pretty much won that match and I was crestfallen.

At dinner that night while I licked my wounds, my father said, why don't you be Willie Mays? I'd never heard of Willie Mays at that point but dad filled me in on him and so that began an affection with the Say-Hey Kid.

Ironically, it wasn't long after that Carl and his folks went to Chicago to visit some relatives and while in the Windy City took in a Cubs game. When they returned, Carl only wanted to be Ernie Banks and so Mantle was out the door since I was already Willie Mays.

And on my 9th birthday Mays made "the catch" in the first World Series that I paid attention to and I was hooked! Shortly after the sweep of the Indians, we got a new puppy and named it Willie.

In pickup games at Crystal Park during my elementary school days, I always wanted to play center field and several of my friends would just call me Willie. The nickname "Willie" lasted for several years through not only my high school days but over my lifetime. Our 60th high school reunion is scheduled in 2023 and I can almost guarantee that at least three of my buddies from the good old days will still call me Willie! We've held reunions every five years and it seems some things just never change.

Oh, despite my desire for center field, I was moved to third base, a position I played for four seasons in American Legion ball. By this time the Twins had moved to neighboring Minnesota and since I played third, favored Harmon Killebrew while retaining Mays as number 1. My last year in Legion ball, possibly the last two, I played third base, hit third, and wore number 3, Killebrew's uniform number.

Unfortunately, I never got to see Mays play in person. I did, however, meet him on a one-to-one basis on two occasions.

The first time was at the 1975 All-Star Game in Milwaukee, and credit for the introduction goes to Clark Griffith, son of then Twins owner Calvin Griffith. Clark was just a few years older than me and often spent time around the media. Good, cordial guy.

I was the Associated Press bureau sportswriter in the Twin Cities and the Twins were among my beats during the mid-1970s. I was assigned to help cover the All-Star Game that year and came to Milwaukee in the early afternoon the day before.

Clark arranged that I come down to a dinner at a Milwaukee hotel on the eve of the game where Mays would be in attendance. He pulled Willie from the group of roughly 18 or 20 folks (Stan Musial and Bowie Kuhn among them) and introduced me. It was pretty brief but long enough for me to share my appreciation to Mays and let him know (I was 29 years old at the time) how much I'd enjoyed cheering for him for the past 20-plus years.

*Willie Mays with Brent Kallestad, at Tallahassee on February 26, 2006 following a Black History Month celebration. Mays was among several sports celebrities to visit that day as guests of former Governor Jeb Bush. Photograph courtesy of Brent Kallestad.*

And the second time was in 2005 or possibly 2006 when Gov. Jeb Bush invited me to attend a welcome for Mays at the Florida state capitol. By now I was AP's senior political writer in Florida and had known Governor Bush since 1986, when he began his ascent in politics. Again, a short but sweet meeting with Mays, but this time our AP photographer got a picture of us visiting. It sits under glass with other significant career pictures in my home retirement office.

I'll go to my grave believing that Mays was the most complete and most exciting baseball player of the twentieth century. And eternally grateful to my dad for giving his young baseball-loving son a lifetime hero.

# MAYS SINGLES HOME THE WINNER IN EXTRA INNINGS IN GAME ONE OF THE NEGRO AMERICAN LEAGUE CHAMPIONSHIP SERIES

## September 11, 1948: Birmingham Black Barons 5, Kansas City Monarchs 4 (11 innings), at Rickwood Field, Birmingham, Alabama

BY JEB STEWART

ON SATURDAY, SEPTEMBER 11, 1948, Rickwood Field in Birmingham, Alabama, hosted Game One of the Negro American League Championship Series between the Birmingham Black Barons and the Kansas City Monarchs. The series featured a matchup between first-year managers and was expected to be a hotly contested because both teams had "plenty of hitting, power, pitching and fielding."[1]

Birmingham was managed by player-manager Piper Davis. The Black Barons had won the championship of the first half of the NAL and finished with a league-best record of 63-28-2 (.692).[2]

The Black Barons' powerful offense included shortstop Artie Wilson, who won the league batting title with a sizzling .433 average; Davis, who primarily played second base and batted .393; and right fielder Ed Steele, who hit .357 with 3 home runs. Rookie Willie Mays, who was just 17 years old, became the team's center fielder after regular starter Norman Robinson broke his ankle, and hit .262.[3] The club also had a solid pitching staff led by Jimmie Newberry (14-5, 2.18 ERA), Bill Powell (11-3, 3.30), Bill Greason (6-4, 3.30), and Alonzo Perry (10-2, 4.73).[4]

Their counterparts from Kansas City had won the second-half championship of the NAL and finished with a record of 67-34-3 (.663). The Monarchs were managed by player-manager Buck O'Neil and had an intimidating lineup of their own with perhaps the

*Willie Mays and Roy Campanella were two of the many Negro League stars who later enjoyed Hall of Fame careers in MLB. SABR/The Rucker Archive.*

best-hitting outfield in the NAL. The Monarchs were led by center fielder Willard Brown, who hit .408 and crushed 7 home runs; Hank Thompson in right field, who hit .337 with 5 homers and 12 steals; and left fielder Johnie Scott, who batted .300. Another outfielder, 19-year-old rookie Elston Howard, would later gain fame as a catcher with the New York Yankees.

The Monarchs' pitching staff was every bit as good as Birmingham's. It was led by Jim LaMarque (15-5, 1.96 ERA), Ford Smith (10-5, 2.64), Gene Collins (9-3, 2.23), and Gene Richardson (5-6, 4.40).[5]

Future Hall of Fame pitcher Hilton Smith was 41 years old. Depending on the source, he may have had a terrible season or an above-average one. According to the Howe News Bureau, Smith posted a 1-2 record in the NAL with an ERA of 8.02 in 46 innings pitched. Though Seamheads seems to contradict Howe, showing Smith with a 4-2 record and a 3.96 ERA in 62⅔ innings, baseball historian Gary Ashwill explains that the Seamheads numbers include seven regular-season games against NAL teams (in which Smith went 2-2 with a 5.92 ERA in 38 IP), along with four appearances in interleague games against NNL teams, in which he was 2-0 with a 2.10 ERA in 25⅔ IP). According to Ashwill: "It looks like he had some good performances in interleague games that didn't count in the official NAL stats, plus a few bad innings against NAL opponents that were counted in official league stats, but that are not represented in our statistics because no box scores were published. If the interleague games with box scores included in Smith's Seamheads totals are added to Howe's official NAL statistics, Smith finished either 3-2 or 4-2 with a 5.90 ERA in 71⅔ IP against major Negro League teams in the 1948 regular season."[6]

In Game One, Davis handed the ball to his reliable right-hander, Powell, while O'Neil countered with left-hander LaMarque, who had a reputation as a soft-tosser with pinpoint control.[7] A reported crowd of 5,300 passed through the turnstiles to see the Saturday night game.[8] After four innings, the game was scoreless but hardly a pitchers' duel as the teams had already combined to strand 12 baserunners.

The Monarchs squandered their best early opportunity to score when shortstop Gene Baker led off the game with a walk and Herb Souell singled. Facing an early deficit and with their run-producers, Thompson, Brown, and Howard, coming up, Powell settled down and recorded three straight outs, although the details of how he escaped the inning are lost to history.

Birmingham's hitters were even more frustrated early in the game as LaMarque proved easy to hit but difficult to score against. The Black Barons stranded two baserunners in each of the first four innings. In the bottom of the fifth, they finally broke through.

Davis and Mays opened the inning with singles. Steele reached on an error by pitcher LaMarque to load the bases. The pitcher began to struggle with his control. He walked left fielder Jim Zapp and then hit catcher Pepper Bassett with a pitch. With the Black Barons now leading, 2-0, with no outs and the bases still loaded, first baseman Joe Scott hit into a force, and Steele was thrown out at home. LaMarque was able to record the second out of the inning against the next batter, Powell. However, leadoff hitter Wilson got a base hit, scoring Zapp. The Monarchs then got out of the inning but trailed, 3-0.

Kansas City immediately stormed back, scoring three runs in the top of the sixth to tie the score.[9] Thompson opened the frame with a walk. Needing to give his team a spark, he stole second. With one out, Howard singled, moving Thompson to third. After Monarchs' first baseman Tom Cooper made an out, second baseman Curtis Roberts singled, scoring Thompson and moving Howard to third. Roberts made a heads-up play by hustling into second as the ball was thrown to third. Catcher Earl Taborn followed with a single to score Howard and Roberts and tie the game, 3-3. Powell got LaMarque for the final out, but the damage was done.

The Black Barons threatened again in the sixth and seventh innings but again stranded runners and the game remained tied. But in the top of the eighth, the Monarchs' Brown hit a leadoff single and ratcheted up the pressure on the Black Barons' defense by stealing second. Howard's single moved him to third. After an out, Roberts singled again, driving in Thompson to give the Monarchs a 4-3 advantage. But with two on and only one out, the Monarchs failed to add to their lead as Powell induced back-to-back outs from Taborn and LaMarque.

Birmingham failed to score in the bottom of the eighth, and Powell recorded three straight outs in the top of the ninth. Birmingham's Bassett opened the bottom of the ninth with a double. Manager Davis replaced his slow-footed 37-year-old catcher with a pinch-runner, second baseman Wiley Griggs. The move paid off when Greason, pinch-hitting for Powell, singled and drove home Griggs to tie the game, 4-4. However, the Black Barons' threat soon ended and the game went into extra innings.

Griggs remained in the game at second in place of the versatile Davis, who moved behind the plate with Bassett out of the game. Greason stayed in the game to pitch and breezed through the Monarchs' order in the 10th. The Black Barons also couldn't score in the frame and the game remained tied.

In the 11th, Newberry relieved Greason. Roberts reached on an error but the crafty left-hander picked him off and the threat soon ended. In the bottom of the inning, O'Neil removed LaMarque and brought Richardson into the game. Scott led off with a single. After Newberry popped out, Wilson walked. Richardson then uncorked a wild pitch and both runners moved up. Richardson then walked John Britton to fill the bases with one out. The next batter, Davis, popped up to second.

With two outs and the bases loaded, Mays came to the plate. The Black Barons had already stranded a whopping 20 or 21 runners to just 8 for Kansas City.[10] Mays was unfazed and ended the game with a sharp single to second, which scored Scott. Author John Klima described the moment in *Willie's Boys*:

> "It didn't matter how you pitched to Mays because he didn't care. He hit like he was trying to hurt someone. This time, Mays hit a full-count pitch hard behind second base. Roberts was extraordinarily fast, so he was able to scramble to his right to knock down the drive as he slid on the seat of his pants. He stopped the ball but could not control it. When he saw Mays dashing down the first base line with the hat flying off his head, he knew he had no chance to stop Scott, who charged home with the winning run in Birmingham's dramatic 5-4 victory.
>
> "The Black Barons streamed from their dugout and surrounded Mays on the infield grass, celebrating the child, who basked in the moment."[11]

Davis led the Black Barons with four hits, while Wilson had three. Four other players (Mays, Bassett, Powell, and Scott) contributed two hits each. Powell struck out eight over his nine innings pitched and Newberry was credited with the win.

Howard led the Monarchs with three hits, while Brown and Cooper added two hits each. LaMarque struck out 8 in 10 innings pitched and Richardson got the loss.

## SOURCES

In addition to the sources cited in the Notes, the author consulted the box score and play-by-play of the game presented by Retrosheet. This piece mostly uses official NAL pitching statistics compiled by the Howe News Bureau, as they cover more games than Seamheads, which includes only games for which box scores could be found.[12]

https://retrosheet.org/NegroLeagues/boxesetc/1948/B09110BIR1948.htm

## NOTES

1 "Kansas City Ready for Black Barons Play-Off," *Birmingham Weekly Review,* September 11, 1948: 7.

2 William J. Plott, *Black Baseball's Last Team Standing: The Birmingham Black Barons, 1919–1962* (Jefferson, North Carolina: McFarland & Company, Inc., 2019), 180.

3 https://seamheads.com/NegroLgs/team.php?yearID=1948&teamID=BBB&LGOrd=3. Except as noted, most of the statistics in this biography are from Seamheads or Retrosheet.org.

4 Official Negro American League Statistics for 1948, compiled by the Howe News Bureau (Chicago).

5 Official Negro American League Statistics for 1948, compiled by the Howe News Bureau.

6 Email from Gary Ashwill, February 14, 2023.

7 John Klima, *Willie's Boys* (Hoboken, New Jersey: John Wiley & Sons, Inc., 2009), 154.

8 "Birmingham Grabs First 2 Games in Playoff Series," *Chicago Defender*, September 18, 1948: 11; "Repeats Over Monarchs," *Kansas City Times*, September 13, 1948: 15.

9 "Birmingham Grabs First 2 Games in Playoff Series."

10 "Birmingham Grabs First 2 Games in Playoff Series." The newspaper reported 20 runners; Retrosheet shows 21.

11 Klima, 158.

12 According to Gary Ashwill, "Seamheads statistics and the official Howe News data are not directly comparable, as Seamheads is based only on games for which box scores were published at the time (roughly half of Negro league games in the 1940s), and Seamheads regular season statistics include official NAL games as well as two categories of games that were not counted in the official numbers: unofficial games against NAL opponents, and interleague games against NNL teams. The Howe News Bureau statistics, by contrast, cover only official NAL regular season games, though they are more complete than Seamheads numbers in that category, as they include many games for which box scores were not published at the time." Email from Gary Ashwill, February 14, 2023.

# MAYS' TWO-OUT DOUBLE IN THE NINTH SAVES THE DAY FOR THE BLACK BARONS

## September 12, 1948: Birmingham Black Barons 6, Kansas City Monarchs 5 (10 innings), at Rickwood Field, Birmingham, Alabama

## Negro American League Championship Series, Game Two

BY JEB STEWART

THE BIRMINGHAM BLACK Barons and the Kansas City Monarchs met at Rickwood Field for Game Two of the Negro American League Championship Series on September 12, 1948. Birmingham won the first game, 5-4, in 11 innings the previous day.

For Game Two, Monarchs manager Buck O'Neil started a 29-year-old right-hander Ford Smith, who had won 10 games during the season and posted a 2.64 ERA. Birmingham's Piper Davis gave the nod to right-hander Alonzo Perry, a 26-year-old who had also won 10 games, but whose 4.73 ERA was significantly higher than Smith's.

Sunday games were always popular in Birmingham, and 8,000 fans poured into Rickwood to witness the matchup.[1] Unlike the previous game, which had been scoreless through four innings, both teams scored early in this one. Artie Wilson led off the bottom of the first with a triple and John Britton drove him in, giving Birmingham an early 1-0 lead.

In the top of the second, the Monarchs' bats came alive. Willard Brown opened with a single to left and advanced to third on an error by Jim Zapp. Another error, this one by third baseman Britton, allowed the next hitter, Johnie Scott, to reach first as Brown scored the tying run. Elston Howard then walked. After Gene Baker made an out, Curtis Roberts walked, and the bases were loaded. After another out, Herb Souell singled to bring home Scott and Howard. O'Neil made the last out of the inning, but the Monarchs led, 3-1.

In the fourth inning, Gene Baker homered over the left-field fence to increase Kansas City's lead to 4-1. Willie Mays, who drove home the winning run in Game One, singled in the bottom of the inning and was on base with two outs when Davis stepped to the plate. With the Black Barons' hopes beginning to fade, "Davis hit one of the longest balls in Rickwood history ... a terrific drive well above the right end of the 33 foot scoreboard which is 381 feet from home plate."[2] The home run cut the deficit to 4-3.

Davis was not only having a big series as a hitter. As Birmingham's manager, he had already made several key decisions to help his team win Game One. Before the top of the fifth started, he knew he had to make a decision. Perry had struggled during his four innings on the mound. Although he had stuck out five, his performance was uneven as he had walked four, given up three hits, and surrendered four runs. Davis had no choice but to replace him.

Davis called on 23-year-old right-hander Bill Greason. Greason had pinch-hit the previous day and had already pitched one inning in the series.[3] He immediately rewarded Davis for his decision by recording two outs, setting down Buck O'Neil and Hank Thompson. Brown, however, hit a home run to left field; and Greason gave up consecutive singles to Scott and Howard. With two on and two out, Greason retired Baker to end the fifth inning, but the Monarchs had padded their lead to 5-3.

Neither team scored over the next two innings, though both threatened. In the bottom of the sixth, Mays led off with a walk, but Ed Steele grounded into a 6-4-3 double play. In the top of the seventh, Thompson walked with one out but was caught trying to steal second base.

The Monarchs had an even better chance to score when Howard doubled to open the eighth, He was left stranded at second, though, after Greason retired the next three batters. In the bottom of the inning, the Black Barons scored a run on consecutive singles by Britton, Mays, and Steele. However, after loading the bases with one out, neither Pepper Bassett nor Jim Zapp could get a hit, and the Monarchs clung to a 5-4 lead.

The Monarchs failed to score in the top of the ninth as Greason hung tough. In the bottom of the inning, Wilson hit a one-out double and made it to third on Britton's groundout. With two outs, Mays hit a double to right that scored Wilson and tied the game at 5-5.[4] For the second day in a row, the teams played extra innings.

In the 10th inning, Greason flirted with trouble. Scott led off with a walk but Greason picked him off. Greason got Howard out, but Baker singled and advanced to second on an error by Britton. Roberts singled to right, but Steele's throw to Bassett caught him at the plate and kept the score tied.

In the bottom of the 10th, Souell's error at third allowed Davis to reach first. Scott moved him to second on a well-executed bunt down the third-base line. Catcher Bassett, who had been involved in arguably the biggest defensive play of the game in the previous inning, singled to score Davis. The Black Barons won, 6-5.

Wilson, Mays, and Davis proved to be a three-headed monster: Each had three hits. Despite his somewhat rocky start, Greason scattered eight hits over seven innings in a gutsy performance, allowing only one run and gaining the win. Brown led the Monarchs with three hits and Howard and Baker had two hits each. Ford Smith gave up 14 hits and walked three over 9⅓ innings and took the loss.

The best-of-seven championship series continued with Birmingham winning, 4-3, in Memphis on September 15. The Monarchs won Game Four, 3-1, at Blues Stadium in Kansas City on the 19th. The teams played a 3-3 tie on the 20th with the game called because of rain in the sixth inning. The Monarchs won, 5-4, on September 21 and again, 5-3, on the 22nd. The deciding game was also in Kansas City, on September 26. Behind the three-hit pitching of

Bill Greason, Birmingham won, 5-1, and celebrated a championship.

## SOURCES

In addition to the sources cited in the Notes, the author consulted the box score and play-by-play of the game presented by Retrosheet. This piece mostly uses official NAL pitching statistics compiled by the Howe News Bureau, as they cover more games than Seamheads, which includes only games for which box scores could be found.[5]

https://retrosheet.org/NegroLeagues/boxesetc/1948/B09120BIR1948.htm

## NOTES

1 "Repeats Over Monarchs," *Kansas City Times*, September 13, 1948: 15.

2 Tim Cary, "Slidin' and Ridin', at Home and on the Road with the 1948 Birmingham Black Barons," *Alabama Heritage*, Fall 1986: 31.

3 https://retrosheet.org/NegroLeagues/boxesetc/1948/B09110BIR1948.htm.

4 "Birmingham Grabs First 2 Games in Playoff Series," *Chicago Defender*, September 18, 1948: 11.

5 According to Gary Ashwill, "Seamheads statistics and the official Howe News data are not directly comparable, as Seamheads is based only on games for which box scores were published at the time (roughly half of Negro League games in the 1940s), and Seamheads regular season statistics include official NAL games as well as two categories of games that were not counted in the official numbers: unofficial games against NAL opponents, and interleague games against NNL teams. The Howe News Bureau statistics, by contrast, cover only official NAL regular season games, though they are more complete than Seamheads numbers in that category, as they include many games for which box scores were not published at the time." Email from Gary Ashwill, February 14, 2023.

# MAYS LEADS THE BLACK BARONS TO POSTSEASON VICTORY

## September 30, 1948: Birmingham Black Barons 4, Homestead Grays 3, at Rickwood Field, Birmingham, Alabama

## Game Three of the 1948 Negro League World Series

BY RICHARD J. PUERZER

**THE 1948 NEGRO** League World Series was both an ending and a beginning. It was the last Negro League World Series. With the precipitous demise of the Negro Leagues following the desegregation of the National and American Leagues, the prominence and structure of the Negro Leagues were already in decline. However, this Series was also an important beginning. It was the first event of national prominence for a 17-year-old Birmingham Black Barons center fielder and superstar in the making, Willie Mays. Game Three provided glimpses of the greatness that Mays would display on baseball diamonds for more than the next two decades.

Two of the great teams in the history of the Negro Leagues, the Homestead Grays and the Birmingham Black Barons, faced off in the 1948 Series. The talent in the Negro Leagues had begun to thin as players left for the formerly all-White major and minor leagues, although the rosters of the Black Barons and Grays had not yet been directly affected. The Black Barons featured stars Lorenzo "Piper" Davis, Artie Wilson, Lloyd "Pepper" Bassett, and their youngest player, Willie Mays. The Homestead Grays were a strong veteran team, with power hitters Buck Leonard, Luke Easter, and Bob Thurman, along with veteran Sam Bankhead, making for a formidable lineup.

The Negro League World Series was played before the major-league World Series began. the press coverage of the Negro League games was somewhat overshadowed by the other World Series, which featured the Cleveland Indians, starring former Negro Leaguers Larry Doby and Satchel Paige, and the Boston Braves. The African American press, including the *Pittsburgh Courier*, *Chicago Defender*, and the *Afro American* of Baltimore, did provide coverage and game stories for the Negro League World Series, but failed to provide box scores, let alone pay much attention to the games. For example, the October 9 issue of the *Afro American* featured a preview authored by Sam Lacy of the Cleveland-Boston World Series on the front page.[1]

Additionally, many sportswriters were filing stories about the performances of Brooklyn Dodgers stars Jackie Robinson and Roy Campanella, as well as Don Newcombe, who was pitching in the Dodgers' minor-league system. In fact, the October 9 *Afro American* featured pictures of Newcombe, Sam Jethroe, and Dan Bankhead in anticipation of the "Little World Series" between the Montreal Royals and the St. Paul Saints, both minor-league affiliates of the Dodgers.[2] Meanwhile, the story for Game Four of the Negro League World Series was relegated to a brief description of the game, and lacked even a line score.

The Homestead Grays won the first game of the Series, 3-2, and the second, 5-3. The only known box score is for Game One. It lists Mays as batting third and playing center field. Mays went 0-for-3 at the plate in that game. He did reach base in the eighth inning on a fielder's choice, and scored on Piper Davis's triple. Mays is not mentioned in the Game Two accounts.[3]

Game Three was played on Thursday night, September 30, at the Black Barons home ballpark, Rickwood Field, in Birmingham, Alabama. Tom Parker started the game for the Grays against Alonzo Perry of the Black Barons. It was in this game that Mays showed glimpses of his future greatness on both offense and defense. He made three plays that became etched in the memories of players and fans present for the game.

The Black Barons took a 1-0 lead in the bottom of the third. In the fourth, Grays slugger Luke Easter slugged a home run to tie the game. Next up was power-hitting Bob Thurman, who drove a ball deep to center field for what appeared to be a sure double. Mays, however, got a great jump on the ball and made the catch against the center-field fence.[4]

In the bottom of the fourth, Grays pitcher Parker pulled a muscle and was relieved by R.T. Walker. In the top of the sixth, Mays made another defensive gem. With Buck Leonard on first base, the next batter singled to center field. Leonard tried advancing to third base on the young center fielder. However, Mays was quick to field the ball and fired a bullet to third, cutting down Leonard.[5]

Walker pitched well for the Grays until he gave up two runs in the sixth, giving the Black Barons a 3-1 lead. Ted Alexander relieved Walker in the seventh. Meanwhile, Alonzo Perry put up a strong performance pitching for the Black Barons until he gave up two runs in the eighth inning before being relieved by Bill Greason.

Greason held the Grays in the top of the ninth. In the bottom half, Jim Zapp grounded out to lead off the inning and Greason followed with a single. Artie Wilson flied out, but third baseman John Britton followed with a walk. This brought up Mays, who had already demonstrated his defensive prowess twice in the game. With two out and two on, and a chance to win the game, he now had a chance to shine on offense. He promptly drove a ball up the middle, reportedly through the pitcher's legs, to score Greason with the game-winning run.[6]

Game Three proved to be the only win for the Black Barons. The Grays dominated Game Four and won 14-1. Game Five was a slugfest, with the Grays prevailing in 10 innings, 10-6, and winning the Series four games to one. Newspaper accounts for the final two games do not mention Willie Mays.[7] After making his mark on Game Three, Mays returned to the Black Barons for the 1949 and 1950 seasons and then signed with the New York Giants.

## SOURCES

Portions of this article were taken from Richard J. Puerzer, "The 1948 Negro League World Series," in Frederick C. Bush and Bill Nowlin, eds., *Bittersweet Goodbye: The Black Barons, The Grays, and the 1948 Negro League World Series* (Phoenix: Society for American Baseball Research, 2017), 386-390.

## NOTES

1 Sam Lacy, "AFRO Picks Indians to Win in 7 Games," *Baltimore Afro American*, October 9, 1948: 1.

2 "They'll Play in 'Little World Series,'" *Baltimore Afro-American*, October 9, 1948: 8.

3 For Game One, the following references were used: "Grays Score Win in World Series," *Baltimore Afro American*, October 2, 1948: 9, and "National League Champions Clinch Game In Second With 3-Run Rally," *Kansas City Call*, October 1, 1948: n.p. For Game Two, the following references were used: "Grays Shade Black Barons by 5-3 Score," *Birmingham Age-Herald*, September 30, 1948: n.p., and "Black Barons Seek Initial Win Tonight," *Birmingham News*, September 30, 1948: n.p.

4 John Klima, *Willie's Boys* (Hoboken, New Jersey: John Wiley and Sons, 2009), 181-182.

5 Buck Leonard with Jim Riley, *Buck Leonard: The Black Lou Gehrig* (New York: Carroll and Graf, 1995), 201-202.

6 For Game Three, the following newspaper references were used: "Black Barons Nip Grays, 4-3, for First Series Win," *Birmingham Age-Herald*, October 1, 1948: n.p., and "Black Barons Nip Grays, 4-3," *Birmingham News*, October 1, 1948: n.p.

7 For Game Four, the following references were used: "Black Barons, Grays Tangle In N.O. Today," *Birmingham News*, October 3, 1948: n.p.; "Grays Hold 3-1 Lead in Series," *Baltimore Afro American*, October 9, 1948: 8; "Grays Rout Birmingham in Series," *Pittsburgh Courier*, October 9, 1948: 12; and "Homestead Grays Swamp Black Barons, 14-1," *Chicago Defender*, October 9, 1948: 10. For Game Five, the following references were used: "Black Barons Take On Grays," *Birmingham News*, October 5, 1948: n.p.; "Grays Nip Black Barons, Win Series," *Birmingham Age-Herald*, October 6, 1948: n.p.; "Grays Blast Black Barons," *Birmingham News*, October 6, 1948: n.p.; and "Grays Win, 10-6 in World Series," *Afro American*, October 16, 1948: 8.

# WILLIE MAYS HAS THREE HITS, MAKES SPECTACULAR CATCH IN MILLERS HOME OPENER

## May 1, 1951: Minneapolis Millers 11, Columbus Red Birds 0, at Nicollet Park, Minneapolis

BY DAVE LANDE

**WILLIE MAYS HAD** three hits, Ray Dandridge had four, and Hoyt Wilhelm threw seven shutout innings as the Minneapolis Millers defeated the Columbus Red Birds, 11-0, in the Millers' home opener of the 1951 American Association season. Dubbed the "Black Mush Bowl," the game was played in rain-soaked conditions in front of 6,477 fans.[1] Included in the crowd was Max Levy, who had attended every Millers Opening Day since 1902.[2]

Newspapers across the country ran articles about Mays' arrival with the Millers after he played in 1950 for the Trenton Giants of the Interstate League. This from the *Capital Journal* of Salem, Oregon: "American Association fans are already tabbing Willie Mays, 19-year-old center fielder at Minneapolis, as the league's brightest prospect this season. He has a great arm and can run like the Dickens."[3]

From the *Birmingham News*: "Willie Mays, Former Black Baron, hit 10 for 21 for Minneapolis – six of the blows going for extra bases, three doubles, one triple and two home runs. Mays was a natural ball player from the first day he showed up at Rickwood while a student at Parker High School."[4] And from the *Black Dispatch* of Oklahoma City: "... and Willie can do everything an outfielder is supposed to do. Only his lack of experience is holding him back. That would be terrific – seeing this young colored star, trained by the Giants coming up to the Polo Grounds. He's be sensational and a whale of a drawing card."[5]

Recognition for Mays continued at Nicollet Park as the Millers players walked from the dressing room under the right-field stands to the dugout. Ray Dandridge, the veteran third baseman nicknamed Old Bow Legs, preceded Mays from the dressing room, and the early-arriving fans in the stands applauded him. Dandridge, in turn, tipped his cap. Shortly after, Mays left the dressing room and also received applause from the fans. A *Minneapolis Morning Tribune* writer noted, "The customers wanted to let Mays know they had heard about him."[6]

Before his team even came to bat, Mays gave Millers fans a thrilling demonstration of his baseball skills when he ran to deep center field, 435 feet from home plate, and caught Vern Benson's long drive[7] against the flagpole.[8] According to one fan's reminiscence of this play decades later, there were less than two outs and the Red Birds had a runner on third. When Mays made the catch, the runner tagged and ran for home. Mays' throw from center field bounced once before it was caught by the catcher. The baserunner, who was halfway to home, stopped and ran back to third, where he slid to avoid being tagged out.[9]

The Millers put across a trio of runs in the bottom of the first. The leadoff hitter, Pete Milne, walked and two batters later Mays singled to center. With two outs in the inning, Milne and Mays both scored when Dandridge singled to left. The Red Birds pitcher, Herb Moford, walked the next three hitters, Davey Williams (his first of four walks in the game), John Kropf, and Jake Early, to force in Dandridge with the final run of the inning.[10]

Dandridge opened the bottom of the fourth with a single and Williams walked. One out later, Early walked to load the bases. The next hitter, the ninth hitter in the batting order, was pitcher Wilhelm. In the *Minneapolis Morning Tribune*, Halsey Hall wrote, "Mr. Wilhelm, who has sometimes been known to 'pull' a ball as far as second, didn't bother about it this time and sliced a runaway double to right." Wilhelm's hit scored two runs. A third run scored when Milne singled to center, and a force out by Rudy Rufer scored the fourth run of the inning.[11]

The second Red Birds pitcher of the game, Maurice Garlock, gave up the final Miller runs in the sixth inning. Dandridge led off with a home run, for which he was given a watch by the National Jewelry Company after the game for hitting the first Millers homer of the season in Nicollet Park. After Williams walked and Kropf doubled, Early homered over Nicollet Avenue to score the final three runs of the game for the Millers.[12]

Before the start of the seventh inning, the lights at Nicollet Park were turned on – a first in the history of Nicollet Park for an afternoon game, according to Millers business manager George Brophy.[13] Wilhelm struck out light-hitting Howie Phillips in the top of the seventh with the bases loaded to end the half-inning. With two outs in the bottom of the seventh and Dandridge on first base, umpire Pat Padden finally called the game due to field conditions described as abominable and a "bowl of soup."[14]

Mays finished the game going 3-for-5 with a double and one run scored. Dandridge went 4-for-5 with a home run, three runs scored, and three runs batted in.[15] Catcher Jake Early said "[T]he secret of Hoyt's success was not better stuff but better control than in previous starts.[16] Wilhelm gave up five hits and walked two in seven innings.[17]

The next day in the *Minneapolis Star*, columnist Charles Johnson wrote that the Red Birds weren't upset about the soggy field conditions until they fell behind after the first inning. "Then they acted like a lot of mistreated corner lot ball players who apparently didn't realize yet (sic) gate receipts make possible their salaries. Crowds in the minor leagues of 6,500 paid aren't every day happenings."[18]

After the game, Mays described it as "just another game." He added, "I didn't go for power today. I just wanted hits. How can you miss with such grand fans? There is no strain in playing in front of people like you." Asked how difficult it was to play center field in Nicollet Park, Mays said, "The right field fence is so close you don't get a chance to run to your left. Outside of that, it's no different."[19]

To another writer, Mays complained that he didn't lift one over the short right-field fence. "That fence, that fence, said gentleman Willie in a high-pitcher voice in the club house." First baseman Mike

Natisin told Willie to "forget the fence" and added, "It's been there sixty years and it'll probably be there sixty more years."[20]

Millers manager Heath was effusive in his praise of Mays: "That's the way Mays has played all year. You think the boy isn't that good, but he comes up with impossible plays every day. He does something to help us win every game. He can hit, throw and run. What more can you ask? The boy is the greatest prospect I have ever seen."[21]

Slightly over three weeks later, on May 25, Mays' time with the Millers came to an end when he was called up to the New York Giants. He was batting a robust .477 (71-for-149) with a .524 on-base percentage. During his time in Minneapolis, the Millers went 21-14, which was good for third place in the eight-team American Association.[22] After May 25 and without Mays in the lineup, the Millers went 56-61 to finish in fifth place at 77-75. Two days later, Horace Stoneham, owner of the Giants, arranged to have a letter to Miller fans printed in a Sunday newspaper explaining why Mays was called up to the Giants after playing only 25 games with the Millers. Mays' "record of performance" is why he was entitled to the promotion, explained Stoneham in the letter.[23]

## NOTES

1 Halsey Hall, "Mays in Torrid Debut, Dandy Raps Four Hits," *Minneapolis Morning Tribune*, May 2, 1951: 19.

2 Jim Byrne, "Dandridge's 4 Hits Cheer Heath," *Minneapolis Star*, May 2, 1951: 41. Thew newspaper capitalized the word Dickens in this instance.

3 "Oak Player Gets Nod as Coast's Top Rookie of '51," *Salem* (Oregon) *Capital Journal*, April 30, 1951: 12.

4 Zipp Newman, "Dusting 'Em Off," *Birmingham News*, May 1, 1951: 28.

5 Al White, "New York Giants May Call Up Negro Star, Willie Mays, to Fill Right Field Post," *Black Dispatch* (Oklahoma City), April 28, 1951: 6.

6 Joe Hendrickson, "Sports Views," *Minneapolis Morning Tribune*, May 2, 1951: 20.

7 Byrne, "Dandridge's 4 Hits Cheer Heath."

8 Hall, "Mays in Torrid Debut, Dandy Raps Four Hits."

9 Ben Welter, "May 2, 1951: Willie Mays 'Torrid' in Minneapolis Debut," *Star Tribune* Blog, May 31, 2017.

10 Hall, "Mays in Torrid Debut, Dandy Raps Four Hits."

11 Hall, "Mays in Torrid Debut, Dandy Raps Four Hits."

12 Hall, "Mays in Torrid Debut, Dandy Raps Four Hits."

13 Byrne, "Dandridge's 4 Hits Cheer Heath."

14 Hall, "Mays in Torrid Debut, Dandy Raps Four Hits."

15 Hall, "Mays in Torrid Debut, Dandy Raps Four Hits."

16 Byrne, "Dandridge's 4 Hits Cheer Heath."

17 Hall, "Mays in Torrid Debut, Dandy Raps Four Hits."

18 Charles Johnson, "Lowdown on Sports," *Minneapolis Star*, May 2, 1951: 41.

19 Sid Hartman, "Just Another Game, Says Millers' Mays," *Minneapolis Morning Tribune*, May 2, 1951: 19.

20 Byrne, "Dandridge's 4 Hits Cheer Heath."

21 Hartman, "Just Another Game, Says Millers' Mays."

22 *Minneapolis Morning Tribune*, May 25, 1951: 20.

23 *Minneapolis Sunday Tribune*, May 27, 1951: 34.

# HIS FIRST NATIONAL LEAGUE HIT WAS A TOWERING HOMER

## May 28, 1951: Boston Braves 4, New York Giants 1, at Polo Grounds, New York

BY RICHARD BOGOVICH

**IF YOU BEGIN** your National League career going hitless in three road games, you may as well go for broke and swing mightily early in your first home game. That's what Willie Mays did against the Boston Braves on May 28, 1951, and beat writers for both teams chose their strongest adjectives to describe his contact with the pitch in question, which happened to be against another future Hall of Famer. He produced his team's only run, but also figured in its subsequent failures on offense that night.[1]

In 1950 Mays hit .353 in 81 games for the Trenton Giants of the Class-B Interstate League, and to start the 1951 season he was promoted to the Minneapolis Millers of the Triple-A American Association. Before he was called up by the New York Giants for his debut, he batted a staggering .477 with 8 homers and 30 RBIs in 35 games. In fact, Mays left the Millers with a 16-game hitting streak in which he hit a blistering .569. Of his 41 hits during the streak, 17 were for extra bases.[2]

Mays said he and Millers teammate Ray Dandridge, another future Hall of Famer, were watching the movie *Lightning Strikes Twice* in Sioux City, Iowa, when a voice over the theater's loudspeaker asked him to report to its office immediately. "I was shocked and thought real lightning had struck when I found Tommy (Tommy Heath, his manager) waiting. ... He told me I was to come to New York and they had to get me on a plane as soon as possible," Mays told Sam Lacy of the *Afro-American* a few days later. "Wasn't scared at first, but it sure was a surprise."[3]

Alas, his first three games in the National League were duds. He went hitless in 12 at-bats at Philadelphia before his home debut on Monday, May 28. "Phils' pitchers gave him little in the way of 'fat ones' or even 'good ones' to swing at," wrote an anonymous sportswriter with the *Philadelphia Tribune* (in 2022 the oldest continuously published African American newspaper in the country).[4]

Expectations for Mays were already very high. Probably by coincidence, on May 29, sports editor Zipp Newman of the *Birmingham News* (near the rookie's hometown of Fairfield, Alabama) noted that "the Giants believe that if Mays can come through, he will be as big a drawing card as the Yankees' Mickey Mantle." Newman declared that Mays was "a better fielder than Mantle and scouts will tell you very quickly there isn't a throwing arm in all baseball like Mays'."[5] Alvin Moses of the *Atlanta Daily World*, another African American paper, echoed the first of Newman's points when he wrote that Mays "figures to bring out thousands of kids just as Mickey, Casey Stengel's freshman, has done at Yankee Stadium."[6]

After the futility Mays experienced in his first three games, a *Philadelphia Tribune* reporter worried aloud that the pressure might be too much. On a positive note, however, with the Giants he became one of "four Negro players, three of whom are regulars." The other three weren't named in that article, but were presumably third baseman Hank Thompson, outfielder-first baseman (and future Hall of Famer) Monte Irvin, and Cuban catcher Ray Noble. Black shortstop Artie Wilson had played his final game for the Giants on May 23 and was sent down to the minors to make room for the addition of Mays on May 24. Thompson and Irvin both started with Mays on May 28, and Noble pinch-hit. Despite the fact that Mays wasn't cracking an all-White lineup, the *Tribune* reporter worried about the newcomer's age and experience. "It may be that young Mays, he is only 20, will not be able to make the grade," the writer observed. "He has only been in organized baseball 18 months."[7] Mays' 20th birthday was May 6.

On the evening of May 28, the temperature was 68 degrees Fahrenheit at 6:00, and little more than a trace of rain fell in New York City that day.[8] Boston's record was 19-18 at the start of play, while the Giants began at 20-19. The attendance was 23,101.[9]

The starting pitcher for the Giants was Sheldon Jones, in his sixth season with the team. His two best years were in 1948 and 1949, when he went 16-8 and 15-12 respectively, with ERAs below 3.40.[10] Jones struck out Boston's leadoff hitter, Roy Hartsfield, but the third strike rolled about 10 feet from New York catcher Wes Westrum. He threw low to first baseman Whitey Lockman, who dropped the ball and was charged with an error. Willard Marshall tripled, and one out later Bob Elliott homered to drive in the second and third runs for the visitors. Jones retired two of the next three Braves to sidestep an additional threat.[11]

The Giants' leadoff hitter, Eddie Stanky, drew a walk from Warren Spahn, who was well on his way to becoming the sixth-winningest pitcher of all time. Stanky was soon erased on a 3-6-3 double-play grounder hit by Lockman. Willie Mays thus batted with the bases empty. The relatively new Giant "was given a rousing welcome," reported Hy Hurwitz in the *Boston Globe*. "He took a ball and then smashed a Spahn fast ball over the whole works in left which was [as] genuine a homer as they come."[12]

By contrast, Henry McKenna of the *Boston Herald* wrote, "It appeared he hit a curve on a 3-1 pitch and thereafter he saw nothing but fast balls."[13] Mays himself told Dale Wright of the *New York Amsterdam News*, a Black paper, that it was an outside curve. "I can get more of them if National

*Willie Mays hit 20 home runs and won NL Rookie of the Year honors in 1951. Promoted May 24, he batted .274 with 68 RBIs for New York. 1951 Bowman card, courtesy of Topps.*

League pitchers don't hand me too many passes," Mays said. Well-known actress Laraine Day, wife of Giants manager Leo Durocher, gave Mays a nice wristwatch to welcome him to the club that day, and he reportedly earned a second one from a chewing gum company for the homer.[14] In addition to curve vs. fastball, newspapers disagreed on whether Mays hit the sphere *onto* the left-field roof or *over* it, as both Boston sportswriters characterized it. For example, Joseph Sheehan of the *New York Times* wrote that the "towering poke landed atop the left-field roof."[15]

Only one more runner scored that night. In the third inning, Jones gave up singles to the first two batters and was replaced by Al Gettel. The new pitcher got Elliott to ground into a double play, but the lead runner scored to make it 4-1. Elliott complained demonstrably about being called out at first to complete the double play, and umpire Lou Jorda ejected him.[16]

Gettel, who was primarily a starting pitcher with three American League teams from 1945 through 1948, finished the game for the Giants. He surrendered only two hits and a walk in his seven innings. Spahn hurled a complete game and scattered six more hits. The Braves were 1-for-4 with runners in scoring position and left four men on base. The Giants were 0-for-8 with runners in scoring position and left 11 teammates stranded on the basepaths. The game took 2:28 to complete.[17]

Jim McCulley of the *New York Daily News* summarized the Giants' best chances against Spahn. With one out in the fourth, the Giants had two men on base, but "Irvin and Thompson failed to keep this threat alive," McCulley wrote. "In the fifth, with one down, Stanky singled and, with two down, Mays drew a walk. But Spahn, who fanned eight, made Westrum his fourth straight strikeout victim at this point."[18]

To begin the seventh inning, Durocher seemed close to pinch-hitting for his pitcher, but he didn't. "Gettel fanned, then much to Durocher's dismay, Stanky and Lockman followed with singles," McCulley reported. "Spahn took care of this situation by striking out Mays and Westrum, the latter for the third straight time."[19] In the bottom of the ninth, Mays batted with two outs and Lockman on first base. He popped out to end the game.[20]

Hurwitz said Mays reacted quite negatively after whiffing but apparently didn't direct hostility toward home-plate umpire Larry Goetz. "He was boiling mad at himself in the seventh" for not producing in that at-bat, Hurwitz observed. Mays hadn't swung and missed, but rather "took a called third strike and jumped up and down in disgust."[21] After that first-inning blast for his first National League hit, he contributed only that walk among his four other plate appearances. (In fact, Mays went into a 0-for-13 slump after hitting his first homer as a Giant and began his career 1-for-26.) On defense he had one chance, a putout on a fly to begin the second inning.[22]

By winning, Boston improved to 20-18 and moved into a virtual tie with Chicago for third place in the eight-team National League. The Giants, at 20-20, were one game behind.[23] As is widely known, the Giants ultimately won the pennant that season in an incredibly dramatic manner. But as for Willie Mays on May 28, 1951, it was one homer down, 659 to go in his National League career.

## SOURCES

In addition to the sources cited in the Notes, the author consulted Baseball-Referencc.com and Retrosheet.org.

https://www.baseball-reference.com/boxes/NY1/NY1195105280.shtml

https://www.retrosheet.org/boxesetc/1951/B05280NY11951.htm

## NOTES

1 Back in 1948, Mays played for the Birmingham Black Barons of the Negro American League (NAL), which in 2020 became recognized by Major League Baseball as a major league. As of 2023 the Seamheads Negro Leagues database online shows Mays with no home runs with that team. However, newer research documents homers by Mays in at least two NAL regular-season games, according to Tom

Thress, "Tracking Down Willie Mays's 1948 Game Log," *Willie Mays – Five Tools*, ed. by Bill Nowlin and Glen Sparks (Phoenix: SABR, 2023).

2 "Willie Mays, Miller Sensation Brought .477 Ave. to Giants," *The Sporting News*, May 30, 1951: 6. This article also said Artie Wilson was sent down to Ottawa of the International League to create a roster spot for Mays.

3 Sam Lacy, "From A to Z," *Baltimore Afro-American,* June 2, 1951: 17. Speaking of movies, in this column Mays credited footage of Joe DiMaggio with teaching him how to bat. (Mays credited his own father with teaching him how to catch a ball.)

4 "Mays Impresses as Philly Fans Get First Look," *Philadelphia Tribune*, May 29, 1951: 11. For his minor-league stats in 1950 and 1951, see https://www.baseball-reference.com/register/player.fcgi?id=mays--002wil.

5 Zipp Newman, "Dusting 'em off," *Birmingham News*, May 29, 1951: 19.

6 Alvin Moses, "Beating the Gun," *Atlanta Daily World*, May 30, 1951: 5. A colleague of Moses' may have been among the very first sportswriters to predict superstardom for Mays, back in 1948: "Willie Howard Mays ... is the wonder kid of the Negro American League. Nobody has voted him the find of the year, rookie of the year or most valuable player. ... But in my book, he is the most promising youngster to play baseball at Rickwood Field since I've been around." – Emory O. Jackson, "Hits and Bits," *Atlanta Daily World*, October 15, 1948: 5.

7 "The Case of Willie Mays," *Philadelphia Tribune*, June 2, 1951: 4. See Note 1 regarding Artie Wilson.

8 "Daily Almanac," *New York Daily News,* May 28, 1951: 2. "Daily Almanac," *New York Daily News*, May 29, 1951: 2.

9 Jim McCulley, "Braves Check Giants, 4-1; Mays Hits 1st HR," *New York Daily News*, May 29, 1951: 46.

10 For the career stats of Sheldon Jones, see https://www.baseball-reference.com/players/j/jonessh01.shtml.

11 Henry McKenna, "Spahn, Braves Defeat Giants, 4-1," *Boston Herald*, May 29, 1951: 15.

12 Hy Hurwitz, "Spahn 7-Hitter, Elliott's Homer Top Giants, 4-1," *Boston Globe*, May 29, 1951: 1, 17.

13 McKenna.

14 Dale Wright, "Willie Mays Feels at Home in Polo Grounds," *New York Amsterdam News*, June 2, 1951: 14.

15 Joseph M. Sheehan, "Braves Trip Giants at Polo Grounds; Dodgers Triumph; Yanks Bow," *New York Times*, May 29, 1951: 29.

16 Sheehan.

17 For the baserunning stats, see https://www.baseball-reference.com/boxes/NY1/NY1195105280.shtml. Career stats for Gettel and all the other players are readily available by clicking on their names in the two batting orders.

18 McCulley.

19 McCulley.

20 Sheehan.

21 Hurwitz.

22 Sheehan.

23 "Standings in the Major Leagues," *Boston Herald*, May 29, 1951: 15. This daily's standings were presented in a chart showing each team's performance against all the other teams.

# "IT WAS THE MOST PERFECTEST THROW I EVER MADE"

## August 15, 1951: New York Giants 3, Brooklyn Dodgers 1, at Polo Grounds, New York

BY DAN FIELDS

THREE YEARS BEFORE Willie Mays made perhaps the most famous catch in baseball history, he made a throw for the ages. Although Mays's iconic over-the-shoulder catch of a long drive by Vic Wertz in Game One of the 1954 World Series is better known, the finest defensive play of his career might have been on August 15, 1951, when Mays was a 20-year-old rookie who had played fewer than 80 games in the majors.

The night before, the Giants had won the first game of a three-game series against the Dodgers, giving them four wins in a row, but they still trailed their crosstown rivals by 11½ games in the race for the NL pennant. A crowd of 21,007 showed up at the Polo Grounds for the Wednesday afternoon game. The Giants scored first, in the bottom of the first inning. Al Dark hit a line drive to right field off Ralph Branca and stretched the hit into a double when Carl Furillo threw behind him. Dark moved to third base on a groundout by Don Mueller and came home when Monte Irvin singled to center field.

The Dodgers evened the score in the top of the seventh inning. Pee Wee Reese singled to center field off starter Jim Hearn, running his hitting streak to 22 games, and advanced to second base on a wild pitch to Duke Snider. After Snider and Andy Pafko flied out, Roy Campanella hit a ground-ball single to center and drove Reese home.

With one out in the top of the eighth, Brooklyn's Billy Cox was on third, Branca was on first, and Furillo was at the plate. Furillo was a right-handed pull hitter, so New York center fielder Mays positioned himself in left-center. Instead, Furillo hit a fly to right-center. "It looked plenty deep enough to bring in Cox, especially since Mays had to run a long way to get the ball," wrote Joseph M. Sheehan in the *New York Times*. "But Willie, making a complete whirling pivot on the dead run, cut loose with a tremendous peg that boomed into [Wes] Westrum's mitt in perfect position for the catcher to tag the sliding Cox."[1] Westrum, not imagining a play at home, hadn't bothered to remove his mask. According to Mays's biographer James S. Hirsch, the catcher "estimated that when the ball reached him, it was traveling 85 mph, and if the umpire had called it, it would have been a strike."[2]

As the crowd erupted, "Cox sat staring at the plate in disbelief."[3] After the inning-ending double play, Mays's teammates met him on the dugout steps, and he "shrugged his way through, as though uncomfortable with all the fuss."[4] Mays was first up in the bottom of the eighth, and he received a standing ovation when he emerged from the dugout with his bats. He lined a single to center and got another standing ovation. After Bobby Thomson struck out swinging, Westrum homered over the left-field scoreboard. The Dodgers went down in order in the ninth inning, with Mays catching a fly ball by Pafko for the last out, and the Giants won 3-1.

Eddie Brannick, the Giants' traveling secretary, who had been with the team for more than 40 years, made a rare visit to the clubhouse to congratulate Mays and compared him favorably with some legendary center fielders. "I've seen [Tris] Speaker, [Joe] DiMaggio, [Terry] Moore, all of them," Brannick said, "but I've never seen anything like that throw. This kid made the greatest throw I ever looked at."[5] Furillo, then considered to have the best arm in baseball, was less charitable: "Luck. That was the luckiest throw I ever saw in my life. He can try that 50 times and he won't come close again."[6] Sports columnist Bill Corum went so far as to suggest that Mays tried the throw because he wasn't very bright: "A thinking ball player probably would have thought ... that the play was impossible and never have attempted it."[7]

Six years later, Furillo simply expressed astonishment. As players reminisced before the last game ever played at the Polo Grounds between the Giants and the Dodgers, on September 8, 1957, Furillo said, "I saw the impossible happen here ... when Willie Mays made that catch on me, whirled in a complete circle and threw out Billy Cox at home plate. It was a play that couldn't happen. But it did."[8]

And years after that, Mays told the *New York Times*' Arthur Daley, "It was the most perfectest throw I ever made."[9]

The Giants win was their fifth in a row, in a streak that continued through 16 games, placing them just five games behind the Dodgers when it concluded.

## NOTES

1 Joseph M. Sheehan, "Mays Helps Hearn Topple Brooks, 3-1," *New York Times*, August 16, 1951.

2 James S. Hirsch, *Willie Mays: The Life, The Legend* (New York: Scribner, 2010), 124.

3 Hirsch, 124,

4 Hirsch, 124,

5 Jason Aronoff, *Going, Going ... Caught! Baseball's Great Outfield Catches as Described by Those Who Saw Them, 1887-1964* (Jefferson, North Carolina, and London: McFarland & Company, Inc., Publishers), 155.

6 Aronoff, 155.

7 Hirsch, 125.

8 Aronoff, 157.

9 Arthur Daley, "Farewell to Willie," *New York Times*, September 23, 1963: Sports 2.

# MAYS MAKES HIS GREATEST CATCH – NO, NOT THAT ONE

## April 18, 1952: Brooklyn Dodgers 7, New York Giants 6 (12 innings), at Ebbets Field, Brooklyn

BY GLEN SPARKS

WILLIE MAYS SPRINTED deep into the Polo Grounds outfield to make his memorable over-the-shoulder catch of a Vic Wertz fly ball in Game One of the 1954 World Series. As soon as the ball settled into his glove more than 400 feet from home plate, Mays whirled around and threw a dart into the infield. Larry Doby, the lead runner for the Cleveland Indians, ran to third base but did not score, while Al Rosen stayed at first.[1]

Gayle Talbot called the catch "truly amazing."[2] New York Giants manager Leo Durocher said, "It was great. The wind was blowing, he had his back to the diamond, and I don't know how [*sic*] if he can do that."[3] Broadcaster Jack Brickhouse described the robbery as "an optical illusion."[4]

Today, The Catch, as many insist it be spelled, is the stuff of legend, and footage of the play is available on YouTube and other social media channels. But was it really the greatest catch of Mays' incredible career? Vin Scully said that Mays made an even better one more than two years earlier, and the Say Hey Kid agreed.

The Giants were playing their fiercest rival, the Brooklyn Dodgers, at Ebbets Field on April 18, 1952. A crowd of 31,032 filed into the cozy ballpark on Sullivan Place. The host Dodgers had a record of 3-0 after sweeping their opening road series against the Boston Braves. The Giants, meanwhile, opened at home against the Philadelphia Phillies and split a two-game set.

Brooklyn manager Charlie Dressen named 25-year-old right-hander Clem Labine as his starting pitcher. Durocher countered with 31-year-old righty Jim Hearn, the one-time St. Louis Cardinal.

New York took an early lead with a big first inning. Labine failed to retire even a single batter. Davey Williams led off with a double and scored on Al Dark's base hit. Bobby Thomson's single put runners on first and second. With Hank Thompson batting, Labine uncorked a wild pitch that veered far enough from catcher Roy Campanella for Dark to score and Thomson to advance one base. Hank Thompson grounded an RBI single to right field.

After Mays walked, Labine's day was done. Dressen called on Carl Erskine to provide some relief. The first batter "Oisk" faced, Don Mueller, struck out swinging. Whitey Lockman and Wes Westrum followed with RBI singles, and New York took a 5-0 lead.

Brooklyn got one run back in the bottom of the first when Campanella singled home Billy Cox, who had lined a one-out triple.

The Dodgers scored three more times in the second. Andy Pafko drew a leadoff walk and Gil Hodges singled. Carl Furillo followed with an RBI base hit but was thrown out trying to stretch his single into a double. Hearn left the game after walking Erskine.

Durocher summoned Hoyt Wilhelm from the bullpen. The knuckleball pitcher from North Carolina was making his big-league debut at the age of 29. He went on to pitch 21 seasons and earn a spot in the National Baseball Hall of Fame. Nicknamed "Old Sarge," Wilhelm served in World War II and was wounded in the Battle of the Bulge. He taught himself the knuckleball while still in high school.

Brooklyn shortstop Pee Wee Reese, the first batter Wilhelm faced, drove a pitch deep enough into center field for Hodges to tag and trot home. Cox's double advanced Erskine to third. Wilhelm, maybe with some first-game jitters, walked Jackie Robinson and, with Campanella batting, threw a wild pitch that scored Erskine. Wilhelm's shaky debut concluded after he walked Campanella. Dave Koslo entered the game with two outs. Duke Snider, Brooklyn's reliable slugger, ended the rally by grounding out. New York led, 5-4.

The game settled down after that early action. Neither team scored over the next four innings. Brooklyn put runners on first and third with one out in the sixth, but Koslo got Robinson to hit into a double play.

New York scored once in the seventh after Erskine loaded the bases with two out and Don Mueller at bat. This time, it was the Brooklyn pitcher's turn to uncork a wild pitch, the third of the game. Thomson, who started the rally with a two-out walk, ran safely home.

Pafko narrowed the Giants' lead with his two-out solo home run in the bottom of the seventh. Brooklyn had acquired the hard-hitting outfielder from the Chicago Cubs in June 1951, and the new Dodger hit 18 homers in just 84 games. After Pafko's big hit, Hodges singled and Furillo drew a walk. Dressen sent Bobby Morgan, a second-year infielder, to pinch-hit for Erskine.

Morgan ripped a liner into left-center-field and Mays began his sprint toward the wall. According to a reporter from Baltimore's *Afro-American*, "[I]t was doubtful that anyone in the park, even the most optimistic of the Giant rooters, entertained a hope that (Mays) would catch it."[5]

Mays "grabbed Morgan's blast with a desperation lunge."[6] Dick Young wrote that Mays made "another one of his description-defying catches." The second-year player "left his feet. He actually bounced, crashed into the wall on the first hop,

*Fans loved the exciting young outfielder who could do it all. SABR/The Rucker Archive.*

and rolled over on his back. But he held the ball."[7] Young's colleague at the *New York Daily News*, Dana Mozley, insisted "Willie Mays just had no right" to catch Morgan's liner.[8]

Brooklyn's new pitcher, Billy Loes, retired the Giants one-two-three in the top of the eighth. In the bottom half, with George Spencer now on the mound for New York, Robinson homered to tie the score, 6-6.

Neither team mounted much of a threat over the next 3½ innings. The Giants managed two singles, one in the ninth and one in the 10th, while the Dodgers were held hitless. Pafko led off the bottom of the 12th and drove a Spencer pitch over the right-field fence to give Brooklyn a 7-6 victory. "This one disappeared amid the advertising signs and chicken wire at the far end of the scoreboard," wrote the *Brooklyn Eagle's* Harold C. Burr.[9] Spencer's won-lost record fell to 0-2; Loes went to 1-0.

After the game, the talk turned more to Mays' catch than Pafko's heroics. "The greatest catch I ever saw in my life," Reese said. "He came with it. I know that. There's no argument. It was in his glove when he turned over, and Thomson went over and picked it out."[10]

According to Burr, "It looked as if the best Willie could do with the drive was to hold it to the double."[11] Morgan, still in disbelief after being robbed of extra bases, said, "I guess he must have caught it. You could have knocked me over with a feather when the ump waved me out. I was going for three for sure when I saw him on the ground."[12] Durocher called the catch "great, great, the greatest."[13]

In between sips from his soft drink, Mays told reporters, "I didn't think I had a chance at all to get it. It was sinking fast and seemed to be curving away. But I stayed with it and got it on the dive – with both hands together. Slid along the ground and got shaken up, that's all. Little bruise here on my right side."[14]

Compare those comments to the ones that Mays made after he snagged Wertz's drive. In 1954, Mays shrugged off any praise directed at him for that catch. "I had that ball all the way," he said. "There was nothing too hard about that one. … That catch today, you should never miss those kind."[15]

In an interview decades later, Mays said, "In my mind, I was always going to catch the ball. It was just a matter of how I'm going to get the ball back to the infield. I think I was more proud of the throw than I was of the catch. … I think a lot of people saw it in the World Series. They picked that catch as the catch of the century."[16]

Mays celebrated his 85th birthday on May 6, 2016. On that day, Scully was in the early months of his 67th and final season broadcasting Dodgers games. He told his television audience, "I was privileged to see Willie make the greatest catch of his career, and he agrees with me that it was."

Scully said that as soon as Morgan hit the ball "you knew it was an extra-base hit. Everyone knew that except Willie." Scully described how Mays ran and leapt parallel to the ground "like an arrow" to snare the ball. Mays hit the gravel warning track and "bounced headfirst into the concrete wall." He rolled onto his back but held on to the ball. "That," Scully said, "was the greatest single play I've ever seen."[17]

In 2020 Mays wrote the book *24: Life Stories and Lessons from the Say Hey Kid*, with John Shea. He tells readers, "That (the catch off Morgan) was a good catch, better than the World Series catch. I believe my best catch."[18]

## SOURCES

In addition to the specific sources cited in the Notes, the author used the Baseball-Reference.com and Retrosheet.org websites for general player, team, and season data and the box scores for this game.

https://www.baseball-reference.com/boxes/NYN/NYN197308170.shtml

https://www.retrosheet.org/boxesetc/1973/B08170NYN1973.htm

## NOTES

1 Sal Maglie started Game One for the Giants against the Indians and allowed two runs over seven-plus innings. He allowed two runners in the eighth and made way for reliever

Don Liddle, who gave up the fly ball to Vic Wertz. Giants manager Leo Durocher lifted Liddle and brought in Marv Grissom. Grissom walked Dale Mitchell to load the bases but struck out Dave Pope and got Jim Hegan to fly out. New York won the game, 5-2, and swept the World Series.

2 Gayle Talbot, "Dusty Rhodes' Homer Big Blow, But Mays' Catch Saved Giants," *Elmira* (New York) *Star-Gazette,* September 30, 1954: 40.

3 Ted Smits, "Wasn't Trying for a Homer, Confesses Giants Hero Rhodes," *Elmira* (New York) *Advertiser,* September 30, 1954: 11.

4 James S. Hirsch, *Willie Mays: The Life, the Legend* (New York: Scribner, 2010), 195.

5 Hirsch, 149.

6 Dick Young, "Flock Nips Giants in 12th, 7-6." *New York Daily News*, April 19, 1952: 140.

7 "Flock Nips Giants in 12th, 7-6." *New York Daily News*, April 19, 1952: 143.

8 Dana Mozley, "Mays' Catch Greatest, Dodgers, Giants Agree," *New York Daily News*, April 19, 1952: 28.

9 Harold C. Burr, "Pafko's Bat Can Spell Pennant for Flock," *Brooklyn Daily Eagle*, April 19, 1952: 6.

10 Mozley.

11 Burr, "Pafko's Bat Can Spell Pennant for Flock."

12 Burr, "Mays' Catch Greatest, Dodgers, Giants Agree."

13 Burr, "Mays' Catch Greatest, Dodgers, Giants Agree."

14 Burr, "Mays' Catch Greatest, Dodgers, Giants Agree."

15 Jim McCulley, "Mays Catch Saves Game; Indians Blame Wind," *New York Daily News*, September 30, 1954: 81.

16 Willie Mays reflects on "The Catch" in 1954 World Series – YouTube

17 Vin Scully tells great Willie Mays story on the Giants legend's 85th birthday | FOX Sports.

18 Willie Mays with John Shea, *24: Life Stories and Lessons from the Say Hey Kid* (New York: St. Martin's, 2020), 90.

# WILLIE MAYS LEADS GIANTS OVER DODGERS AS ARMY INDUCTION APPROACHES

## May 27, 1952: New York Giants 3, Brooklyn Dodgers 0, at Ebbets Field, Brooklyn

BY JOHN FREDLAND

AN ALABAMA DRAFT board summoned Willie Mays almost immediately after his debut season with the New York Giants in 1951, triggering a conscription process, necessitated by America's military intervention in Korea, that dragged through the winter and into the early weeks of the 1952 season. With orders finally in hand and his Army swearing-in two days away, Mays flashed the star quality about to be absent from the majors for nearly two seasons, as he connected on a home run and two doubles in the Giants' 3-0 win over the Brooklyn Dodgers at Ebbets Field on May 27.

Joining the Giants from the American Association's Minneapolis Millers five weeks into the 1951 season, Mays – manager Leo Durocher's starter in center field from day one – sparked New York to an improbable pennant,[1] anchored the first all-Black outfield in a formerly segregated major league,[2] and received National League Rookie of the Year honors.[3] At age 20, his future appeared bright.

But world events slowed his rise. North Korea had invaded South Korea in June 1950, and the United States, spearheading the United Nations' military response, was inducting young men into its armed forces. America's conscription laws subjected men aged 18½ through 25 to 24-month service terms.[4]

On October 12, two days after the Giants' loss to the New York Yankees in the 1951 World Series, the *New York Daily News* reported that Mays had been classified "1-A" – "eligible for military service" – by his hometown draft board in Alabama.[5] "The day I got home [after the 1951 season] the mail brought a letter to me from the Selective Service Board," Mays noted in his autobiography. "I was told to report to my draft board … within ten days."[6]

Seven months of uncertainty – spanning the offseason and spilling into the 1952 schedule – followed. Mays, who had graduated in the top half of his high-school class, made unwelcome headlines in October for failing a written Army aptitude test.[7] He was not accepted for duty until he passed the test in mid-January of 1952.[8]

The draft board had already met its quota of inductees for February, which pushed Mays' departure into the spring.[9] He requested a hardship deferment, asserting that his baseball income was needed to support four of his siblings,[10] but officials denied it on April 10 and set a May 17 induction date.[11]

Induction was delayed once again to transfer his files to a draft board in New York.[12] Finally, on May 21, Mays received orders to report to the Army on May 29.[13]

Against this backdrop, Mays – who missed a week of spring training in March after what the newspapers called "minor surgery"[14] – struggled on the field, batting only .161 in 17 games from April 22 through the first game of a May 16 doubleheader. Durocher dropped Mays from fifth to seventh in the order for several games, then alternated him between fifth and sixth, depending on whether a righty or lefty started against New York. The Giants also were without Mays' mentor, 1951 NL RBI king Monte Irvin, who had broken his ankle in a spring-training game.[15]

Still, their bid to repeat as NL champs rolled on. A 4-2 win over the Dodgers at the Polo Grounds on May 26 gave the Giants a 24-8 record and a half-game advantage over Brooklyn for first place in the league.[16]

The action moved to Ebbets Field on May 27 for the middle game of the crosstown series, expected to be Mays' next-to-last appearance before he left for the Army. With righty Ben Wade on the mound for Brooklyn, Mays, who had played every inning of every game in center, batted sixth.

New York's starter, 35-year-old right-hander Sal Maglie, had been integral to the Giants' early success. He entered with wins in all eight of his starts in 1952 and an 11-decision winning streak dating to September 1951.[17] The unblemished stretch included a two-hit shutout of the Dodgers on April 20.[18]

*Willie Mays missed nearly two full seasons due to military service. Courtesy National Baseball Hall of Fame.*

Wade – in a major-league rotation for the first time at age 29 after wartime Army service and nine seasons in the minors[19] – had been on the losing side of Maglie's April shutout. He fanned three Giants in the first inning of the rematch, working around Whitey Lockman's bad-hop single off Pee Wee Reese's chest at short and catching Bobby Thomson and Hank Thompson looking at fastballs on the outside corner for the final two outs.

But Don Mueller opened the second by driving his fifth homer of the season over the scoreboard in right-center, giving the Giants a 1-0 lead.

Mays followed with a drive near the wall in right. Carl Furillo went back and, as Dick Young reported in the *New York Daily News*, "backed to the scoreboard, reached high, and got his glove on the ball. But at that precise moment, Carl brushed the scoreboard and couldn't hold the pill."[20] Mays stopped at second with a double.

Alvin Dark hit a liner toward short. Reese, Young observed, "[took] his eye off the ball for a split second size-up of his chances of doubling Mays off second," and the ball hit off Reese's glove.[21]

As Reese retrieved the ball from the edge of the grass, Mays disregarded Durocher's stop sign at third and headed home. Reese fired to Rube Walker, who tagged Mays out, holding on despite Mays' knee accidentally striking him in the face.[22]

Mays did produce a run in the fourth, clubbing a two-out solo homer to right. It was his fourth home run of the season, and the Giants led, 2-0.

In the meantime, Maglie again held the upper hand over Brooklyn. Through four innings, the home team was hitless and no Dodger had reached second base. Several Dodgers, including Jackie Robinson, asked home-plate umpire Dusty Boggess to inspect the ball for illegal substances – a frequent allegation against Maglie[23] – but Boggess found nothing improper.

Furillo ended Maglie's no-hit string by singling to lead off the fifth. One out later, Walker hit a grounder between first and second. Davey Williams ranged far to his left, fielded it, and threw to Maglie covering first for the out.[24] Furillo took second, but Maglie fanned Wade to strand him there.

Brooklyn stirred again with two outs in the sixth. Duke Snider walked on a full-count pitch. After a strike, Robinson again made his case to Boggess, who threw the ball out.

Robinson singled on the next pitch. Snider went to third, giving Brooklyn two runners on base for what turned out to be the only time of the game, but Andy Pafko's popup to Williams ended the inning.

Another potential Dodgers' rally fizzled in the seventh. After Furillo walked to lead off the inning, Thompson made a leaping catch of Gil Hodges' fly ball near the stands in left, and Williams turned Walker's grounder into a double play.

By then, Mays had recorded his third opposite-field extra-base hit of the game, a one-out double to right in the seventh. He advanced no farther than second, but the Giants added an unearned run in the ninth off reliever Johnny Rutherford. Reese committed his second error of the game, as Dark's grounder went through his legs, allowing Mueller, who had singled and taken second on Mays' groundout, to score from second.

Robinson doubled to open the ninth, but Maglie retired the next three Dodgers to cap the four-hit shutout and extend his winning streak.[25]

A day later, Mays went hitless as Durocher's team completed the three-game sweep.[26] Ebbets Field cheered its foe, sending Mays off with what the *New York Daily News* characterized as "a farewell that was tinged with more affection than any Giant has been accorded in Brooklyn since King Carl Hubbell's bow out."[27]

"The New York Giants won the ball game ... but in the process lost the guy who is probably the best young ball player to come up to the majors in the past ten years, Willie Mays," added the *Pittsburgh Courier*'s Wendell Smith.[28]

Mays reported for the Army on May 29, bound for training in New Jersey, then duty at Fort Eustis, Virginia.[29]

Famed sportswriter Grantland Rice devoted his syndicated column to Mays that week. "No young ballplayer has shown greater promise in recent years," Rice wrote. "His day isn't over. He has time enough for baseball when he leaves the Army, around [age] 23."[30]

Mays' 1952 season went into the books with a .236 batting average and four homers in 34 games. Without him, the '52 Giants lost eight of their next 10 games and fell out of first place to stay. They finished second in the NL, 4½ games behind the Dodgers; they were fifth in 1953.

Mays twice requested hardship release from the Army but was denied both times.[31] He remained in uniform until March 1, 1954 – eight months after the armistice ending the Korean War – when he received his honorable discharge and returned to the Giants.[32]

While playing for a service team at Fort Eustis, he developed what soon became his trademark "basket catch" and hungered for a return to major-league competition.[33]

"[W]hen I left for the Army, the Giants had been a first-place club," Mays recalled in his autobiography. "While I was away, they were little more than mediocre. I planned to turn this around right away."[34]

*Acknowledgments*

The author thanks Gary Belleville for his comments on an earlier version of this article.

## SOURCES

In addition to the sources cited in the Notes, the author consulted Baseball-Reference.com and Retrosheet.org for pertinent information, including the box score and play-by-play. The author also reviewed game coverage in the *Brooklyn Eagle*, *New York Daily News*, and *New York Times* newspapers.

https://www.baseball-reference.com/boxes/BRO/BRO195205270.shtml

https://www.retrosheet.org/boxesetc/1952/B05270BRO1952.htm

## NOTES

1 When Mays debuted with the Giants on May 25, they were in fifth place, 4½ games behind the Dodgers. They trailed the Dodgers by 13 games on August 11 before winning 37 of their final 44 regular-season games to force a three-game playoff for the pennant. They won the pennant on Bobby Thomson's dramatic ninth-inning homer in Game Three of the tie-breaker. John Drebinger, "Giants Capture Pennant, Beating Dodgers 5-4 in 9th on Thomson's Three-Run Homer," *New York Times*, October 4, 1951: 1.

2 In Game One of the 1951 World Series, the Giants started Mays in center, Monte Irvin in left, and Hank Thompson in right. American Negro Press, "All-Sepia Outfield May Be Key to Indian Win: Pope Joins Doby, Smith in Outfield," *Pittsburgh Courier*, August 21, 1954: 21.

3 "Mays, Mac Win Rookie Awards," *New York Daily News*, November 16, 1951: 21C.

4 Harold B. Hinton, "Draft-U.M.T. Bill Signed by Truman," *New York Times*, June 20, 1951: 1.

5 Joe Trimble, "Reynolds and Raschi Face Operations Next Week," *New York Daily News*, October 12, 1951: C22.

6 Willie Mays with Lou Sahadi, *Say Hey: The Autobiography of Willie Mays* (New York: Simon & Schuster, 1988), 99.

7 "Army 'Releases' Mays: He Flunks Aptitude Test," *New York Daily News*, October 30, 1951: 72. Mays biographer Mary Kay Linge suggests the draft board believed Mays had failed the Armed Forces Qualification Test (AFQT) on purpose. Mary Kay Linge, *Willie Mays: A Biography* (Westport, Connecticut: Greenwood, 2005), 48.

8 "Army Passes Mays; Reports in March," *New York Daily News*, January 17, 1952: C20.

9 According to the *New York Daily News*, an Army public information officer "said that normally Mays would be ordered to report in 21 days but would be delayed because of a full quota from the [local draft] board." "Army Passes Mays; Reports in March."

10 Hyman C. Turkin, "Mays May Escape Army Draft," *New York Daily News*, April 8, 1952: 60.

11 "Mays No Hardship Case, Joins the Army May 17," *New York Daily News*, April 11, 1952: 61. "I ... did not qualify for either of the two requirements the Army had established for consideration as a hardship case," Mays indicated in his autobiography. "Either you had to be a married man with a child, or you had to be living in the home looking after the people you claimed as dependents. That ... I was helping my mother and four of my nine stepbrothers and sisters out didn't count. Nor did the fact that my stepfather was out of a job." Mays with Sahadi, *Say Hey*, 100.

12 This delay was reported on the eve of Mays' expected departure. Newspaper coverage on May 15 still asserted that "Mays reports to the Army following tomorrow's [May 16] game." Dana Mozley, "Delay Mays' Induction Month," *New York Daily News*, May 16, 1952: 21C; Associated Press, "21 Players, Including Stan Rojek, Shipped to Minor Leagues," *Buffalo Evening News*, May 15, 1952: IV, 52.

13 Jim McCulley, "Diamond Dust – Army Takes Mays May 29," *New York Daily News*, May 22, 1952: 94.

14 Jim McCulley, "Indians' Triple Play Aids Bob; Giants Beaten," *New York Daily News*, March 31, 1952: C20.

15 Mays with Sahadi, *Say Hey*, 100.

16 Jim McCulley, "Giants Hurdle Dodgers, 4-2; Bob Homers Before 40,456," *New York Daily News*, May 27, 1952: 72.

17 Jim McCulley, "Maglie Tops Braves 5-3, for 8 in a Row," *New York Daily News*, May 24, 1952: 28.

18 Dick Young, "Maglie 2-Hitter Halts Flock: Williams, Thompson HRs Air Giant Ace," *New York Daily News*, April 21, 1952: 46.

19 Tommy Holmes, "Wade Must Wait for the Big Day," *Brooklyn Eagle*, April 17, 1952: 19.

20 Dick Young, "Sal Blanks Dodgers 3-0, for 9th in Row," *New York Daily News*, May 28, 1952: 80.

21 Young, "Sal Blanks Dodgers 3-0, for 9th in Row."

22 Walker was in the lineup for Roy Campanella, sidelined with a broken thumb. "Diamond Dust – Loes Flock's Last Resort," *New York Daily News*, May 28, 1952: 87.

23 Dana Mozley, "Brooks Charge 'Spitter'; Just Their Sweat: Sal," *New York Daily News*, May 28, 1952: 80.

24 The 24-year-old Williams was new in the Giants' lineup in 1952, having replaced veteran second baseman Eddie Stanky, who was traded to the St. Louis Cardinals in the offseason. "Davey Williams has been the best possible replacement for Ed Stanky, the loss of whom was going to be the ruination during the Winter of the Giants," the *Brooklyn Eagle* concluded. Harold C. Burr, "Maglie's Razor Gives Us Barber's Itch," *Brooklyn Eagle*, May 28, 1952: 17.

25 Maglie's winning streak ended in his next start, a 5-4 loss to the Cardinals on June 2. He finished 1952 with an 18-8 record and made the NL All-Star team.

26 Dick Young, "Hearn 4-Hits Flock, Giants Sweep, 6-2," *New York Daily News*, May 29, 1952: C20.

27 Hall of Famer Hubbell pitched for the Giants from 1928 through 1943. Hyman C. Turkin, "Lip Gives Army-Bound Willie a 5-Star Rating," *New York Daily News*, May 29, 1952: C20.

28 Wendell Smith, "Wendell Smith's Sports Beat," *Pittsburgh Courier*, June 7, 1952: 12.

29 "Recruit Mays," *New York Daily News*, May 30, 1952: 42; "Everyone Hated to See Willie Go," *Pittsburgh Courier*, June 7, 1952: 14.

30 Grantland Rice, "Baseball Will Miss Willie," *Birmingham News*, May 28, 1952: 31.

31 Mays first requested a hardship release in January 1953, which the Army denied in March. On April 11, 1953, Mays' mother, Annie Satterwhite, died during childbirth at age 37. Mays again asked for his release, but the Army declined to release him. Dana Mozley, "Mays May," *New York Daily News*, January 13, 1953: C24; Associated Press, "Army Won't Let Mays Play for Giants in '53," *New York Daily News*, March 17, 1953: 52; Associated Press, "Mays Home for Mother's Funeral," *New York Daily News*, April 16, 1953: 97; Mays with Sahadi, *Say Hey*, 101.

32 "Mays on the Way," *New York Daily News*, March 2, 1954: C20.

33 Willie Mays and John Shea, *24: Life Stories and Lessons from the Say Hey Kid* (New York: St. Martin's Press, 2020), 72-77.

34 Mays with Sahadi, *Say Hey*, 103. Mays earned NL MVP honors in his 1954 return to the Giants, leading New York to a World Series sweep of the Cleveland Indians.

# WILLIE MAYS'S TWO HOMERS, THREE HITS, AND FOUR RBIS SINK PHILLIES

## May 24, 1954: New York Giants 5, Philadelphia Phillies 4, at Connie Mack Stadium, Philadelphia

BY HOWARD ROSENBERG

**IN 1954, FEW** teams needed a player to return from military service during the Korean War as much as the Giants needed Willie Mays. In 1951, though he had played in only 121 games, Mays was the National League Rookie of the Year on a team that made it to the World Series, finishing the regular season with a 98-59 record and a .624 winning percentage. During the games Mays played, the Giants were 81-40 (.669). In games without him, the team lost more than they won, their record 17-19.

In 1952 Mays was able to play in 34 games from April 16 to May 28 before he had to report to the US Army induction center in New York City on May 29.[1] The Giants finished in second place with a 92-62 record. In his games, the Giants were 26-8, their .765 winning percentage 170 points higher than their season's winning percentage of .597.

Without Mays in 1953, the Giants fell to fifth place, winning only 70 of their 155 games, their fewest wins since 1946. (They lost 84 games and had one tie.) They were not the same team without the Say Hey Kid.[2]

During spring training in 1954,[3] manager Leo Durocher told the team that Mays was "that rare kind of player who can single-handedly lead us to the pennant," and added, "This is like getting us a twenty-game winner."[4] And shortstop Alvin Dark predicted, also while the team was in Phoenix, Arizona, "We're going to be a much better team this year with Willie Mays back from the Army."[5]

While in the Army, Mays stayed in shape. "Willie came out of the Army bigger and stronger than when he had reported for duty,"[6] and though he was "stronger," he was also leaner. "'All his baby fat was gone,' recalled outfielder Monte Irvin. 'Not that there was a lot of it to begin with.'"[7]

"The Army's daily regimen of calisthenics, running, and baseball had kept Willie in superb condition," according to Allen Barra, author of *Mickey and Willie*.[8]

On Tuesday, April 13, the Giants began their season in the Polo Grounds against the Dodgers, Sal Maglie facing Carl Erskine. Dick Young wrote, "Giant fans have been saying that 'Mays is the difference,' and that's exactly what Wondrous Willie was" in a 4-3 Giants win.[9]

In Mays' second Opening Day game, he played center field and batted fifth. The teams went back and forth into the sixth. In the top half of that inning, Mays' miscue on Gil Hodges' sacrifice fly – Mays made a poor throw to the plate – allowed Duke Snider to score and tie the game. But as luck would have it, Mays led off the bottom of the sixth and, on Erskine's first pitch, atoned for his failure to prevent Snider from scoring, smacking it out of the park, his 425-foot shot clinching the win for the Polo Grounders.[10] Dick Young called the game a "stomach-bubbling scrap."[11]

It was both Mays' first hit of the season and his first homer since May 27, 1952. The future superstar had gotten off to a slow start and was batting just .247 through his first 20 games. He also started slowly in 1952 and hit just .211 through 20 games.

In 1954 over his next 20 games, Mays hit .420 with 9 homers and 24 runs batted in, more than doubling his production.

*Fans cheered on their hero during his great 1954 MVP season. SABR/The Rucker Archive.*

Mays more than met the high expectations of Giants fans in a game again the Philadelphia Phillies at Connie Mack Stadium on May 24. He put together his first game with two homers, three hits, and four RBIs. Mays was one of only three National League players to do that in 1954 and the only Giant.[12]

The game started with the Giants in fourth place, two games behind the league-leading Milwaukee Braves. The Phillies' Murry Dickson got the game rolling by striking out Whitey Lockman. Al Dark flied out to center. Hank Thompson singled. Monte Irvin flied out.

In the bottom of the first, Maglie allowed one batter, Earl Torgeson, to reach first, on a walk. Dickson retired the side one-two-three in the second, striking out Mays, batting sixth.

In the Phillies' half of the second inning, Smoky Burgess doubled with two outs but was left stranded after Ted Kazanski grounded out. Dickson continued to dominate the New York batters in the top of the third. He got three batters to ground out and walked Maglie.

The Phillies stirred fans' attention in the bottom of the third. After Maglie walked Willie Jones, Richie Ashburn singled. Torgeson, a left-handed batter, doubled, plating both Jones and Ashburn, in a play that brought fans to the edge of their seats "when Henry Thompson let Mays' throw [to third] get away for an error,"[13] and Torgeson hurried to third. (Thompson was given the error, not Mays.) Del Ennis hit a fly ball to "deep centerfield."[14] As soon as Mays caught it, Torgeson tagged up and ran for home, but Mays' throw nailed him at the plate.

The Giants scored a run in the fourth. With two outs, Don Mueller hit a grounder to second. Granny Hamner threw wildly to first, and Mueller reached second base. Mays stepped into the batter's box for the second time, the first with a runner on base. He singled to center, driving in Mueller, and advanced to second on Ashburn's "poor throw to the plate."[15] But Davey Williams's groundout ended the inning.

*Willie Mays topped the National League in slugging percentage five times. Courtesy National Baseball Hall of Fame.*

The Phillies increased their lead by two in the bottom of the fifth, although Kazanski's single was the team's only base hit, putting them ahead 4-1. Philadelphia benefited from two intentional walks, a Maglie error, and a passed ball.

"As the encounter moved into the seventh, Sal Maglie was trailing Murry Dickson, 4 to 1, and the crowd of 7,899 regarded this one as in the bag for [Phillies manager] Steve O'Neill," wrote the *New York Times's* John Drebinger.[16] But it wasn't. In the Giants' seventh, Mays hit his ninth homer of the season and got his second RBI of the game. Ray Katt's double and a single by Dusty Rhodes narrowed the Phillies' lead to one run.

Two extra-base hits changed the game in the eighth. With two outs, Mueller doubled. Then, Mays hit the game-winning homer on a 2-1 count, the ball landing on the left-field roof. The four-bagger resulted in two more RBIs, giving Mays four RBIs in a game for the fourth time in his career.

Knuckleballer Hoyt Wilhelm sealed the Giants' 5-4 win in the bottom of the ninth. All three batters he faced grounded out to shortstop.

It was the first game in Mays' career in which he slammed two homers, got three hits, and had four RBIs.

The Giants finished the season 97-57, five games ahead of the Dodgers and 27 wins more than their 1953 total. The preseason predictions of both Durocher and Dark came true. In fact, New York won the pennant and swept the Cleveland Indians in the World Series. Mays, the 1954 National League Most Valuable Player, batted .286 against Cleveland pitching and made maybe the most famous catch in Series history.

## SOURCES

In addition to the specific sources cited in the Notes, the author consulted Baseball-Reference.com and Retrosheet.org for player, team, and season data.

https://www.baseball-reference.com/boxes/PHI/PHI195405240.shtml

https://www.retrosheet.org/boxesetc/1954/B05240PHI1954.htm

## NOTES

1 "Willie Mays Through the Years," *USA Today*, May 6, 2020. https://www.usatoday.com/picture-gallery/sports/mlb/2020/05/06/hall-famer-willie-mays-through-years/5173358002/.

2 Larry Schwartz, "The Say Hey Kid," ESPN.com, accessed July 11, 2022. https://www.espn.com/sportscentury/features/00215053.html.

3 Mays arrived in the Giants' spring-training camp on March 2, 1954. Bill Madden, *1954* (Boston: Da Capo Press, 2014), 47.

4 Madden, 39.

5 Jim McCulley, "Giants Future Depends on Williams, Says Dark," *New York Daily News*, May 25, 1954: C20.

6 Allen Barra, *Mickey and Willie* (New York, Crown, 2013), 200.

7 Barra, 201.

8 Barra, 201.

9 Dick Young, "Mays' 425-Ft. HR Nips Flock, 4-3, *New York Daily News*, April 14, 1954: C20.

10 Jack Hand (Associated Press), "Giants Whip Brooklyn's Erskine on Mays' 435 Foot Circuit Clout, 4-3," *San Francisco Examiner*, April 14, 1954: 37.

11 Young, "Mays' 425-Ft. HR."

12 https://stathead.com/tiny/KSh60.

13 John Drebinger, "Polo Grounders Rally to Win, 5-4," *New York Times*, May 25, 1954: 30

14 Stan Baumgartner, "Willie's 2d Clout with One on in 8th Wins Game," *Philadelphia Inquirer*, May 25, 1954: 28.

15 McCulley, "Giants Future." As a center fielder, Ashburn had a great glove but not "a strong throwing arm." – Walter Bingham, "A Long Career of Short Base Hits," *Sports Illustrated*, March 23, 1959, https://vault.si.com/vault/1959/03/23/a-long-career-of-short-base-hits.

16 Drebinger.

# WILLIE MAYS SAYS "HEY" TO THE NATIONAL LEAGUE BATTING TITLE

## September 26, 1954: New York Giants 3, Philadelphia Phillies 2 (11 Innings), at Connie Mack Stadium, Philadelphia

BY FREDERICK C. BUSH

WILLIE MAYS, the "Say Hey Kid," made a big splash in his 1951 debut season with the New York Giants and was named the National League Rookie of the Year. After Mays played in 34 games in 1952, Uncle Sam drafted him into the Army to serve during the Korean War, which caused him to miss the remainder of 1952 and all of 1953. Mays returned with a vengeance in 1954 and became "the year's most publicized player" as he slashed and dashed his way to the NL batting championship and the first of two career MVP awards.[1] Mays also did his best impression of Ted Williams by going 3-for-4 at the plate on the final day of the regular season to claim the batting crown.

Although Williams had aimed to keep his batting average above .400 to claim his first AL batting title, rather than stave off two challengers as Mays was doing, there were interesting similarities between the two players and their feats. Williams, too, played the last two games of 1941 in Philadelphia, where the Red Sox were at Shibe Park to take on the Athletics in a doubleheader on September 28. Williams followed a 4-for-5 performance in the first game with a 2-for-3 batting line in the second and finished the season at .406. Mays had only a single game to play for the Giants against the Phillies at the renamed Connie Mack Stadium. In half the number of games, Mays finished with half the number of hits (he also walked once) in half the number of at-bats as Williams had in 1941, and his .345 average beat out teammate Don Mueller's .342 and the Brooklyn Dodgers' Duke Snider's .341 marks.[2]

The Giants already had the NL pennant wrapped up and the Phillies were jockeying for fourth place at best; thus, only 7,992 fans attended.[3] In addition to Mays and Mueller competing for an individual honor, Phillies ace Robin Roberts took the mound to try to earn a major-league-best 24th win; as it turned out, he settled for the leading the NL with 23 victories, which tied him with Cleveland Indians hurlers Bob Lemon and Early Wynn for the major-league lead.

Johnny Antonelli, whom the Giants had acquired from the Milwaukee Braves before the season and who had won 21 games, was on the hill for New York, though only for the first two innings. He and Roberts put zeros on the scoreboard during those frames, although there was excitement in the top of the first inning. Mueller hit a two-out single and Dusty Rhodes followed with a base hit to left field. Mueller became reckless and tried to take an extra base but was gunned down by left fielder Mel Clark at third to end the Giants' early scoring attempt.

Mays led off the top of the second inning with his first hit of the game, a single to left field. He advanced to second when Phillies first baseman Johnny Wyrostek booted Hank Thompson's grounder and then went to third on Davey Williams's groundout to second baseman Granny Hamner. However, that was as far as Mays got as Roberts struck out Wes Westrum and retired Antonelli on a fly ball to right field.

Jim Hearn took over the mound duties from Antonelli, who had completed his "final world series tune-up,"[4] in the bottom of the third and continued to match goose eggs with Roberts until the bottom of the fifth. During that interval, Mays registered his only out in the game by grounding to Hamner in the top of the fourth.

In the bottom of the fifth, Roberts was determined to help his own cause and banged out a leadoff double. Richie Ashburn followed with a single to right field, but Roberts held up at third base. With runners on the corners, Clark hit into a double play and Roberts scored for a 1-0 Phillies lead. Hearn then walked Smoky Burgess but retired Hamner to end the inning.

Hearn ran into further trouble the next inning, and Roberts again was involved in the scoring as he tried to hit and to pitch his team to victory. Bobby Morgan knocked a one-out single to left field, and Willie Jones followed with a double that put two Phillies in scoring position. Giants manager Leo Durocher had Hearn issue an intentional walk to Wyrostek that loaded the bases for Roberts. The Phillies pitcher laid down a perfect sacrifice bunt that drove in Morgan and advanced Jones and Wyrostek. Durocher ordered another intentional walk, this time to the dangerous Ashburn; once again, the bases were filled with Phillies. Hearn escaped further damage by retiring Clark on a fly to Mueller in right field for the third out.

Philadelphia's 2-0 lead turned out to be short-lived as Mays stepped to the fore in the top of the seventh and banged out a leadoff triple. The three-bagger was the Giants' first hit since Mays' second-inning single, and the New Yorkers had managed only one additional baserunner in the interim – Thompson, who had walked in the fourth

This time, Thompson grounded out to Wyrostek at first, and Mays ran home for New York's first tally. After Williams and Westrum hit back-to-back singles, with Williams advancing to third on Westrum's hit, Joe Garagiola pinch-hit for Hearn and lofted a sacrifice fly to right field that drove in Williams to tie the game, 2-2. Whitey Lockman

*Teammates Willie Mays and Don Mueller battled it out for the 1954 batting title. SABR/The Rucker Archive.*

then worked a walk from Roberts, but the Phillies' stalwart ace retired Billy Gardner to preserve the tie for the moment.

Marv Grissom became the Giants' third pitcher of the day in the bottom of the seventh, and he threw two uneventful innings. Roberts allowed doubles to Mays in the top of the eighth – his third hit of the game – and to Garagiola in the ninth but kept the Giants from scoring any additional runs.

After lifting Grissom for a pinch-hitter in the top of the ninth, Durocher sent Al Worthington to the hill to continue the duel with Roberts in the bottom of the inning. Worthington flirted with trouble, but a little strategy and a bit of luck sent the ballgame into extra innings. Worthington walked Ashburn to lead off the ninth, and Ashburn advanced to second on Clark's sacrifice. Durocher ordered an intentional walk to Burgess, and Hamner flied out to center with neither runner being able to advance. Worthington then walked Del Ennis, and Durocher pulled the hurler in favor of George Spencer, who retired Morgan for the third out.

Mueller led off the 10th with a double off Roberts, and Mays drew an intentional walk that put runners on first and second with one out. Roberts bore down and got the two outs he needed to keep the game going. After Spencer worked around two bases on balls (one intentional) in the bottom of the frame, it was time for the Giants to end the game and the regular season.

Garagiola hit a one-out double in the top of the 11th – his second of the game – and the next batter, Lockman, drew the seventh intentional walk of the game (four by the Giants' hurlers and three by Roberts). This time, the free pass backfired as Gardner lashed a single to left that brought Garagiola home for a 3-2 New York advantage. Roberts retired Mueller and Rhodes, but the handwriting for a Philadelphia defeat was now on the wall. Spencer surrendered a leadoff walk to Burgess in the bottom of the frame, but Hamner hit into a double play, and Ennis popped out to end the game.

The Giants finished with a 97-57 record, and "wondrous Willie," as the *Philadelphia Inquirer* dubbed him, won the NL batting championship.[5] In an interesting quirk that coincided with Mays' accomplishment, Ted Williams had finished the season with an identical .345 batting average that was the highest in the AL, but he had too few at-bats to qualify for the official title.[6] Before Mays learned that he had also garnered his first MVP award, he etched his name into baseball lore with a play in World Series Game One that will forever be known simply as "The Catch." Mays' unbelievable running catch of Cleveland Indians batter Vic Wertz's deep drive, and his throw that held Larry Doby at third base, propelled the Giants to an upset in the game and the Series against a powerful Cleveland squad that had won 111 games in the AL that season.

## SOURCES

The author consulted baseball-reference.com and retrosheet.org for the box score and play-by-play of the game as well as for team standings, player statistics, and awards.

https://www.baseball-reference.com/boxes/PHI/PHI195409260.shtml

https://www.retrosheet.org/boxesetc/1954/B09260PHI1954.htm

## NOTES

1 United Press, "'Hey' Kid Bat King/Williams' .345 Tops for Americans But –," *Pasadena Independent*, September 27, 1954: 17.

2 Mueller went 2-for-6 for the Giants against the Phillies while Snider was 0-for-3 for the Dodgers against the Pittsburgh Pirates at Brooklyn's Ebbets Field on the final day of the season.

3 Although the Phillies lost to the Giants, they finished in fourth place, one game ahead of the Cincinnati Reds, after the Reds lost their finale to the Chicago Cubs.

4 "Mays Wins Batting Title as Giants Defeat Phils; Dodgers Topple Pirates/Roberts is Loser in 11 Innings, 3-2," *New York Times*, September 27, 1954: 25.

5 Ryan Baumgartner, "Mays Wins Bat Title as Phils Lose to Giants, 3-2, Take Fourth," *Philadelphia Inquirer*, September 27, 1954: 21.

6 A minimum of 400 at-bats was required to qualify for the batting title, and Williams finished with 386. Cleveland's Bobby Avila, who batted .341 over 555 at-bats, was the official AL batting champion in 1954.

# WILLIE MAYS MAKES 'THE CATCH'

## September 29, 1954: New York Giants 5, Cleveland Indians 2, at the Polo Grounds, New York (Game One of the 1954 World Series)

BY GREGORY H. WOLF

"WE WERE BEATEN by the longest out and the shortest home run of the year," said an incredulous Al Lopez, skipper of the Cleveland Indians, who had just lost to the New York Giants in Game One of the 1954 World Series, featuring two of the most iconic plays in baseball history.[1] Following Willie Mays' over-the-shoulder, run-saving catch in deep center field to preserve a tie game in the eighth inning, Dusty Rhodes belted a walk-off, pinch-hit, three-run homer into the short right-field porch in the 10th inning to give the Giants a dramatic 5-2 victory in the Polo Grounds. "It was just another game for us," said Giants pitcher Johnny Antonelli. "We won the pennant with finishes like this all season long."[2]

According to the Associated Press, the Giants (who were 97-57 during the regular season) were 8-5 underdogs against the Indians, winners of a then AL-record 111 games.[3] But a closer look at the squads reveals two very similar teams. The Indians pitching staff was their shining diamond. Two 23-game winners, Bob Lemon and Early Wynn, helped Cleveland lead the American League with a stellar 2.78 earned-run average. New York's pitching staff, though less glamorous than Cleveland's, paced the National League in ERA (3.09), but unlike its opponent relied heavily on its relief corps, the best in baseball. Both squads were average-hitting teams that led or co-led their respective league in round-trippers.

On a warm autumn afternoon, Wednesday, September 29, 1954, the venerable Polo Grounds was packed with 52,751 spectators. Singer Perry Como, supported by Artie White's orchestra, sang the national anthem. Jimmy Barbieri, the 12-year-old captain of Schenectady's Little League world championship baseball team, threw out the ceremonial first pitch.[4]

Cleveland wasted no time getting to New York's 37-year-old unflappable curveballer, Sal Maglie (14-6 during the regular season), who drilled leadoff hitter

*The Giants swept the 1954 World Series against the Cleveland Indians. Among the champions were, left to right, Willie Mays, Davey Williams, Billy Gardner, Whitey Lockman, Monte Irvin and Alvin Dark. SABR/The Rucker Archive.*

Al Smith on his fourth pitch. Bobby Avila, who had led the AL with a career-high .341 batting average, lined a single in front of charging right fielder Don Mueller, who fumbled it, allowing Smith to scamper to third. After Larry Doby and Al Rosen popped up, Vic Wertz smashed a long fly ball over Mueller's head. It "caromed off the wall," wrote John Drebinger of the *New York Times*, "and bounded gaily past the Giants bullpen," before Willie Mays gathered it.[5] Wertz slid easily into third as Smith and Avila scored, giving the Indians a 2-0 lead. Giants manager Leo Durocher, expecting the worst, had swingman Don Liddle warm up in the bullpen. But the "Barber," so named for his command of the inside of the plate, shrugged off the two runs and settled down.

New York faced Cleveland's 33-year-old ace, right-hander Bob Lemon, who had recorded a major-league-leading 148 victories in the previous seven seasons. He squelched a Giants threat in the first with runners on first and third, and cruised into the bottom of the third inning with a 2-0 lead. Described by Irving Vaughan of the *Chicago Tribune* as "only steady at times," Lemon struggled with control throughout the game.[6] The Giants' Whitey Lockman and Al Dark led off the third with singles. Mueller, who enjoyed a career year, batting .342 and leading the NL with 212 safeties, grounded into a force out as Lockman scored. After a walk to Mays, Hank Thompson blasted a single to right, driving in Mueller to tie the game. While Cleveland's Art Houtteman warmed up in the bullpen, Lemon set down Monte Irvin and Davey Williams to extinguish another rally. Lemon, who had been Cleveland's Opening Day center fielder in 1946 before being converted into a pitcher, gathered his composure and allowed only four baserunners (three hits) from the fourth inning through the ninth.

New York dodged a bullet in the sixth inning when Wertz led off with a single to right field. Mueller attempted to throw him out at first, but the ball shot over Lockman's head. Wertz should have made it to third, thought skipper Lopez, but the slow-footed slugger's protective shin guard "broke loose and stopped him" at second base.[7]

Two innings later, the left-hand-hitting Wertz faced Don Liddle, who had just replaced Maglie, with two on and no outs. He belted the southpaw's fourth pitch deep into center field. Mays, just 23 years old, took sight of the ball and raced with his back facing the diamond toward the wall in front of the bleachers, just a shade right of center field. Mays "travel[ed] on the wings of wind,' wrote Drebinger, "to make one of his most amazing catches."[8] Mays, the NL Most Valuable Player in his first full season after spending most of the previous two in the armed forces, whirled around and heaved the ball to the infield as Doby tagged and raced to third. "Durocher was standing in front of me in the dugout," former Giants batboy Bobby Weinstein told the author. "He turned around and said, 'Oh no.' And then he saw Mays run the ball down."[9] After the game Mays took his fielding exploit in stride, "I had it all the way," he said. "There was nothing too hard about it."[10]

The forgotten star of what Gayle Talbot of the Associated Press called a "real hard rock of a baseball game" was Giants reliever Marv Grissom, who snuffed out Cleveland's rallies in the eighth, ninth, and 10th innings.[11] Relieving Liddle after Mays' "preposterous catch" of Wertz's fly ball, Grissom walked pinch-hitter Dale Mitchell to load the bases.[12] After pinch-hitter Dave Pope fanned looking, catcher Jim Hegan smashed a fly ball to deep left field. "It looked like a homer," said Al Lopez, "but the wind, blowing from left to right, pulled the ball in."[13] With two outs in the ninth, left fielder Irvin dropped Avilla's popup for a two-base error, putting a man in scoring position for slugger Doby, who had topped the AL in homers (32) and runs batted in (126). Grissom issued an intentional pass to face Rosen, the 1953 American League MVP, who flied out to end the threat.

In the "throat-clutching" final inning, Wertz led off the 10th with his fourth hit, a double to the gap in left-center.[14] Pinch-runner Rudy Regalado moved to third on Sam Dente's sacrifice. With nerves of steel, "Old Tomato Face" Grissom intentionally walked Pope, then fanned Bill Glynn and induced Lemon, arguably the best hitting pitcher in baseball, to line out to first to end the inning with the go-ahead run 90 feet from home. The Indians tossed away multiple scoring chances and left seven runners on base in the last three innings.

The bottom of the 10th provided, in the words of John Drebinger, a "breath-taking finish to as nerve-tingling a struggle as any world series had ever seen."[15] After striking out Mueller, Lemon issued a

*Willie Mays sprinted deep into the Polo Grounds outfield and made his most famous catch off a Vic Wertz flyball in Game One of the 1954 World Series. SABR/The Rucker Archive.*

walk to Mays, who moved into scoring position by stealing second. Lemon issued an intentional pass to Hank Thompson to play for an inning-ending twin killing. The next batter, Dusty Rhodes, pinch-hitting for Irvin, swung at Lemon's first pitch and hit a pop fly down the right-field foul line. "We all thought the ball was going to twist foul," said Lopez after the game.[16] Instead, the ball traveled 270 feet and barely cleared the right-field stands, bouncing off a fan, and rolling back onto the field. Rhodes' three-run, walk-off homer gave the Giants a stunning 5-2 victory.

Hailed as a "Chinese homer" (a cheap home run) in the insensitive parlance of the time, Rhodes' round-tripper was just the fourth pinch-hit homer in World Series history and the first to end a game. A poor fielder, Rhodes enjoyed a career year in 1954, batting .341 with 15 homers and 50 RBIs in just 164 at-bats. He also hit two of the Giants' record 10 pinch-hit home runs that season.

"It was difficult to find the No. 1 hero in the Giants' clubhouse," said sportswriter Roscoe McGowen of the New York Times.[17] From "team electrifier" Mays and the clutch-hitting Rhodes to Grissom's relentless, pressure-packed pitching, the Giants made a heroic statement in their Game One victory.[18]

## SOURCES

In addition to the sources listed in the Notes, the author consulted Baseball-Reference.com, Retrosheet.org, and accessed video of "The Catch" on YouTube:

https://www.baseball-reference.com/boxes/NY1/NY1195409290.shtml

http://www.retrosheet.org/boxesetc/1954/B09290NY11954.htm

https://www.youtube.com/watch?v=7bLt2xKaNH0

## NOTES

1 Ed Corrigan (Associated Press), "Giants Jubilant After 10th Inning Series Win; Longest Out, Shortest HR Blamed by Lopez," *Newport* (Rhode Island) *Daily News*, September 30, 1954: 12.

2 Corrigan.

3 Jack Hand (Associated Press), "Rhodes Pinch Hit Homer, Mays' Magnificent Catch Trip Tribe," *Sarasota Herald-Tribune*, September 30, 1954: 12.

4 Barbieri is among the few players who played in the Little League World Series and the big leagues. In 1966 he saw action in 39 games with the Los Angeles Dodgers.

5 John Drebinger, "Giants Win in 10th From Indians, 5-2, on Rhodes' Homer," *New York Times*, September 30, 1954: 1.

6 Irving Vaughan, "Giants' Homer in 10th Beats Indians, 5-2," *Chicago Tribune*, September 30, 1954: D1.

7 Hand.

8 Drebinger.

9 Author's telephone interview with Bobby Weinstein on May 28, 2014.

10 Corrigan.

11 Gayle Talbot (Associated Press), "Giants Win Series Opener, 5-2, on Rhodes' Pinch Homer, *Newport* (Rhode Island) *Daily News*, September 30, 1954: 12.

12 Dan Daniel, "Mays' Catch gets Nod," *Newport* (Rhode Island) *Daily News*, September 30, 1954: 13.

13 Louis Effrat, "Cleveland Contends Wind Contributed to Downfall on Two Important Points," *New York Times*, September 30, 1954: 54.

14 Hand.

15 Drebinger.

16 Effrat.

17 Roscoe McGowen, "Heroics of Mays, Rhodes, Grissom Regarded as Routine by Happy Giants," *New York Times*, September 30, 1954: 40.

18 Talbot.

# WILLIE MAYS TIES JOHNNY MIZE'S GIANTS RECORD WITH 51ST HOME RUN

## September 25, 1955: New York Giants 5, Philadelphia Phillies 2 (first game of doubleheader), at the Polo Grounds, New York

BY TIM ODZER

AFTER SHOCKING THE baseball world in 1954 by defeating the 111-win Cleveland Indians in the World Series, the Giants entered 1955 expecting to contend for another championship. But despite the triumph in 1954, not all was well with the Giants. Manager Leo Durocher was in the final year of his contract, and tension between the skipper and Giants owner Horace Stoneham made it unlikely Durocher would return in 1956. To stick around, he needed another pennant. But injuries and underperformance created a frustrating season for the Giants.

The double-play combination of Davey Williams and Alvin Dark both missed significant time with injuries (and Williams retired in midseason due to an arthritic back condition). Pitcher Sal Maglie was claimed on waivers by Cleveland, and star outfielder Monte Irvin was demoted to Triple-A Minneapolis after getting off to a slow start. With the Brooklyn Dodgers off to a blazing start, the Giants never were in the race.

On September 23, the Giants welcomed the Phillies to town for a season-ending series. In the first game, Philadelphia won 5-1 behind a complete game from Saul Rogovin. On September 24, with the Giants a distant third behind the pennant winners in Brooklyn, news broke that Durocher was resigning as Giants manager. Stoneham accepted the resignation and announced that Bill Rigney would take over as skipper in 1956. Though the Giants and Phillies were scheduled to play the second game of their season-ending series the same day, the teams were rained out. The Phillies and Giants concluded the 1955 campaign in a season-ending doubleheader on September 25.

On paper, the pitching matchup for the first game of the doubleheader favored Philadelphia.

The Phillies started Robin Roberts, who was in a dominant multiseason run during which he rated as perhaps the best pitcher in baseball. Roberts put together a stellar 1955 campaign and came into his final start of the season with a 3.29 ERA and a 23-13 record.

New York countered with rookie left-hander Pete Burnside. A graduate of Dartmouth College, Burnside had made his major-league debut five days earlier, on September 20, against the Pittsburgh Pirates. After retiring the side in the first, Burnside struggled mightily, surrendering seven runs on three hits and six walks over 3⅔ innings.

Leading off for the Phillies against Burnside was center fielder Richie Ashburn. Ashburn came into the season-ending doubleheader hitting .342, comfortably on his way to winning the 1955 NL batting title.[1] Burnside retired Ashburn on a groundout, second baseman Wayne Terwilliger to first baseman Gail Harris, to open the contest. Weak-hitting Phillies shortstop Bobby Morgan singled to left for the game's first hit but was stranded at first as Burnside retired the next two men.

*The Giants fell to third place in 1955. Even so, Willie Mays slammed 51 home runs. Courtesy National Baseball Hall of Fame.*

In the bottom of the first, Roberts retired Giants leadoff hitter Billy Gardner on a groundout before surrendering a single to right fielder Don Mueller. That brought up Willie Mays. Mays, the reigning 1954 National League MVP, came into 1955 with sky-high expectations, only to hit under .300 during the 1955 campaign's first three months. But Mays played superbly over the season's final few months and came into the season-ending doubleheader hitting .316/.399/.652 with 50 home runs.[2] Roberts worked the count on Mays to 1-and-2 before challenging him with a fastball. Mays hit the ball just inside the foul pole and into the upper deck in left field.[3] The home run was Mays' 51st of the season and tied Johnny Mize's team single-season record.[4] It was also the league-leading 41st home run hit off Roberts during the season. Roberts retired the next two Giants batters, Hank Thompson and Whitey Lockman.

Staked to an early lead, Burnside cruised through the second and third innings. After making it through the second frame unscathed, Roberts ran into trouble in the third. Gardner reached second on an error by shortstop Morgan. With one out, Mays came up to bat. The *New York Daily News* wrote that "Mays tried to break [Mize's] record with every swing" for the remainder of the doubleheader in front of 6,848 fans at the Polo Grounds. Though Mays failed to homer this time, he singled and drove Gardner home before stealing second, for his 23rd stolen base of the season. Mays came around to score New York's fourth run of the game on a single by Lockman. At the end of three, the Giants led 4-0.

With two out in the top of the fourth, Phillies left fielder Del Ennis tripled to right. It was his seventh triple of the season and allowed Philadelphia a chance to get back into the game. But the Phillies stranded Ennis at third as Burnside got Willie Jones to ground out.

The Giants added their fifth run of the game in the bottom of the fifth when 21-year-old rookie Joey Amalfitano drove in Gardner with a triple.[5]

The late innings were uneventful as Burnside continued to retire the Phillies with ease. Roberts also pitched scoreless ball during his last two innings of 1955, with New York's only hit coming off Mays' double. Roberts finished his season going seven innings, allowing eight hits, and giving up five runs (three earned).

The Giants entered the ninth inning with a 5-0 lead as Burnside looked to finish the shutout. After he retired Ennis on a comebacker, Willie Jones singled and Stan Lopata hit his 22nd home run to make the game 5-2. With the shutout over, Burnside finished the complete-game victory. Unscored upon until the ninth, Burnside secured his first career victory, having allowed seven hits to go with the two runs.

In the second half of the doubleheader and the final game of Durocher's tenure as Giants skipper, the Phillies entered the bottom of the ninth with a 3-1 lead behind eight stellar innings from Curt Simmons and home runs by Ted Kazanski and Marv Blaylock. Jack Meyer took over in the ninth, and was greeted with a single from Amalfitano. Amalfitano advanced to second on a wild pitch and Lockman walked. Down two runs, the Giants had men on first and second with nobody out. As described by the *Philadelphia Inquirer*, the next man up, Bob Hofman "sent a fast ball screaming toward left-center. [Shortstop] Kazanski caught the ball and Amalfitano and Lockman were so far advanced they had no chance to scramble back. Kazanski flipped to Morgan, who threw to Blaylock. It was over that quickly."[6] A triple play to end the season.

Durocher walked back across the outfield grass to the center-field clubhouse. As he left the Polo Grounds, Durocher "received a rousing send-off from several hundred fans."[7] His departure deeply affected Mays, Durocher's favorite player. "I feel terrible," said Mays. "It's like losing a great friend. I can't even begin to tell you how much I am going to miss him."[8]

## SOURCES

In addition to the sources cited in the Notes, the author consulted Baseball-Reference.com and retrosheet.org.

https://www.baseball-reference.com/boxes/NY1/NY1195509251.shtml

https://www.retrosheet.org/boxesetc/1955/B09251NY11955.htm

## NOTES

1 Ashburn went 0-for-7 in the season-ending doubleheader, which dropped his batting average to .338. He still finished far ahead of Mays and Stan Musial, who both hit .319, to become Philadelphia's first batting champion since Harry Walker in 1947.

2 Mays finished second behind Mickey Mantle in Wins Above Replacement in 1955.

3 The author's description of the at-bat comes from Dana Mozley, "Triple Play Closes Out Lip; Mays Ties HR Mark at 51," *New York Daily News*, September 26, 1955: 346.

4 Mize hit 51 home runs for the Giants in 1947 and finished third in National League MVP voting. His personal best in home runs came 10 years later, when he hit 52 home runs for the 1965 San Francisco Giants.

5 Amalfitano had entered the game at third base as a replacement for Hank Thompson the previous half-inning.

6 Art Morrow, "Phillies Edge Giants, 3-1, After Roberts Loses, 5-2," *Philadelphia Inquirer*, September 26, 1955: 22.

7 William J. Briordy, "Giants Split With Phillies as Durocher Tenure Ends," *New York Times*, September 26, 1955: 28.

8 Joe Reichler (Associated Press), "Durocher Gives T.V. Fans His Farewell as Giants' manager," *Allentown* (Pennsylvania) *Morning Call*, September 26, 1955: 13.

# A TALE OF THE KID AND THE MAN AND THE SAY HEY KID AND THE COMMERCE COMET

## July 10, 1956: National League 7, American League 3

## Major League All-Star Game – Griffith Stadium, Washington, DC

BY ALAN COHEN

**GRIFFITH STADIUM PLAYED** host to the 23rd All-Star Game on July 10, 1956. A sellout crowd of 28,843 saw the National League win its sixth decision in the past seven encounters, 7-3. The overflow crowd filled the seats behind the center-field wall, creating a bad background for the batters, and there were 17 strikeouts in the game. Nevertheless, the game lived up to its billing with home runs being hit by four of the greatest players in the history of the game.

Casey Stengel and Walter Alston led their charges. It was Alston's second turn as manager. He had managed in 1954 after the Dodgers won the NL pennant in 1953. Stengel was no stranger to the leadership role, having already led the AL five times.

Each team had a veteran presence. Ted Williams, selected to his 13th All-Star Game, manned left field for the American League, and St. Louis's popular Stan Musial, also in his 13th trip to the event, started the game in right field for the NL.

Pittsburgh's Bob Friend started on the mound for the National League and stymied the opposition in his three innings. Speaking of his success that day, he said he "had a real good fast ball but didn't use it often on account of their left-handers." He "threw mostly breaking stuff, except when I struck out Mickey Mantle on a fast one."[1] According to Harold Kaese of the *Boston Globe*, Friend threw nine curves and two knuckleballs as Ted Williams struck out and grounded out.[2]

The winners were sparked by the fine defensive play of third baseman Ken Boyer of St. Louis. Boyer, in only his second year in the National League, was playing in his first All-Star Game, and it didn't take him long to start making an impression. In the bottom of the first inning, diving to his left, he grabbed a line drive off the bat of leadoff batter Harvey Kuenn of the Detroit Tigers. It was the beginning of a great day for Boyer.

The starting pitcher for the American League was Billy Pierce of the Chicago White Sox, and he, like Friend, performed well, striking out five batters in his three innings on the mound. He struck out the Redlegs' rookie sensation Frank Robinson twice. However, the National League was able to manufacture a run in the third inning. Roy McMillan of Cincinnati walked, was sacrificed to second by Friend, and came home on a single by Johnny Temple.

The fans' votes determined the starters and the Redlegs were represented by five players from their league-leading lineup. Robinson was in left field, McMillan and Temple patrolled the middle infield, Ed Bailey was behind the plate, and Gus Bell was the center fielder. Also representing the Redlegs was substitute first baseman Ted Kluszewski. Cincinnati manager Birdie Tebbetts served as one of Alston's coaches.

In the top of the fourth inning, Yankees lefty Whitey Ford came on to pitch. He fanned Musial and then was greeted by Boyer's single. Bell, a left-handed batter, was due up, and manager Alston elected to go to his bench for a right-handed hitter. Pinch-hitter Willie Mays, after swinging through the first pitch, deposited Ford's second pitch into the seats in left-center field, putting his team in front 3-0. After the game, Alston said, "Mays's pinch homer was the turning point. It gave us a comfortable lead and put them on the defensive. After that it was just a matter of getting good pitching from everybody."[3]

The NL extended its lead to 5-0 with runs in the fifth and sixth innings. In the fifth, after righty Jim Wilson had replaced Ford on the mound, Temple led off with a bunt single down the third-base line, took second on a comebacker by Musial, and scored on the third of Boyer's three singles. An inning later, Tom Brewer was on the mound for the AL and was greeted by Kluszewski, pinch-hitting for the NL's starting first baseman, Dale Long. Kluszewski launched the first of his two doubles, went to third when Cincinnati teammate McMillan hit a bloop single to right field, and scored when Brewer uncorked a wild pitch. During his at-bat, Kluszewski fouled a ball off catcher Yogi Berra's right hand. After the side was retired, Berra returned to the dugout and showed his bruised hand to manager Stengel. Yogi's day was over.[4]

In the bottom of the fifth, Boyer, having already made a great defensive play and gone 3-for-3 at the plate, added to his résumé. With two out, Harvey Kuenn scorched a groundball down the third-base line destined for the left-field corner. Diving to his right, Boyer grabbed the ball and threw to first for the inning-ending out.

The AL did all of its scoring in the sixth inning, victimizing Warren Spahn. The Milwaukee ace was the second pitcher to hurl in the game for the National League. He entered the game in the fourth inning. Nellie Fox of the White Sox singled to center off Spahn to open the sixth and two loud swings later, the AL had three runs. Williams sent a towering blast to right, making the score 5-2. Next up was Mickey Mantle of the Yankees. Playing on a bad knee and fighting the glare from the shirts in the center-field bleachers, he had struck out in his first two at-bats. This time, he homered off Spahn for the AL's third run.

The AL got no closer. Manager Alston called on Johnny Antonelli and the Giants' ace extinguished the fire, but not without some drama. Sherman Lollar batted for Berra and singled to center field and Detroit's Al Kaline singled to left. With the tying runs on base and none out, Stengel sent up Vic Power to bat for Mickey Vernon, but Power hit a short fly ball to Musial in left field. Then Cincinnati's tandem of McMillan and Temple converted George Kell's grounder into a 6-4-3 double play, the only DP of the game, to end the threat. Temple, in throwing to first, leapt high to elude the spikes of the hard-sliding Kaline.

Infielders Temple, McMillan, and Boyer were performing so well defensively that manager Alston left them in for the entire game. Reserve infielders Junior Gilliam, Ernie Banks, and Eddie Mathews didn't see action.

The NL, which scored in each inning after breaking the ice in the third, was not about to take its foot off the accelerator, especially with its lead cut to two runs. In the bottom of the seventh inning, after Tom Brewer had struck out Duke Snider, the voice on the press-box loudspeaker announced: "The home run by Ted Williams in the previous inning ties Stan Musial's record for All-Star Games. They now have four apiece."[5] Musial stepped in. He took his distinctive stance at the plate, looking over his right shoulder toward the mound. Brewer, a left-hander, threw a pitch that was moving away from the lefty swinging Musial. Musial sent the pitch toward left-center field, and it cleared the fence, extending his team's lead to 6-3. The voice on the loudspeaker came on once again: "Cancel the previous announcement. Musial just took his record back."[6] (Musial extended his record to six with a homer in 1960's second game.)

Willie Mays walked with two outs. Kluszewski hit his second double in as many at-bats and Mays, who was running on the play, didn't stop running. His 270-foot scamper resulted in his team's seventh run, and to nobody's great surprise as related to his readers by Tommy Holmes, "Willie sailed out from under his cap as he slid across the plate."[7]

Boyer, whose perfect day at the plate ended when he grounded out for the second out of the seventh inning, was back to flashing his glove in the bottom of the inning. Detroit's Ray Boone, pinch-hitting for Brewer, sent a liner to third base that was grabbed by the leaping Cardinals third baseman.

Williams began the bottom half of the inning hitting against the shift and launching a fly ball to short left field. Musial charged and caught the ball, colliding with Boyer in the process. Stan came up grabbing his thigh and Alston, choosing to err on the side of the caution, removed his left fielder from the game. Milwaukee's Henry Aaron took over in left field. In his only at-bat, he flied to right field.

In the bottom of the ninth, with one out, Vic Power legged out an infield single. George Kell's single to right field was corralled by Mays, who launched a perfect throw to third base, keeping the runners at first and second.[8] Antonelli got the final two outs, and the NL had the win.

## SOURCES

https://www.baseball-reference.com/allstar/1956-allstar-game.shtml

In addition to Baseball-Reference.com and the sources shown in the Notes, the author used the following:

Bowen, George. "Boyer Is Standout for National Nine," *Bergen* (New Jersey) *Evening Record*, July 11, 1956: 30.

Considine, Bob. "Nationals Tip Americans in All-Star Game, 7-3," *Arizona Republic* (Phoenix), July 11, 1956: 24.

Drebinger, John. "National League Beats American as Mays and Musial Set Pace with Homers," *New York Times*, July 11, 1956: 22.

Lee, Bill. "With Malice Towards None," *Hartford Courant*, July 11, 1956: 17.

## NOTES

1 Associated Press, "Walt Alston Picks Boyer as Game's Top Performer," *Hartford Courant*, July 10, 1956: 17.

2 Harold Kaese, "Friend Dazzles Ted, Who Plans 1957 Play," *Boston Globe*, July 11, 1956: 11.

3 Joe Reichler (Associated Press), "Mgr. Walt Alston Praises Redlegs," *Bergen Evening Record*, July 11, 1956: 30.

4 Louis Effrat, "Berra Joins List of injured Stars," *New York Times*, July 11, 1956: 22.

5 Arthur Daley, "Sports of the Times: Sprinkled with Stardust," *New York Times*, July 11, 1956: 23.

6 Daley.

7 Tommy Holmes, "NL Pitching Halts AL Stars Again, 7-3," *Boston Globe*, July 11, 1956: 11.

8 Gerry de la Ree, "For the Record," *Bergen Evening Record*, July 11, 1956: 30.

# MAYS STEALS FOUR BASES, HOMERS AGAINST REDLEGS

## May 18, 1957: New York Giants 6, Cincinnati Redlegs 3, at Crosley Field, Cincinnati

BY GLEN SPARKS

ALWAYS CAPABLE OF doing the spectacular, Willie Mays stole four bases and hit a home run against the Cincinnati Redlegs on May 18, 1957. The New York Giants won, 6-3, before a ladies day crowd of 8,538 at Crosley Field.

The Giants began the day in sixth place with a record of 12-17. Cincinnati was 19-8 and atop the National League, 1½ games ahead of the second-place Milwaukee Braves. This was the finale of a three-game series, and the Redlegs were looking for a sweep. They won the opener, 3-2, and the follow-up, 11-1.

(This was fourth straight season that the Cincinnati club used the Redlegs designation as a way to distance itself from any association with communism, derided by many as the Red Menace. The team went back to being the Reds in 1959.)

Of note, Cincinnati catcher Ed Bailey threw out Mays once in each of the first two games trying to steal. Maybe the Say Hey Kid had some incentive to get the best of Bailey this time.

Ruben Gomez, a 29-year-old right-hander from Puerto Rico, started on the mound for New York. Joe Nuxhall, a 28-year-old lefty from nearby Hamilton, Ohio, who made his big-league debut at the tender age of 15 in wartime 1944, took the ball for Cincinnati.

Mays entered the action with a .304 batting average and got off to a running start. He came up to bat with two out in the first inning and singled to right field. With Hank Sauer at bat, Mays stole second base and then third. The Giants, though, could not take advantage of their superstar's speed. Sauer walked, but Ray Katt struck out to end the threat.

The Giants broke out on top with a solo run in the top of the second inning. Daryl Spencer and Foster Castleman led off with consecutive singles. Dusty Rhodes hit into a force out that scored Spencer. Gomez singled but was forced out when he went

*Willie Mays stole four bases in a game twice in his career. Courtesy National Baseball Hall of Fame.*

into second base standing on Red Schoendienst's groundball. Nuxhall hit Whitey Lockman with a pitch, but Mays flied out to center field. "The failure of Gomez to slide into second prevented the Giants from racking up two or three more runs," Lou Smith of the *Cincinnati Enquirer* wrote.[1]

The Redlegs took a 2-1 lead in the bottom of the second and scored their first run the same way the Giants did. Frank Robinson, who had a .376 batting average, and George Crowe began the rally with base hits. Smoky Burgess hit into a force out that scored Robinson. After Don Hoak popped out, Roy McMillan knocked a triple to center field that brought home the not-so-speedy Burgess. Nuxhall grounded out to end the inning.

Mays had nearly turned McMillan's triple into an out. He "had the ball all the way," according to *New York Daily News* sportswriter Jim McCulley. As the great defender backed up near the Crosley Field wall, he fell down. According to McCulley, "Mays tried to make the catch while lying flat on his back, but the ball bounced out of his glove."[2] Lou Smith insisted, "Mays almost contributed the circus catch of the season."[3]

New York took the lead in the fourth. Rhodes singled and advanced to second base on Gomez's sacrifice. That brought Schoendienst up to bat. The Giants had acquired the nine-time All-Star infielder from the St. Louis Cardinals on June 14, 1956, in an eight-player deal.[4] Upon hearing about the trade, the Germantown, Illinois, native said simply, "That's the way the ball bounces, I guess."[5] *St. Louis Globe-Democrat* columnist Robert L. Burnes wrote, "We're going to miss him and if that's the wrong attitude, it's just too doggone bad."[6]

Schoendienst entered this game with a .310 batting average and singled in his third at-bat. The ball scooted through Nuxhall's legs, allowing Rhodes to score. Nuxhall kicked himself for not making the play. "It went right through my legs," he said. "I flinched thinking it was hit harder than it actually was. And it got by me. That was a double-play ball and instead of being out of the inning, they get three runs."[7]

Lockman's groundball forced Schoendienst right before Mays slammed a "Ruthian"[8] two-run homer deep into the right-center-field seats. It was his fourth homer of the season but his first since April 22, and it gave New York a 4-2 lead. The round-tripper also ended Nuxhall's afternoon. Reliever Art Fowler, who served as pitching coach for several big-league teams after his playing career ended in 1964, struck out Sauer to end the inning.

Neither team scored again until Crowe hit a solo homer off Gomez with one out in the seventh. The Giants answered with a run in the top of the eighth. Schoendienst drove home his second run of the day with a two-out single that brought home Castleman, who had begun the inning with a double to left.

The final run came across in the ninth. Mays led off with a single. Once again with Sauer at the plate, the "mercury-footed"[9] Mays took off for second. Safe, he next ran to third for his fourth stolen base of the day and 14th of the season. (This was the second and only other time in Mays' career that he swiped four bases in a game. He also performed the feat on May 6, 1956, against the St. Louis Cardinals on his 25th birthday. However, he did not hit a home run in that one.) Sauer popped out, though, and Katt hit a lazy fly ball to center field. Mays scored when Spencer doubled to left.

Gomez pitched a scoreless ninth to seal the victory and run his won-lost record to 6-1. He was the first pitcher in baseball to reach that mark and now had nearly half of New York's 13 victories. The fifth-year veteran also boasted a 2.30 ERA. The previous season, Gomez was just 7-17 with a 4.58 ERA.

In his game story, the *Cincinnati Enquirer*'s Smith heaped praise on Gomez. "If one has to lose," he wrote, "there always is some comfort in having the job done by an expert."[10] Reds manager Birdie Tebbetts confirmed, "He didn't give us many chances."[11]

Nuxhall, the losing pitcher, dropped to 1-1 with a 6.00 ERA. Unlike Gomez's strong effort, Smith commented, "the Redleg pitching left much to be desired."[12] The Giants nearly broke open the game a few times. Smith wrote, "Sloppy baserunning, especially in the second frame kept the Giants from racking up more runs."[13] New York put at least one runner on base in every inning except the seventh.

Lou Smith called Mays "the Giants' demon of speed." He told his readers that Mays and Bailey were engaged in a "feud" of sorts. Bailey explained: "When he steals one on me, he pops off. When I throw him out, I pop off."[14]

The Reds, despite their impressive start, finished the season in fourth place with an 80-74 mark. Robinson led Cincy with a .322 batting average and a .529 slugging percentage. George Crowe topped the club with 31 homers and 92 RBIs.

For the Giants, Mays batted a team-high .333 and led the league with 38 steals. He hit 35 home runs and 26 doubles and also topped the circuit with 20 triples and a .626 slugging percentage. Only three other National League or American League players in the twentieth century had ever reached at least 20 doubles, triples, and home runs in the same season.

The Giants finished 69-85 in their final year in New York. They slipped into sixth place on May 3 and never left that lowly position.

The NL's two New York-based teams left for California in 1958, the Giants to San Francisco and the Dodgers to Los Angeles. Giants owner Horace Stoneham waited until July 18 to make his decision, but Mays biographer James H. Hirsch wrote that "by spring training, Stoneham had already decided to move the team."[15]

Attendance at the Polo Grounds, once robust, had dwindled. The ballclub that drew 1,600,793 in 1947 attracted just 653,923 fans in the lame-duck season of 1957, actually an improvement over the previous year (629,179). Lockman said that "playing before crowds of twelve hundred was like walking through a morgue."[16]

In addition, several Giants lost faith in manager Bill Rigney. By late summer, according to Hirsch, "his team had quit on him." Mays and the skipper, though, had patched up some of their differences from the previous season when they clashed several times. In 1957, Hirsch wrote, "Mays didn't quit, and for that reason alone 1957 may have been his finest year."[17]

## SOURCES

Besides the specific sources cited in the Notes, the author used the Baseball-Reference.com and Retrosheet.org websites for general player, team, and season data and the box scores for this game.

https://www.baseball-reference.com/boxes/NYN/NYN197308170.shtml

https://www.retrosheet.org/boxesetc/1973/B08170NYN1973.htm

1 Lou Smith, "Giants' Gomez Tames Reds' Power," Cincinnati Enquirer, May 19, 1957: 57.

2 Jim McCulley, "Giants Leading Redlegs; Gomez Faces Nuxhall," New York Daily News, May 19, 1957: 56.

3 Lou Smith, "Pirates 'Debut' at Crosley Field in Double Bill," Cincinnati Enquirer, May 19, 1957: 57.

4 The Cardinals later sent Bob Stephenson and Gordon Jones to the Cardinals to complete the deal and make this a 10-player transaction.

5 Robert L. Burnes, "Schoendienst Traded to Giants in 8-Player Deal," St. Louis Globe-Democrat, June 15, 1956: 27.

6 Robert L. Burnes, "The Benchwarmer," St. Louis Globe-Democrat, June 15, 1956: 27.

7 Bill Ford, "Didn't Get a Chance to Get to Ruben," Cincinnati Enquirer, May 19, 1957: 57.

8 Smith, "Giants' Gomez Tames Reds' Power."

9 Smith, "Giants' Gomez Tames Reds' Power."

10 Smith, "Giants' Gomez Tames Reds' Power."

11 Ford, "Didn't Get a Chance to Get to Ruben."

12 Smith, "Giants' Gomez Tames Reds' Power."

13 Smith, "Giants' Gomez Tames Reds' Power."

14 Smith, "Pirates 'Debut' at Crosley Field in Double Bill."

15 James S. Hirsch, Willie Mays: The Life, the Legend (New York: Scribner, 2010), 260.

16 Hirsch, 257.

17 Hirsch, 257.

# END OF AN ERA AS GIANTS PLAY FINAL HOME GAME IN NEW YORK

## September 29, 1957: Pittsburgh Pirates 9, New York Giants 1, at Polo Grounds, New York

BY STEPHEN V. RICE

THE NEW YORK Giants played their first game on May 1, 1883, and their last game on September 29, 1957. On August 19, 1957, Horace Stoneham, the Giants owner since 1936, announced that the team would move to San Francisco for the 1958 season. Why leave New York after 75 seasons? "Lack of attendance," he said bluntly.[1] Of the eight National League teams, the Giants were last in attendance in 1956 and 1957.

At Stoneham's invitation, Giants of the past gathered in New York the night before the final game and reminisced. Among them were Jack Doyle, age 87; Hooks Wiltse, 78; Hans Lobert, 75; Red Murray, 73; Larry Doyle, 71; and Rube Marquard, 70.[2]

Fred Engel, 82, recounted his time as a team mascot in the 1880s. His favorite Giants were John Ward, Jim O'Rourke, Mickey Welch, and manager Jim Mutrie. Welch, the pitcher who won the first Giants game in 1883, liked to sing about food and beer, said Engel. And Mutrie was quite a showman: "He would arrive at the park dressed formally — high hat, tails and all — and parade around the park shouting, 'Who are the people?' Without waiting for a reply, he would scream, 'The Giant fans are the people!'"[3]

On Sunday, September 29, the last day of the 1957 season, the Giant fans were sad people. As if attending a funeral, 11,606 of them came to the Polo Grounds to grieve and bid their team farewell. The game against the Pittsburgh Pirates was secondary.

During the pregame ceremony, about 20 former Giants were introduced, including the old-timers mentioned above, and a bouquet of roses was given to Blanche McGraw, the 74-year-old widow of longtime Giants manager John McGraw. She was introduced as "the First Lady of the Polo Grounds."

On this day of nostalgia, Bill Rigney, the current Giants manager, fielded a lineup in which seven of nine starters were members of the 1951 or 1954 NL-champion Giants. George Levy, 81, announced the batteries using a megaphone, just as he had done in 1924: "Ladies an' gentulmen — Battrees for to-day's game — for Noo Yawk: Antonelli, pitchin'; Westrum, catchin'; for Pittsburgh: Friend, pitchin'; Peterson, catchin'."[4]

It was a battle of also-rans. The Giants were in sixth place. The Pirates were tied with the Chicago Cubs for seventh. Left-hander Johnny Antonelli and right-hander Bob Friend had lost 17 and 18 games, respectively, during the season. In the National League, only Robin Roberts of the Philadelphia Phillies had lost more.

The game began at 2:00 P.M. on a pleasant afternoon with the temperature in the low 60s. The Pirates' Gene Freese led off with a single, and Bill Mazeroski followed with another. Dick Groat lined the ball into the hands of Whitey Lockman at first base, who stepped on the bag for an unassisted double play. Freese scored when Bob Skinner catapulted a triple to center field. Skinner tried to make it an inside-the-park home run but was thrown out at the plate by a strong throw from the Giants center fielder, the incomparable Willie Mays.

In the bottom of the first inning, Don Mueller singled and moved to third base on Mays' single. Dusty Rhodes sent a fly ball to center field, where it was caught by Roberto Clemente. Mueller tagged up and made it home ahead of Clemente's throw to catcher Hardy Peterson. As Mays headed for second base, Peterson threw to Mazeroski, the second baseman, who tagged Mays out.

Frank Thomas led off the top of the second inning with a home run into the left-field stands. Clemente doubled and John Powers was hit by a pitch. Peterson singled to right field, scoring Clemente and sending Powers to third base. Peterson, though, was thrown out trying to stretch it to a double. Powers scored on Friend's single, and the Pirates led, 4-1.

After allowing four runs on seven hits in two innings, Antonelli was replaced by Curt Barclay, a rookie right-hander. The Pirates scored two runs off Barclay in the fourth inning, with singles by Clemente and Friend and a double by Powers. In the sixth inning, consecutive singles by Clemente, Powers, and Peterson produced another run. Meanwhile, Friend silenced the Giants offense. Mays got his second hit of the day, a single in the seventh inning, but did not score.

The Pirates tacked on two more runs, getting one in the eighth on Friend's single and Mazeroski's double, and another in the ninth on Powers' home run, a mammoth shot off right-hander Ramón Monzant. The powerful blast sailed over the roof in right field, close to the foul line.

Friend was still going strong as the Giants came to bat in the bottom of the ninth. Mueller flied to Powers in right field for the first out. Then Mays stepped to the plate. The fans gave him a standing ovation, realizing this was his final at-bat as a New York Giant. Though he grounded weakly to Friend and was easily thrown out, the fans continued their applause. Mays said later, "With the crowd cheering me and everything, it was the only time in my entire career I could feel the bat shaking in my hand."[5]

Rhodes made the final out on a grounder to Groat, the shortstop. The final score was Pirates 9, Giants 1. Friend allowed six hits in his complete game. It was his "bachelor's party," said the *Pittsburgh Post-Gazette*, because he was set to get married the next day.[6]

The *New York Times* called the game "an inelegant thrashing."[7] But "inelegance" understates what happened immediately after the game. As soon as the final out was made, fans rushed onto the field. The players fled to the clubhouse in center field, ahead of the mob.

Fans ran amuck in a frenzy of souvenir collecting. They took the bases and pitcher's rubber; demolished the wooden bullpen shelter; tore pieces of foam rubber off the outfield fences; scooped up dirt from the infield; and pulled sod from the outfield. Several teens pried the bronze plaque off the Eddie Grant memorial monument, but the police were able to recover it. At one point, the fans chanted in unison, "We want Stoneham, with a rope around his neck!"

Sportswriter Morris McLemore witnessed the ugly scene. He said he was born a Giants fan but wished he "hadn't shown up for the last twitches of a dying tradition."[8]

Regarding the players' run to the clubhouse, a jaded fan remarked, "That is the only time I've seen them guys run hard all year. Let 'em run right on to 'Frisco." "All but Willie," said another fan. "Yeah, all but Willie," said the first.[9]

Mrs. McGraw watched the devastation from the stands. "It would have broken John's heart," she said.[10]

## SOURCES

Game coverage in the September 30, 1957, issues of the *New York Times*, *New York Daily News*, *Pittsburgh Press*, *Pittsburgh Post-Gazette*, and *Pittsburgh Sun-Telegraph*.

baseball-reference.com/boxes/NY1/NY1195709290.shtml

https://www.retrosheet.org/boxesetc/1957/B09290NY11957.htm

## NOTES

1 Walter Judge, "History Is Made! S.F. in Big Leagues!" *San Francisco Examiner*, August 20, 1957: II-10.

2 "Pirates Whip Giants, 9 to 1," *Baltimore Sun*, September 30, 1957: 16.

3 Howard M. Tuckner, "Giants' First Batboy Is Not Entirely Alone," *New York Times*, September 29, 1957: S3.

4 "Ready for To-Day's Game," *Brooklyn Standard Union*, October 8, 1924: 16.

5 Curley Grieve, "S.F. Giants Born in N.Y. mid Rioting," *San Francisco Examiner*, September 30, 1957: I-1, II-5.

6 Jack Hernon, "Pirates Win Final Game, 9-1," *Pittsburgh Post-Gazette*, September 30, 1957: 27, 30. Friend married Pat Koval on September 30, 1957.

7 "Giants, in Farewell to New York, Lose to Pirates before Crowd of 11,606," *New York Times*, September 30, 1957: 36.

8 Morris McLemore, "Only Game in Town," *Miami* (Florida) *News*, September 30, 1957: 8.

9 Bill Bryson, "Giant Fans to Miss Mays," *Des Moines* (Iowa) *Tribune*, September 30, 1957: 20.

10 Arthur Daley, "Sports of the Times," *New York Times*, September 30, 1957: 37.

# MAYS 'SEALS' THE WIN WITH HOMER

## April 26, 1958: San Francisco Giants 3, Chicago Cubs 1, at Seals Stadium, San Francisco

BY DANIEL WINKLER

**FOR WILLIE MAYS,** the April 26, 1958, game between his San Francisco Giants and the Chicago Cubs was historic, as the game saw the Say Hey Kid's first-ever home run as a San Francisco Giant.

The Cubs arrived in San Francisco that weekend playing well, having won consecutive series against the St. Louis Cardinals and Los Angeles Dodgers. But the Giants proved a stiff challenge, defeating the Cubs 2-0 in the opener at Seals Stadium.

The next day the Cubs again challenged the Giants. The Cubs were 6-3 so far, while the Giants were slightly better at 7-3. Because they had started the season off well, both teams were undoubtedly hopeful.

In efforts to turn that hope into reality, Giants manager Bill Rigney started Johnny Antonelli, while the Cubs skipper, Bob Scheffing, went with Glen Hobbie.

As Antonelli strode to the mound, a crowd of 19,284 ambled about, ready to support their new team. That was a titanic draw in 1958, and a prime reason why Giants owner Horace Stoneham had moved the team to the West Coast. New York City was the Giants' birthplace, and the team had played most of its home games at the glorious Polo Grounds. But attendance had dwindled, and in 1957 the Giants averaged a paltry 8,493 fans per game, second lowest in the majors.

And so the Giants left New York City and moved to San Francisco, in search of more fans, more money, and more wins. The 19,284 fans present on April 26 definitely helped bring in more fans and money, while Johnny Antonelli hoped to add more wins.

But winning ain't easy, and for Antonelli, the game started inauspiciously. The Cubs' first-year second baseman, Tony Taylor, smacked a single to center field. The young Cuban infielder would have a notable career and was a threat to steal bases. Having him prowl about on first base was no way for Antonelli to begin his afternoon, especially as sluggers Lee Walls and Ernie Banks were lurking.

Yet, Antonelli was able to recover and face the minimum three batters in the inning, when with one out Banks grounded into a double play to retire the side.[1]

With Antonelli resting on the bench, the Giants offense began in futile fashion as Cubs starter Hobbie retired the hitters in order in the bottom of the first. Hobbie, who had just made the Cubs rotation that spring training, even retired Mays, who hit a "screaming line drive" that shortstop Banks jumped "high to grab." This was the only time Mays recorded an out in the game.[2]

Ernie Banks had come into Seals Stadium playing well, hitting above .300 and slugging above .600. Banks was radiantly hot throughout the 1958 season, and ultimately led the National League in slugging, home runs, runs batted in, and total bases. Such dominance helped the slugger win the Most Valuable Player Award, one he would win again the next season.

After he snagged snagging Mays' line drive, Banks and his teammates ambled into the dugout, doubtlessly eager to resume their offensive efforts. Again, the Cubs' leadoff man, now Walt Moryn, reached base via a hit-by-pitch. Antonelli made up for the mistake, inducing the next three Cubs to fly out, including former Giant Bobby Thomson.

During the early innings, the game generally followed this pattern. Runners would get on, but the rally was quickly squelched. Mays helped break this pattern, leading off the fourth inning with a double to right field. Left fielder Hank Sauer, a former Cub and the 1952 MVP, singled, and Mays flew around the bases, reaching home and scoring the game's first run.

Along with power, speed was an essential and excellent part of Mays' game. His iconic catches and baserunning relied on his speed. Mays led the league in steals every year from 1956 through 1959. Thanks to such speed, the Giants now had the lead to the delight of the Seals Stadium faithful.[3]

After Mays scored, the Giants were retired. The Cubs seemed about to retaliate, with their first two batters, Johnny Goryl and El Tappe, both hitting singles to start the top of the fifth inning. But again, despite allowing two baserunners, Antonelli was unfazed and retired the next three batters in order.

The Giants could not add to their lead in the bottom of the fifth, and again the Cubs wasted another runner in the top of the sixth, this time due to a double play. Mays again broke the monotony in the bottom of the sixth.

He led off again and crushed a 370-foot home run to left field. It was his first home run of the season, the first West Coast home run he ever hit, and his first home run as a San Francisco Giant. In the immediate context, the home run proved to be the winning run in the game, as the Cubs scored just once.

In 1958 Mays hit 29 home runs, tied for the fewest he hit during the stretch between his return from military service in 1954 and 1966. Despite the relatively lower home-run total, Mays still led the league in both OPS (1.002) and OPS+ (165) in 1958. He hit .347, the highest batting average of his career, and he finished second in MVP voting to Banks.

According to form, the Cubs stranded a runner in the top of seventh, unable to respond to Mays' blast. Hobbie then left the game and was replaced by Dolan Nichols, who retired the Giants in the bottom of the seventh.

The Cubs scored their only run in the eighth. Right fielder Lee Walls smashed a 375-foot home run. It was the fifth of the young season for Walls, who hit 24 home runs in 1958, led the league in HBP (8), had a 4.4 WAR, and had a .304/.370/.493 slash line. He was an All-Star as well.

Banks stepped up the plate right after Walls and smashed a double. Antonelli was in trouble. Again, though, Antonelli ended the inning and stranded Banks. For the entire game, "Walls was the only Cub to touch third base."[4]

In the Giants' half of the eighth, Mays led off for the third time and recorded his third straight extra-base hit. But while his earlier hits were powerful, this double was no line drive but a "high fly to short right" that "Walls could not handle."[5]

A reporter commented that the wind took the ball "out of the hands of Walls" and "Willie kept right on going to turn what at first appeared to be an out into a double."[6] Mays hit 33 doubles in 1958, and during his 15 seasons as a San Francisco Giant, he hit 30 or more two-baggers five times.

Mays scored another run for the Giants, this time driven in by Daryl Spencer's two-out double. Ed Mayer relieved Nichols and recorded the final out of the inning.

Down by two runs, Chicago had only three outs left. And Antonelli retired the Cubs in order, for the first time since the fourth inning. (The fourth and ninth were the only two innings in which the Cubs had no baserunners.)

Antonelli's ability to pitch through trouble helped him complete a "minor masterpiece," and Emmons Byrne noted that "Lovable John, always a control pitcher, has seldom been better as his 91 pitches in nine innings indicate."[7]

Yet, despite his apt performance, the postgame clubhouse scene was not a love affair for Antonelli, who had a tumultuous relationship with the San Francisco-area press. On that day he was "still having no part of the Bay Area press, and angrily ordered a cameraman, who wanted to take his picture, out of the clubhouse."[8]

For his part, Antonelli excelled as a Giant until his last season in New York in 1957, when his struggles culminated in a 12-18 record. Sportswriter Byrne wrote that the "irritation" began with "printed speculation as to the condition of his arm" during these struggles. Antonelli seemed to at least concede that his grievance with the press was new, noting that "this is the first time I can't get along with the press."[9] Sadly for Antonelli, he has often been remembered for such conflicts rather than for his pitching acumen.

As for Mays, Byrne said that the center fielder "literally ran away with the game."[10]

Another reporter had similar praise, describing Mays' performance as "a one-man show."[11]

## SOURCES

In addition to the sources cited in the Notes, the author consulted Baseball-Reference.com

https://www.baseball-reference.com/boxes/SFN/SFN195804260.shtmlhttps://www.retrosheet.org/boxesetc/1958/B04260SFN1958.htm

## NOTES

1 Antonelli was talented, and certainly capable of retiring Banks and stranding runners. Like Willie Mays, Antonelli had been a star prospect, having signed a massive contract out of high school. In the majors, though, he had languished with the Boston/Milwaukee Braves until 1954 when the Giants traded Bobby Thomson and catcher Sammy Calderone for Antonelli, Don Liddle, Ebba St. Claire, Billy Klaus, and $50,000. Antonelli noted that the trade was "the best break of my career." Alexander Edelman, "Johnny Antonelli," SABR BioProject.

2 Alan Kline, "Mays Homers, Doubles Twice, as Giants Edge Chicago 3-1," *Santa Cruz* (California) *Sentinel*, April 27, 1958: 14.

3 This opening of the scoring doubtless pleased the Seals Stadium crowd, who were used to their team scoring runs in their beautiful downtown stadium. As noted in Eric Enders' *Ballparks Then and Now*, Seals Stadium had hosted the vaunted San Francisco Seals minor-league team for years, a squad that won 15 Pacific Coast League titles and always had good players, including the San Francisco native and legendary DiMaggio brothers, Dom, Vince, and Joe DiMaggio. Eric Enders, *Ballparks Then and Now* (London: Pavilion Books, 2019), 144-45. Joe DiMaggio was an idol of Mays as Joe Posnanski noted in his book, The *Baseball 100* (New York: Avid Reader Press, 2021), 819.

4 Kline, "Mays Homers, Doubles Twice, as Giants Edge Chicago 3-1."

5 Kline.

6 Emmons Byrne, "Mays Hits First Homer as Giants Beat Cubs," *Oakland Tribune*, April 27, 1958: 57, 60.

7 Byrne.

8 Byrne.

9 Byrne.

10 Byrne.

11 Kline.

# MAYS COMPLETES TORRID STRETCH AGAINST RIVAL DODGERS

## May 13, 1958: San Francisco Giants 16, Los Angeles Dodgers 9, at Los Angeles Coliseum

BY GLEN SPARKS

WHAT WAS WRONG with Willie Mays?

Sure, the Say Hey Kid was batting .372 through May 7, but he had just one home run in his first 22 games as a San Francisco Giant. According to one reporter, "A lot of his hits have been cheapies – the seeing-eye kind."[1] Mays hit 35 homers in 1957, the Giants' final season in New York, and a major-league-high 51 in 1955. A United Press reporter called the center fielder "something of a disappointment in San Francisco because he was not hitting the long ball."[2]

Mays picked a good time to start swinging for the fences. The Giants began a four-game set against the Los Angeles Dodgers on May 9, the first two at Seals Stadium and next two at the LA Coliseum. Mays hit two homers and collected five RBIs in the opener, an 11-3 win against the Giants' bitter rival and the other National League team that left New York City for California after 1957, the Dodgers from the borough of Brooklyn. The *San Francisco Examiner* reported, "Willie Mays finally broke out with the big one tonight."[3]

Mays hit another home run in the second game, and the Giants won, 3-2, behind Johnny Antonelli. After an offday, the teams met in Los Angeles. The Giants won in lopsided fashion, 12-3. Ruben Gomez struck out 10 Dodgers and walked just one in a complete-game effort. Don Drysdale lasted only two innings for LA and gave up three runs and six hits. Mays hit two more home runs, including a grand slam, and once again drove home five. He was now batting .398. "Walloping Willie Mays was at it again tonight," Walter Judge wrote in the *San Francisco Examiner*.[4]

Could the superstar center fielder keep up his hot hitting in the finale? After those three straight wins against LA, San Francisco had a record of 16-9 and was in second place, just a half-game behind the Milwaukee Braves. The Dodgers were struggling with a 9-16 mark and looking up from the National League cellar. "The Dodgers struck rock bottom last night," Frank Finch of the *Los Angeles Times* told his readers on May 13. The team hadn't sunk this low since July 2, 1948, Finch reported.[5] "They spent only one day in the dungeon on that doleful date," Finch continued, "but the way the bedraggled Dodgers are playing now it may be that they will never see daylight again."[6]

Giants skipper Bill Rigney sent 19-year-old left-hander Mike McCormick, a native of nearby Pasadena, to the mound. The ballclub signed McCormick in 1956 as a so-called bonus baby out of Mark Keppel High School in Alhambra, California, and he made his big-league debut as a 17-year-old. The Dodgers countered with veteran right-hander Don Newcombe, who was less than two years removed from his 27-win season and Cy Young Award campaign in 1956.

*Willie Mays batted .309 lifetime against the Dodgers and hit 98 home runs. Courtesy National Baseball Hall of Fame.*

Only 10,507 fans filed into the vast Coliseum on a Tuesday afternoon, almost 20,000 fewer than attended the previous evening's game and 90,000 or so short of capacity. McCormick and Newcombe struggled from the start. Newcombe surrendered five runs in the top of the first inning. Mays hit a one-out, two-run homer deep into the center-field seats. Jim Davenport, who led off the game with a walk, also scored.

Hank Sauer, the Giants' next batter, reached on an error by third baseman Dick Gray. Orlando Cepeda, San Francisco's hard-hitting rookie first baseman, followed with a single. Daryl Spencer tripled into right field, and the road team led 4-0. After Bob Schmidt struck out looking, Danny O'Connell singled home Spencer. McCormick ended the inning by grounding out.

The Dodgers got back three runs in their half of the first. Jim Gilliam, known for his good eye at the plate, began the rally with a walk. McCormick added to his problems by hitting Gino Cimoli with a pitch. After Charlie Neal struck out, Carl Furillo deposited a pitch into the seats. Gil Hodges followed with a base hit that ended McCormick's afternoon. Rigney brought in right-hander Ramon Monzant, a 25-year-old from Venezuela, who retired Gray and Don Zimmer.

San Francisco scored twice in the second. Don Taussig reached on Gray's second error of the game, and Mays hit his second homer. Neal knocked a three-run homer for the Dodgers in the bottom half of the inning, narrowing San Francisco's lead to 7-6.

Hodges tied the game when he hit a homer in the third inning off Al Worthington, San Francisco's third pitcher. Hodges and Furillo now had four home runs apiece for the season.

The Giants pulled ahead 11-7 in the fourth. Mays led off by tripling into center field off Fred Kipp, who had relieved Newcombe with one out in the third. Sauer walked and Cepeda followed with an RBI single. That hit ended Kipp's day. LA skipper Walter Alston called on Ed Roebuck, who immediately gave up a three-run homer to Spencer.

Mays led off the San Francisco fifth by singling to right field and stealing second base with Sauer at bat. After the left fielder popped out, Mays was caught trying to steal third, this time with Cepeda at the plate. Cepeda, the son of Puerto Rican baseball legend Pedro "Perucho" Cepeda, promptly launched his ninth homer of the season. Spencer doubled and scored on Schmidt's two-base hit. The Giants now led 13-7.

The Dodgers launched another rally with Worthington still pitching in the fifth inning. Hodges singled and Gray and Zimmer walked. Joe Pignatano lined out, and Alston sent up Duke Snider to pinch-hit for Roebuck. The fabled Duke of Flatbush, who hit at least 40 homers every year from 1953 to 1957, grounded into a force out, which scored Hodges. The next batter, Gilliam, flied out to center field.

Alston sent in the talented but wild-armed left-hander Sandy Koufax to pitch in the sixth inning. The Brooklyn native was, like McCormick, a bonus baby and trying to learn the game as a major leaguer without benefit of minor-league seasoning.. This was his fourth season with the Dodgers. San Francisco mounted a quick rally off the 22-year-old. After Worthington grounded out, Davenport doubled and Taussig singled. Mays walked to load the bases. Koufax, always prone to giving out free passes, also walked Sauer and the Giants took a 14-8 lead. Cepeda hit into a double play to end the frame.

Spencer greeted Koufax with a home run in the seventh, the shortstop's second round-tripper of the day. Koufax also gave up a one-out single to O'Connell. Worthington, though, hit into a force out, and Davenport struck out looking. The Giants now led 15-8, and scored their final run in the eighth inning with lefty Danny McDevitt on the mound. Mays hit his second triple of the day and sprinted home on Willie Kirkland's sacrifice fly.

The Dodgers' last run came on Neal's homer off Worthington in the eighth inning. Neither team scored in the ninth with McDevitt still pitching for Los Angeles and Marv Grissom performing those duties for San Francisco. Worthington got the win in this high-scoring 16-9 affair, improving his record to 3-1, and Grissom picked up his fourth save. Kipp took the loss and dropped to 1-3.

San Francisco batters rang up 26 hits. Cepeda, O'Connell, Schmidt, and Spencer had four apiece, and Spencer drove home six runs. Mays had five hits, four RBIs, and four runs scored. The Giants collected 50 total bases, the most in the modern era (post-1900) in the National League.[7] Judge wrote, "This was a great day of glory for the Giants."[8] Mays raised his batting average to .427. "I guess I would say it was my biggest day," he said afterward.[9]

Over his past four games, Mays was 12-for-17 (.706) with 7 homers, 2 triples, a double, 10 runs scored, and 15 RBIs. He had 38 total bases. About his sudden power surge, Mays said, "I didn't change anything. I just started to hit."[10] Judge called Mays "baseball's most exciting player."[11]

While Southern California's new big-league team struggled ("What's wrong with the Dodgers?" *Los Angeles Times* columnist Al Wolf wrote after the four-game debacle against the Giants. "It's a good question – a pertinent question. But there doesn't seem to be a satisfactory answer – a finger-on-the-spot answer."[12]), the ballclub from up north had found a happy home.

*Examiner* sports editor Curley Grieve wrote, "Hot or cold in the future, up or down the National League ladder, we can point to this period of big league induction as one that hit the highest and finest notes on the baseball scale. … I'm going to say that so far the Giants have played 'world series baseball.'" As for Mays, Grieve wrote, he "did not dominate at the outset as expected, although performing excellently. And then, suddenly almost, he burst forth like a Roman candle, lighting up the scene with a new brilliance."[13]

## SOURCES

Besides the sources cited in the Notes, the author used the Baseball-Reference.com and Retrosheet websites for general player, team, and season data and the box scores for this game.

https://www.baseball-reference.com/boxes/LAN/LAN195805130.shtml

https://www.retrosheet.org/boxesetc/1958/B05130LAN1958.htm

## NOTES

1 Charlie Park, "Movies Cure Problems over Hitting of Mays," *Los Angeles Mirror*, May 10, 1958: 10.

2 United Press, "Willie Mays Convinces Giant Fans; Mantle Powers Long Homer," *Salinas Californian*, May 10, 1958: 10.

3 Walter Judge, "Mays Clouts 2 Homers in 11-3 Win," *San Francisco Examiner*, May 10, 1958: 17.

4 Walter Judge, "Giants Erupt 12-3 – Mays Grand Slam," *San Francisco Examiner*, May 13, 1958: 28.

5 The Dodgers were tied for last place on July 2, 1948, .004 percentage points behind the Chicago Cubs.

6 Frank Finch, "29,770 See Giants Tumble Dodgers into Cellar, 12-3," *Los Angeles Times*, May 13, 1958: 53.

7 Walter Judge, "Giants Win 16-9, Lead NL," *San Francisco Examiner*, May 14, 1958: 36. (Three teams have since surpassed the Giants' total and one team matched that figure The Expos compiled 58 total bases on July 30, 1978, against the Atlanta Braves. The Cincinnati Reds had 55 on May 19, 1999, against the Colorado Rockies. The New York Mets had 51 total bases on August 24, 2015, against the Philadelphia Phillies, and the Washington Nationals had 50 against the New York Mets on July 31, 2018.)

8 "Giants Win 16-9, Lead NL."

9 "My Best Day Ever," *San Francisco Examiner*, May 14, 1958: 36.

10 "LA Sees Too Much Mays in 16-9 Loss," *Valley Times* (San Fernando Valley, California), May 14, 1958: 12.

11 "Giants Win 16-9, Lead NL."

12 Al Wolf, "Dodgers Wonder What's Wrong with Dodgers," *Los Angeles Times*, May 14, 1958: 65.

13 Curley Grieve, "Most Exciting Month of Sports Entertainment in City's History," *San Francisco Examiner*, May 14, 1958: 39.

# MAYS VIES FOR AN IMPROBABLE BATTING TITLE ON THE SEASON'S FINAL DAY

## September 28, 1958: San Francisco Giants 7, St Louis Cardinals 2, at Seals Stadium, San Francisco

BY JAMES FORR

SAN FRANCISCO ADOPTED Willie Mays like a stepson. He was fine and all, but he wasn't theirs.

Sure, he was hitting .433 in early June, but as the summer went on, his average tumbled, the Giants stumbled, and fans began to boo. New Yorkers never booed Willie Mays. No one booed Willie Mays.

As Jim Murray of the *Los Angeles Times* put it, "They didn't expect Willie Mays to land there; they expected the waters of the Golden Gate to part and let him walk ashore."[1]

The city liked Mays, respected him, but it loved Orlando Cepeda, a 20-year-old rookie unsullied by any association with New York. Before the final game of the year, against the St. Louis Cardinals at Seals Stadium, he received a spirited ovation as he accepted the team's Most Valuable Player Award, as voted on by Giants fans. Mays, who bested Cepeda in almost every offensive category, settled for a consolation prize, albeit a nice one: a shot at the National League batting championship.

As of September 11, four future Hall of Famers huddled atop the list of National League batting leaders. St. Louis's Stan Musial led the way with an average of .338, Richie Ashburn was three points back, Henry Aaron of the Braves was at .333, and then came Mays with a mark of .328.

The September 15 issue of *Sports Illustrated* laid odds on the race. Writer Roy Terrell didn't think much of Ashburn's chances, concluding, "Ashburn is a not a good bet for one of those 5-for-5 days, which the other three occasionally provide."[2]

Terrell wrote a lot of nice things about him, too, but all Ashburn could focus on was that last sentence. "It really got me peeved," he said years later.[3]

Aaron tailed off during the final few weeks. Musial missed nine games with a leg injury and, although he hit well upon his return, he couldn't keep up with the stampeding pace set by Ashburn and Mays. From September 11 to September 27, Ashburn batted .460 and came into the season finale with five consecutive multihit games. Mays, during the same span, batted .500. The Sunday papers on the 28th were calculating their averages to four decimal points – Ashburn stood at .3469, Mays at .3445.

Mays had been here before. He began the final game of 1954 in a virtual tie with his teammate, Don Mueller, and Brooklyn's Duke Snider. (Mueller was batting .3426, Snider .3425, and Mays .3422.) Mays' 3-for-4 effort against Robin Roberts in Philadelphia earned him the crown.

This was going to be a steeper climb because he entered the day trailing slightly, but even if he fell short, Mays knew he had made a point. "I think I tried to prove something in '58 because when I first came out, the writers said, 'Well, here's a kid coming from New York. We don't know what he can do.' So I said, OK, I'll just go for batting average this year."[4]

While Mays was heading for the ballpark, Ashburn was back east in Pittsburgh facing the Pirates' Bennie Daniels. He grounded to short his first time up. "I remember going back to the dugout and kind of thinking, 'It's going to be one of those days.'"[5]

It wasn't. Ashburn met the challenge. He lashed three singles, including one in the 10th inning that sparked a two-run rally and propelled Philadelphia to a 6-4 victory.

Although the Giants had been out of contention since August, a crowd of 19,435 came out, enticed by Mays' chance at glory and by the unseasonable 80-degree weather. (The 92-degree temperatures the day before sent 125 parboiled fans wobbling into the first-aid room.)

Most of the crowd was unaware of exactly where the batting race stood. The Giants made no announcements about what Ashburn had done, but Mays knew. "I heard it on the radio just before we went out. I knew I needed [to go] 5-for-5 to win."[6] Manager Bill Rigney knew, too. He batted Mays leadoff instead of in his usual third spot to provide him with a better shot at that fifth at-bat.

The miracle would have to come against St. Louis's 14-game winner, Sam Jones, who was tall, fast, wild, and generally a little terrifying. He was no easy mark for anyone, including Mays, who had only seven hits in 39 career at-bats against him.

Mays took the initial step on his unlikely journey with a ringing double to deep left field in the first inning. Jim Davenport's infield grounder advanced him to third. Then, with Willie Kirkland at the plate, Jones's pitch squirted away from catcher Gene Green. The ball didn't roll far, but Mays broke immediately. Green slipped as he threw toward home, Jones was late getting there anyway, and Mays sneaked in with the game's first run.

San Francisco scored two more in the second, but Mays' hopes came to an end in the middle of that rally. He got a reprieve after tapping a weak groundball toward first base; umpire Frank Secory immediately sprang in front of the plate, waved his arms, and shouted that Green had called time before the pitch. The stay was only temporary, however. Moments later Mays lofted a lazy fly ball to Ellis Burton in left. "I knew then what chance I had was gone," he said.[7]

San Francisco starter John Fitzgerald was making his major-league debut. He was a prospect the Giants wanted to take a look at, even though he had just gotten out of the US Army and hadn't pitched professionally in two years. The kid held up. He allowed just one walk and a solo home run to Joe Cunningham in his three innings of work. Dom Zanni, also making his first big-league appearance, relieved Fitzgerald in the fourth. Mays helped him with a solo home run in the bottom of that inning to increase San Francisco's lead to 4-1.

After Bobby Gene Smith cut the lead to 4-2 with a fifth-inning home run, the Giants rose up again in the sixth and Mays was right in the middle of it. With one away, he trickled a grounder up the third-base line. Ken Boyer's throw was wild, and Mays ended up at second with an infield hit and an error charged to Boyer. Davenport doubled to left to bring home Mays, and one out later, Leon Wagner doubled to right-center to plate Davenport. The Giants added another run in the seventh to set the final score at 7-2 and give Zanni a victory in his debut. Mays lined out to center in his final at-bat in that seventh inning.

Mays went 3-for-5 and scored three runs. The runs elevated him past Ernie Banks to the top of the National League in that category, but he fell three points short of Ashburn – .350 to .347.

Mays was in a rush to get out of the clubhouse and catch an evening flight home to Manhattan, where he planned to kick back for a few days before going out again on an offseason barnstorming tour. He brushed aside a question about whether he had felt any extra pressure: "Of course, I wasn't pressing. Anytime I get three hits I'm not pressing. I just went out and played my regular game."[8]

"No, I wasn't disappointed," he said. "After all, I didn't have it won. If I hit .347 every year I'll be satisfied."[9]

Ashburn found it to be a scintillating final month. "The other time I won the title (in 1955) it wasn't close. This year was different. I feel better about winning a race with four guys in there," he said.[10]

"I don't know how I ever finished ahead of [Mays]," Ashburn marveled. "It seemed Willie kept getting hits by the handful."[11]

"Willie sure made a good run for it," said Rigney, who preferred to focus more on the progress his club had made, improving from 69-85 in their desultory last season in the Polo Grounds to a third-place 80-74 record in sunny California.[12] "[N]ext year we'll win 90 if we get some pitchers. I hoped for the first division this year and I said so and am pleased with third."[13]

It took a while for the Giants to fulfill Rigney's exuberant vision – and he was gone by the time they did. It also took a while for San Francisco to fully embrace Willie Mays. He was a Black man in a city that was surprisingly inhospitable to African Americans. He played the same position as the local hero, Joe DiMaggio, and suffered by the comparison. He was an unwelcome reminder of the Giants' New York roots, which the new fan base preferred to forget. No batting race, no matter how thrilling, could magically sweep all that away. But it was a start.

## SOURCES

In addition to the newspaper sources cited in the Notes, the author used Baseball-Reference.com and Retrosheet.org for play-by-play and other information:

https://www.baseball-reference.com/boxes/SFN/SFN195809280.shtml

https://www.retrosheet.org/boxesetc/1958/B09280SFN1958.htm

The author also reviewed the following sources:

Connolly, Will. "Mays' 3-for-5 Not Good Enough," *San Francisco Chronicle,* September 29, 1958: 1H, 6H.

Lewis, Allen. "Ashburn's .350 Wins Batting Title, Phils Finish With 6th Victory in Row," *Philadelphia Inquirer*, September 29, 1958: 22, 27.

## NOTES

1 Jim Murray, "Wonderful Willie," *Los Angeles Times*, May 23, 1962: Part III, 1.

2 Roy Terrell, "For Silver and Gold," *Sports Illustrated,* September 15, 1958: 52-53.

3 Larry Shenk, "Ashburn Edges Mays for Batting Title," MLB.com, September 28, 2016, https://www.mlb.com/news/richie-ashburn-beats-out-willie-mays-in-1958-c203891470.

4 Steve Bitker, *The Original San Francisco Giants: The Giants of '58* (Champaign, Illinois: Sports Publishing, LLC, 2003), 185.

5 Shenk.

6 Jack Fiske, "Willie Knew, but 19,435 Fans Didn't," *San Francisco Chronicle*, September 29, 1958: 1H, 6H.

7 Walter Judge, "3 Hits! – Mays' Bid Fails," *San Francisco Examiner,* September 29, 1958: Sec II, 4.

8 Fiske.

9 Judge.

10 Allen Lewis, "Freese Billed to Plug Phils' Keystone Gap," *The Sporting News,* October 8, 1958: 13.

11 Lewis.

12 Judge.

13 Fiske.

# WILLIE MAYS HITS FOR THE CYCLE IN ALL-STAR DOUBLEHEADER

## July 13, 1960: National League 6, American League 0, at Yankee Stadium, New York

BY MIKE HUBER

**IN HIS SECOND** at-bat of the second All-Star Game in 1960, Willie Mays made history by completing the All-Star Game cycle. In the span of just two days, Mays had collected the four necessary hits to hit for the cycle: a single, double, triple, and home run. No major leaguer has ever hit for the cycle in one All-Star Game. Mays became the first (and only) ballplayer to hit for the cycle in an All-Star doubleheader, when both games were played in the same season.

From 1959 through 1962, a four-season experiment, there were two All-Star Games played each year. Why? According to mlb.com writer Bill Center, "Profits from the second All-Star Game went directly into the players' pension fund under the Collective Bargaining Agreement with the Major League Baseball Players Association."[1] In 1960 the games were only two days apart (July 11 and 13), and they were played in two American League venues (Kansas City's Municipal Stadium and New York's Yankee Stadium).

The gametime temperature at Yankee Stadium was 88 degrees, but it was very humid. Still, this was 12 degrees cooler than it had been in Kansas City,[2] where the National League handily defeated the American League, 5-3, before a crowd of 30,619. Pittsburgh's Bob Friend started for the NL and pitched three one-hit, shutout innings. Friend had tied for the major-league lead in wins in 1958 with 22 wins; he also tied for the most losses (with 19) the following season.[3] He rebounded in 1960, winning 10 games in the season's first half to gain his third All-Star selection. For the AL, Boston's Bill Monbouquette started; he had won eight games coming into the All-Star break. The Red Sox right-hander was tagged for four runs on five hits in just the first two frames. Mays led all batters with a

3-for-4 performance, consisting of a single, double, and triple. He made four putouts in center field.

The starting pitchers in Game Two were the Yankees' Whitey Ford and the Pirates' Vern Law. Ford had struggled a bit in the first half of the season, winning only five of 10 decisions. His ERA was over three runs per nine innings, higher than in any of his first eight seasons with New York. But he was the Yankees' ace, and the game was in New York. Law and Friend were the stars of the Pirates staff. Law had won 11 games leading up to the break, with a 2.52 ERA. A crowd of 38,362 came through the gates of Yankee Stadium.

Before the game, Mays supposedly joked with American League All-Star Yogi Berra, "Hey Yog. Do you mind if I steal on you?"[4] Berra responded with "Go ahead, Willie." Mays swung at the first pitch of the game, singling to left field. Bob Skinner banged a Baltimore chop for another hit, and Mays advanced to second. With Hank Aaron in the batter's box, Mays "expressed his talent for baseball larceny"[5] and stole third base. On the next pitch, Skinner broke for second on a missed hit-and-run. Berra faked the throw to second and instead threw to third base, as Mays came down the line toward home. According to the *New York Times*, Berra "hung him up on the third-base line, as exposed as the Monday wash,"[6] and later told reporters, "That'll learn yuh not to go horsin' around with me."[7]

The senior circuit squad tallied in the second inning. Joe Adcock led off with a single and Eddie Mathews followed with a homer. Law faced the minimum through two innings. Although Bill Skowron singled with one out in the bottom of the second, Berra hit a comebacker to Law, who started a double play to end the inning.

Mays led off the third inning facing Ford for the second time. He swung at a curve that was low and away and "blasted a towering homer deep into the lower left-field stands,"[8] extending the NL advantage to 3-0. Ford told reporters that Mays "just reached out and pulled the ball into the seats."[9] With the round-tripper, Mays had completed hitting for the All-Star Game cycle in just his sixth at-bat.

With Johnny Podres now pitching, the AL loaded the bases with a single and a pair of walks in the bottom of the third, but Roger Maris popped out to the catcher for the third out. The score remained 3-0 until the top of the seventh. Perennial All-Star Stan Musial pinch-hit for pitcher Stan Williams and belted a homer well beyond the right-field barrier. It was his sixth All-Star Game home run.

In the home half of the seventh, Maris had another chance to put the AL on the scoreboard. Larry Jackson was now on the mound. Frank Malzone walked and two outs later, Ted Williams singled. Brooks Robinson entered as a pinch-runner for 41-year-old Williams, playing in his final season. Jackson walked Al Kaline to load the bases, bringing Maris to the plate. This was his second at-bat with the bases loaded. Maris hit a fly ball to center that "enabled Mays to treat his admirers to one of his familiar basket catches."[10] Mays played the game with a glove borrowed from Roy Face, saying, "Somebody stole my glove in Kansas City."[11] Showing the glove to reporters, he said, "Look at it. It's a little boy's glove."[12]

Mays led off the top of the eighth. In the fifth he had popped out to first baseman Skowron, but in the eighth he singled to center to start a rally, An out later, Roberto Clemente walked, but Dick Groat, pinch-hitting for Ernie Banks, grounded into an inning-ending 4-6-3 double play. Vada Pinson entered the game, replacing Mays in center. Mickey Mantle singled to begin the bottom of the eighth. After Vic Power flied out, Sherm Lollar lined a ball to right field that bounced over the fence for a ground-rule double. Mantle had to hold at third base. Bill Henry retired the next two batters to preserve the shutout.

The NL team had a little magic left. Norm Larker started the ninth inning with a walk. Ken Boyer followed with a blast to deep left for a two-run homer. The Nationals led, 6-0. Two more batters reached in the ninth, but no more would score.

Lindy McDaniel came on to pitch the bottom of the ninth for the NL. Although Kaline managed a single, McDaniel retired the other three batters he faced with groundballs. Maris ended the game with a grounder to first. In three at-bats, the 1960 Most Valuable Player had left seven men on base.

The National League team had swept the 1960 All-Star doubleheader, giving them nine wins in the past 13 contests. In this second game, they had scored six runs, all driven in by the long ball; hit by four different stars: Mathews, Mays, Musial, and Boyer. The American Leaguers had been held to eight hits, all singles except Lollar's double.

Combining his totals for the two 1960 All-Star Games, Mays batted .750, getting six hits in eight at-bats. Those hits included the four necessary for a cycle. His OPS was 2.250! He drove in a run and scored twice. Al Lopez, skipper for the American League team, said, "We didn't have a pitching book on Willie Mays."[13]

In his career, Mays played in 24 All-Star Games, including two each year from 1959 to 1962. As of the 2022 season, Mays still held the record for most career singles (15) in All-Star Games. In addition, he clouted two doubles, three triples, and three home runs.

Ted Williams was obviously not happy with the two losses, but he told the press, "There's nothing much wrong with playing two All-Star Games. Any guy who's a ballplayer wants to play ball."[14]

### *Author's Note*

Mays' historic feat is phenomenal, considering that he accomplished hitting for the cycle in the same season's All-Star Games. His sequence for the four hits needed was triple-single-double-home run.[15]

Other players have accomplished a career All-Star Game cycle, including Ernie Banks, Roberto Clemente, Ted Williams, Mike Schmidt, Steve Garvey, Lou Whitaker, George Brett, Prince Fielder and Mike Trout. In the two 1960 games, Banks was 3-for-7, collecting a single, double, and home run, putting him just a triple shy of tying Mays' historic mark.

Just over a half-century after Mays, Trout hit for a natural All-Star cycle[16] in four consecutive All-Star Games. In 2012 he singled against R.A. Dickey in the sixth inning (and then stole second base). In 2013 he doubled to right off Matt Harvey to lead off the game. In 2014 he tripled to center field on a full count off Adam Wainwright in the top of the first, driving in a run; he also doubled to left in the fifth inning. In 2015, again leading off the game, he homered on a line drive off Zack Greinke, to complete the career All-Star Game cycle.

## SOURCES

In addition to the sources mentioned in the Notes, the author consulted Baseball-Reference.com, MLB.com, Retrosheet.org, and SABR.org.

https://www.baseball-reference.com/allstar/1960-allstar-game-1.shtml

https://www.retrosheet.org/boxesetc/1960/B07110ALS1960.htm

https://www.baseball-reference.com/allstar/1960-allstar-game-2.shtml

https://www.retrosheet.org/boxesetc/1960/B07130ALS1960.htm

## NOTES

1 Bill Center, "Leagues Split Two All-Star Games Played in 1959," found online at www.mlb.com/news/leagues-split-two-all-star-games-in-1959-c163719750. Accessed September 2022. Center also wrote, "The result didn't exactly measure up to the level of Midsummer Classics, and the dual All-Star Game experiment ended in 1962." *New York Times* writer Leonard Koppett denounced the two-game idea, writing that the "[p]layers had revealed themselves in a mercenary light." See Leonard Koppett, "All-Star Review: Ho-Hum Affair," *New York Times*, July 25, 1974: 39.

2 John Drebinger, "Mays Stands Out in 6-0 Contest," *New York Times*, July 14, 1960: 30.

3 Warren Spahn had 22 wins for the Milwaukee Braves in 1958, while Pedro Ramos had 19 losses with the Washington Senators in 1959.

4 Arthur Daley, "Sports of the Times," *New York Times*, July 14, 1960: 14.

5 Lou Hatter, "N.L. Wallops Four Home Runs to Defeat A.L. All-Stars, 6 to 0," *Baltimore Sun*, July 14: 22.

6 Daley.

7 Daley.

8 Daley.

9 Louis Effrat, "Pitching Shares in Victory Credit," *New York Times*, July 14, 1960: 30.

10 Drebinger.

11 Daley.

12 Daley. Face was 5-feet-8, 155 pounds.

13 "A.L. Lacked Mays's 'Book,'" *Baltimore Sun*, July 14: 19.

14 Hatter.

15 As of the 2022 All-Star break, the triple-single-double-home run (3-1-2-4) sequence of hits is one of the rarest in regular-season play, occurring in just 10 of the 316 known sequences (3.16 percent). Of the 339 official cycles in major-league history to this date, the sequence of hits is known for only 316 games Almost all of the unknown sequences took place in nineteenth-century games, where play-by-play is not available and newspaper recaps of the games are vague. Only two other sequences (2-3-4-1 and 4-2-3-1) have occurred less frequently than that hit by Mays.

16 A natural cycle occurs when the batter gets the hits (single, double, triple, and home run) in that order.

# GIANTS TOP PHILLIES BEHIND THREE TRIPLES BY WILLIE MAYS

## September 15, 1960: San Francisco Giants 8, Philadelphia Phillies 6 (11 Innings), at Connie Mack Stadium, Philadelphia

BY BOB WEBSTER

THE GIANTS WERE in the middle of a 21-game road trip when they took on the Phillies at Connie Mack Stadium in Philadelphia (formerly Shibe Park) on Thursday, September 15, 1960. The road trip began with a doubleheader against the Dodgers in Los Angeles on September 5. There were four doubleheaders on a road trip that finally ended on Monday, September 26, back in Los Angeles, where it began.

The Phillies took game one of the series the night before, 5-1. The fifth-place Giants were 69-71 going into game two, with Sam Jones on the mound against Jim Owens. The Phillies were 52-88 and in eighth place.

The Giants' Don Blasingame led off the game with a double to left. Jim Davenport grounded out, bringing center fielder Willie Mays to the plate. Mays tripled to right, scoring Blasingame. Felipe Alou walked and Willie McCovey, starting at first base in place of Orlando Cepeda, who was nursing a groin injury,[1] flied out to center field, scoring Mays. With Willie Kirkland batting, Alou stole second. Kirkland walked, and catcher Hobie Landrith singled Alou home while Kirkland stopped at second. Eddie Bressoud's triple drove in Kirkland and Landrith. Sam Jones, the ninth batter of the inning, grounded out to end the inning, but not before the Giants had a 5-0 lead.

Jones gave up a single, a double, and a walk in the bottom of the first but got out of the inning without surrendering a run.

Mays beat out a bunt single with two outs in the second, but Alou grounded out to end the inning.

The Phillies got on the board in the bottom of the third as Tony González singled in Johnny Callison, who led off with a single and took second on a walk to Bobby Malkmus. The Giants got the run back in the top of the fourth. Blasingame singled but was erased when Davenport grounded into a fielder's choice. Mays struck out. Alou singled to center and Davenport stopped at second. McCovey doubled into the gap in right-center, scoring Davenport, but Alou was thrown out trying to score from first.

The score remained 6-1 until the bottom of the sixth. Cal Neeman reached first on an error by shortstop Bressoud to lead off the inning. Jim Woods struck out but Clay Dalrymple, batting for shortstop Rubén Amaro, walked. Joe Koppe ran for Dalrymple. Pitcher Dallas Green singled to load the bases and with only one out, the Phillies had a rally in the making. Callison singled in Neeman. Second baseman Malkmus made his first major-league home run a grand slam.[2] That hit chased the Giants' Jones from the game and Johnny Antonelli came in to pitch. Antonelli struck out Bobby Del Greco and got González to ground out to second to end the inning, but the Phillies had tied the score, 6-6.

Dallas Green, who had replaced Owens on the mound in the top of the fifth, retired the first six batters he faced before Mays singled to lead off the Giants' seventh. He advanced to third on groundouts by Alou and McCovey but was left stranded when Kirkland flied out to right.

Antonelli struck out the side in the bottom of the seventh, and Green retired the side in the top of the eighth. In the bottom half, Koppe drew a walk from Antonelli. Green sacrificed, and with Koppe on second, Ken Walters, pinch-hitting for Callison, walked. But Malkmus struck out and Del Greco hit a ground ball back to Antonelli, who threw to first base to end the inning.

Green, in his fifth inning in relief, retired Blasingame and Cepeda (batting for Davenport) on groundouts to open the Giants' ninth before Mays laced his second triple of the game, to right field. But Green retired Alou on a popup to keep the score tied.

In the bottom of the ninth, Joey Amalfitano replaced third baseman Davenport. Leadoff batter González flied out to Mays in center. Pancho Herrera doubled to center. After Neeman flied out to right, Antonelli intentionally walked Woods, then struck out Koppe to send the game into extra innings.

In the top of the 10th, Green retired McCovey and Kirkland on fly balls to González in center field. Landrith singled and Bressoud walked. Green retired Antonelli on a popup to second, ending the inning. In the bottom of the inning, Malkmus singled but Antonelli kept the Phillies scoreless.

Turk Farrell came in to pitch for the Phillies the top of the 11th inning. Blasingame walked, but Amalfitano struck out attempting to bunt. Mays, batting next, sent a drive to deep center field. The 440-foot drive[3] took a hop before hitting the wall. Blasingame scored easily. It was the third triple of the game for Mays. McCovey drove in Mays with a fly ball to center, making the score 8-6. Kirkland's strikeout ended the half-inning.

After Antonelli walked González to start the bottom of the 11th, reliever Billy Loes replaced him. He got Herrera to ground into a 6-4-3 double play and retired Neeman on a grounder to short, giving the Giants an 8-6, 11-inning victory.

Mays finished the night going 5-for-6, with two runs scored and two RBIs, and raised his batting average from .319 to .325, placing him behind only Norm Larker (.328) and Dick Groat (.325) in the NL batting race. (Roberto Clemente was right behind at .322.)[4]

After both starting pitchers were knocked out of the game early, the relievers for both teams did an excellent job. Antonelli for the Giants pitched 4⅔ scoreless innings, surrendering two hits and striking out six to record the win. Green pitched six innings in relief for the Phillies, giving up no runs on three hits. Loes picked up the save for the Giants, while Farrell took the loss for the Phillies.

The third triple in the game for Mays would have been a home run in most ballparks, but the center-field wall at Connie Mack Stadium was 448 feet from home plate, and the ball stayed in play.[5]

Mays hit one more triple in the 1960 season and finished tied with the Reds' Vada Pinson with 12, one behind league leader Bill Bruton of the Milwaukee Braves. Mays' season high in that category was a league-high 20 in 1957, the Giants' final season in New York. He also led the NL in triples in 1954 and 1955 with 13 apiece.

## SOURCES

In addition to the sources cited in the Notes, the author accessed Retrosheet.org, and Baseball-Reference.com for player and game information.

https://www.baseball-reference.com/boxes/PHI/PHI196009150.shtml

https://www.retrosheet.org/boxesetc/1960/B09150PHI1960.htm

## NOTES

1 Walter Judge, "S.F. Wins, 8-6; 3 Mays Triples Do Job," *San Francisco Examiner*, September 16, 1960: 53.

2 Allen Lewis, "Giants Beat Phils in 11th on Mays Triple; Willie's 5th Hit Defeats Farrell in Relief, 8-6," *Philadelphia Inquirer*, September 16, 1960: 36.

3 George Kiseda, "Mays May Not Want Batting Crown, but His Bat Surely Does," *Philadelphia Daily News*, September 16, 1960: 87.

4 United Press International, "Willie Mays Pushes Giants to 8-6 Win With 3 Triples," *Stockton* (California) *Evening and Sunday Record*, September 16, 1960: 30.

5 Philip J. Lowry, *Green Cathedrals* (Phoenix: SABR, 2019), 234. After 1969 renovations to the ballpark, the distance was reduced to 410 feet.

# THE SAY HEY KID'S FOUR-HOMER GAME

## April 30, 1961: San Francisco Giants 14, Milwaukee Braves 4, at County Stadium, Milwaukee

BY NELSON "CHIP" GREENE

THE 1961 MAJOR-LEAGUE season was barely three weeks old the day 29-year-old Willie Mays produced perhaps the greatest offensive performance of his legendary career. Led by Mays, the San Francisco Giants came to Milwaukee for a three-game series with the hometown Braves. Just a year away from the World Series, the Giants were a team on the rise. Besides Mays they boasted future Hall of Fame batters Orlando Cepeda and Willie McCovey, as well as pitcher Juan Marichal, also destined for enshrinement at Cooperstown. For their part, the Braves featured their own future Hall of Famers, Hank Aaron, Eddie Mathews, and Warren Spahn. In this, the two teams' first series of the season, the stars of both squads were about to put on an awesome display.

The Giants entered the series in first place, one game ahead of the third-place Braves. However, in the first game, on Friday night, April 28, the Braves defeated the Giants behind the seemingly ageless Warren Spahn. Just seven months earlier, on September 16, 1960, the 39-year-old Spahn had tossed his first career no-hitter, blanking the Phillies, 4-0, in Milwaukee. Now, just past his 40th birthday, Spahn threw his second no-hit gem, giving the Braves a 1-0 victory. It was the 290th win of his illustrious career.

The next afternoon, offense ruled the day, and this time the Giants' bats were potent, as the team collected 15 hits in support of their ace, Marichal. As Marichal allowed three runs and eight hits in a complete-game win, the Giants blasted five home runs, four off Braves starter Bob Buhl and one off Don McMahon, and crushed the Braves, 7-3. The next day would be the series tiebreaker – and Mays would take center stage.

On Sunday, April 30, a crowd of 13,114 was on hand to witness the historic performance.[1] Milwaukee's starting pitcher was Lew Burdette. With 146 wins for the Braves, the right-handed Burdette was a mainstay in the rotation, a fierce and talented competitor. Today, however, was not to be his day. The Giants' Chuck Hiller singled to open the game, but was quickly erased on a double play. That brought Mays to the plate. Over the first two games of the series, Mays had gone 0-for-7, leaving him with a .291 batting average for the young season; he'd hit two home runs and driven in six runs. While those numbers might have been acceptable after 15 games for a mortal player, for Mays it constituted a slow start. Indeed, after the game Mays claimed that he'd been in a slump. "I couldn't hit the ball hard before," he said. "But before today's game I had an idea I was going to snap out of it. I was about due to do something."[2]

Indeed he was. Burdette threw a fastball, and Mays drilled it 420 feet to deep center field, where it cleared the fence, staking the Giants to a 1-0 lead.

Pitching for the Giants was veteran right-hander Billy Loes. Loes was the perfect hurler to face the Braves. In 12 previous decisions vs. Milwaukee, he was 11-1; his only defeat had come in 1953. Early on, however, it appeared that Loes might be in store for his second loss to the Braves. In the bottom of the first, with one out and two men on, Hank Aaron drilled a home run to put Milwaukee ahead 3-1. Yet, using a very effective changeup, Loes recorded the next two outs without incident.

Neither team scored in the second inning. To start the third, Burdette faced light-hitting José Pagán, who in his 113 major-league at-bats had amassed just 23 hits (a .204 batting average), none a home run. On any other day, in the absence of Mays' heroics, Pagan would have been the game's star. He hit his first major-league home run in the third and cut the Braves' lead to 3-2. Burdette retired the next two batters, but then hit Jim Davenport with a pitch. That again brought Mays to the plate, and he drove a Burdette sinker 400 feet for his second home run of the game. With the damage done, Burdette retired McCovey on a groundout. The Giants now led, 4-3.

From there, Loes once again proved a Braves killer. Down in order went Milwaukee in the bottom of the third. As the fourth inning began, Burdette had to face another slugger, Orlando Cepeda, to start the inning. In the previous day's Giants slugfest, Cepeda had contributed one of San Francisco's four homers off Bob Buhl. Now he did the same to Burdette, and increased the Giants' lead to 5-3. Perhaps mercifully, Burdette's afternoon was ended.

Right-hander Carl Willey relieved Burdette; yet, little changed for the Giants. Right-handed hitter Felipe Alou was the first man to face the new Braves pitcher. Alou, too, had homered the day before against Buhl. Now, he homered off Willey. It was 6-3, Giants.

Against his second batter, Ed Bailey, Willey coaxed a grounder to first and recorded the inning's first out. To the plate strode Pagán, and he homered again. Although Hiller doubled between groundouts, he was stranded at second base. As the game moved to the bottom of the fourth, the Giants led 7-3.

For the second inning in a row, Loes set down the side in order in the fourth. As the Giants came to bat in the top of the fifth, with Mays leading off, right-hander Moe Drabowsky came on for the Braves. For the first time, Mays failed to hit a home run, instead flying out to center field. Drabowsky walked McCovey, then retired the Giants on a fly ball and a popup.

In machine-like fashion, Loes retired the side again in the fifth, and then the Giants' slugging resumed in the sixth. Drabowsky had been lifted for a pinch-hitter, so left-handed reliever Seth Morehead entered the game for the Braves. Things soon went awry. After striking out Bailey, Morehead allowed a single to Pagán. Loes sacrificed and was safe at first when the Braves couldn't get Pagán at second. Hiller's grounder that forced Loes scored Pagán, who raced home all the way from second. Morehead walked Davenport. For the fourth time, Mays stepped to the plate.

Over the course of his five-year major-league career, Morehead allowed 34 home runs, only one to Mays. Against Morehead's slider, this was the one, and it was monstrous. The left-field power alley in County Stadium was 376 feet from home plate, with newly installed bleachers atop the left-field wall. Along the left-field line was a new picnic area called Braves Reservation.[3] As the ball cleared the wall, its trajectory was high enough that it could have cleared the bleachers and left the ballpark; however, it veered left and landed between the asphalt and grass in the picnic area. The ball was estimated to have traveled 450 feet. The score was now Giants 11, Braves 3.[4]

There would be one more homer for Mays. After Aaron's second homer of the game brought the score to 11-4, the seventh inning was scoreless. Left-hander Ken MacKenzie worked that inning for Milwaukee, then was lifted for a pinch-hitter in the bottom of the inning. As the Giants came to bat in the eighth, Braves right-hander Don McMahon took over. After retiring the leadoff hitter, McMahon allowed a double to Hiller and a triple to Davenport to make it 12-4, and then Mays returned. With Davenport at third, Mays blasted a McMahon slider[5] an estimated 430 feet to left-center field for his fourth home run, driving in the final two of his eight RBIs in the game. That capped the game's scoring; the Giants won convincingly, 14-4. The team hit eight home runs in the game, itself tying a record; the 13 homers they had hit in back-to-back games set a new one.[6] The *Milwaukee Journal* said, "The best thing that could be said about the Braves Sunday is that none of them got hurt."[7]

Mays might have gotten a fifth home run. In the top of the ninth, he knelt in the on-deck circle as Davenport batted with two outs. When Davenport grounded out, the fans booed. After the game Mays said of the attempt that never materialized, "To tell the truth, I don't think I would have hit anything. You see, I started to think about it when it was announced over the public address and I know I'd be pressing, trying to go for another one."[8]

Mays said he'd never hit more than two home runs in a game before.[9] His explanation for the four home runs, however, was as clear as had been the day. "It was the first time this year that I hit the ball real good. It seems that I could see the ball plainly."[10]

He certainly did.[11]

## SOURCES

In addition to the sources cited in the Notes, the author consulted Baseball-Reference.com and Retrosheet.org. Thanks to Dennis Degenhardt for assistance with the *Milwaukee Sentinel*.

https://www.baseball-reference.com/boxes/MLN/MLN196104300.shtml

https://www.retrosheet.org/boxesetc/1961/B04300MLN1961.htm

An earlier version of this article appears in Gregory H. Wolf, ed., *From the Braves to the Brewers: Great Games and Exciting History at Milwaukee's County Stadium* (Phoenix: SABR, 2016).

## NOTES

1 Red Thisted, "Mays Gets 4; Mates 4 More!," *Milwaukee Sentinel*, May 1, 1961: Part 2, 2.

2 Thisted. The *San Francisco Chronicle* quoted Mays as saying before first pitch, "I know people are saying I'm in a slump. But, I'll come out of it. I may go out there today and get myself four singles." "Giants Smash Hit Records, Take Lead in 14-4 Beating of Braves," *San Francisco Chronicle*, May 1, 1961: 43.

3 Philip J. Lowry, *Green Cathedrals: The Ultimate Celebration of Major League and Negro League Ballparks* (New York: Walker & Company, 2006), 130-31.

4 After the game Mays was asked if this had been his longest home run. He replied, "I think I've only hit one as long or longer. That was the one I socked over the eagle on the Anheuser-Busch sign against the Cardinals at Busch Stadium." Thisted.

5 "When asked what pitches he had hit in his four-home-run barrage, Mays rattled off, 'Sinker, sinker, slider, slider.' He hesitated about Don McMahon's fatal pitch on his fourth blast but finally settled on a slider. … The Braves' pitching chart later revealed: "Fast ball (Burdette); sinker (Burdette); slider (Morehead); and slider (McMahon)." Thisted.

6 Bob Stevens, "Mays Equals All-Time Mark," *San Francisco Chronicle*, May 1, 1961: 43. Jose Pagán hit two homers and Orlando Cepeda and Felipe Alou hit one each.

7 Bob Wolf, "Mays Gets Four Home Runs as Giants Maul Braves,14-4," *Milwaukee Journal*, May 1, 1961: 12.

8 Thisted.

9 "I've never had a day like this. The biggest until now came when I got my first major-league hit back in 1951. It was off Warren Spahn and you know what it was? A home run – how

about that?" Lou Chapman, "My Greatest Day – Mays," *Milwaukee Sentinel*, May 1, 1961: Part 2, 2.

10 Thisted.

11 Mays became the 10th major-league player to hit four home runs in a game. In the more than 60 years since Mays' feat, through the 2022 season, nine others have had four-homer games: Mike Schmidt (April 17, 1976), Bob Horner (July 6, 1986), Mark Whiten (September 7, 1993), Mike Cameron (May 2, 2002), Shawn Green (May 23, 2002), Carlos Delgado (September 25, 2005), Josh Hamilton (May 8, 2012), Scooter Gennett (June 6, 2017), and J.D. Martinez (September 4, 2017).

*Roger Maris, Willie Mays, and Mickey Mantle gave fits to big-league pitchers. Courtesy National Baseball Hall of Fame.*

# MAYS HITS THREE HOMERS, INCLUDING THE GAME-WINNER IN THE 10TH

## June 29, 1961: San Francisco Giants 8, Philadelphia Phillies 7, at Connie Mack Stadium, Philadelphia

BY THEO TOBEL

ONE WEEK AFTER a legendary four-homer performance,[1] the Say Hey Kid stood on the steps of Connie Mack Stadium, looking out at a cool, foggy May 6 night. He patiently waited for the rain that poured down onto the field to stop, but after a lengthy delay, the showers would not cease, and the game was rescheduled.

And so at 6:07 P.M. on June 29, the Philadelphia Phillies and the San Francisco Giants lined up once again to take the field. Both teams desperately needed a win: The Giants were four games out of first place, and the cellar-dwelling Phillies sported a measly record of 22 wins and 42 losses.

The night before, the two teams had battled through 14 innings until San Francisco pulled ahead with three runs to make the score 7-4 in the top of the 15th. But in the bottom half, the Phillies tied the game. After 5 hours and 11 minutes and 10 pitchers used between both teams (a significant amount at the time), including Phillies ace Robin Roberts, the game was ruled a no-decision. With few pitchers to choose from, Philadelphia manager Gene Mauch picked Ken Lehman but put two additional pitchers in the starting lineup in an attempt to platoon to the Giants' pitcher, who had not yet been announced. Once the lefty Billy O'Dell was slated to toe the rubber, Mauch replaced his two pitchers in the lineup with two right-handed batters.

The Giants came out swinging, forcing Mauch to pull Lehman after only two batters, both of whom reached base with a single and a walk. Mauch opted for long reliever Dallas Green, who successfully induced a double play from Orlando Cepeda to bring up Willie Mays with one baserunner on and two outs. Mays wasted no time putting the Giants on the board, driving a two-run shot to the center-field bleachers.

But the Phillies would not go down easy. After a leadoff single by center fielder Bobby Del Greco, O'Dell was pulled for Sam Jones. Mauch, again playing the platoon, substituted in two left-handed batters – Tony González and Clay Dalrymple – who added two more singles. Philly scored three runs and went ahead, 4-2.

In the top of the third, Mays decided to carry the Giants on his back by hitting another two-run shot to center field, tying the score, 4-4.

After being put down in order in the bottom of the third, the Phillies rallied in the fourth with a walk, a hit batsman, and two singles to go ahead again by two runs, 6-4.

The Giants fell quiet for two innings until the sixth, when Mays hit a single to left field but was caught stealing by catcher Dalrymple. Even so, consecutive singles by Willie McCovey, Ed Bailey, and Jim Davenport reduced the Phillies' lead to one run at 6-5. In the next inning, the Giants caught a huge break when Philadelphia second baseman Tony Taylor made an error on a ball off the bat of Jim Marshall and Chuck Hiller doubled. With Hiller at second and Marshall at third, Harvey Kuenn hit a sacrifice fly and Cepeda doubled, leading to both an unearned and earned run, putting the Giants in the lead by one, 7-6.

*Willie Mays became just the fourth major leaguer to hit at least three home runs twice in one season. Courtesy National Baseball Hall of Fame.*

After pitching two one-two-three innings and tasked with facing the top of the lineup in the bottom of the seventh, Jones was pulled by Alvin Dark in favor of veteran pitcher Billy Loes. And again, the Phillies battled back – a single, a sacrifice, a hit batsman, and a single by outfielder Don Demeter knotted the score, 7-7.

The next two innings, both teams' bats went quiet ... that is, until Mays stepped up to the plate in the 10th.

It was as if the score had been reset and a new game had started: Each team's win probability was 50 percent. With the score at 7-7 – the same as the final score the night before – Willie Mays belted his third home run of the game, off Frank Sullivan, to catapult the Giants' win probability to 84 percent and put them in the lead for good.[2]

When Mays completed his trip around the bases and touched home plate, he finished his night with four hits, three of which were home runs, and with five of the team's eight RBIs.

Yet on this late afternoon game, another star for San Francisco continued to creep out of the shadows of Mays' success: Juan Marichal, who would become the winningest pitcher in the major leagues during the 1960s. At only 23 years old, this game proved to be the first relief appearance in Marichal's young career. Tasked with protecting the lead given by Mays, Marichal closed out the game and earned the win with two no-hit innings.

In the second game of the doubleheader, the Giants beat the Phillies 4-1. After driving in two runs and going 2-for-3, the ever-understated Mays said to reporters, "I just like to go out and play."[3] The sweep of the Phillies raised Mays' batting average 13 points, to .331.

Across the country, newspapers lauded the performance: The Associated Press exclaimed that "Willie Mays is back to beltin' the ball again."[4] The *Radford* (Virginia) *News Journal* headlined, "Fabulous Willie Mays Riding High in Hit Department Again."[5] The historic performance by Mays was not only a sign that he was one of the pastime's best ever but also served as an indication that the San Francisco slugger's prime was far from over – he went on to total more than 10 wins above replacement (WAR) in each of the next four seasons (1962-1965), finishing with his second MVP award in 1965.

In retrospect, the go-ahead home run for Mays came as no surprise, for the star center fielder was the king of extra-inning homers. According to Ray Gonzalez's article in the 1976 *Baseball Research Journal*, Mays is the all-time leader in both extra-inning home runs (22, with the runner-up, Babe Ruth, second with 16) and in home runs in the 10th inning, with 11.[6]

With the sweep, the Giants moved into second place over the Los Angeles Dodgers. However, the team hit a slump in July and failed to recover in August and September, finishing in third place in the NL pennant race with a record of 85-69-1. The Phillies crumbled in July and August – they sported a .242 winning percentage in those two months – posting a dismal 47-107 record and a last-place finish in the National League.

With this three-homer game following a four-homer game on April 30, 1961, Willie Mays became the fourth major leaguer to belt three (or more) home runs twice in the same season, joining Johnny Mize, Ralph Kiner, and Ted Williams.

## SOURCES

In addition to the sources cited in the Notes, the author consulted Baseball Reference, Retrosheet, and Baseball Almanac for general game information and play-by-play data.

https://www.baseball-reference.com/boxes/PHI/PHI196106291.shtml

https://www.retrosheet.org/boxesetc/1961/06291961.htm

https://www.baseball-almanac.com/box-scores/boxscore.php?boxid=196106291PHI

## NOTES

1 Nelson Greene, "April 30, 1961: The Say Hey Kid's Four-Homer Game." Society for American Baseball Research, https://sabr.org/gamesproj/game/april-30-1961-the-say-hey-kids-four-homer-game/.

2 For win probability, see "San Francisco Giants vs Philadelphia Phillies Box Score: June 29, 1961." https://www.baseball-reference.com/boxes/PHI/PHI196106291.shtml.

3 "Willie Mays Shrugs Off Praise After Hitting, Fielding Display," *Hanover* (Pennsylvania) *Evening Sun*, June 30, 1961: 10.

4 Associated Press, "Willie Mays Hits Three Homers as Giants Beat Phils Twice," *Terre Haute* (Indiana) *Tribune*, June 30, 1961: 14.

5 United Press International, "Fabulous Willie Mays Riding High in Hit Department Again," *Radford* (Virginia) *News Journal*, June 30, 1961: 2.

6 Ray Gonzalez, "Extra Inning Home Runs," *Baseball Research Journal*, 1976 (Society for American Baseball Research). https://sabr.org/journal/article/extra-inning-home-runs/.

# "HEY YOU GUYS, WHERE YOU BEEN?"[1]

## June 1, 1962: San Francisco Giants 9, New York Mets 6, at the Polo Grounds, New York

BY ALAN COHEN

**ON AUGUST 18,** 1957, came an anticipated yet numbing announcement. After 75 years in New York at various incarnations of the Polo Grounds, the Giants were moving to San Francisco.

New York was without National League baseball for four long seasons. Four seasons of listening to radio re-creations of day games by Les Keiter on WINS. As for the night games, they were "just getting underway" at bedtime for the fans back in New York.

National League baseball returned to the Polo Grounds on April 13, 1962, when the Mets, after opening their inaugural season on the road, took up residence in the Polo Grounds. Attendance was only 12,447. Things really wouldn't be right until the Dodgers and Giants came back, if only to visit. The Dodgers arrived first, playing before 55,704 fans on Memorial Day.

On the evening of June 1, Willie Came Home. There were 43,742 fans, many of whom remembered the "Miracle of Coogan's Bluff" in Willie's first year and "The Catch" in center field in the 1954 World Series. Willie Mays returned to New York wearing a uniform that seemed to have just too many letters, and announcer Russ Hodges was in a booth reserved for visiting announcers.

The landscape had changed some since 1957. The ballpark had been given a much-needed coat of paint and the elevated subway station was now below ground. The crowd first saw Willie when he joined his teammates for infield practice. Unbeknownst to his New York admirers, it was not uncommon for Mays to partake in infield drills. Hank Sauer, who had homered at the Polo Grounds on September 8, 1957, against the Dodgers for the last New York Giants homer at the ballpark, was now a coach with San Francisco. He pitched batting practice before the game. Also throwing a bit in batting practice was Johnny Antonelli, ace of the 1957 mound staff, who had retired after the 1961 season. Antonelli, in the last Giants home game at the Polo Grounds, had yielded a homer to Frank Thomas, who was now hitting homers for the Mets.

At 7:11 P.M., Number 24 came up to take his batting-practice swings. The crowd showered him with applause as he sent three balls into and beyond the stands, one going over the roof in left field.

Before the game manager Al Dark and his players were introduced and stood along the third-base line.

When the game began, Roger Craig (2-6), a former Dodger, was on the mound for the Mets. Billy Pierce (7-0) started for the Giants. Pierce, who had been in the American League through 1961, had not played at the Polo Grounds as a big leaguer. However, he appeared at the ballpark on August 7, 1944, in the Esquire's All-American Boys' Baseball Game. In that game, he started and pitched six shutout innings as his East All-Stars defeated the West All-Stars, 6-0.

In the top of the first inning, Willie McCovey came to bat with one out and lashed a ball off the roof in right field, just inside the foul pole, for his sixth homer of the season. The Giants added to their lead in the third inning. Chuck Hiller singled with one out and McCovey's second blast off Craig, this time just eluding the foul pole in left and landing on the roof, made the score 3-0.

In the top of the fifth, the crowd got what they came to see. After Craig finally got McCovey out, Mays came to the plate and lined a homer into the right-field stands, his 17th of the season, best in the National League. After the game a sportswriter asked him about his most memorable hit at the Polo Grounds. Mays responded, "The first one."[2] In 1951, after going hitless in his first 12 at-bats, Willie had homered off Milwaukee's Warren Spahn for his first big-league hit, and it was that homer he was referring to. However, his first trip to the Polo Grounds had been on May 29, 1949, when the 18-year-old was with the Birmingham Black Barons. He had homered then, as well.

Craig left the game for a pinch-hitter in the bottom of the fifth inning. The pinch-hitter was Richie Ashburn, who had first appeared at the Polo Grounds as a catcher in the 1944 Esquire's Game, making the last out of that contest. Willard Hunter, in his first game with the Mets, came on to pitch in the sixth inning.

New York, after winning nine of 12 games from May 6 through May 20 and rising as high as eighth place, had slipped on the proverbial banana peel, and lost 11 straight games. The Mets' record coming into the game was 12-30. Despite that record, they had not been shut out all season. Manager Casey Stengel loaded his lineup exclusively with right-handed batters against the Giants lefty, but Pierce was in control, and it looked as though he would keep the Mets from scoring on this night.

But the budding stars of the Mets were as adept at finding ways to score as they were at finding ways to lose. Rod Kanehl hit his first career homer, a solo shot, to put the Mets on the board in the sixth inning. They would not be shut out this night.

The Giants broke things open and built a seemingly unsurmountable lead in the seventh inning. In a righty-lefty switch, Dark sent up Harvey Kuenn to pinch-hit for McCovey. Kuenn opened the inning with a single and Mays singled for his second hit of the game. After Orlando Cepeda struck out, Felipe Alou scored Kuenn with a single on which Mays raced from first to third. Predictably, Willie's hat went flying as he passed second base. After a walk to Tom Haller, Jim Davenport launched a grand

*Willie Mays remained a beloved figure in New York even after moving 3,000 miles away to San Francisco. SABR/The Rucker Archive.*

slam that made the score 9-1. Hunter got out of the inning without further damage and pitched scoreless ball in the eighth inning.

The Mets clawed their way back into the game with an eighth-inning rally. After Pierce struck out pinch-hitter Cliff Cook, Elio Chacon, who the prior weekend in San Francisco had a shoving contest with Mays, reached on a throwing error by Giants shortstop Jose Pagan. Kanehl ripped a single up the middle for his second straight hit, and Charlie Neal sent a double into the bullpen in distant left-center field. A two-run single through the left side by Thomas cut the lead to 9-4, and Giants manager Dark went to the mound to change pitchers.

The fans remembered Dark. He had joined the Giants in 1950 and keyed their 1951 Miracle of Coogan's Bluff pennant and 1954 World Series championship before being traded to St. Louis during the 1956 season. They cheered him when he brought out the lineup cards before the game, but when he came out to change pitchers, spectators gave him a chorus of boos. The rallying Mets had won over much of the crowd. The "New Breed" of Mets fans, initially outnumbered by the old Mays and Giants fans, had gained more than a few converts.

Bobby Bolin came in for the Giants with a runner on base and yielded a first-pitch two-run homer to Felix Mantilla that capped the Mets' scoring. Bolin navigated his way through the balance of the inning without further damage. Stengel sent up lefty-hitting Ed Bouchee to pinch-hit for catcher Harry Chiti, and Bolin struck him out. After walking Joe Christopher, Bolin got Marv Throneberry, pinch-hitting for Jim Hickman, on a popup. When Bolin began the ninth inning with two pitches to Sammy Taylor that were far out of the strike zone, Dark brought in ace reliever Stu Miller, who had pitched two innings at the Polo Grounds in the finale on September 29, 1957.

Miller took care of business, although the Mets mounted a threat. A walk to Taylor and a two-out single by Neal put runners at first and second for Thomas, who represented the tying run. His hard grounder was corralled by third baseman Davenport, whose throw to second base forced Neal and brought the game to a close in 3:01.

Over the weekend, the Giants and Mets played before 118,845 fans. It was the best-attended series at the Polo Grounds during the Mets' first season.

The Giants, with their win, stayed in a first-place tie with Los Angeles, and the teams were still tied at season's end. After defeating the Dodgers in a best-of-three playoff, the Giants were in the World Series against the New York Yankees. Mays came back to Yankee Stadium for his first meaningful game at that venue (the Giants had played an exhibition there in 1961) since the 1951 World Series.

For the Mets, the loss put their record at 12-31. They finished their first season at 40-120.

## SOURCES

In addition to Baseball-Reference.com and the sources cited in the Notes, the author used the following:

Jupiter, Harry. "Giants 'Capture' N.Y.: 1 for Mays and 2 for McCovey," *San Francisco Examiner*, June 2, 1962: 37-38.

Richman, Arthur (*New York Daily Mirror*). "Mays Admits – 'Goose-Bumps' All Over," reprinted in *San Francisco Examiner*, June 2, 1962: 37.

Sheehan, Joseph M. "43,742 See Giants Turn Back Mets 9-6, Despite New York's 5 Runs in 8th," *New York Times*, June 2, 1962: 12.

Teague, Robert L. "Q: Who's Who Here? A: No. 24 – Polo Grounds Fans Cheer Mays Even for Doing Nothing," *New York Times*, June 2, 1962: 12.

## NOTES

1 Harry Jupiter, "Hey You Guys, Where You Been: Even Antonelli Welcomes S.F.," *San Francisco Examiner*, June 2, 1962: 38.

2 Norman Miller (United Press International), "Like I Never Left Home," *San Francisco Examiner*, June 2, 1962: 38.

# MAYS' 8TH-INNING HR FORCES 3-GAME PLAYOFF FOR NL PENNANT

## September 30, 1962: San Francisco Giants 2, Houston Colt .45s 1, at Candlestick Park, San Francisco

BY PAUL HOFMANN

THE LOS ANGELES Dodgers held a four-game lead over the San Francisco Giants with eight games left in the 1962 regular season and were cruising to a National League pennant. However, by the end of the next-to-last day of the season, Los Angeles had lost two to Houston and two to St. Louis and the Giants had narrowed the lead to a single game. Yet, needing only a win, the Dodgers still controlled their own destiny.

Houston manager Harry Craft, whose expansion club was finishing its first season, reflected on his team's recently completed three-game series with the Dodgers in which the Colt .45s won two of three games. "Golly, they were tight," said Craft, "tight and tired."[1]

After their series with the Dodgers, Houston went to San Francisco for a season-ending series with the Giants. The teams split a Saturday afternoon doubleheader. San Francisco won the opener, 11-5, and Houston came back to win the nightcap, 4-2. The Giants needed a win to have any hope of extending their season.

Houston started the hard-throwing veteran right-hander Turk Farrell (10-19, 3.04 ERA). Before the game a confident Farrell promised to end the Giants' season and told reporters, "I don't intend to lose."[2] The Giants started 19-game winner Billy O'Dell. The left-handed O'Dell was attempting for the second time to win his 20th game of the season.

The game-time temperature at Candlestick Park was 70 degrees, the wind blowing out of the northeast at just 5 MPH, and the skies were fair when O'Dell delivered the game's first pitch to Houston center fielder Carl Warwick.

The game remained scoreless until the bottom of the fourth, as both pitchers navigated their way through the opposing team's lineup. O'Dell gave up two singles and issued two walks over the first four innings. Farrell worked around two doubles, a single, and a walk in his first three innings of work. Farrell retired Willie McCovey on a popout to third to start the bottom of the fourth. Giants catcher Ed Bailey then hit a fastball over the right-field fence fair, just after hitting one foul. "He threw me the same pitch again," said Bailey after the game. "Needless to say, I was grateful."[3] It was the five-time All-Star's 17th home run of the season.[4]

Houston mounted a quick threat in the fifth. J C Hartman singled to lead off the inning and stole second. However, he was stranded there when O'Dell retired the next three Houston batters. Farrell put the Giants down in order in the bottom of the inning.

Houston tied the score in the top of the sixth. Román Mejías opened with a single to left. He remained at first when first baseman Norm Larker popped out to shortstop. Mejias took second when Bob Aspromonte lined a single to left, his second hit of the game. Left fielder Jim Pendleton followed with a single to center to drive in Mejias.

The Giants threatened in the bottom of the seventh. Chuck Hiller and José Pagan hit back-to-back one-out singles. With runners at first and third, rookie Tom Haller, batting for O'Dell, flied out to right and Pagan advanced to second. The Giants loaded the bases when Harvey Kuenn was hit by a pitch. Farrell escaped unscored upon when Matty Alou popped out to second baseman Johnny Temple and ended the inning.

Right-handed junkballer Stu Miller came on in relief in the top of the eighth. Miller had pitched in both ends of a doubleheader the day before, working six scoreless innings as the teams split the first two games of the series.[5] Miller picked up where he left off and retired Larker, Aspromonte, and Panamanian Dave Roberts, who was pinch-hitting for Pendleton.

Willie Mays stepped to the plate to lead off the bottom of the eighth. The Giants center fielder, who had drawn a first-inning walk off Farrell and was 0-for-2 for the afternoon, "had played himself into nervous exhaustion" over the season's final two weeks as the Giants desperately chased the Dodgers.[6]

Farrell, working very carefully, sprinkled in some off-speed pitches in an attempt to keep the Giants star off-balance. Mays "took an easy swing at the curve ball" but was late on the pitch and sent it far down the right-field line, "foul by perhaps 30 feet." Then came Farrell's signature fastball, "down the pipe, perhaps a little higher than Farrell wanted it." Mays' 400-foot blast cleared the wire fence in left field and "hit the bleacher wall some 50 feet farther back" to give the Giants a 2-1 lead. The home run was Mays' 47th of the season, giving him one less than American League leader Harmon Killebrew.[7] Farrell retired the next three Giants batters, and the game headed to the top of the ninth.

Miller, who had an up-and-down year while sharing late-inning duties with the veteran right-hander Don Larsen and young side-armer Bobby Bolin, came through when it counted most.[8] Miller retired Houston catcher Hal Smith on a fly ball to left. Merritt Ranew, who batted for Hartman, lofted a popup that Bailey handled in foul territory. With the Colt .45s down to their final out, Craft sent in veteran Billy Goodman to pinch-hit for Farrell. Miller closed the game by striking out Goodman.[9]

Miller earned the victory and improved to 5-8, lowering his ERA to 3.88. Farrell took the loss, his 20th during Houston's inaugural campaign. He became just the fifth pitcher to be selected to an All-Star team in the same season in which he went on to lose 20 games.[10] Three others have subsequently joined this small group of hurlers.[11] The time of the game was 2 hours and 28 minutes.

After the victory, the Giants retreated to the clubhouse to listen to the Cardinals-Dodgers game on the radio. Mild pandemonium broke loose after the final out of the Cardinals' 1-0 victory over the Dodgers, "and the happiest of all were Mays and manager Alvin Dark."[12]

With the Giants' victory and Dodgers' loss, the two teams finished with identical records of 101-61 and headed to a best-of-three playoff that would determine the NL pennant winner.

The Giants won the first game 8-0 as Billy Pierce went the distance and the Giants got to Sandy Koufax early. Mays hit two home runs, off Koufax in the first inning and Larry Sherry in the sixth.

The Dodgers took the second game, 8-7, when Ron Fairly lined a walk-off sacrifice fly to center that scored Maury Wills.

The Giants captured the National League pennant with a 6-4 victory in the third game. However, in one of the closest votes ever, Wills edged out Mays for the National League Most Valuable Player Award.[13]

## SOURCES

In addition to the sources cited in the Notes, the author also relied on Baseball-reference.com and Retrosheet.org.

## NOTES

1 "A Giant Shot That Forced a Playoff," *Sports Illustrated*, October 10, 1962. Retrieved from www.vault.si.com/vault/1962/10/08/a-giant-shot-that-forced-a-playoff.

2 "A Giant Shot That Forced a Playoff."

3 "A Giant Shot That Forced a Playoff."

4 Bailey was an All-Star again in 1963.

5 Warren Corbett, "Stu Miller," SABR BioProject, https://sabr.org/bioproj/person/stu-miller/.

6 Bill Becker, "Wallop by Mays Downs Colts, 2-1; 400-foot homer in eighth puts Giants in playoff – Miller Pitching Star," *New York Times*, October 1, 1962: 42.

7 Mays hit two more home runs in the three-game playoff against the Dodgers to finish the "regular" season with 49 home runs.

8 Corbett.

9 This was the final at-bat of Goodman's career. He played in 1,623 games in his major-league career, collecting 1,691 hits and a lifetime batting average of precisely .300.

10 David Skelton, "Turk Farrell," SABR BioProject, https://sabr.org/bioproj/person/turk-farrell/.

11 As noted by David Skelton, besides Farrell, those pitchers are Hugh Mulcahy, 1940 Philadelphia Phillies; Edgar Smith, 1942 Chicago White Sox; Ken Raffensberger, 1944 Phillies; Bob Rush, 1950 Chicago Cubs; Sam Jones, 1955 Cubs; Mel Stottlemyre, 1966 New York Yankees; and Steve Rogers, 1974 Montreal Expos.

12 Bill Becker.

13 Despite Mays' 10.5 WAR compared with Wills' 6.0 WAR, Wills outpolled Mays 209 votes to 202.

# MAYS AND PIERCE LEAD GIANTS TO WIN IN GAME ONE OF TIEBREAKER SERIES

## October 1, 1962: San Francisco Giants 8, Los Angeles Dodgers 0 (Game One, National League tiebreaker), at Candlestick Park, San Francisco

BY BRIAN M. FRANK

THE SAN FRANCISCO Giants made a late-season charge to catch the slumping Los Angeles Dodgers in the 1962 National League pennant race. Leading the Giants by four games with only seven games left to play, the Dodgers lost six of seven games and didn't score a run in their final 21 innings. San Francisco won five of its final seven games, including the one on the final day of the schedule, when Willie Mays hit a solo home run in the bottom of the eighth inning to help defeat the Houston Colt .45s, 2-1. The Giants' dramatic victory coupled with the Dodgers' 1-0 loss to the St. Louis Cardinals brought the two rivals into a first-place tie and forced a best-of-three tiebreaker series to decide the NL pennant.

It was the first time the two teams had squared off in a tiebreaker game since 1951, when Bobby Thomson's famed "Shot Heard 'Round the World" sent the Giants to the World Series. That was, of course, before both clubs relocated from New York City to the West Coast.

A pair of southpaws took the mound in the first game of the tiebreaker series. The Giants sent 35-year-old veteran Billy Pierce to the mound to face 26-year-old Dodgers ace Sandy Koufax. Pierce was 15-6 with a 3.72 ERA – but notably went 11-0 with a 3.08 ERA in 11 starts at Candlestick Park. Koufax came into the series 14-6 with a 2.41 ERA. However, despite his impressive numbers, he was in the process of battling back from an injury to his pitching hand that put him out of action from July 17 until September 21. Since returning from the disabled list, he'd uncharacteristically struggled, allowing seven earned runs in just 7⅔ innings pitched.

There was a bit of controversy before the first pitch when Giants manager Alvin Dark and umpire Jocko Conlan got into a heated discussion over whether the Giants had sanded and watered down the Candlestick Park infield in order to slow down the speedy Dodgers baserunners. The *Oakland Tribune* reported that "for a time it looked like the two men might come to blows."[1] As a result, the grounds crew, on Conlan's orders, worked on the field for more than 20 minutes, "rolling down the soft spots around home plate and near the bases with small bulldozers."[2]

After Pierce set down the Dodgers in order in the top of the first, Koufax retired the first two batters he faced before Felipe Alou "hit a scorcher down the left-field line" for a double to bring Mays to the plate.[3] The Giants' star hit a 2-and-1 pitch over the fence in left-center field to give San Francisco a 2-0 lead. It was Mays' 48th home run of the season and his second homer in two at-bats, after his shot to help beat Houston the day before.

"I hit a fastball off Koufax," Mays said, "but I've seen Sandy throw a lot harder."[4]

Jim Davenport led off the Giants' second inning by hitting a ball that "just barely cleared the left-field fence."[5] The next batter, Ed Bailey, singled to right and Dodgers manager Walter Alston sent coach Leo Durocher to the mound to take Koufax out after he'd faced just seven batters.

*Willie Mays' strong play helped the Giants catch the Dodgers in the exciting 1962 NL pennant race. Courtesy National Baseball Hall of Fame.*

"I have an idea of what I want to do out there, but I can't seem to do it," Koufax told sportswriters. "I try to throw hard, but the ball doesn't come out as hard as it used to, and my control is way off. Right now I'm in about the same stage as I would be in the third week of spring training."[6]

Ed Roebuck came in from the Dodgers bullpen to try to stop the bleeding. He did a stellar job, allowing only one hit over four shutout innings before being removed for a pinch-hitter in the sixth inning.

Larry Sherry came in to work the bottom of the sixth for the Dodgers. He retired Alou on a popup before Mays blasted his second home run of the game – this one into the right-center-field bleachers. It was Mays' 49th home run of the season, putting him one ahead of Minnesota Twins slugger Harmon Killebrew for the major-league lead. (Statistics from the tiebreaker series counted as regular-season statistics.)

"I passed Killebrew's 48 homers and lead both leagues?" a seemingly surprised Mays said after the game. "I don't worry about what's going on in the other league. Not 'til Thursday, anyway."[7]

"The crowd hadn't resettled itself" when the next batter, Orlando Cepeda, made it back-to-back home runs by driving a high fly ball over the left-field fence.[8] It was the slugger's 35th home run of the season and gave the Giants a 5-0 lead.

Meanwhile, Pierce was having little trouble with the Dodgers' struggling lineup and seemed to get stronger as the game went on.

"I never get tired," Pierce said. "After Willie hit that first one, I got stronger. By the time I had five runs, I was like a tiger."[9]

The Giants rallied for three insurance runs in the eighth inning. Phil Ortega walked Mays to start the frame. After Cepeda flied out, Mays stole second. (The *Oakland Tribune's* George Ross commented that Mays stole "just to show Maury Wills and Walt Alston that the track isn't so slow after all."[10]) Davenport drew a walk, and after Ortega hurled three balls to Ed Bailey, Ron Perranoski was summoned from the Dodgers bullpen. Perranoski threw ball four to complete the walk and load the bases. José Pagán finished the scoring for the day by hitting "a sharp grounder into right-center."[11] Pagán raced around first as Frank Howard chased down the ball and fired to Wills covering second. The throw hit Wills in the face, breaking his sunglasses and leaving him with a bruised nose. Pagán was awarded a double on the play, but Howard was charged with an error on the throw, allowing Bailey to come home and make the score 8-0.

Pierce completed the shutout by retiring the Dodgers in order in the ninth inning, fanning Howard for the final out. The veteran southpaw ended up allowing just three hits and a walk, while striking out six, to improve his record at Candlestick Park to 12-0.

"My control on the corners was good," Pierce said. "I was getting it in and out on the batters real well, and my fastball was working good."[12]

Giants catcher Bailey gave a glowing assessment of his hurler's performance.

"I've been in the major leagues nine years," Bailey said, "and I've never caught a better pitched game. I've caught two-hitters and one-hitters, but I never before saw anybody get as much out of his stuff as Pierce. The way he was moving the ball in and out, hitting spots and keeping the batters off balance was really something."[13]

A veteran of 16 seasons, who'd pitched over 3,000 innings, won 205 games, made seven All-Star games, and pitched in the 1959 World Series with the White Sox, Pierce ranked his performance against the Giants high on his list of impressive achievements.

"But all in all," Pierce said, "this had to be my most satisfying win. It's got to be. It meant so much to me, the ballclub, and was so important in general."[14]

Pierce's performance helped hand the Dodgers their fifth consecutive loss and extended their scoreless streak to an astounding 30 innings.

San Francisco's offense was led by Mays. After his home run the previous day helped force the playoff series, the Giants slugger went 3-for-3 with two home runs, a single, walk, three RBIs, three runs scored, and a stolen base.

The amazing performances by Pierce and Mays brought the Giants to within one victory of securing their first pennant since moving to San Francisco and earning the right to face the New York Yankees in the World Series. However, Mays wasn't ready to count out the slumping Dodgers. When asked if he thought the Dodgers looked bad, the Giants superstar responded: "Any club looks bad when it's not hittin'. But I'm not countin' my Series cut yet. We could lose the next two easy."[15]

As for his own play, Mays ranked it as one of his best games ever. "I've had some big days, like when I hit those four homers in one game at Milwaukee last year," he said, "but this game today meant a lot more."[16]

Dark agreed with his star player's assessment.

"He's the greatest all-around player I've ever seen," Dark said. "Was this his greatest day? I can't compare. He has great days so often. But over 12 years, how can you pick out a best? This one certainly meant more than many others."[17]

## SOURCES

In addition to the sources cited in the Notes, the author consulted Baseball-Reference.org and Retrosheet.org.

https://www.baseball-reference.com/boxes/NYA/NYA195310050.shtml

https://www.retrosheet.org/boxesetc/1953/B10050NYA1953.htm

## NOTES

1 "Ump, Dark Battle over Sandy Field," *Oakland Tribune*, October 2, 1962: 36.

2 "Ump, Dark Battle Over Sandy Field."

3 Paul Zimmerman, "Pierce Flips 3-Hitter, as Willie Hits Two; Koufax Knocked Out," *Los Angeles Times*, October 2, 1962: Part 3, 1.

4 Leo Peterson (Associated Press), "Mays, Pierce Lead SF to 8-0 Win in Opener," *Fresno Bee*, October 2, 1962: 22-A.

5 Zimmerman.

6 "We're Beat if We Don't Go on a Two Game Winning Streak," *Los Angeles Times*, October 2, 1962: Part 3, 1.

7 George Ross, "Giants Banking on Mays Red-Hot Bat," *Oakland Tribune*, October 2, 1962: 38.

8 Harry Jupiter, "Dodgers Blasted, 8-0; Mays, Pierce Brilliant," *San Francisco Examiner*, October 2, 1962: 56.

9 Curley Grieve, "If I'm Going to Smile, Says Billy, It's Today," *San Francisco Examiner*, October 2, 1962: 56.

10 Ross, "Giants Banking on Mays Red-Hot Bat."

11 Zimmerman: Part 3, 3.

12 Ross.

13 Emmons Byrne, "Giants Win on Homers," *Oakland Tribune*, October 2, 1962: 38.

14 Grieve.

15 Frank Finch, "Mays Tired but Keeps Wearing Out Pitchers," *Los Angeles Times*, October 2, 1962: Part 3, 1. The Giants lost the next day at Los Angeles, 8-7, before winning the series' decisive game at Dodger Stadium, 6-4, to advance to the World Series, where they fell to the Yankees in seven games.

16 Finch.

17 Curley Grieve, "Fun Day for Plain Tired Willie Mays," *San Francisco Examiner*, October 2, 1962: 54.

# THE GIANTS WIN THE PENNANT, PART TWO!

## October 3, 1962: San Francisco Giants 6, Los Angeles Dodgers 4 (Game Three, National League tiebreaker), at Dodger Stadium, Los Angeles

BY TIM OTTO

ON SEPTEMBER 22, 1962, the second-place San Francisco Giants trailed the Los Angeles Dodgers by four games, with seven contests remaining in the regular-season schedule.

One week later the Giants had closed the deficit to one game. In the final game on September 30, Willie Mays' eighth-inning home run gave San Francisco a 2-1 victory at home against Houston, while Los Angeles was losing at home to St. Louis, 1-0. Gene Oliver's eighth-inning homer sent the Dodgers to their fourth straight defeat and sixth loss in their last seven games. Second in the league to San Francisco in runs scored, they were in the midst of a batting slump and hadn't scored in 21 innings.[1]

A three-game playoff would decide the winner of the National League pennant.[2] Dodgers manager Walter Alston selected Sandy Koufax as his starting pitcher for the first playoff game, at Candlestick Park on October 1. Koufax, sidelined in mid-July because of numbness in his left index finger, had been ineffective since returning in mid-September. Mays hit a two-run homer in the first inning,[3] and San Francisco went on to win, 8-0.

The teams moved to Dodger Stadium the next day. The score was 5-0 in San Francisco's favor when Los Angeles finally broke its scoring drought with seven runs in the sixth inning. The Giants tied the game in the eighth, but the Dodgers won, 8-7, when Maury Wills scored the winning run in the ninth on a sacrifice by Ron Fairly.

For the decisive third game, Dodgers coach Leo Durocher, who had managed the 1951 Giants to their dramatic playoff victory over the Dodgers when both teams were in New York, brought the same T-shirt he wore 11 years earlier when Bobby Thomson hit his pennant-winning home run. Current Giants manager Alvin Dark, Durocher's starting shortstop in 1951, was asked if he had brought anything from that game. He replied, "Yeah, Willie Mays."[4]

Johnny Podres, pitching on two days' rest for the first time in his career,[5] held the Giants scoreless in the first two innings, allowing only a single by leadoff hitter Harvey Kuenn. Wills singled to start the bottom of the first, but he was the only baserunner allowed by San Francisco starter Juan Marichal in the initial two frames.

Jose Pagan singled to open the top half of the third. Podres fielded Marichal's bunt and threw past second base into center; Pagan took third on the error. Pagan scored on Kuenn's single to left, with Marichal holding at second.

Chuck Hiller missed a bunt attempt. Marichal was caught off second on the play, but John Roseboro's throw sailed into center for another error, putting Marichal at third.

Hiller flied out to left. Marichal bluffed for home, and Duke Snider's throw was cut off by third baseman Tommy Davis, who threw to Jim Gilliam at second, catching Kuenn in a rundown. Kuenn scrambled back toward first; Gilliam's throw hit him in the back. Kuenn was safe at first, and Marichal scored on Los Angeles's third error of the inning for a 2-0 lead.

In the Dodgers' half of the third, Wills singled with two outs and stole second. He was stranded there after Gilliam's fly out. Consecutive two-out singles in the fourth put Giants runners on first and second, but Kuenn fouled out to the catcher, ending the threat.

Snider doubled to start the Dodgers fourth and advanced to third on a single by Tommy Davis. One out later, Frank Howard grounded to third. Davis slid hard into second base, breaking up a potential double play and allowing Snider to score. The Giants' lead was down to 2-1.

In the sixth, the Giants loaded the bases with no outs on Orlando Cepeda's line-drive single to right, Ed Bailey's smash off Wills's glove, and Jim Davenport's bunt single. Ed Roebuck, making his sixth appearance in the Dodgers' last seven games, relieved Podres. Pagan grounded to Wills, who threw home for the force out. Marichal hit into a groundball double play; the Dodgers escaped, still training by only a run.

Roebuck's clutch relief looked like a turning point after Snider led off the Dodgers' half of the sixth with a single. Tommy Davis hit a 3-and-1 pitch deep into the left-center-field seats, putting the Dodgers in front, 3-2.[6]

The Giants failed to score in the seventh, leaving runners stranded at first and second, and the Dodgers added a run in the bottom of the inning. With one out, Wills hit his fourth straight single and stole second on Marichal's first pitch to Gilliam, who then flied out to left. Wills stole third on the first pitch to the next batter, Larry Burright, and came home when Bailey's errant throw bounced past Davenport into left field.[7] Los Angeles now led 4-2.

Roebuck kept the Giants scoreless in the eighth. In the Dodgers half of the inning, Marichal, after throwing three pitches to Tommy Davis, all balls, was relieved by Don Larsen, whose first pitch was a low curve for ball four. A sacrifice by Fairly moved Davis to second. He stole third on Frank Howard's swinging strikeout. Larsen intentionally walked the next two batters, bringing up the pitcher. Roebuck grounded out, but the Dodgers were three outs from the World Series.

Matty Alou, pinch hitting for Larsen, singled on Roebuck's first pitch in the top of the ninth. Kuenn forced Alou at second on a grounder but beat the throw to first, avoiding a double play. Pinch-hitter Willie McCovey walked on four pitches, then Felipe Alou walked on a 3-and-2 count to load the bases.

Alston visited the mound, but left Roebuck in the game. Mays lined a single off Roebuck's glove, scoring Kuenn to cut the gap to 4-3.

Stan Williams relieved with the bases still loaded. Cepeda's sacrifice fly to right tied the score, with Felipe Alou advancing to third.

Williams threw a strike to Bailey, then sailed a high pitch over Roseboro's glove. Alou held at third as Mays advanced to second on the wild pitch. Alston called for an intentional walk to Bailey, and the bases were again loaded.

Davenport walked on five pitches, sending Alou home with the go-ahead run.

Ron Perranoski relieved Williams, and Jose Pagan hit a grounder toward second. Burright, a defensive replacement in the seventh, bobbled the ball for an error – Los Angeles' fourth error of the game. Mays scored for a two-run lead.

After watching his team score four runs on two hits, four walks, an error, and a wild pitch to take the lead, 6-4, Billy Pierce relieved and retired the Dodgers in order in the home half of the ninth. The Giants were headed to the World Series for the first time since moving to California after the 1957 season.

The Dodgers kept the press out of their locker room for nearly an hour after the loss. Team captain Snider, one of the few to dress in order to congratulate the Giants, said, "Don't hold it against the guys. They just want to cool off. They agreed they didn't feel like talking. They're still in a daze."[8]

A stunned Roebuck let Wally Moon explain to reporters what happened on the line drive hit by Mays in the ninth. "Ed told me the ball just hit the web of his glove and he didn't see it."[9]

Alston said he let Roebuck hit in the eighth with the bases loaded and two out because Roebuck was the best pitcher to protect the Dodgers' two-run lead. Stating that his pitchers finally "ran out of gas," Alston added, "We just came close, that's all. Ed Roebuck did one helluva job as long as he lasted. I think everybody gave it everything he possibly could."[10]

Dark defended his counterpart's strategy. "Maybe some will think he should have taken Ed Roebuck out of the game earlier in the ninth inning, but I don't think he could have, the way Roebuck was pitching," Dark said. "When McCovey went to bat with a man on first, Alston could have called in Ron Perranoski, his lefthander, but he knew that my next three batters after McCovey were righthanders, so he couldn't take a chance with a lefthanded pitcher in a spot like that."[11]

San Francisco and the New York Yankees split the first six games of the 1962 World Series. Down 1-0 in the bottom of the ninth in Game Seven, the Giants had runners on second and third with two outs and McCovey at the plate. Their hopes of another comeback were silenced when McCovey's line drive was caught by Bobby Richardson.

Despite speculation that he would be replaced by either Durocher or Pete Reiser,[12] Alston signed his 10th one-year contract to manage the Dodgers the day after the World Series ended.[13] Koufax made a complete recovery in 1963, winning 25 games and the Cy Young Award.[14] He was also named the National League's Most Valuable Player. Los Angeles held off a late-season challenge by the St. Louis Cardinals to win the pennant. San Francisco finished in third place. The Dodgers swept the Yankees in the 1963 World Series.

## SOURCES

The author accessed Baseball-Reference.com and Retrosheet.org. for box scores/play-by-play information, player, team, and season pages, pitching and batting game logs, and other data:

https://www.baseball-reference.com/boxes/LAN/LAN196210030.shtml

https://www.retrosheet.org/boxesetc/1962/B10030LAN1962.htm

The author also accessed YouTube's *Classic Baseball on the Radio* for NBC's national broadcast of this game by Al Helfer and George Kell:

https://www.youtube.com/watch?v=3jHOlcH1GiM

## NOTES

1 Dan Hafner, "Stunned Dodgers Can't Believe It," *Los Angeles Times*, October 1, 1962: C4.

2 It was the fourth time the NL season ended with two teams tied for first place, necessitating a best-of-three-games playoff to decide the pennant winner. In 1946 the Dodgers and Cardinals tied, with St. Louis winning the first two playoff games. In 1951 the Dodgers and Giants needed three games to determine a winner, with Bobby Thomson's home run in

the bottom of the ninth giving the Giants the pennant. In 1959, the Dodgers won the first two playoff games against the Braves. Dodgers outfielder Duke Snider and Giants center fielder Willie Mays were the only active players remaining from the 1951 playoff. Leo Durocher, now a coach for Los Angeles, managed the Dodgers in 1946 and the Giants in 1951. Current San Francisco manager Alvin Dark and coaches Whitey Lockman, Wes Westrum, and Larry Jansen all played for the Giants in 1951.

3 Results of the playoff games counted in the players' season statistics. At the end of the 162-game schedule, Mays led the National League in home runs, with 47, but Harmon Killebrew of the American League's Twins led the majors with 48. In addition to his first-inning home run, Mays hit one off Larry Sherry in the sixth inning, giving him a major-league-leading total of 49.

4 "Playoff Pearls," *The Sporting News*, October 13, 1962: 10.

5 Bob Hunter, "Dodger Slab Staff Cracks in Showdown," *The Sporting News*, October 13, 1962: 7.

6 The two RBIs gave Davis 153 for the season, tops in the majors. Davis started the game with a .344 batting average, two points ahead of Cincinnati's Frank Robinson. He ended the day with a .346 average after two hits and a walk in four plate appearances.

7 Wills had four steals in the playoff series, bringing his season total to 104, a major-league record at the time. He edged out Mays for the National League MVP award (209 points with 8 first-place vote to 202 points with 7 first-place votes for Mays).

8 "Dodgers Want to Be Alone," *San Francisco Examiner*, October 4, 1962: 65.

9 "Dodgers Want to Be Alone."

10 "Dodgers Want to Be Alone."

11 "Playoff Pearls," *The Sporting News*, October 13, 1962: 10.

12 Sid Ziff, "Walt Will Be Back," *Los Angeles Times*, October 11, 1962: B3.

13 Paul Zimmerman, "Alston Keeps Job, OK's Durocher Stay," *Los Angeles Times*, October 18, 1962: B3.

14 Until 1967, only one Cy Young Award, covering both the National and American Leagues, was given.

# MARICHAL OUTDUELS SPAHN IN 16-INNING THRILLER

## July 2, 1963: San Francisco Giants 1, Milwaukee Braves 0 (16 innings), at Candlestick Park, San Francisco

BY LOU HERNÁNDEZ

AS THE 1963 National League season moved into its fourth month, the Milwaukee Braves visited San Francisco for the second time. On July 2 San Francisco sent 25-year-old Juan Marichal out against Warren Spahn, 17 years his senior, in the Tuesday night opener of a three-game set.

The Giants starter was looking to avenge a 3-1 loss on April 28 to the antediluvian left-hander, by then pitching in his 19th major-league campaign. The third-place Giants (44-34) were 1½ games behind the first-place St. Louis Cardinals, while the 38-38 Braves were sixth, 6½ games out of first. Marichal had won 12 games in 15 decisions for his team, and Spahn was sporting an 11-3 record.

At slightly past 8 o'clock, Marichal took the Candlestick Park mound. More than 4 hours and 15 innings later, he was still toiling there. And so was Warren Spahn – in a scoreless pitching duel.

The Braves had mounted a serious scoring threat in the top of the fourth inning. Marichal disposed of the first two batters before trouble arose. The right-hander walked Norm Larker, and Mack "The Knife" Jones followed with a single to left, moving Larker to second. Del Crandall hit a soft single to center that Willie Mays fielded, then lasered to the plate to nail Larker trying to score. It had been a charmed half-inning for the Dominican pitcher. Henry Aaron led off the frame with a drive to deep left field that Marichal later said he thought was gone.[1] Willie McCovey hauled the ball in a few feet from the fence, as Candlestick Point's strong westerly winds knocked it down.

McCovey nearly ended the game in the bottom of the ninth. The Giants left fielder smoked a pitch deep to right field, just missing a home run – or so said the first-base umpire. Local beat writer Curly Grieve expanded: "McCovey was so enraged when Chris

Pelekoudas called the blast a foul that momentarily it appeared he would push the arbiter around the outfield and wind up ejected in the clubhouse. McCovey, [manager] Alvin Dark and [first-base coach] Larry Jansen surrounded Pelekoudas, claiming the ball left Candlestick fair. Pelekoudas stuck to his call, which took courage."[2]

"I followed the ball all the way out but evidently the umpire didn't. As hard as I hit the ball it didn't have a chance to curve before leaving the ballpark," McCovey said after the game.[3] When he stepped back into the batter's box, a miffed McCovey grounded out to first base, with Spahn covering. After a two-out single by Felipe Alou, Orlando Cepeda popped up to third base, and the scoreless game moved into extra innings.

With two outs in the top of the 13th, Braves second baseman Frank Bolling singled off Marichal, ending a string of 16 batters in a row retired by the Giants' workhorse since a walk to Aaron in the eighth. Bolling was left stranded by the next hitter, Aaron, who popped up to first baseman Cepeda in foul ground.

Marichal was scheduled to bat third that inning. Cepeda later recalled the moment in a 1998 memoir. Alvin Dark asked Marichal if he had had enough. Cepeda remembered Marichal barking at Dark, "A 42-year-old man [Spahn] is still pitching. I can't come out!"[4] Dark accepted – or was startled into acceptance by Marichal's ardor – and let him bat. Marichal flied out to complete the inning, and the game pushed forward.

The Giants made a strong bid to get Marichal a win in the bottom of the 14th. With two outs, they loaded the bases on a double, a walk, and an error by Denis Menke, in at third base for Eddie Mathews, who was removed after two at-bats due to a sore right wrist. Spahn then coolly retired Giants catcher Ed Bailey on a fly to center, ending the inning and extending the deadlock.

Marichal shook off his catcher's failure and assailed the mound for the 15th time. As if he had gained strength against his team's impotency, the fourth-year pitcher resolutely retired the side in order, his counterpart the second out on a foul popup. Spahn duplicated the orderly effort and set down the three hitters he faced in the bottom half of the frame, Marichal the third out on a strikeout.

Marichal and Spahn had recorded 90 outs, equally divided through 15 innings of pitching grandeur. Had it been a championship prizefight, a draw could have been called to no one's contention. Had they been two enslaved gladiators, the reigning Caesar would have been compelled to free both of them. Such magnificence from the hill had rarely been displayed in baseball annals by two pitchers in the same game.[5]

As was his custom and as he had done in each of the prior 15 innings, Juan Marichal sprinted to the mound in the top of the 16th with all the appearance of a schoolboy released from classes for the summer, except that he clutched a baseball glove instead of a glowing report card. Inning after inning after inning, Juan Antonio Marichal had scaled the hilly sandbox that acted as his playground and disposed of batters with a brimming confidence that bordered on nonchalance. How much longer could the bravado of youth sustain him?

Marichal set down the first two batters of the 16th on fly outs to right field and center field respectively. He gave up a two-out hit to Menke, the eighth and final hit he allowed in the game and only the second by the Braves since the seventh inning. Marichal then registered, on a comebacker, his 48th out, on his 227th pitch of what was now, according to the scoreboard clock, a new day.

As was his custom and as he had done in each of the prior 15 innings, Warren Spahn strolled to the mound in the bottom of the 16th with all the appearance and enthusiasm of a factory worker walking to his next shift, except that he toted a baseball glove instead of a lunch pail. Inning after inning after inning, Warren Edward Spahn had reached his elevated, dirt-compressed workstation and methodically doled out reject-tags to an assembly line of hitters. How much longer before the albatross of advanced age claimed him?

Braves outfielder Don Dillard nestled under a fly ball hit by leadoff batter Harvey Kuenn, and with the catch Spahn recorded the first out of the bottom of the 16th inning. The shrewd southpaw prepared to pitch to the next armed challenger, Willie Mays. The cruelty of baseball for a starting pitcher is that one bad pitch can often ruin the cumulative effort of 100 good ones. In Spahn's case, at a few minutes past midnight, it was 200 good ones. The same ball Kuenn had swung under and lifted to Dillard in center field, Spahn threw as his 201st pitch to Mays.

Mays' bat met Spahn's first pitch with a crackling fury that sent the ball shooting high and far into the heavy San Francisco night, soaring on a shimmering arc of triumph not even the treacherous Candlestick Park winds could betray. And just like that, the dramatically pitched game dramatically ended – Marichal the exhausted victor, Spahn, the valiantly defeated.[6]

Only once, in the six decades since, has one pitcher thrown as many innings in one major-league game as Marichal did that night against Spahn.[7]

Over the 16 innings, Marichal allowed the eight hits along with four walks, and struck out 10. Spahn yielded nine hits and walked one (intentionally, Mays), with only two strikeouts.

Both stalwarts, who were pitching on three days' rest, made their next appointed starts with no ill aftereffects (the Sunday before the All-Star Game). Spahn complained of a sore elbow, which apparently flared up on him enough to land him twice on the disabled list. He still went on to lead the league in complete games with 22 at season's end, while garnering his 13th and final 20-win campaign with a mark of 23-7.

Three days into September, Marichal became a 20-game winner for the first time. In all, he started 40 games for the Giants and finished the season with a sterling 25-8 record and 18 complete games.

After the game, Spahn's teammates greeted their aged warrior – the last player to enter the clubhouse because of an interview session – with their own tribute. Quoting Spahn's fellow starting pitcher Bob Sadowski, writer Jim Kaplan described it: "When Spahn arrived, everyone stood, applauded, and lined up to shake his hand. 'If you didn't have tears in your eyes, you weren't nothing.'"[8]

The game would not be complete without returning to that baseball savant known as Willie Mays. In the fourth inning of this contest, Mays threw a runner out at the plate from center field, which allowed this game for the pitching ages to develop, then won the game in the 16th inning with a home run.

This was Willie Mays, every day.

## SOURCES

In addition to the sources cited in the Notes, the author consulted Baseball-Reference.com, Retrosheet.org, the *San Francisco Examiner*, and the *Milwaukee Journal.*

Keri, Jonah. "The Greatest Pitching Duel in Human History," Grantland.com, July 9, 2013. https://grantland.com/the-triangle/the-greatest-pitching-duel-in-human-history. Accessed on May 26, 2022.

https://www.baseball-reference.com/boxes/SFN/SFN196307020.shtml

https://www.retrosheet.org/boxesetc/2004/B06250BOS2004.htm

## NOTES

1 Curly Grieve, "Juan, Spahn, All Agree: 'Twas Terrific Game,'" *San Francisco Examiner*, July 4, 1963.

2 Grieve.

3 Grieve.

4 Orlando Cepeda and Herb Fagen, *Baby Bull: From Hardball to Hard Time and Back* (Dallas: Taylor Publishing Company, 1998), 93.

5 On August 13, 1954, Jack Harshman of the Chicago White Sox defeated Al Aber of the Detroit Tigers, 1-0, in 16 innings at Comiskey Park. Both pitchers went the distance. Harvey Kuenn was the Tigers' shortstop. Nine years later, Kuenn was the Giants' third baseman behind Marichal. The infielder played the entire way in both marathons. Two seasons after the Marichal-Spahn classic, the Phillies' Chris Short and the Mets' Rob Gardner locked up in a scoreless duel for 15 innings on October 2, 1965, at Shea Stadium. Both pitchers retired

after the 15th, and the game (the second of a doubleheader) ended in a 0-0 tie after 18 innings, halted by curfew.

6 Bob Wolf, "Spahn Loses Shutout on Homer by Mays," *Milwaukee Journal*, July 3, 1963. Mays' blast was his 15th of the season and 353rd of his storied career. Spahn had accumulated a scoreless string of 27⅓ innings before Mays ruined it, and had thrown 31⅔ innings without walking a batter before intentionally passing Mays in the 15th.

7 On September 1, 1967, Marichal's moundmate Gaylord Perry, a right-hander, started and pitched 16 scoreless innings in Cincinnati – the last time (as of the 2022 season) that a pitcher has thrown as many innings in a baseball game. Goose eggs galore reigned in that game, which lasted 20 scoreless innings before the Giants pushed across a run in the top of the 21st inning to win, 1-0. "When Gaylord trudged off the diamond after hurling all those 16 memorable innings, the crowd at Crosley Field gave him a standing ovation. Perry acknowledged the ovation by tipping his cap – with his left arm. 'I couldn't raise my right,' he said." Bob Stevens, "Hat's Off," *The Sporting News*, September 30, 1967: 19. (Five days later, Perry had no trouble with his arm. He pitched a 2-0 shutout in his regularly scheduled start against Houston.)

8 Jim Kaplan, "The Best-Pitched Game in Baseball History: Warren Spahn and Juan Marichal," *The National Pastime*, No. 27, 2007.

# THE SAY HEY KID STEALS THE SHOW

## July 9, 1963: National League 5, American League 3, at Cleveland Municipal Stadium

BY CRAIG GARRETSON

**"THEY INVENTED THE** All-Star Game for Willie Mays," Ted Williams said,[1] and Mays showed why in the 1963 All-Star Game. Wondrous Willie didn't hit a home run, but the rest of his formidable tools were on display as he had a hit and a walk, stole two bases, scored two runs, knocked in two runs, and had two defensive gems to become the All-Star Game MVP.

After four years of double All-Star Games – between 1959 and 1962, two games were played, anywhere from a month apart (1959) to two days (1960) – the 1963 midsummer classic was again a one-game affair.

It was the second year that an All-Star MVP was named. (The Dodgers' Maury Wills had won it the previous year after the NL had a 3-1 win in Game One, and the Angels' Leon Wagner when the AL won Game Two, 9-4.) So while 1963 was the first of the two All-Star MVP Awards won by the 32-year-old Mays, one can imagine the 24-time All-Star would have won a few more had the award been in existence for his entire career.

There was one disappointment for Mays going into the 1963 Game: Whitey Ford wouldn't be there. In five All-Star Games, Mays had gone an incredible 6-for-7 against Ford, with two home runs and a triple;[2] in the 1962 World Series, he had four hits and a walk, with two runs scored and an RBI, in 10 plate appearances against Ford.

(In 1997 Mays was asked if there was a pitcher he wished he could have batted against in the days before interleague play. "Whitey Ford," he replied. "He couldn't get me out. 3-for-4, 4-for-4. He was my man."[3])

But the Yankees hurler, despite being 13-3 with a 2.94 ERA at the time, had been left off the roster by AL All-Star (and Yankees) manager Ralph Houk. The 34-year-old lefty had battled a sore arm and a circulatory issue with his left index finger earlier that season,[4] and perhaps Houk wanted to save him for October.

The "Chairman of the Board" had made his appearance known anyway. The final Yankees series before the All-Star Game had them playing the Indians in Cleveland, where the All-Star Game would be played. Ford, after closing out a 7-4 win over the Indians with a perfect ninth inning, left a handwritten note for Mays: "Sorry I didn't make team, but Houk didn't want me to make you look bad."[5]

Mays managed to look good even without him.

The game was played in front of 44,160 fans at Cleveland Municipal Stadium, the same ballpark in which Mays had made his All-Star Game debut nine years earlier.

After a scoreless first inning thrown by Jim O'Toole of the Reds and Ken McBride of the Angels, Mays led off the top of the second by drawing a five-pitch walk, the NL's first baserunner of the day. On a 3-and-1 pitch to the Giants' Ed Bailey, Mays stole second off catcher Earl Battey of the Twins. Bailey then walked, the Cardinals' Ken Boyer popped out, and Dick Groat of the Cardinals hit a seeing-eye single through the left side scoring Mays from second with the first run of the game. McBride then retired the next two batters.

In the bottom of the second, with Leon Wagner on second and the Twins' Zoilo Versalles on first, McBride helped his own cause with a two-out single to tie the score.

Mays came up again in the top of the third with two outs and Milwaukee's Henry Aaron on second after reaching on a fielder's choice. Facing McBride for a second time, Mays lined a single up the middle on a 3-and-1 pitch to knock in Aaron. Once again Mays stole second base with Bailey batting, and he scored on Bailey's single to right-center. The stolen base, his second of the game, set an All-Star Game record for the most by a player in a game (since tied, but not broken), and extended Mays' record for the most career All-Star Game stolen bases to five; he added another in 1964, and his six career stolen bases are still the All-Star career record.[6] (He was caught only once, in 1960.)

In the bottom of the frame, the Angels' Albie Pearson lined a gapper to left-center off the Cubs' Larry Jackson to lead off the inning. "The fans are applauding for two things," Cleveland Indians broadcaster Bob Neal, calling the game for NBC Radio, said over the cheering crowd. "One, the power and placement of that base hit by Albie Pearson that went all the way to the fence, and the other, the spectacular fielding by Willie Mays who on the dead run circled around behind (Tommy) Davis at the fence, came up with the ball, came out from behind and fired it into third all in the same motion."[7] Pearson scored on a single by Frank Malzone of the Red Sox, and then Malzone scored the tying run on a single by Battey.

The game stayed tied until the fifth inning, when Mays came up with one out and runners on the corners, facing Detroit's Jim Bunning. Mays topped a bouncer to first baseman Joe Pepitone of the Yankees, who could only step on the bag for the second out as Davis scored the go-ahead run.

It remained a 4-3 game until the eighth. Mays, batting second in the inning, came up with the Cardinals' Bill White on first after a base hit.

"Well, Willie has done just about everything here today," Neal told his audience. "He walked, he singled, he grounded out, he batted in two runs, he scored two, and he has stolen two bases."[8]

After taking a huge cut on the first pitch from Boston's Dick Radatz and fouling it off – "Mays was gonna try to hit that one in the lake," Neal said[9] – Mays swung and missed at the 1-and-2 pitch with White running on the pitch. White was safe at second, and he scored the final run of the game on a single by Chicago's Ron Santo.

In the bottom of the eighth, the Dodgers' Don Drysdale struck out Elston Howard of the Yankees and Carl Yastrzemski of the Red Sox. That brought up Pepitone, who crushed a ball to the right of the 380-foot sign in center field that Mays ran into the outfield wall – actually a wire fence – to catch. He came away limping. *The Sporting News* reported: "Willie Mays was a near All-Star Game casualty when he caught his foot under the center field wire fence as he dashed to the barrier for a catch of Joe Pepitone's long, eighth-inning drive. Willie hopped around for a few moments, then jogged to the dugout and reported later that he was not injured."[10]

"I knew he was all right when I saw him limping," NL (and San Francisco Giants) manager Alvin Dark said. "If he'd really been hurt, he would have been trying to hide it."[11]

The AL had one last gasp in the bottom of the ninth, after Baltimore's Brooks Robinson singled with one out off Drysdale. That brought up New York's Bobby Richardson as the potential tying run. He hit a groundball to White at first base for a game-ending 3-6-3 double play. The win was the first of eight straight wins, and 19 of the next 20, for the Senior Circuit.

Mays, who was hitting .271/.352/.468 before the All-Star Game, went on a tear over the second half of the season, hitting .362/.412/.709 with 20 doubles, 6 triples, and 22 home runs to finish the year with a .314/.380/.582 line in 671 plate appearances. He was fifth in the MVP balloting and won his seventh straight Gold Glove.

## SOURCES

In addition to the sources cited in the Notes, the author consulted Baseball-Reference.com and Retrosheet.org.

https://www.baseball-reference.com/allstar/1963-allstar-game.shtml

https://www.retrosheet.org/boxesetc/1963/B07090ALS1963.htm

## NOTES

1 Willie Mays biography, The National Baseball Hall of Fame and Museum. Accessed November 3, 2022.

2 Mays went 2-for-2 (with two runs scored) off Ford in the 1955 All-Star Game; 1-for-1 (with a two-run home run) in 1956; 1-for-1 (with an RBI triple) in 1959 (Game One); 2-for-2 (with a home run and a stolen base) in 1960 (Game Two). Ford finally retired him the last time they faced each other in an All-Star Game, in the first inning of the first game in 1961. In an oft-retold story, including in *The Baseball Codes* by Jason Turbow and Michael Duca, Giants owner Horace Stoneham had paid for Ford and Mickey Mantle's $400 tab at a golf club, and when they tried to pay him back, Stoneham offered a "double or nothing" bet on whether Ford could finally get Mays out. After two long foul balls, Ford threw a breaking ball (Turbow said it was a spitball) that was taken for a called strike three for the final out of the first inning. Jason Turbow and Michael Duca, *The Baseball Codes* (New York: Anchor Books, 2011), 59-61.

3 Berry Tramel, "Mays Loved Facing Whitey, and Didn't Fear Drysdale," *The Oklahoman* (Oklahoma City), June 15, 1997.

4 C. Paul Rogers III, "Whitey Ford," SABR BioProject.

5 The note was taped to a mirror in the visitors' locker room along with a newspaper clipping of a photo of a shirtless Mays. Asked about the stunt by *The Sporting News*, Willie said: "That Whitey's a nice boy. I wish he had made the team again this year." "Star Dust From Lake Erie," *The Sporting News*, July 20, 1963: 20.

6 https://www.baseball-reference.com/allstar/leaders_bat.shtml. Mays also holds the All-Star Game career records with 24 games played (tied with Aaron and Stan Musial); at-bats, 75; plate appearances, 82; runs scored, 20; hits, 23; total bases, 40 (tied with Musial); triples, 3 (tied with Brooks Robinson); and singles, 15.

7 NBC Radio call as heard on https://www.youtube.com/watch?v=8XtKO-NkxYs.

8 NBC Radio call.

9 NBC Radio call.

10 Photo caption accompanying "Star Dust From Lake Erie," *The Sporting News*, July 20, 1963: 20.

11 Bob Broeg, "N.L.'s Swifties Scamper Past A.L. All-Stars," *The Sporting News*, July 20, 1963: 5.

# A REVITALIZED WILLIE MAYS HOMERS TWICE AND DRIVES IN FIVE EN ROUTE TO MVP AWARD

## August 7, 1965: San Francisco Giants 10, St. Louis Cardinals 4, at Busch Stadium, St. Louis

BY CHAD MOODY

"I WANT TO talk about slumping and pressing," Willie Mays said in a 1966 article. "I'm supposed to be famous for them."[1] Perhaps Mays' most infamous slump occurred as a rookie in 1951 when he could muster only one hit in his first 26 at-bats for the New York Giants.[2] In 1965, another doozy of a slump, in which the (now San Francisco) Giants center fielder found himself mired, undoubtedly contributed to his reputation for being an "unusually streaky" hitter.[3]

The beginning of Mays' struggles in this instance can be traced to a brutal home-plate collision with Philadelphia Phillies catcher Pat Corrales on July 10. Left with a banged-up right hip that he further aggravated in the All-Star Game three days later, Mays hit only .125 over the rest of the month with just one home run and one RBI.[4] "I'm not saying I would have been hitting if I hadn't hurt myself, but I couldn't swing freely," he later explained.[5] During his post-injury struggles, Mays had to endure an incredible 0-for-24 stretch that helped drop his batting average from .339 to .308 by the end of July. "When you go into a slump you have a tendency to swing at bad balls despite yourself," he acknowledged.[6]

"But if fans know about his slumps they also know he usually comes out of them with a bang – a hot streak as terrifying to pitchers as his slumps are to manager Herman Franks," sportswriter Jack McDonald wrote.[7] Indeed, a fresh new month seemed to provide the spark that produced the "bang" for the 34-year-old. Over the first six days of August 1965, a revitalized Mays hit .419 with 3 home runs and 5 RBIs. And any remaining doubts as to whether Mays' recent slump had been completely busted were put to rest on August 7, in the second game of a road series against the St. Louis Cardinals. The Giants had won the opener, 3-2.

Despite reigning as World Series champions, St. Louis entered the midseason contest in seventh place and eight games out of first. Hoping to even the series, the Cardinals asked right-hander Tracy Stallard to cool off the hot Giants, who were winners of four straight, aided by the rejuvenated Mays. A 20-game loser for the New York Mets in the previous season, Stallard was nonetheless working his way into becoming St. Louis's second-best starter behind future Hall of Famer Bob Gibson. San Francisco countered with Bob Shaw, a reliable veteran who was also having a fine campaign as the number two man in the Giants' starting rotation behind Juan Marichal, another future Hall of Famer. A crowd of 18,737 watched the nationally televised afternoon contest at Busch Stadium.

The visiting Giants wasted no time jumping on Stallard. Dick Schofield's walk to lead off the top of the first was subsequently followed by Jesús Alou's single to put a runner in scoring position. Mays, the number-three batter, continued his recent hitting spree with an opposite-field base hit that scored Schofield. Despite the shaky start, Stallard was able to work his way out of the jam without further damage. Things quieted down over the next inning and a half, with neither team mustering a threat.

The top of the third also started uneventfully with Stallard retiring the first two Giants. However, a walk to Mays set the table for cleanup slugger Willie McCovey's "tremendous, 420-foot" round-tripper to the right-center-field bleachers.[8] The home run, McCovey's 25th of the season, extended the visitors' lead to 3-0, which held for the subsequent two half-innings.

St. Louis broke through against Shaw in the bottom of the fourth. With one out, Curt Flood walked. Bill White added a bad-hop single over first baseman McCovey's head that advanced Flood to third. Veteran star Ken Boyer, "although aching all over with a bad back that would have made Quasimodo wince," followed with a three-run homer to left field that deadlocked the game.[9]

Leading off the top of the fifth, Schofield reached base on an error by first baseman White. With one out, Mays – "no longer aching" from his bad hip – deposited a "towering drive" into the left-center-field bleachers for a tie-breaking two-run homer.[10] The distance of his "tape-measure job" was estimated at as much as 450 feet.[11] Although Stallard retired the next two San Francisco hitters to end the inning, the right-hander's day was over.

With the score 5-3 in favor of the Giants, the bottom of the sixth began with a single by Cardinals shortstop Dick Groat, who moved into scoring position on a wild pitch by Shaw. However, Groat ran himself into a double play – and effectively put "the Cards out of business" – after trying to advance from second to third on Flood's tapper to third baseman Jim Ray Hart.[12] After Hart threw to first to get an out, an "alert Willie [McCovey] slammed the ball back across the diamond to Hart and Groat was market meat."[13] Shaw retired the next batter to bring St. Louis's promising frame to a close without allowing a run.

San Francisco padded its lead in the top of the seventh courtesy of the hot-hitting Mays, who was "rolling once more."[14] After rookie Cardinals reliever Nelson Briles set down the first two Giants in order, Jesús Alou ripped a line-drive double down the right-field line that kept things alive. Capping his outstanding afternoon, Mays pulled Briles' first offering into the left-field-corner bleachers for his second two-run homer of the day and major-league-leading 29th of the campaign. It was the 53rd time in his career that he had hit two or more home runs in a game.

Despite now working with a comfortable 7-3 lead, Giants hurler Shaw, "again bothered constantly by accusations that he was throwing the evil spitter," began to "wilt slightly in the 90-degree heat" in the bottom of the seventh.[15] Facing a two-on, one-out situation, manager Franks called upon "relief whiz" Frank Linzy, who quickly squelched the potential St. Louis rally with a double-play ball.[16] "If there ever was a pitcher who looked like he throws a spitball but doesn't, it's Linzy," Giants catcher Dick Bertell said after the game. "His heavy sinker is the best I've ever seen."[17]

San Francisco's offensive onslaught turned the tilt into a laugher in the top of the eighth.[18] After Briles had loaded the bases with nobody out, Cardinals manager Red Schoendienst brought in bullpen arm Don Dennis. Hal Lanier greeted the rookie moundsman with a two-run single that scored Hart and Matty Alou, who was playing with a ruptured blood vessel in his right ankle after making an awkward slide. Two batters later, an RBI fielder's choice off Schofield's bat scored Tom Haller for the third and final tally of the frame.

With the contest now well in hand, the Giants replaced the "amazing" Mays in center field with rookie Ken Henderson in the bottom of the eighth.[19] During that half-inning, the Cardinals attempted a half-hearted comeback against the bespectacled Linzy but could muster only a lone run on Flood's RBI single that scored Bob Skinner, who had doubled to lead off the frame. Neither team mounted any offensive threats in the final stanza, resulting in a 10-4 victory for San Francisco.

The win was the fifth straight for the Giants, advancing them to second place all alone in the National League. "Herman [Franks] has been keeping the guys together, and we maintained a good feeling even when we were losing," Mays said regarding keys to the Giants' recent success.[20] However, perhaps the biggest reason for the club's upswing was a now-healthy Mays being "back in stride."[21] "The hot weather in Milwaukee and around the road trip helped, and I spent a lot of time under the lamp," he explained of his hip rehabilitation.[22]

Mays' two home runs and five RBIs in the game gave him five and 10, respectively, over a six-game span. Additionally, he was now riding an eight-game hitting streak that had elevated his batting average 15 points since the beginning of the month. The reenergized slugger went on to hit a then-NL record 17 home runs during August and finished his superb season with 52 round-trippers, 112 RBIs, and a .317/.398/.645 slash line.

Although San Francisco eventually lost out to the Los Angeles Dodgers in a tight pennant race, Mays won the NL's Most Valuable Player Award – despite the fallout of his dreadful injury-induced July collapse. However, the slump seemed to provide the future Hall of Famer with a teachable moment. "Maybe next time I'll tell them I know I can't play up to my best ability and I feel I can help the club and myself better by resting up," Mays observed.[23]

## SOURCES

The author accessed Baseball-Reference.com (https://www.baseball-reference.com/boxes/SLN/SLN196508070.shtml) for box scores/play-by-play information and other data, as well as Retrosheet. (https://www.retrosheet.org/boxesetc/1965/B08070SLN1965.htm). In addition to the sources cited in the Notes, the author also accessed GenealogyBank.com, NewspaperArchive.com, Newspapers.com, Paper of Record, and Stathead.com.

## NOTES

1 Willie Mays, "Mays Gives Advice on Little Leaguers," *St. Louis Post-Dispatch*, April 4, 1966: 3D.

2 Mays had rookie status in 1951 under the prevailing rules at the time; after Major League Baseball revised its view of what constituted a major league in 2020, Mays' major-league debut is deemed to have occurred in 1948 as a member of the Negro American League's Birmingham Black Barons.

3 James S. Hirsch, *Willie Mays: The Life, The Legend* (New York: Scribner, 2010), 254.

4 Harry Jupiter, "Mays Says Fall Made Him Dizzy," *San Francisco Examiner*, July 11, 1965: IV-1; Associated Press, "Marichal, Mays Shed Woes, Gain Series Lead for League," *Newport News* (Virginia) *Daily Press*, July 14, 1965: 15.

5 George Ross, "Pennant Adrenalin," *Oakland Tribune*, August 10, 1965: 39.

6 Ross.

7 Jack McDonald, "Mays Snaps Skid – Giants Step on Gas," *The Sporting News*, August 14, 1965: 16.

8 Bob Stevens, "Two Mays Homers – Giants Win Again," *San Francisco Chronicle*, August 8, 1965: 31.

9 Stevens.

10 Harry Jupiter, "Mays Rips 2; Giants Roll, 10-4," *San Francisco Examiner*, August 8, 1965: IV-5; Neal Russo, "Cards Lose to Giants," *St. Louis Post-Dispatch*, August 8, 1965: 1C.

11 Stevens, "Two Mays Homers – Giants Win Again."

12 Stevens, 34.

13 Stevens.

14 Jupiter, "Mays Rips 2; Giants Roll, 10-4," IV-1.

15 Stevens, 31.

16 Russo, "Cards Lose to Giants."

17 Russo.

18 Stevens, 34.

19 Stevens, 31.

20 Ross, "Pennant Adrenalin," 40.

21 Jupiter, "Mays Rips 2; Giants Roll, 10-4," IV-5.

22 Ross, "Pennant Adrenalin," 39.

23 Ross.

# WILLIE MAYS SWATS TWO HOME RUNS, CLOSES IN ON NUMBER 500, AS GIANTS TAKE FIRST PLACE

## September 8, 1965: San Francisco Giants 12, Houston Astros 3, at Candlestick Park, San Francisco

BY MIKE HUBER

**BEFORE A CROWD** of 8,922 at Candlestick Park, Willie Mays hit his 44th and 45th home runs of the season to lead the San Francisco Giants over the Houston Astros, giving San Francisco the outright lead in the National League standings with a half-game advantage over both the Cincinnati Reds and Los Angeles Dodgers.

After a slow start to the 1965 season (winning just seven of 16 games in April), San Francisco had won close to 60 percent of its games over the next three months (going 48-34). Series sweeps against both the Reds and St. Louis Cardinals in early August had brought the Giants to within one game of first place. By winning five of their first seven contests in September, the Giants suddenly found themselves tied for first place with the Dodgers, locked in a pennant race that would not be settled until the season's final week.

The Astros won 10 of 16 to begin the season and were a half-game out of first place when April ended. They didn't have another winning month, though, and by the time they played the Giants in September, they were 60-79, having lost three of their past four games.[1]

The 34-year-old Mays was batting .339 at the All-Star break, with 23 home runs and 59 RBIs. He homered to lead off the midseason classic, and then he went on a tear, batting .363 in August with 17 home runs and 29 RBIs, leading his team's climb in the standings.

The Giants hosted the Astros in a two-game series beginning on September 8. Right-hander Bobby Bolin had the mound duties for San Francisco. This was his 37th appearance of the season but only his ninth start. Sporting a 2.60 ERA, he was in search of his ninth victory. Another righty, Don Nottebart,

*Willie Mays hit a career-high 52 home runs in 1965. Courtesy National Baseball Hall of Fame.*

started for the Astros. He was struggling (4-13 with a 4.29 ERA). In two outings against the Giants that season, he absorbed the loss both times; in neither outing did he pitch more than five innings.

Lee Maye led off the game with a single to right, but Bolin retired the next three Astros batters on fly balls. The Giants wasted no time in jumping on Nottebart. After Dick Schofield struck out, three consecutive singles by Jesús Alou, Mays, and Willie McCovey produced the game's first run. Nottebart then walked Jim Ray Hart to load the bases. Len Gabrielson singled into right-center field. Mays scored easily, but McCovey was thrown out at home trying to score. The Giants led, 2-0.

In the second inning, with two on and two out, Mays blasted a three-run homer over the left-field fence. With the score 5-0, the Giants "had their first laugher in a long, long time."[2] Ron Taylor was called in from the Houston bullpen to relieve Nottebart and remained on the mound for the rest of the game.

Through three innings, Bolin allowed just two singles. The top of the fourth presented an unusual play. With one down, Bolin hit Jim Gentile with a pitch. Bob Aspromonte singled and Gentile advanced to second. Rusty Staub belted a drive to deep center. Gentile, running on the play, had passed third base when Mays made a sensational catch, and Gentile had to backtrack to second base. According to the *San Francisco Examiner*, "the Giants appealed that Jim hadn't retagged third base and for once the umps agreed."[3] The double play ended Houston's threat.

No reason was given in the newspapers, but Astros skipper Lum Harris inserted Walt Bond for Gentile to play first base in the bottom half of the fourth. Hal Lanier tripled and scored on Bolin's single to left. The Giants now owned a six-run lead.

Houston finally scored in the sixth. Maye tripled and Joe Morgan walked. Jim Wynn's sacrifice fly to center plated Maye. Bond followed with a home run, well beyond the right-field fence, and Houston now trailed by just three runs.

Nothing happened for each team's next two turns at bat. In the bottom of the eighth inning, the Giants doubled their run total. Taylor loaded the bases on singles by Gabrielson and Tom Haller and a walk to Lanier. Bolin grounded out to second baseman Morgan for his second RBI of the game. Schofield doubled to drive in Lanier and Haller. The deciding blows came when Mays and McCovey smacked back-to-back homers over the fence in right. This was the 498th career home run of Mays' 15-year career.[4] According to the *San Francisco Examiner*, McCovey's tape-measure blast, his 33rd of the season, traveled "almost 500 feet."[5]

Then came the frightening moment, as "everyone in the park but Jim Hart must have known what was going to happen on Astro hurler Ron Taylor's next pitch."[6] Curley Grieve, sports editor for the *Examiner*, detailed how Hart "went down in a heap"[7] to avoid Taylor's pitch, which just missed his head. Hart grounded out to Morgan to end the inning.

Bolin approached the mound in the ninth with a nine-run lead. His manager, Herman Franks, brought in a few defensive substitutions. Bob Burda replaced McCovey and Matty Alou entered for Mays.[8] Bolin had pitched only two three-up, three-down innings, and in the ninth he faced four batters, yielding a one-out single to Eddie Kasko. Joe Gaines pinch-hit for Taylor and, with his team trailing by nine runs, sacrificed Kasko to second with a bunt. Bolin struck out Maye to end the game, notching his ninth win of the season. In the clubhouse, the pitcher said, "That was the big game of the year for me. I wasn't especially fast, but I had good control."[9]

Every San Francisco starter except Hart participated in the 15-hit attack. Mays was 3-for-5, with three runs scored and five runs batted in. Jesus Alou had three singles, and Schofield, McCovey, and Gabrielson each added two hits. San Francisco had won its fifth game in a row.[10]

The Dodgers played even better than the Giants down the stretch and secured the pennant with a 97-65 record. (The Giants finished 95-67, two games behind.)

With his five runs batted in, Mays had 98 for the season. This was second-best in the National League, behind Cincinnati's Deron Johnson, who had 116.[11] Further, with 25 scheduled games left in the season,[12] reporters started speculating whether Mays could break his personal record of 51 home runs in a single season, set in 1955 when he led the National League. He was just two homers shy of 47, the number of round-trippers he hit in 1964 to lead the league.[13] After the game, Mays told reporters, "These last 25 games are going to be real tough. I think I can do the club better when I get a day off."[14] Mays played in 24 of those 25 games. His average dropped four points to .317, his on-base percentage stayed the same (.398), but his slugging percentage fell from .662 to .645.

The Say Hey Kid hit seven more home runs to finish 1965 with 52, setting a new season high. That gave him 505 for his career. The NL record for career homers was 511, set by New York Giants slugger Mel Ott.[15] From 1960 through 1965, in just six seasons, Mays clobbered 255 home runs, more than half his career total. In 1965 he led all players in the majors with an 11.2 WAR and 1.043 OPS, and he was rewarded with his second Most Valuable Player Award, beating three Dodgers stars.[16]

## SOURCES

In addition to the sources mentioned in the Notes, the author consulted Baseball-Reference.com, MLB.com, Retrosheet.org, and SABR.org.

https://www.baseball-reference.com/boxes/SFN/SFN196509080.shtml

https://www.retrosheet.org/boxesetc/1965/B09080SFN1965.htm

## NOTES

1 Houston won just five of its final 22 games of the season, finishing the National League in ninth place.

2 Harry Jupiter, "Fifth Straight Keeps SF on Top," *San Francisco Examiner*, September 9, 1965: 59. The Giants had not scored more than nine runs in a game since August 15.

3 Jupiter.

4 Mays hit number 499 four days later (September 12), in the second game of a doubleheader against the Chicago Cubs. On the next day (September 13), he launched his 500th career home run, against the Astros, also off Houston's Nottebart. Mays became the fifth major-league slugger to belt 500 career home runs, after Babe Ruth (August 11, 1929), Jimmie Foxx (September 24, 1940), Mel Ott (August 1, 1945), and Ted Williams (June 17, 1960).

5 Jupiter.

6 Curley Grieve, "Giants Played Like Flag Winner," *San Francisco Examiner*, September 9, 1965: 61.

7 Grieve.

8 Matty Alou took over in right field, and Ken Henderson moved from right to play center for Mays.

9 "Mays Moves Within 2 of 500-Homer Club," *Corpus Christi* (Texas) *Times*, September 9, 1965: 25.

10 The Giants' win streak grew to 14 straight before a September 17 loss to Milwaukee.

11 As of the end of play on September 8, 1965. Johnson finished the season with 130 RBIs, best in the National League. Cincinnati's Frank Robinson was second with 113, while Mays was third with 112.

12 The Giants played 163 games in 1965. On August 25 they tied the Pittsburgh Pirates.

13 Mays led the NL in home runs in 1964 with 47, and he led all major leagues in both 1955 (51 home runs) and 1962 (49).

14 *Corpus Christi Times.*

15 With the 52 home runs in 1965, Mays' career total stood at 505. On April 24, 1966, he launched his 511th career round-tripper, off Houston's Jim Owens (see https://www.baseball-reference.com/players/event_hr.fcgi?t=b&id=mayswi01 for Mays' career home-run log). On May 4 Mays hit an opposite-field homer off Los Angeles Dodgers hurler Claude Osteen, in front of the home crowd at Candlestick Park, giving him the record for most home runs hit in the National League.

16 Mays finished with 224 Vote Points, while Los Angeles' Sandy Koufax had 177, Maury Wills had 164, and Don Drysdale had 77. Cincinnati's Johnson finished fourth in the voting with 108 points.

# MAYS BREAKS GIANTS' RECORD WITH 52ND HR, CALLS IT A DAY

## October 3, 1965: San Francisco Giants 6, Cincinnati Reds 3, at Candlestick Park, San Francisco

BY JAKE BELL

**THERE WAS NO** big champagne celebration in the locker room after the game in which Willie Mays blasted his 52nd home run of the 1965 season, the highest season total of his career. For that matter, there was no Mays in the locker room either.

Any plans for celebration died the previous evening when the Los Angeles Dodgers clinched the National League pennant, rendering the final game of the 1965 season largely meaningless for the Giants.

Just over two weeks earlier, on September 16, San Francisco was sitting atop the National League, 4½ games ahead of the Dodgers and the Cincinnati Reds. The Giants had just beaten the Houston Astros for their 14th consecutive win, their longest winning streak of the season. But the now-second-place Giants, who'd gone 23-10 in September and October, their best finish since moving to San Francisco,[1] could hardly be accused of choking. "I don't think the kids panicked and collapsed," offered Giants manager Herman Franks. "That club down south simply wouldn't stop winning."[2]

The Dodgers had won the night of the 16th as well, kicking off a historic run. Of the final 16 games of 1965, Los Angeles won 15, a feat only accomplished previously by the 1960 New York Yankees.[3] In that span, opponents scored only 17 runs, were shut out eight times, and had just 15 extra-base hits.[4]

The Dodgers pitching staff had a combined ERA of 0.85 during the run, led by Sandy Koufax and Don Drysdale. In going a combined 8-0, Koufax pitched three shutouts and a 3-1 complete game – and earned a save to boot – while Drysdale had two shutouts and surrendered just one earned run in his other two starts for a 0.28 ERA.

Koufax was on the mound, bidding for his NL-leading 26th win, as the Giants gathered around a radio in the locker room after their 3-2 win over the Reds in Candlestick Park. The longer the game wore on without a Milwaukee runner advancing beyond first base, the more Giant players accepted their fate, grabbed their things, and left. "He's got a two-run lead in the seventh inning?" Franks acquiesced. "I'll listen to the rest of it in my car."[5]

With their place in the standings cemented, Franks planned to give his star players the day off, but was told the league would take issue because the Reds were tied with the Pittsburgh Pirates for third place. "I rested 'em when I was going for a pennant, didn't I?" Franks argued. "Do you want me to kill them now because somebody else is going for third place?"[6]

Mays was the player Franks most wanted to rest. The 34-year-old had sprained his left thumb against a fence while trying to nab a Hank Aaron home run in Milwaukee on September 17, but had donned a padded golf glove and played though pain that made it difficult to even grip a bat. With the pennant chase over and Mays's fourth home run title secured – teammate Willie McCovey was second in the NL with 39, trailing him by 12 – it seemed unnecessary, perhaps even reckless, to start Mays. But the difference between finishing third or fourth in the standings could mean about $500 per player out of the World Series pool. So Franks conceded that he'd start his regulars but wouldn't play them the full game.

Despite San Francisco's dashed playoff hopes, a crowd of 39,489 filled the stands at Candlestick Park, many motivated by five new cars that would be raffled off as part of Fan Appreciation Day.[7] The Giants started Dick Estelle, a September call-up making his first start of 1965 after five relief appearances; the Reds countered with relief ace Billy McCool, making his second start of his 62 games pitched. Both retired the side in order in the first inning, with Mays capping off the bottom of the inning with a fly ball to center fielder Vada Pinson.

Estelle got himself into some trouble in the second, walking Frank Robinson and Deron Johnson, then surrendering a single to Don Pavletich. Jesus Alou bailed him out, albeit briefly, when Robinson tested the right fielder's arm and was thrown out at home as the other runners advanced. After intentionally walking Tony Pérez to load the bases, Estelle gave up a sacrifice fly to Leo Cardenas that scored Johnson. The pitcher eventually escaped the inning down only one run despite putting five runners on base.

The Giants got the run back in the bottom of the inning. Jim Ray Hart and Alou led off with back-to-back singles, and Hart later scored on a two-out Hal Lanier triple.

Estelle allowed three runners in the third but maintained the tie. McCool dismissed the Giants in order in the bottom half of the frame, getting the third out on a McCovey fly ball to center field.

In the fourth, the exodus began. Franks sent McCovey out on defense, but after the first out, the manager dispatched Orlando Cepeda to first base to relieve him, allowing McCovey to bask in the outpouring of affection from the Giants faithful. Two more Reds runs scored in the inning, one on an error by San Francisco shortstop Tito Fuentes and a second on a single by Robinson. That ended Estelle's day as Franks called Bobby Bolin from the bullpen.

The right-hander was looking for some redemption. In his previous start, two day earlier, the Reds had knocked him out after only a third of an inning. Bolin had given up four runs on four hits, including two homers, before being pulled. The Reds went on to win, 17-2.[8]

Bolin silenced the Cincinnati bats the rest of the way, giving up just one hit while striking out nine in 5⅓ innings and earning the win, but later, in the clubhouse, he lamented, "It was two days late."[9]

The Giants responded by tying things up again. Mays led off the fourth by driving McCool's first pitch deep and into the left-field bleachers. He rounded the bases, now in sole possession of the Giants' single-season record for home runs, besting the previous mark of 51 set by Johnny Mize in 1947 and matched by himself in 1955. It was another in a succession of home-run milestones for Mays in the previous five weeks.

His home run on August 29 broke Ralph Kiner's NL record for homers in a month (17) and also pushed Mays past Lou Gehrig for sole possession of fifth place on the career home-run list (494). Two weeks later, in Houston, he became the fifth major leaguer to hit 500 home runs. On September 25, his 50th homer of the season made him the fifth player with multiple 50-home-run seasons and only the second to do it in the National League.

And more were coming. Home run number 52 of the season was also number 505 of Mays' career, setting him up to surpass Mel Ott as the most prolific home-run hitter in National League history with his seventh home run of 1966. Ten more would overtake Ted Williams, and with another 13 after that, Mays would surpass Jimmie Foxx as the second greatest power hitter in major-league history.

After touching home plate, Mays acknowledged the cheering crowd and stepped back into the dugout. Franks planned to send Mays back into the field, then replace him as he'd done with McCovey, but Mays declined and hit the showers. "They gave me an ovation after I hit the home run and ... I didn't want to milk the fans for applause," he would later recount.[10]

Franks wasn't far behind. Wanting to get on the road for his long drive home to Salt Lake City, he put coaches Charlie Fox and Cookie Lavagetto in charge and left the ballpark.

Mays wasn't the only player with a milestone to chase. Hart started the day batting .296 and stood to earn a hefty pay raise in 1966 if he could finish the season with a .300 average. He followed Mays's homer with a double, his 176th hit of the year in his 589th at-bat. He later tied the game, 3-3, scoring on a two-out single by Bob Barton.

One of the Giants called the press box to ask where Hart stood. The Giants statistician let them know he was batting .2988 and would need another hit. Hart responded with a leadoff triple to right in the sixth inning, giving him an average of precisely .300.

The next inning, McCool lost his ability to get anyone out. Two singles, a walk, an error, and another single plated three San Francisco runs, and the Reds turned to reliever Dom Zanni to face Hart, who was a home run shy of the cycle.

Instead, Hart flied out to right, bringing his average back down to .299 (.29949 to be precise). When acting manager Fox learned of the final outcome, he was livid with the press-box staff, suggesting that someone should have called the dugout to let them know Hart's average would slip below .300 with an out. "If I'd known that, Jimmy," Fox apologized, "I would have had you bunt."[11]

## SOURCES

In addition to the sources cited in the Notes, the author also accessed Baseball-Reference.com, Retrosheet.org, and Stathead.com.

https://www.baseball-reference.com/boxes/SFN/SFN196510030.shtml

https://www.retrosheet.org/boxesetc/1965/B10030SFN1965.htm

## NOTES

1 Four New York Giants teams had 24 or more wins in their final 33 games: 1916 (27-5), 1921 (24-9), 1928 (25-8), and 1951 (25-8). Sports Reference LLC, https://stathead.com/tiny/wS9TB.

2 Associated Press, "Franks: 'We Didn't Collapse,'" *Redwood City* (California) *Tribune*, October 4, 1965: 11.

3 Sports Reference LLC, https://stathead.com/tiny/LLH1G.

4 Five of which (three home runs and two doubles) came in an anomalous 7-6 11-inning affair against the Milwaukee Braves on September 22.

5 George Ross, "Champagne in L.A. – Party's Over in S.F.," *Oakland Tribune*, October 3, 1965: 39.

6 Willie Mays and Charles Einstein, *Willie Mays: My Life In and Out of Baseball* (New York: E.P. Dutton, 1972), 297.

7 Prescott Sullivan, "A Show of Gratitude," *San Francisco Examiner*, October 3, 1965: III-1; Bill Ford, "Reds Lose, 6-3, Finish 4th," *Cincinnati Enquirer*, October 4, 1965: 41; "5 Giant Fans Win New Cars," *Oakland Tribune*, October 4, 1965: E43.

8 The next day some Reds players upset the Giants by engaging in a game of touch football during batting practice, a taunt

referencing the "football score" they'd managed. "Reds Warm Up with Ball That Befits Score," *Sacramento Bee*, October 3, 1965: F1.

9 Ford, "Reds Lose, 6-3, Finish 4th."

10 Mays and Einstein, *Willie Mays: My Life*, 297.

11 Associated Press, "Franks: 'We Didn't Collapse.'"

# “THAT ONE KIND OF SANG ITSELF OUT OF THE PARK”: MAYS PASSES FOXX WITH 535TH CAREER HOMER

## August 17, 1966: San Francisco Giants 4, St. Louis Cardinals 3, at Candlestick Park, San Francisco

BY CREG STEPHENSON

IT WASN'T THE most important hit of the day for the San Francisco Giants, but it was the most historic.

On August 17, 1966, Willie Mays hit career home run number 535 at Candlestick Park in San Francisco, moving past Jimmie Foxx into second place on the all-time list behind only Babe Ruth's 714. The Giants won the game 4-3 on a pinch-hit, walk-off single by Jesús Alou in the bottom of the ninth.

The 35-year-old Mays connected in the fourth inning off Cardinals starter Ray Washburn, hitting a slider over the right-field wall for a solo home run. The blast cut an early St. Louis lead to 3-1.

“That one kind of sang itself out of the park,” Mays told the *San Francisco Examiner*.[1]

Mays had tied Foxx just the previous afternoon, going deep off St. Louis left-hander Al Jackson in the third inning of a 3-1 Giants victory. No other right-handed hitter in American or National League history had hit more home runs to that point.[2]

San Francisco was also in a closely contested battle for the NL pennant in August 1966, at the time hot on the trail of the first-place Pittsburgh Pirates. The Giants eventually finished 1½ games behind the Los Angeles Dodgers, with the Pirates three games back.

The Cardinals reached Giants ace Juan Marichal for three runs in the first two innings, with Lou Brock leading off the game with a home run to right field. St. Louis added two more runs in the second, the first on three straight singles by Charley Smith, Julian Javier, and Dal Maxvill, the second coming home when Washburn grounded into a double play.

Marichal retired Brock on a fly ball to end the inning but apparently reinjured a sore left ankle at some point during the at-bat. Lindy McDaniel came out of the bullpen for the fourth inning with his team down 3-1.

"My left ankle hurt me every time I followed through on a pitch," Marichal told reporters after the game. "I couldn't get the ball down. All the hits off me came on high pitches."[34]

McDaniel got through the third and fourth innings without giving up a run, allowing a two-out hit each time. Washburn retired the Giants one-two-three in the bottom of the third to keep his team on top 3-0.

Len Gabrielson led off the Giants' fourth by grounding out to second base. That brought up Mays, who had struck out on Washburn's slider in his first-inning plate appearance.

Washburn had no such good fortune this time, as Mays tagged his 3-and-2 offering into the wooden right-field bleachers. A 16-year-old East Oakland resident named Joseph Hustace tracked down the ball and returned it to Mays in exchange for $25 and two autographed baseballs.[5]

*Willie Mays took over second place on the all-time home run list when he passed Jimmie Foxx on August 17, 1966. SABR/ The Rucker Archive.*

"The pitch he hit was a slider that got up around the waist over the plate," Washburn told the *St. Louis Post-Dispatch*. "I got him out on the same pitch the first time but that one was lower.

"It was just one of those things. But I figured it was gone when he hit it with the wind blowing to right field the way it was."[6]

Mays, whose homer was his 30th of the season, got a standing ovation from the 21,956 in attendance.[7] He doffed his cap in appreciation after rounding the bases and before entering the dugout.[8]

History had been made, but the Giants still had a game to win. San Francisco got back-to-back two-out singles from Jim Ray Hart and Tom Haller later in the inning, but Ollie Brown grounded into a force out to end the threat with St. Louis still on top 3-1.

Meanwhile, McDaniel continued to hang zeroes on the Cardinals. He retired them in order in the fifth, and got out of the sixth by inducing Smith to hit into a 5-4-3 double play.

Mays struck out on a Washburn curveball in the bottom of the sixth, in which the Giants went down one-two-three. Both teams were sent down in order in the seventh, then McDaniel allowed only a two-out Tim McCarver single in a scoreless top of the eighth.

Washburn retired pinch-hitter Jim Davenport to start the eighth, but Bob Burda followed with a pinch-hit single and took second on an error by Brock in left field. Don Mason pinch-ran and came home when Tito Fuentes singled to center field, cutting the Cardinals' lead to 3-2.

Left-hander Joe Hoerner replaced Washburn and got Cap Peterson to fly out to center for the second out.[9] Mays worked a walk to move Fuentes into scoring position, and Willie McCovey followed with a single to center to score Fuentes and tie the game.

Nelson Briles then replaced Hoerner, who had retired just one of the three batters he faced. Briles struck out Hart to end the eighth.

Frank Linzy entered the game to pitch the ninth for San Francisco, with Davenport staying in to play second and Peterson remaining on in left. Linzy got Mike Shannon to fly out to right, then retired Smith and Javier on infield grounders, sending the game into the bottom of the ninth.

Haller singled off Briles to start the Giants' ninth. After Brown struck out. Davenport delivered what was described as a "perfect hit and run single"[10] that send Haller to third.

That brought up Alou,[11] who lined a single to right field that scored Haller and put San Francisco ahead. It was the Giants' fourth consecutive win and fifth in their past six games.

Pittsburgh lost later that night in New York to allow San Francisco to move within a half-game of first. Despite the Giants winning a key game in a pennant race, most of the postgame media attention was on Mays' home run.

California Governor Pat Brown[12] sent a congratulatory telegram to Mays, which read, "My heartiest congratulations on your tremendous achievement today in becoming second only to the great Babe Ruth in number of lifetime homers. We were with you all the way on that three and two pitch off Ray Washburn in the fourth. Keep going. In California we are used to setting records. My best personal regards and hopes that one day you will hit number 715."[13]

According to the *San Francisco Examiner*, an unidentified "well-wisher" in the Giants' clubhouse told Mays, "The pressure's off now, Willie. You won't have to worry anymore now until you hit No. 713." Mays quickly responded, "You guys are the ones who do the worrying, not me. I never worry."[14]

Dick Dietz, then a Giants rookie backup catcher who had just one hit (a single) in 22 at-bats that season, quipped, "What's all the fuss about? I'm only 535 home runs behind Mays right now. If I get real hot I might catch him."

Mays laughed and replied, "He's ahead of me in one department. I got a $5,000 bonus to sign. He (Dietz) got about $85,000."[15]

After an offday, Mays hit a two-run shot off Atlanta's Denny Lemaster on August 19 in an 8-5 Giants loss. He went deep again on August 20 – a solo blast against Tony Cloninger – in a 6-1 Giants win, giving him homers in four straight games.

Mays homered just three times in September and once on October 2, the final day of the regular season. He finished with 37 homers in 1966, and had 542 in his career to that point.

Mays' final batting line in 1966 was .288/.368/.566, with 29 doubles, 99 runs scored, and 103 RBIs in 629 plate appearances spread across 152 games. He finished third in the National League Most Valuable Player balloting behind Pittsburgh right fielder Roberto Clemente and Los Angeles pitcher Sandy Koufax, and won the 10th of his 12 consecutive Gold Gloves for fielding excellence.[16]

## SOURCES

In addition to the sources mentioned in the notes, the author consulted baseball-reference.com.

https://www.baseball-reference.com/boxes/SFN/SFN196608170.shtml

https://www.retrosheet.org/boxesetc/1966/B08170SFN1966.htm

## NOTES

1 James K. McGee, "It Sang Out of Park – Mays," *San Francisco Examiner*, August 18, 1966: 49.

2 Henry Aaron had hit career home run number 431 in Atlanta three days earlier and did not homer again until August 22 in Los Angeles, meaning he was more than 100 behind Mays at the time Mays hit his 535th. Aaron surpassed Mays with his 649th home run on June 10, 1972, in Philadelphia, then overtook Ruth with number 715 on April 8, 1974, in Atlanta. He finished his career in 1976 with a then-record 755.

3 "Marichal Re-Injures Ankle," *San Francisco Examiner*, August 18, 1966: 50.

4 Marichal returned to the rotation on August 23 and proceeded to pitch complete games in eight of his final 10 starts that season. The only two in which he didn't go the distance were when he worked eight innings in a 6-0 loss to the Cubs on September 9 and when he pitched nine in a 6-4, 10-inning victory over the Mets on September 17. He finished the season 25-6 with a 2.23 ERA and 25 complete games in 36 starts.

5 McGee, "It Sang Out of Park – Mays."

6 Ed Wilks (Associated Press), "Mays's Bag – 1 Foxx, 9 Birds," *St. Louis Post-Dispatch*, August 18, 1966: 14.

7 The home run was Mays' fourth in his previous six games. The Giants went 5-1 in those games.

8 Charles Doherty photos, *San Francisco Examiner,* August 18, 1966: 49-50.

9 Washburn pitched 7⅓ innings, allowing three runs on five hits with no walks and five strikeouts. He earned no decision, lowering his ERA to 3.74. Briles took the loss to fall to 4-12.

10 Harry Jupiter, "Don't Forget McDaniel in Tabbing Giants' Heroes," *San Francisco Examiner*, August 18, 1966: 49.

11 The youngest of three Alou brothers who played together with the Giants in 1963, Jesús was the only one remaining in San Francisco by 1966. Oldest brother Felipe Alou had been traded to Milwaukee in December 1963 in a seven-player deal that brought catcher Del Crandall (among others) to the Giants. Middle brother Matty Alou had been swapped to Pittsburgh for pitcher Joe Gibbon and utilityman Ozzie Virgil Sr. in December 1965.

12 Father of Jerry Brown, California's governor from 1975 to 1983 and again from 2011 to 2019.

13 Associated Press, "Great! – Pat Wires Mays," *San Francisco Examiner*, August 18, 1966: 50.

14 McGee, "It Sang Out of Park – Mays."

15 Jupiter, "Don't Forget McDaniel in Tabbing Giants' Heroes."

16 Mays did not receive a first-place MVP vote from members of the Baseball Writers Association of America in 1966 after winning the award for the second time the previous season. Clemente got eight of 20 first-place votes, Koufax nine, Philadelphia third baseman Dick Allen (who finished fourth) one and Felipe Alou – who finished fifth in the MVP voting in his first season with the Atlanta Braves – got two.

# MAYS HITS HIS 600TH HOMER AND FRANK TORRE CAN GO HOME NOW

## September 22, 1969: San Francisco Giants 4, San Diego Padres 2, at San Diego Stadium

BY LUIS BLANDON

HE WANTED TO go home.

Frank Torre had been on the road for weeks, waiting for Willie Mays to hit his 600th homer so Torre could shower him with gifts and go home. Once his baseball career ended, Torre became the manager of the professional division for the Adirondack Bat Company, whose bats Mays used. Torre "estimated he had seen 40 games, covered 12,000 miles and spent $4200 in travel costs, waiting for the historic blow."[1] Before the first of a three-game series between the Giants and Padres at San Diego Stadium on Monday evening, September 22, Torre took his seat behind the Giants dugout. Maybe this was the night.

Mays was stuck on 599 homers, second only to the revered 714. The race to 600 was taxing on Mays: "I had been trying too hard to hit home runs."[2] Mays wished to hit the historic homer at home in Candlestick Park. He started the season with 587 career homers and "[S]ince he needed only 13 to reach the magic mark, it was reasonable to assume that he'd be there by Mother's Day or at least by the Fourth of July."[3]

Although he was muscular and fit, time was creeping up on the 38-year-old Mays.[4] His five-tool supremacy was fading. He played the season with minor injuries, notably an injured left knee suffered in a home plate collision against the Cubs on July 29. The *San Francisco Chronicle*'s Bob Stevens observed, "[P]eople cringed in sympathy when (Mays) went on defense and stumbled and wobbled and did not get to some baseballs he would have gobbled up two years ago."[5] After hitting his 11th homer of the season on August 17, Mays hit his 12th (and his 599th career homer off the Atlanta Braves' Pat Jarvis on September 15.

The Giants and the Braves were in a fight for first place in the National League West and a playoff berth. The Giants were 86-67, in first place by a half-game (.004) over Atlanta. Mays told manager Clyde King that he could not start but was available to pinch-hit. Manager Preston Gomez's expansion Padres were in last place at 48-105, 38 games back, the worst record in baseball. "We can still be a spoiler," Gomez said.[6]

Selected from the Giants in the expansion draft, rookie right-hander Mike Corkins was on the rubber for the Padres in his fourth and last start of the season.[7] Left-handed prospect Ron Bryant was making his eighth start of the season for the Giants. The pitchers were roommates in the minors.[8]

The Giants took a 2-0 lead in the third inning. Bobby Bonds made the record books that frame when he struck out for the 176th time in the season, breaking the season strikeout record set in 1963 by Dave Nicholson of the Chicago White Sox.[9] The Padres responded with a single tally in the bottom of the third.

*Willie Mays began the 1969 season with 587 home runs and hit No. 600 on September 22, 1969. Courtesy National Baseball Hall of Fame.*

Early in the game, the Padres' scoreboard lit up with a promotional message: "Come tomorrow night and see Willie Mays hit no. 600."[10] Mays noticed, telling his teammates "Tomorrow night? I'm going to hit it tonight."[11]

The Padres tied the game in the bottom of the sixth. King replaced Jim Ray Hart in left (bruised right shoulder) with George Foster.[12] Bryant pulled a right rib-cage muscle on a pitch to the leadoff hitter Roberto Peña.[13] Don McMahon came in for relief and gave up the lead. Peña "walloped McMahon's first pitch to deep center for a double."[14] Peña attempted to stretch the hit into a triple but was thrown out after Ken Henderson fielded the ball and fired it to second baseman Ron Hunt, who threw to Tito Fuentes. Ollie Brown doubled to the wall in center. Al Ferrera struck out for the second out.

The next batter, Nate Colbert, laced a low liner down the right-field line toward the Giants' bullpen, driving in Brown to tie the game. Henderson attempted to catch the ball with a diving effort. He lay "stunned on the grass[;] the ball rolled" toward the fence.[15] Colbert rounded third with an apparent inside-the-park home run, when he suddenly retreated back to third after being given the stop sign by third-base coach George "Sparky" Anderson.[16]

"By dashing to the extremities of right field," Hunt caught up to the ball where one rarely sees a second baseman.[17] Hunt tossed the ball toward first base. Instinctively, from his shortstop position, Hal Lanier raced behind first base and threw home after catching Hunt's relay. Hunt and Lanier "did something outstanding on the spot thinking and made two fine relay throws to limit the Padres to one run in the sixth inning when they could have just as well scored three, or probably more runs."[18]

Hunt led off the top of the Giants' seventh and beat out a grounder for a single. King met Mays' eye and said, "[G]rab a bat" and pinch-hit for the rookie Foster.[19] "We didn't want to put too much pressure on the kid," Mays said."[20]

Mays knew little about Corkins: "Heck, he had been five years old when I broke in with the Giants."[21] Gomez and Corkins, though, recalled Mays hitting a homer off Corkins in spring training.[22] Press reports indicated that the first pitch to Mays was a low and outside fastball. Mays wrote that it was a belt-high fastball.[23] Mays "swung prodigiously and blasted the ball into the left field stands, 391 feet from the plate."[24] The baseball "arched toward the left-field seats, a tiny blur beneath the lights, the roar of the crowd swelled as Mays, his head lifted slightly, followed the flight of the historic bomb he had launched."[25] Hunt tracked the ball "going into the stands, he threw up his arms and started to dance in from second."[26] Mays jogged "shoulders sagged slightly and he dog-trotted, limping on his painful left knee. …"[27] It was Mays' second pinch-hit blast of the season.[28]

The Giants led 4-2. His teammates darted to home plate, greeting Mays in joy "screaming, hauling, tugging, laughing…"[29] "That was my biggest thrill. Seeing my teammates" gather at home to greet him, Mays said.[30] The 4,779 fans "clapped, stomped and cheered" with "[W]e Want Mays" chants.[31] Mays was "summoned twice from the dugout for encore bows."[32] He tipped his cap to the cheering Padres fans. Torre had been about to leave "[A]nd then it happened so suddenly … I didn't expect him to pinch-hit," and raced "to meet [Mays] by the time he circled the bases."[33] Giants utilityman Bob Burda snapped photos.[34]

After Willie McCovey singled to center off Corkins, Gomez brought in Frank Reberger to close out the inning. Play was halted at the end of the Giants' half of the seventh. Torre walked with Mays to home plate and presented him a huge trophy commemorating Mays' accomplishment. The *San Francisco Chronicle* editorial page wrote, "[T]his is the sort of performance to which we are accustomed but which also makes men into legends."[35]

Reberger pitched three scoreless relief innings. Mays led off the top of the ninth with a popup to Colbert at first.[36] The Padres were silenced by McMahon, who set them down in order in the last two innings, pitching four innings for his sixth win against six losses.

Corkins asked Gomez, "Why did it have to be me?"[37] Gomez, who had seen his share of Mays as a coach with the Dodgers, consoled him: "Just remember that the same thing has happened to a lot of other pitchers – and some great ones."[38] Corkins suffered his third loss against one win, pitching six uneven innings.[39]

In a game lasting 2:51, Mays' homer gave the Giants a 4-2 victory. Hunt and Lanier's defensive play prevented two Padres runs and a devastating loss during a pennant race on the night of Mays' 600th homer. If not for them, "Mays' homer might have meant no more than a personal achievement."[40]

After the game, Mays would not offer any words on how many home runs he had left in his bat or regarding Babe Ruth's 714: "I don't know how much longer I can play, but I think I'm playing all right now. If I stay healthy, I'll hit a few more home runs."[41] As it transpired, Mays had 60 homers left to hit.[42] On who would next reach 600, "The next one should be Henry Aaron (of the Braves)," Mays predicted.[43]

Mays said he did not care about personal achievements. The win mattered: "It was more of a thrill because the home run won the game."[44] "I knew I'd hit 600, but I was beginning to wonder when," Mays said.[45]

Mays said to the beat writers that his "600th homer means more than any other he had hit. 'It has to. It's worth about $30,000.'"[46] Adirondack gave Mays the trophy, a De Tomaso Mangusta Italian sports car, and 391 shares of company stock for the 391 feet Mays' homer trekked. At $9 a share, the stock was worth $3,519.[47] Mays noted: "For one thing, Frank Torre can go home now."[48]

## SOURCES

In addition to the sources cited in the Notes, the author consulted Baseball-Reference.com, Retrosheet.org, YouTube.com, and mlb.com.

*https://www.baseball-reference.com/boxes/SDN/SDN196909220.shtml*

*https://www.retrosheet.org/boxesetc/1969/B09220SDN1969.htm*

## NOTES

1 James K. McGee, "Mays: '600th Worth 30 G's,'" *San Francisco Examiner*, September 23, 1969: 56.

2 Associated Press, "Pinch Blast Breaks Tie, Saves Half-Game Margin," *Sacramento Bee*, September 23, 1969: B4.

3 Arthur Daley, "Sports of the Times: An Epic Home Run," *New York Times*, October 1, 1969: 50.

4 Mays was once asked what his proudest achievement in baseball was. It was his durability: "I came into the league with a 32-inch waist, and I retired with a 32-inch waist." See James S. Hirsch, "Willie Mays Carries the Torch for His Generation," *New York Times*, May 5, 2021 (Online).

5 James S. Hirsch, *Willie Mays: The Life, The Legend* (New York: Scribner, 2010), 485. In 1998 Bob Stevens was awarded the J.G. Taylor Spink Award by the Baseball Writers' Association of America for outstanding contributions to baseball writing. See http://baseballhall.org/discover/awards/j-g-taylor-spink/bob-stevens, accessed December 6, 2022.

6 Paul Cour, "Giants Bats Pose Woe in Series," *Evening Tribune* (San Diego, California), September 22, 1969: C-1.

7 Mike Corkins was signed by the San Francisco Giants as an amateur free agent before the 1965 season. He was drafted by the San Diego Padres from the Giants as the 31st pick in the 1968 expansion draft. He played for the Padres from 1969 to 1974. Prior to his call-up from the Eastern League Elmira Pioneers on August 12, 1969, Corkins tossed a 16-strikeout no-hitter against the Manchester Yankees. See "Corkins No-Hits Manchester," *Elmira* (New York) *Star-Gazette*, August 13, 1969: 31.

8 Corkins and Bryant were roommates in the Giants' minor-league system at Amarillo of the Texas League and Fresno of the California League.

9 Bobby Bonds ended the 1969 season with 187 strikeouts. He broke his record the following season with 189. As of 2023 Mark Reynolds held the record, striking out 223 times in 2009. For more about Dave Nicholson, see https://sabr.org/journal/article/dave-nicholson-revisited/. Willie Mays is the godfather of Bonds' son, Barry Bonds.

10 United Press International, "Willie Called 600th Homer," *San Francisco Examiner*, September 23, 1969: 53.

11 "Willie Called 600th Homer."

12 Pat Frizzell, "600th Didn't Come Easy," *Oakland Tribune*, September 23, 1969: 42.

13 Bryant pitched in relief in two more games in the season.

14 United Press International, "Mays Belts 600th Homer, S.F. Wins, 4-2," *Argus* (Fremont, California), September 23, 1969: 9.

15 James K. McGee, "Hal and Ron Share Giants' Hero Role," *San Francisco Examiner*, September 23, 1968: 53. After the game, Henderson learned that he had bruised his left shoulder on the attempt.

16 Phil Collier, "Mays' 600th HR Whips Padres, 4-2," *San Diego Union*, September 23, 1969: C-4.

17 Pat Frizzel, "Hunt's Hustle Giant Thing of Wonder," *The Sporting News*, October 11, 1969: 7.

18 McGee, "Hal and Ron Share Giants' Hero Role."

19 Hirsch, *Willie Mays: The Life, The Legend*, 486.

20 Ron Fimrite, "End of the Rainbow," *San Francisco Chronicle*, September 23, 1969: 45.

21 Willie Mays with Lou Sahadi, "*Say Hey*" (New York: Simon & Schuster, 1988), 241.

22 Frizzell, "600th Didn't Come Easy."

23 Mays, 242.

24 Pat Frizzell, "Willie Saves 4-2 Win," *Oakland Tribune*, September 23, 1969: 41.

25 Bob Stevens, "Mays' 600th HR Levels Padres, 4-2," *San Francisco Chronicle*, September 23, 1969: 45.

26 McGee, "Mays: 600th Worth 30 G's."

27 Stevens, "Mays' 600th HR Levels Padres, 4-2."

28 To watch Mays' 600th home run, see "Mays Hits His 600th Career Home Run," 2:30, January 28, 2015, MLB, https://www.youtube.com/watch?v=An6KEmXHeEU. Fifteen-year-old Al Frolander Jr. ran through the empty rows and grabbed the Mays ball after it landed. He gave up the ball to stadium ushers. He met Mays and was given a ball autographed by Mays and a new Giants hat. The homer ball was shipped with the bat to the Hall of Fame in Cooperstown. See Rick Smith, "Youth Ready for Mays' Rap, *Evening Tribune* (San Diego, California), September 23, 1969: C1. Also see Fimrite, "End of the Rainbow."

29 Stevens, "Mays' 600th HR Levels Padres, 4-2."

30 Fimrite.

31 McGee, "Mays: 600th Worth 30 G's."

32 United Press International. "Mays Belts 600th Homer, S.F. Wins, 4-2."

33 McGee, "Mays: '600th Worth 30 G's.'"

34 Frizzell, "Willie Saves 4-2 Win."

35 Editorials, "Willie Mays' 600th," *San Francisco Chronicle*, September 28, 1969: 44.

36 Mays had remained in the game playing center field.

37 Collier, "Mays' 600th HR Whips Padres, 4-2."

38 Collier. "It means a lot to me," Gomez said after the game. He saw an 18-year-old Mays play winter ball in Cuba.

39 Corkins allowed eight hits with five walks and four earned runs against four strikeouts. He appeared in a total of six games for San Diego that year with a record of 1-3 and an 8.47 ERA.

40 McGee, "Hal and Ron Share Giants' Hero Role."

41 Frizzell, "600th Didn't Come Easy."

42 Mays made it clear in 1966 that Ruth's 714 was beyond his ability to catch: "[M]an, that's a lot of home runs. I ain't trying to set records. I'm just trying to help the team win some games." See "There's Hope for Willie," *Ebony*, October 1966, Volume 12, Issue 12: 96.

43 Collier.

44 Frizzell, "Willie Saves 4-2 Win." With the win, the Giants remained in first, maintaining their .004 lead over Atlanta. The Giants failed to win the NL West, finishing second going 3-5 in their last eight games, 90-72 overall. Atlanta surged ahead, winning the division by three games.

45 Daley, "Sports of the Times: An Epic Home Run."

46 James K. McGee, "Not After Ruth's Record," *San Francisco Examiner*, September 23, 1969: 53.

47 McGee, "Not After Ruth's Record"; McGee, "Mays: '600th Worth 30 G's.'" For more on the De Tomaso Mangusta, see https://www.autoevolution.com/news/detomaso-mangusta-the-american-powered-italian-supercar-created-to-spite-carroll-shelby-168552.html. In January 2022, a 1969 De Tomaso Mangusta with 6,876 miles was sold for $400,000. See https://www.classic.com/m/de-tomaso/mangusta/, accessed December 16, 2022.

48 Frizzell, "600th Didn't Come Easy."

# WILLIE MAYS JOINS THE 3,000-HIT CLUB

## July 18, 1970: San Francisco Giants 10, Montreal Expos 1, at Candlestick Park, San Francisco

BY DOUGLAS JORDAN

**WILLIE MAYS IS** arguably the greatest baseball player of all time.[1] He was the quintessential five-tool player. He could hit for power (660 career home runs), hit for average (.301 career batting average), run quickly (338 stolen bases), play great defense ("The Catch" in the 1954 World Series), and had a tremendous arm. He was an All-Star for 19 consecutive seasons and won the National League MVP Award in 1954 and 1965. Mays was inducted into the Hall of Fame in 1979.

It took Mays 13 at-bats to get his first hit as a New York Giants rookie in 1951. That initial hit was a home run off future Hall of Famer, and future teammate, Warren Spahn.[2] He averaged an impressive 185 hits a year from 1954 to 1965, and his 190 safeties led baseball in 1960. Mays reached 1,000 hits with a single in his 838th game, on June 23, 1958, the Giants' first season after they moved to San Francisco. He had his 2,000th hit 844 games later, reaching that milestone with an RBI double on September 1, 1963.

By the end of the 1969 season, Mays had played in 894 more games and collected 926 more hits, which left him 74 hits short of 3,000. Mays managed 14 safeties in April 1970 and tallied 29 hits in May and 20 more in June, for a total of 2,989.

As July began, Mays produced one hit in three home games against the Los Angeles Dodgers, then eight more during a seven-game road trip to Atlanta and Houston. After appearing in his 21st career All-Star Game on July 14, Mays began the season's second half with a homestand, needing only two hits to achieve the milestone.

The first game after the All-Star break was played on July 17 against the Montreal Expos. Mays was hitless in his first three at-bats but clobbered a three-run homer in his final at-bat of the game. He was sitting on 2,999 hits going into Saturday afternoon's game with the Expos on July 18.

The Giants were in fourth place in the NL West, four games under .500 at 41-45 and 20 games behind the first-place Cincinnati Reds with their stellar 63-27 record. The Expos, in their second season as an expansion franchise, were in last place in the NL East with a 38-51 record, 12 games behind the Pittsburgh Pirates.

Gaylord Perry started for San Francisco, four days after allowing two runs in two innings in the All-Star Game. The 31-year-old surreptitious spitballer had already won 13 games, and he was on his way to his best season as a Giant, winning 23 games and placing second in the NL Cy Young Award voting.

Montreal countered with Mike Wegener, who was 1-2 going into the tilt, in the second season of his two-year major-league career. The 39-year-old Mays, playing his customary center field, was batting third for the San Franciscans. The 28,879 fans who attended the game at Candlestick Park hoped to witness history.

Perry retired the Expos in order in the first. In the bottom half of the inning, Mays got his first opportunity to reach the milestone, batting with runners on the corners and nobody out. He walked to load the bases for Willie McCovey, who earned an RBI with a fielder's-choice grounder. A sacrifice fly by catcher Dick Dietz – like Mays, Perry, and McCovey, a 1970 NL All-Star – made the score 2-0.

Struggling with his control, Wegener walked the next two batters, bringing shortstop Hal Lanier to the plate with the bases loaded. Lanier's double to left field drove in three runs to put San Francisco ahead, 5-0.

Repeating his first-inning performance, Perry set down the side without allowing a baserunner in the second. Wegener retired the first two batters he faced in the bottom half of the inning, which brought Mays to the plate again, still one hit away from the milestone.

The slugger fell behind in the count, but then pulled a groundball between third and short, bounding across Candlestick Park's artificial turf. It got through untouched for the 3,000th hit of his storied career.

Discussing the at-bat later, Mays said, "I hit a slider. The count was 0-and-2 and I was looking for anything close. None of the pitches Wegener threw me the first time I was up were close."[3]

After stepping on the bag at first, Mays walked slowly toward the Giants dugout on the first-base side as teammates and dignitaries came out to congratulate him. Among the luminaries were National League President Charles Feeney; a fellow member of the 3,000-Hit Club, Stan Musial; Hall of Famer Carl Hubbell; and Monte Irvin, who helped Mays get his start in baseball.

The ball Mays hit had been thrown in, and Feeney handed it to Mays.[4] Mays acknowledged the ovation from the crowd with a tip of his cap.[5] After the celebration, McCovey came to bat. His double to left-center field drove home Mays from first, making the Giants lead 6-0.

Perry again retired the side in order in the third inning. In the bottom half of the inning, Perry came to bat with Lanier on first base. For just the second time in his nine-year career, and the only time that season, Perry slammed a home run. That put San Francisco ahead 8-0.[6]

The Expos did not manage a baserunner against Perry until Mack Jones walked with one out in the fourth. Marv Staehle's double with one out in the sixth was the first hit Perry allowed. The two-bagger scored Jim Fairey with what turned out to be Montreal's only run of the game.

San Francisco responded with two runs in its half of the sixth, with Perry and Mays playing significant roles. Perry led off with his second extra-base hit of the game, a double, and scored when Bobby Bonds followed with a double. One out later, Mays singled for his 3,001st hit, sending in Bonds for a 10-1 lead.

Perry threw a complete game, allowing four hits and one run. He also recorded five putouts, tying a record for NL pitchers.[7]

At the postgame interview Mays said, "Right now, I don't feel excitement about this. A reaction may set in later, and in a few days, maybe I will. But the main thing I wanted to do was to help Gaylord Perry win a game. I don't like to talk about goals, but maybe I have a goal – to help the guys win. I wasn't going to worry about this thing at all. I thought about it sure, there were two photographers at my house this morning. I couldn't help but be reminded."[8]

The team presented Mays with a large cake after the game, and team owner Horace Stoneham promised $3,000 per year for four years toward the college education of Mays's 11-year-old son, Michael.[9]

Mays became the 10th major leaguer with 3,000 hits, reaching the milestone two months after Henry Aaron, who started with the Milwaukee Braves three years after Mays broke in with the Giants in 1951. Before Aaron and Mays, it had been 12 years since the last man to break the barrier, Stan Musial, had done so, in 1958. Mays joined Aaron as only the second major leaguer with 3,000 hits and 500 home runs.[10]

*Willie Mays was the 10th player in MLB history to record 3,000 hits. Courtesy National Baseball Hall of Fame.*

Mays played for three more seasons after his 3,000th safety, finishing his career with 3,283 hits.

***Acknowledgments***

Many thanks to John Fredland for carefully reading the first draft of this article. His suggestions significantly improved the final product. The article was fact-checked by Kevin Larkin and copy-edited by Len Levin.

***Author's note***

Mays had 10 hits for the Birmingham Black Barons of the Negro American League in 1948. In 2020 Major League Baseball included the 1948 Negro American League season among its list of Negro League seasons recognized as "major league." If those hits are added to Mays' total, he reached 3,000 hits 15 days before this game, with a single off fellow Hall of Famer Don Sutton in the Giants' July 3 home game against the Dodgers.

## SOURCES

In addition to the sources cited in the Notes, I used Baseball-Reference.com and Retrosheet.org for team, season, and player pages and logs and the box scores and play-by-plays for this game.

https://www.baseball-reference.com/boxes/SFN/SFN197007180.shtml

https://www.retrosheet.org/boxesetc/1970/B07180SFN1970.htm

## NOTES

1 There is not a definitive answer to who was the best player in baseball history. But there is no question that Willie Mays is in the discussion. Maury Allen (*Baseball's 100*, 1981) and Joe Posnanski (*The Baseball 100*, 2021) have him ranked first in their books of the top 100 players. Bill James (*The New Bill James Historical Abstract*, 2001) has him third. *Baseball Egg* has a comparison of nine different lists of the top 100 players. Mays is first on The Athletic.com list, second at Baseball Egg, ESPN, *Bleacher Report*, and *The Sporting News*, and is third at The Baseball Scholar and Beyond the Boxscore. Baseball Egg, "Comparing Top 100 All-Time Baseball Player Lists, https://baseballegg.com/comparing-baseball-all-time-top-100 (last accessed May 10, 2022).

2 Spahn and Mays were briefly teammates on the San Francisco Giants in 1965, the final season of Spahn's Hall of Fame career.

3 Pat Frizzell, "'No Goals, Just Help Giants Win,' Says 3,000-Hit Willie," *Sporting News*, August 1, 1970: 6.

4 The ball is now in Cooperstown at the Baseball Hall of Fame.

5 The description is transcribed from footage of the hit provided by major league baseball. MLB.com, "Mays Joins the 3,000-Hit Club," https://www.mlb.com/giants/video/mays-joins-the-3-000-hit-club-c14387145 (last accessed March 7, 2022).

6 There's an interesting story associated with Perry's first home run. In 1964 Perry was in his third year with the Giants when a reporter made a favorable comment about Perry's hitting to Alvin Dark (Perry's manager). Dark commented, "Mark my words, a man will land on the moon before Perry hits a home run." Perry was pitching for Giants on July 20, 1969, when Apollo 11 landed on the moon. The landing was announced over the public-address system during the game. Perry hit the first home run of his career about 30 minutes later. The web site is Chris Landers, Cut4, MLB.com, "The Story of Gaylord Perry, the Moon Landing and a Most Unlikely Home Run," https://www.mlb.com/cut4/gaylord-perry-hits-home-run-just-minutes-after-neil-armstrong-moon-landing-c2433 (last accessed May 23, 2022).

7 Jim McGee, "Mays' Memorable Bouncer," *San Francisco Examiner*, July 19, 1970: Section C, 1.

8 Frizzell, "'No Goals, Just Help Giants Win,' Says 3,000-Hit Willie."

9 Frizzell.

10 As of 2022, five more players have reached 3,000 hits and 500 home runs: Eddie Murray, Rafael Palmeiro, Alex Rodriguez, Albert Pujols, and Miguel Cabrera.

# WILLIE MAYS HOMERS IN NEW YORK METS DEBUT

## May 14, 1972: New York Mets 5, San Francisco Giants 4, at Shea Stadium

BY KEVIN LARKIN

IN HIS NOVEL *You Can't Go Home Again*, Thomas Wolfe tells the story of a man returning to his hometown in search of his identity. In May 1972, Willie Mays was sort of a George Webber-like character when he came to the Mets after spending the first 21 years of his career with the Giants – for 15 years in San Francisco and, before that, for six years in New York.

The Mets acquired the future Hall of Famer on May 11 for Charlie Williams and $50,000 and Mays debuted three days later, coincidentally, against the Giants at Shea Stadium. With 646 home runs, 1,859 RBIs, 3,187 hits, and countless defensive gems under his belt, Mays was an unquestioned all-time great.

Now, his role would be far less significant – even though his legend had yet to diminish.

Mets owner Joan Payson was in attendance on this Mother's Day 1972 to watch Mays play. Early in her career Payson had acquired shares in the New York Giants team. Now as part-owner of the New York Mets, she was the third woman to have an ownership stake in a major-league ballclub.[1]

On May 14, Mays played first base and led off against Giants starting pitcher Sam McDowell, who entered the day with a 5-0 record. Pitching for the Mets was Ray Sadecki, without a decision so far in the young season.

Sadecki got the Giants out in the first inning with the only trouble being a double to right field by Tito Fuentes with one out. Fuentes was left stranded and Mays stepped up to the plate for the Mets in the bottom of the first. He walked. So did the next two batters. All three came around to score on a grand slam by Rusty Staub – a four-run New York frame.

Sadecki kept up the good work in the second inning, allowing just a one-out single to Giants third baseman Jim Ray Hart. McDowell settled down, getting the Mets in order including a strikeout of Mays for the third out of the inning.

In the Giants' third, all they could muster for an offense was a one-out single to center field by Fuentes. McDowell then dominated the New York lineup, getting three outs on a fly ball, a strikeout, and a groundout.

It was a 1, 2, 3 inning for Sadecki and the Mets in the top of the fourth. McDowell faltered just a bit for the Giants as he allowed a double to left field by Jim Fregosi. After intentionally walking the Mets catcher, Jerry Grote, McDowell put out this fire by striking out his mound counterpart Sadecki to end the inning.

Sadecki came unraveled in the fifth inning: He walked the leadoff batter, Fran Healy. Bernie Williams pinch-hit for McDowell, and tripled to score Healy with the Giants' first run of the game. Chris Speier, the Giants shortstop, doubled to right field to score Williams and then Fuentes hit a two-run home run to tie the score at 4-4. There were still no outs, but Sadecki struck out Bobby Bonds and got both Dave Kingman and Ken Henderson to fly out.

Don Carrithers replaced McDowell on the mound in the bottom of the fifth, and was to face the number one, two, and three hitters in the Mets lineup: Willie Mays, Bud Harrelson, and Tommie Agee. Mays got his first hit as a Met, a home run to left field that sent the Mets ahead again, 5-4.[2] Agee walked and stole second base. Staub was intentionally walked, but the runners were left stranded when Cleon Jones hit into a 4-6-3 double play to end the inning.

The sixth inning was of little excitement to either team. Hart singled to center field off reliever Jim McAndrew, who had replaced Sadecki. McAndrew got the next three outs to leave Hart stranded at first base. Jim Barr replaced Carrithers and, after giving up a single to Ted Martinez, got Grote to ground into an inning-ending 4-6-3 double play.

Speier led off the seventh inning by grounding out to second base. Fuentes, who had been a pain to every pitcher the Mets used, got his fourth hit of the day, a double to right field. However, he remained at second base as McAndrew got the next two hitters to fly out. With Barr still pitching for the Giants, McAndrew struck out, Mays walked for the second time in the game, but was thrown out trying to steal second base, and Harrelson flied out to right field.

San Francisco was down to its final six outs. McAndrew retired the first two batters in the Giants eighth on a flyout and groundout. Garry Maddox doubled to right field but Dave Rader, batting for Fran Healy, stranded Maddox when he grounded out to the shortstop, Harrelson. In the bottom of the inning, Barr struck out Agee, Staub, and Jones. Now it was the top of the ninth and the Giants were down to their final three outs.

McAndrew was still on the mound for the Mets and the Giants sent up Al Gallagher to hit for Barr. He grounded out to McAndrew on a comebacker. Speier grounded out to shortstop for out number two. Now it was the Giants' last chance. Fuentes, who had tormented the Mets so far, walked to reach base for the fifth time in the game. But Bobby Bonds struck out to end the game.

Mays had pulled out some of that "Say Hey" magic one last time; his home run was the winning margin of victory for the Mets. After the game, Mays said, "That was my first hit as a Met. And my first hit as a Giant was a home run, too."[3]

He played in a total of 135 games for the Mets, he ended his career with 660 home runs (placing him fifth all-time). He also ended up with 3,283 hits and 1,903 runs batted in. Mays announced his retirement after Game Two of the 1973 World Series pitting the Mets against the Oakland Athletics.[4]

## SOURCES

The author consulted Baseball-Reference.com and Retrosheet.org,

## NOTES

1 Payson followed Helene Hathaway Britton who had a ownership with the St Louis Cardinals (1911-1917) and Grace

Comiskey who had partial ownership of the Chicago White Sox between 1940 and 1956.

2 Joseph Durso, "Mets Win on Mays's Homer, 5-4," *New York Times*, May 15, 1972: 47.

3 Ibid. After going 0-for-12 in his first three games as a Giant, Mays homered off future Hall of Famer Warren Spahn of the Boston Braves at the Polo Grounds on May 28, 1951.

4 Phil Pepe, "Willie Mays Retires After Game 2 of the World Series in 1973," *New York Daily News*, October 15, 1973.

# MAYS'S 660TH AND FINAL HR GOES FOR NAUGHT IN NAILBITER LOSS

## August 17, 1973: Cincinnati Reds 2, New York Mets 1 (10 innings), at Shea Stadium, New York

BY KURT BLUMENAU

WILLIE MAYS HIT his first big-league home run in New York City on May 28, 1951, connecting off Boston Braves ace Warren Spahn in the first inning of a game at the Polo Grounds.[1]

His legend entrenched but his skills eroded, Mays also hit the 660th and last homer of his career in New York, on August 17, 1973. He was playing for the New York Mets at Shea Stadium, neither of which existed in 1951.[2]

Further emphasizing the passage of time, the Braves had moved twice since Mays' first homer –to Milwaukee in 1953, then to Atlanta in 1966. Spahn, eight years retired, was employed in August 1973 as the pitching coach of the Cleveland Indians. And the pitcher Mays victimized for his last homer, Cincinnati Reds left-hander Don Gullett, was less than five months old at the time of his first.[3]

Mays' final round-tripper came in the context of a nailbiter game between the Mets and the Reds, the team New York unexpectedly faced in the National League Championship Series later in the season.

Coming into the August 17 game, manager Yogi Berra's Mets sat in sixth (and last) place in the NL East Division with a 53-65 record, 7½ games behind the first-place St. Louis Cardinals. No team had pulled away from the pack: St. Louis, at 62-59, was the division's only team above .500.[4] The Pittsburgh Pirates, three-time defending division champions, were struggling after the death of Roberto Clemente in an offseason plane crash, as well as former pitching ace Steve Blass's baffling, near-complete loss of effectiveness.[5]

The Mets had played sub-.500 ball in May, June, and July, hamstrung by early injuries to key players, including John Milner, Felix Millan, Bud Harrelson, Cleon Jones, and Jerry Grote.[6] Mays, at age 42, suffered from cracked ribs, a right-shoulder injury, and knee problems during what he had already decided

FINAL
DAILY NEWS
NEW YORK'S PICTURE NEWSPAPER ®
MORE THAN TWICE THE CIRCULATION OF ANY OTHER PAPER IN AMERICA

**METS FALL, 2-1; MAYS HRS**

*Willie Mays hit the 660th and final home run of his career against Cincinnati Reds left-hander Don Gullett.*

would be his final season.[7] When he played, he was ineffective. His average stayed below .200 until July 8, and entering the game with Cincinnati, he was hitting just .212 with five home runs.[8]

Manager Sparky Anderson's star-packed Reds were in the thick of the NL West race, one year after losing a hard-fought, seven-game World Series to the Oakland A's. The Reds entered the game with a 74-48 record, 2½ games behind the Los Angeles Dodgers. Pete Rose, in left field in 1973, was leading the league in hits on August 17. Teammates Johnny Bench and Tony Perez were, respectively, first and fourth in RBIs, while Joe Morgan led the league in stolen bases and ranked near the top in doubles and walks. The Reds went 8-4 against the Mets in the regular season, including four wins in six matchups at Shea.

To open a four-game series, New York sent lefty George Stone to the mound. An offseason pickup from the Atlanta Braves, Stone pitched well for the Mets in 1973, entering the game with a 7-3 record and a 2.99 ERA. He'd worked eight innings to beat the Reds on July 14.

Cincinnati countered with Gullett, who entered with a 14-8 record and a 3.59 ERA. While Gullett primarily worked as a starter in 1973, his three previous appearances against the Mets had all come in relief. He'd earned a win on June 5 and taken the loss against Stone on July 14.

The first three innings passed without major incident before a Friday night crowd of 36,803. Home-plate umpire Shag Crawford, suffering flu-like symptoms, left after the first inning. First-base ump Doug Harvey replaced him, and the game proceeded with three umpires.[9]

The Reds collected two singles in the second inning and the Mets one, but both teams hit into double plays that killed momentum. In the third, the Mets' Ted Martinez reached second base on a one-out single followed by a sacrifice, but Wayne Garrett's grounder ended the inning.

First baseman Mays, who had flied out in the first inning, returned to the plate with one out in the fourth. Mays entered the game hitting 2-for-12 lifetime (.167) against Gullett. He'd taken the lefty deep once before, while playing for the San Francisco Giants, in Gullett's first major-league start, on June 22, 1970.[10] That game was also Gullett's first big-league loss, as the Giants chased him in the third inning of an eventual 13-6 victory.

This time, on a 2-and-2 count, Mays drove a Gullett pitch to the opposite field, over the 371-foot marker in right-center, for the game's first run. Only two batters in major-league history had hit more homers at that point: Babe Ruth, with 714, and Henry Aaron of the Braves, who notched number 703 the same night against the Montreal Expos.[11] The Shea scoreboard lit up with the word "WILLIE" while Mays rounded the bases.[12]

As Stone continued to shut down the Reds, the Mets wasted chances to score. Martinez doubled to left in the fifth; Stone and Garrett stranded him. A pair of singles in the Mets sixth put runners at the corners with two out, but catcher Grote's grounder to first ended the rally.

In the Cincinnati seventh, Morgan set the table by drawing a leadoff walk and stealing second. Dan Driessen's fly ball, Perez's liner to Garrett at third, and a grounder to the mound by Bench – playing right field, rather than catcher – kept the score at 1-0.[13]

Stone's throw to first base on Bench's grounder put Mays in Bench's path, setting the stage for a jolting collision between the future Hall of Famers. After a brief pause, both men took to their feet, and Mays returned to play the eighth inning at first base. He was called out on strikes to end the bottom of the eighth, then was replaced by Ed Kranepool for the ninth.[14]

Entering the final frame, Stone had allowed the Reds just two hits – the long-ago second-inning singles by Perez and Andy Kosco. Relying on what one writer called "an enduring assortment of junk,"[15] he dispatched Rose on a liner and Morgan on a grounder, putting the Mets one out away from a 1-0 win.

But rookie Driessen, playing third base, singled into center field. Perez, with an 0-and-2 count, singled him to second with a weak grounder to the left side. And Bench smacked a two-strike single through the left side, scoring Driessen to tie the game, 1-1.[16] Perhaps too late, Berra summoned righty Harry Parker from the New York bullpen. Parker got Bobby Tolan, batting for Kosco, to end the inning with an infield pop.

The Mets wasted a leadoff single by Jones in the ninth. Tolan gathered in Milner's hard-hit fly with a leap at the center-field wall,[17] and Grote hit his second double-play ball of the game. The teams headed into extra innings with Parker on the mound for New York and righty Pedro Borbón working for Cincinnati.[18]

Anderson led off the 10th by summoning a secret weapon of sorts, sending Hal King to hit for catcher Bill Plummer. The *New York Times* described King as "a part-time player who does not hit very often, but who hits home runs almost exclusively when he does."[19] King had collected only four hits thus far in 1973 – but half of them were pinch-homers.[20] King came through again on a 1-and-1 count, drilling a Parker curveball solidly into the right-field bullpen for a 2-1 Reds lead.[21]

The Reds couldn't add to their lead, but the Mets did not rally. In the bottom half of the 10th, Borbón got center fielder Don Hahn to fly out, then got pinch-hitters Ken Boswell and Jim Beauchamp to ground out and strike out. The game ended in 2 hours and 23 minutes, with Borbón earning the win and Parker taking the loss. By coincidence, King's homer – like Mays' – was his last in the majors; he finished his career in 1974 with 24 homers.

After August 17, Mays played 12 more regular-season games, collecting five more hits and four more RBIs. He appeared in only three games in September, the last on September 9. During his near-total absence from the lineup, his teammates mounted a finishing sprint to remember. From September 1 through the end of the regular season, the Mets went 20-8, closing a 5½-game deficit and rising from fifth place to first. New York clinched the NL East title with a 6-4 win over the Chicago Cubs on the season's final day.

Included on the postseason roster, Mays played in one game of the National League Championship Series. He delivered a key pinch-hit on an infield chopper in the decisive Game Five as the Mets upset the favored Reds. Mays then played in three games of the World Series against Oakland, going 2-for-7 (.286) with one RBI. He made his last big-league appearance in Game Three on October 16. Pinch-hitting for Tug McGraw, he grounded into a fielder's choice to end the 10th inning of a game that – like the Series – the Mets lost.

## SOURCES

In addition to the specific sources cited in the Notes, the author used the Baseball-Reference.com and Retrosheet.org websites for general player, team, and season data and the box scores for this game.

https://www.baseball-reference.com/boxes/NYN/NYN197308170.shtml

https://www.retrosheet.org/boxesetc/1973/B08170NYN1973.htm

## NOTES

1 This was Mays' fourth game with the Giants and first home game. The homer off Spahn was Mays' first National League hit, snapping an 0-for-12 hitless streak (including two walks) in his first three games.

2 The Mets entered the NL as an expansion team for the 1962 season, five years after the NL's Brooklyn Dodgers and New York Giants left New York City for Los Angeles and San Francisco. Shea Stadium opened in 1964.

3 Gullett was born January 6, 1951.

4 The Mets were the only NL East team to finish 1973 with a winning record, at 82-79. Second-place St. Louis posted a .500 record at 81-81.

5 Blass went from a 19-8 record and 2.49 ERA in 1972 to 3-9 and 9.85 in 1973, in a downfall he was never able to explain or remedy. He left the majors after a single appearance in 1974 and subsequently became a longtime broadcaster for the Pirates.

6 On June 6, the *New York Daily News* ran a chart of significant Mets injuries to that time, including a broken left hand for Harrelson, a sore right hand for Jones, a jammed left ankle for Millan, and a broken right wrist for Grote – as well as a right-shoulder injury for Mays. The chart omitted Milner, who went on the disabled list in late April with a pulled hamstring, and Ed Kranepool and Harry Parker, who were hampered by pulled muscles around the same time. "Medical Chart: Prognosis Sickly," *New York Daily News,* June 6, 1973: C22; Dick Young, "Mets to Lose Milner; Krane Hurt, Too," *New York Daily News,* April 27, 1973: C22.

7 John Saccoman, "Willie Mays," SABR Biography Project, accessed October 27, 2022; "Medical Chart: Prognosis Sickly."

8 In another measure of his struggles in 1973, Mays ended the season with a Wins Above Replacement total of 0.0. For context, Mays posted double-digit WAR in six seasons, led the NL nine times, and accumulated a career WAR total of 156.1, fifth-best in history as of 2022.

9 Associated Press, "Rally Makes Soothsayer of Shepard," *Springfield* (Ohio) *Daily News,* August 18, 1973: 8.

10 Gullett made 18 relief appearances for the 1970 Reds prior to making his first start. Although he spent most of his big-league career as a starter, Gullett made only two starts in 44 appearances with the Reds in his rookie season. Unusually for him, he had more saves (six) than wins (five) in 1970.

11 Joseph Durso, "Homer in 10th by Hal King Decides It," *New York Times,* August 18, 1973: Sports: 15; Associated Press, "Rally Makes Soothsayer of Shepard." Coincidentally, Frank Robinson of the California Angels hit his 545th homer that same night, moving him ahead of Harmon Killebrew into fourth place at the time. Steve Wilstein (United Press International), "Nolan Ryan's Arm Causing Problems," *Mansfield* (Ohio) *News Journal,* August 18, 1973: 9. For reference, Japanese home-run king Sadaharu Oh, who began his career eight seasons after Mays in 1959, reached 660 home runs during the 1975 season. He finished with 868.

12 Photo and caption, *New York Daily News,* August 18, 1973: 36.

13 Playing a catcher in the outfield or at first base is a common strategy to lighten the workload on the catcher's legs while keeping his bat in the lineup. In 1973 Bench made 23 appearances in right field, 4 at first base, and 1 at third. At the end of his career in 1982-83, the Reds shifted Bench almost exclusively to third and first base.

14 Bob Hertzel, "Reds Win in 'Kingly' Fashion," *Cincinnati Enquirer,* August 18, 1973: 17. Wirephotos of the collision also ran in various newspapers, including the *Sidney* (Ohio) *Daily News,* August 18, 1973: 8.

15 Red Foley, "Reds Pinch Mets with a HR in 10th," *New York Daily News,* August 18, 1973: 28.

16 Hertzel, "Reds Win in 'Kingly' Fashion"; Foley.

17 Foley.

18 Following a brawl between the Reds and Mets in Game Three of the NLCS that fall, Borbón famously picked up a Mets cap left behind in the scuffle and tried to take a bite out of it. Jorge Iber, "Pedro Borbón," SABR Biography Project, accessed October 27, 2022. In "Mets Redux," his essay summarizing the 1973 season, legendary baseball writer Roger Angell of *The New Yorker* reported that the cap belonged to pitcher Buzz Capra. Roger Angell, *Five Seasons: A Baseball Companion* (New York: Simon & Schuster, 1977), 134.

19 Durso, "Homer in 10th by Hal King Decides It."

20 King hit pinch-hit round-trippers against the Dodgers on July 1 and the Expos on July 9. He had also hit a homer in a game he started on June 20 against San Francisco.

21 Hertzel, "Reds Win in 'Kingly' Fashion."

# SAY "OH, NO!" TO "SAY HEY" ONE LAST TIME: WILLIE MAYS HELPS METS PREVAIL IN 12 INNINGS IN WORLD SERIES GAME TWO

## October 14, 1973: New York Mets 10, Oakland Athletics 7, at Oakland-Alameda County Coliseum

BY FREDERICK C. BUSH

**AFTER LOSING A** tight 2-1 decision in Game One of the 1973 World Series, the New York Mets hoped to salvage a split of the first two games against the Athletics in front of 49,151 spectators on a Sunday afternoon in Oakland. The starters for Game Two, the Mets' Jerry Koosman and the Athletics' Vida Blue, were two of the top lefties in the majors, so another pitching duel appeared to be the order for the day. That turned out not to be the case, however, as both starters were long gone by the time New York finished a 10-7 victory in 12 innings that took a record 4 hours and 13 minutes to complete.[1] Though 17 runs were scored in the game, the focus was on the many errors that affected the game's course and final outcome. The A's committed five errors – one short of the record set by the Chicago White Sox in Game Five of the 1917 World Series against the Mets' predecessors, the New York Giants – and their last two errors cost them the game.

The A's struck immediately against Koosman, taking a 2-0 lead in the bottom of the first. Cleon Jones belted a homer to lead off the second and cut the lead in half, but Oakland quickly recouped that run in the bottom of the frame when Joe Rudi's single drove home Bert Campaneris, who had hit a one-out triple. Wayne Garrett launched the Mets' second solo homer of the day in the top of the third to close the gap to 3-2.

In the bottom of the third Gene Tenace drew a one-out walk, Jesus Alou singled, and Ray Fosse was safe on Koosman's errant throw to first baseman John Milner. Manager Yogi Berra gave his starter a quick hook and brought in reliever Ray Sadecki, who managed to escape the bases-loaded jam without allowing another run and then pitched a scoreless fourth.

After Harry Parker kept the A's off the board in the fifth, the Mets took their first lead in the top of the sixth. Blue issued a one-out walk to Jones and allowed a single to Milner, causing his day on the mound also to come to an end. Reliever Horacio Pina threw gasoline on the fire rather than throwing strikes past Mets batters. He hit Jerry Grote with a pitch and allowed consecutive RBI singles by Don Hahn and Bud Harrelson, after which he was quickly pulled from the mound by Oakland manager Dick Williams. Pina's successor, Darold Knowles, did not fare any better as he "awkwardly tumbled down the mound while fielding a bases-loaded comebacker"[2] from Jim Beauchamp and flipped an errant throw to catcher Fosse that allowed two additional runs to score and gave the Mets a 6-3 advantage. Knowles settled down and kept New York from inflicting further damage over the course of 1⅔ innings of work.

Tug McGraw, the Mets' fourth pitcher of the day, took the mound in the bottom of the sixth. From that point through the eighth inning, he allowed only one run, which scored when Reggie Jackson drove home Campaneris with a double in the seventh.

In the top of the ninth, with the score still 6-4, Rusty Staub hit a leadoff single against Blue Moon Odom and was replaced by pinch-runner Willie Mays. The "Say Hey Kid" was playing out his final season and no longer had the spring of youth in his step, a fact that soon became evident. After Jones fouled out, Milner rapped a single to right field on which Mays should have been able to reach third, but Mays missed second base and then stumbled and fell. After the game, the 42-year-old Mays explained, "Rather than embarrass myself, I stopped. I don't know how it happened that I missed the bag. I guess it was trying to do two things at the same time – watch the ball and touch the bag."[3] Mays' misstep

*His career nearly over, Willie Mays batted .286 in the 1973 World Series and drove home one important run. Courtesy National Baseball Hall of Fame.*

on the basepaths turned out to be inconsequential as Grote fouled out and Hahn grounded out to shortstop for the third out.

Of greater importance was Mays' next mishap with his footing after he took his familiar position in center field in the bottom of the inning. Oakland pinch-hitter Deron Johnson led off with a long fly ball to center field. Mays lost sight of the ball and "then slipped, pitching headlong on the turf and tried to reach out at the last instant with his bare hand to grab it"[4] as the ball got past him for a double. Broadcaster Curt Gowdy lamented on air, "Ten years ago he would have put that ball in his back pocket."[5] Mays later admitted, "I didn't see the ball. I tried to dive for it [at] the last second. We had a two-run lead and I shoulda played it safe."[6]

After McGraw retired Campaneris and Rudi, he walked Sal Bando and then surrendered back-to-back RBI singles by Jackson and Tenace that knotted the game, 6-6. McGraw set down Alou for the final out and – in spite of having pitched two innings in Game One the previous day – remained in the game and set the A's down in order in the 10th and 11th innings.

The Mets had a chance to take the lead in the top of the 10th after Harrelson led off with a single, reached second on McGraw's sacrifice bunt, and went to third when Garrett reached base on an error by Tenace at first base. Felix Millan stepped to the plate and hit a fly ball to short left field, but third-base coach Eddie Yost still sent Harrelson home. Almost 40 years later, Harrelson still recalled the play vividly:

> [I] tried to stay up as long as I could to block catcher Ray Fosse's view of the throw. Willie Mays ... was the on-deck hitter and on his knees signaling me to slide, but I saw Fosse reaching down for the ball and I figured my best bet was to go in standing up. ... I was safe, only plate umpire Augie Donatelli didn't agree.[7]

Mays, still on his knees, pleaded Harrelson's case to Donatelli to no avail, as did Berra and the rest of the Mets, and the game remained tied until the top of the 12th.

In the fateful 12th, Mays found redemption for his misplay in the ninth, and the game's goat horns passed to A's second baseman Mike Andrews. Mays came to bat with Harrelson on third, McGraw on first, and two outs. After swinging and missing on Rollie Fingers' first offering, Mays swung at the second pitch and "slapped it straight back, a bounder that hopped high over the pitcher's head and skipped on into center field"[8] and drove in Harrelson with the go-ahead run. Sadecki, by now watching the game in the clubhouse, asserted later, "He had to get a hit. This game was invented for Willie Mays a hundred years ago."[9] It turned out to be the last hit of Mays' storied Hall of Fame career.

After Jones singled to load the bases, Paul Lindblad relieved Fingers. Milner tapped a ball up the middle for what should have been the third out, but the ball bounced through Andrews' legs, allowing McGraw and Mays to score. On the next play, Andrews fielded Grote's grounder cleanly but threw slightly wide of first, where umpire Jerry Neudecker ruled that first baseman Tenace had been drawn off the bag by the throw and that Grote was safe; Andrews was charged with his second error on the play.[10] Television replays showed Neudecker's call to be incorrect – Tenace's foot was still on the bag when he received the throw ahead of Grote's arrival[11] – but it nevertheless allowed Jones to score and increased New York's lead to 10-6. Lindblad retired Hahn, but the A's now found themselves in a deep hole.

A fatigued McGraw allowed a leadoff triple to Jackson and walked Tenace before Berra pulled him in favor of George Stone. Alou promptly knocked home Jackson with a single, but Stone bore down to earn the save – McGraw got the win – after Campaneris grounded to Harrelson for the final out of the game.

## NOTES

1 Lowell Reidenbaugh, "Tug's Battle Cry Inspires Mets: 'You Gotta Believe,'" *The Sporting News*, October 27, 1973: 10.

2 Jason Turbow, *Dynastic, Bombastic, Fantastic: Reggie, Rollie, Catfish, and Charlie Finley's Swingin' A's* (Boston: Houghton Mifflin Harcourt, 2017), 154.

3 "Say-Hey Days Seem Gone for Ol' Willie," *Chicago Tribune*, October 15, 1973: 80.

4 "Say-Hey Days Seem Gone for Ol' Willie."

5 Matthew Silverman, *Swinging '73: Baseball's Wildest Season* (Guilford, Connecticut: Lyons Press, 2013), 175.

6 Red Smith, "The Game They Invented for Willie," *New York Times*, October 15, 1973: 43.

7 Bud Harrelson with Phil Pepe, *Turning Two: My Journey to the Top of the World and Back With the New York Mets* (New York: St. Martin's Press, 2012), 151. Television replays showed that Harrelson was safe; however, in 1973, instant replay was not yet used to confirm or overturn calls on the field, so Donatelli's controversial call stood.

8 Smith, "The Game They Invented for Willie."

9 Smith, "The Game They Invented for Willie."

10 Andrews had been dealing with a long-term shoulder injury, which may explain his poor throw on what should have been

a routine play. Oakland owner Charlie O. Finley was so irate with Andrews that immediately after the game he had Andrews examined by team orthopedist Dr. Harry Walker whom Finley ordered to declare Andrews to be disabled. Walker grudgingly complied, and Finley coerced Andrews into signing a memo in which he agreed with the diagnosis. A's players were so upset with Finley that they threatened to strike and not play Game Three in New York. Commissioner Bowie Kuhn stepped in and ordered Finley to reinstate Andrews in time for Game Three, and the potential disaster of a World Series forfeit by the Oakland A's was averted. (A comprehensive account of the entire episode between Finley and Andrews can be found in Turbow, 155-170).

11 Turbow, 156. Once again, with replay not yet in use on the field, Neudecker's call stood, just as Donatelli's call on Harrelson had in the 10th inning.

# CONTRIBUTOR BIOGRAPHIES

**JAKE BELL** is a former sports journalist, a children's author, and was briefly a media relations intern in the press box of the Milwaukee Brewers, but now he writes and edits government documents. Jake lives in Baltimore, 2.8 miles from Camden Yards.

**LUIS A. BLANDON**, a Washington, DC native, is a producer, writer, and researcher in video and documentary film production and in archival, manuscript, historical, film, and image research. His creative storytelling has garnered numerous awards, including three regional Emmys®, regional and national Edward R. Murrow Awards, two TELLY awards and a New York Festival World Medal. He worked as a producer and/or researcher on several documentaries including *Jeremiah*; *Feast Your Ears: The Story of WHFS 102.3*; and *#GeorgeWashington*. Most recently, he was co-producer of the documentary *The Lost Battalion*. He served as a consultant on documentary film project for the United States Naval Academy's Stockdale Center for Ethical Leadership and Maryland Public Television on the Vietnam War POWs and leadership. He was Senior Researcher and Manager of the Story Development Team for two national programs for Retirement Living Television. He has worked as a historian for two public policy research firms, Morgan Angel & Associates and MLL Consulting LLC. He served as the principal researcher for several authors including for *The League of Wives* by Heath Hardage Lee and her current biography project on First Lady Pat Nixon. He has a Masters of Arts in International Affairs from the George Washington University.

On the day **KURT BLUMENAU** was born, Willie Mays started in center field for the New York Mets. Kurt grew up in western New York, rooting for the Mets and the Triple-A Rochester Red Wings. He works in corporate communications in the Boston area and has written for the SABR Games and Biography Projects. This is his first contribution to a SABR book.

**RICHARD BOGOVICH**'s new book in 2022 was *Frank Grant: The Life of a Black Baseball Pioneer*. For McFarland & Co. he'd previously written *Kid Nichols: A Biography of the Hall of Fame Pitcher* and *The Who: A Who's Who*. He has contributed to such SABR books as *When the Monarchs Reigned: Kansas City's 1942 Negro League Champions* and *The Newark Eagles Take Flight: The Story of the 1946 Negro League Champions*. He works for the Wendland Utz law firm in Rochester, Minnesota.

**THOMAS J. BROWN JR.** is a lifelong Mets fan who became a Durham Bulls fan after moving to North Carolina in the early 1980s. He was a national-board-certified high-school science teacher for 34 years before retiring in 2016. Tom taught science to ELL students in the last eight years of his career and still mentors many of them. He has been a member of SABR since 1995, when he learned about the organization during a visit to Cooperstown on his honeymoon. Tom became active in SABR after his retirement, writing biographies and game stories, mostly about the New York Mets. He loves to travel with his wife, always visiting major-league and minor-league baseball parks whenever possible. Tom also loves to cook and writes about the diverse recipes that he makes on his blog, Cooking and My Family.

**DR. JOHN J. BURBRIDGE JR.** is currently Professor Emeritus at Elon University, where he was both a dean and professor. While at Elon he introduced and taught *Baseball and Statistics*. He has authored several SABR publications and presented at SABR conventions, *NINE*, and the Seymour meetings. He is a lifelong New York Giants baseball fan. The greatest Giants-Dodgers game he attended was a 1-0 Giants' victory in Jersey City in 1956. The sole run was a Willie Mays home run off Don Newcombe. Yes, the Dodgers did play in Jersey City in 1956 and 1957. John can be reached at burbridg@elon.edu.

**FREDERICK C. "RICK" BUSH** has written articles for over two dozen SABR books and, together with Bill Nowlin, has coedited five SABR books about the Negro Leagues, including *The First Negro League Champion: The 1920 Chicago American Giants* (2022) and *When the Monarchs Reigned: Kansas City's 1942 Negro League Champions* (2021), which received the 2022 Robert Peterson Recognition Award. Future volumes about the 1934 Philadelphia Stars (2023) and 1939 Baltimore Elite Giants (2024) are in progress. Rick lives with his wife, Michelle, their three sons, Michael, Andrew, and Daniel, and their border collie, Bailey, in the Houston metro area. He has been an educator for nearly 30 years and has spent the past two decades teaching English at Wharton County Junior College's satellite campus in Sugar Land, which is home to the Astros' Triple-A franchise.

**ALAN COHEN** chairs the BioProject fact-checking committee, serves as vice president-treasurer of the Connecticut Smoky Joe Wood Chapter, and is a datacaster (milb first-pitch stringer) for the Hartford Yard Goats of the Double-A Eastern League. His biographies, game stories and essays have appeared in more than 65 SABR publications. The subject of his earliest *Baseball Research Journal* article was the Hearst Sandlot Classic, at which Willie Mays participated in a home-run-hitting contest in 1957. His story of Mays' return to the Polo Grounds in 1962 with the Giants was first published as part of the SABR website's First Games Back project. He is currently involved with the Retrosheet project on Negro League Games, including Mays' games with Birmingham from 1948 through 1950. He has four children, nine grandchildren, and one great-grandchild and resides in Connecticut with wife Frances, their cats Ava and Zoe, and their dog, Buddy.

**RICHARD CUICCHI** joined SABR in 1983 and is an active member of the Schott-Pelican Chapter. After his retirement as an information technology executive, Richard authored *Family Ties: A Comprehensive Collection of Facts and Trivia about Baseball's Relatives*. He has contributed to numerous SABR BioProject and Games Project publications. He does freelance writing and blogging about a variety of baseball topics on his website, TheTenthInning.com, and is a regular contributor to CrescentCitySports.com. Richard lives in New Orleans with his wife, Mary.

**DAN FIELDS** has contributed to many SABR books He is a senior manuscript editor at the *New England Journal of Medicine* and a longtime volunteer with the Grief Support Services program of Samaritans, Inc. He lives in Framingham, Massachusetts, and can be reached at dfields820@gmail.com.

**JAMES FORR** dreams of sitting under the old Chesterfields sign, watching Willie Mays patrol center field in the Polo Grounds. His book *Pie Traynor: A Baseball Biography*, coauthored with David Proctor, was a finalist for the CASEY Award. He is a winner of the McFarland-SABR Baseball Research Award and has spoken at the Frederick Ivor-Campbell Nineteenth Century Base Ball Conference and the Jerry Malloy Negro League Conference.

**BRIAN M. FRANK** is passionate about documenting the history of major- and minor-league baseball. He is the creator of the website The Herd Chronicles (www.herdchronicles.com), which is dedicated to preserving the history of the Buffalo Bisons and professional baseball in Buffalo. His articles can also be read on the official website of the Bisons. He was an assistant editor of the book *The Seasons of Buffalo Baseball, 1857-2020*, and he's a frequent contributor to SABR publications. Brian and his wife, Jenny, enjoy traveling around the country in their camper to major- and minor-league ballparks and taking an annual trip to Europe. Brian was a history major at Canisius College, where he earned a Bachelor of Arts. He also received a Juris Doctor from the University at Buffalo School of Law.

**JOHN FREDLAND**, an attorney and retired Air Force officer, grew up in a suburb of Pittsburgh. As an undergraduate at Rice University, he covered Rice's nationally ranked baseball teams for the school newspaper, the *Rice Thresher*. John received his law degree at Vanderbilt University, then served as an active-duty attorney in the Air Force's Judge Advocate General's Corps for 20 years. He lives in San Antonio, Texas, and chairs SABR's Baseball Games Project Research Committee.

**ROBERT F. GARRATT** lives on Whidbey Island in Washington State with his wife, Sally. Rob is an emeritus professor of English and humanities at the University of Puget Sound, where he taught courses on modern British and Irish literature and international modernism. He grew up in the San Francisco Bay Area, an ardent fan of the San Francisco Giants. Upon his retirement from university teaching, he began researching the major leagues' move in 1958 to San Francisco and Los Angeles. That initial research resulted in *Home Team: The Turbulent History of the San Francisco Giants* (Lincoln: University of Nebraska Press, 2017), a comprehensive history of the Giants as a Bay Area team. He followed his history of the San Francisco Giants with a biography of Charles A. Stoneham, who owned the New York Giants during the Jazz Age (forthcoming from Nebraska). Rob has been a member of the Society for American Baseball Research since 2007 and is a contributing author in a number of SABR publications including the BioProject and the team histories. He has also published in *NINE*, a journal on baseball and culture.

**CRAIG GARRETSON** was born and raised in New Jersey, where he lives with his wife, two daughters, and a Labrador retriever named Bernie after another New York center fielder. A member of SABR since 2019, this is his second plate appearance in a SABR publication, following his contribution to *Yankee Stadium 1923-2008 - America's First Modern Ballpark*.

**GORDON J. GATTIE** is a lifelong baseball fan and a SABR member since 1998. A civilian US Navy engineer, he includes among his baseball research interests ballparks, historical trends, and statistical analysis. Gordon earned his Ph.D. from SUNY Buffalo, where he used baseball to investigate judgment performance in complex dynamic environments. Ever the optimist, he dreams of a Cleveland Guardians World Series championship. Lisa, his wonderful wife, who roots for the Yankees, and Morrigan, their beloved Labrador retriever, enjoy visiting ballparks and other baseball-related sites. Gordon has contributed to several SABR publications, including various books, multiple issues of *The National Pastime,* and the Games Project.

**STEVEN M. GLASSMAN** has been a SABR member since 1994 and is the secretary of the Connie Mack-Dick Allen Chapter. He wrote articles for *Greatest Comeback Games* and *Baseball's Biggest Blowout Games*. Steven also contributed articles for the SABR Convention Games Project and the Century Committee for the 1921 season. Altogether, he has written six Games Project articles. Steven also wrote eight SABR Convention articles, most recently "The Hidden Potato Trick" (SABR 50). The Temple University graduate in sport and recreation management is currently the director of sports information at Manor College in Jenkintown, Pennsylvania. Steven is also an entertainment staff member/phanstormer for the Philadelphia Phillies, statistics crew member for the Trenton Thunder, and game day staff member for the Trenton Terror. He also serves as first-base coach/scorekeeper for his summer league softball team. Steven was also certified *Microsoft Office Word 2016*. He has attended Phillies games since the 1970s. Born in Philadelphia, Steven lives in Warminster, Pennsylvania.

**DUKE GOLDMAN** is a longtime SABR member whose research focuses on the Negro Leagues and the process of baseball integration. Duke is working on a biography of Monte Irvin for McFarland & Co.; therefore, the article in this volume on Willie Mays and Monte Irvin is right up his alley.

**CHIP GREENE** is a longtime SABR member who has written numerous biographies and game summaries, in addition to editing *Mustaches and Mayhem*, the BioProject book on the three-time-champion Oakland A's. A government contractor and lifelong Orioles fan, Chip lives with his family in Waynesboro, Pennsylvania.

**LOU HERNÁNDEZ** is the author of numerous baseball histories and biographies, and two Young Adult Fantasy novels. He resides in South Florida and follows the Miami Marlins.

**PAUL HOFMANN** has been a SABR member since 2002. He has contributed to more than 25 SABR publications and coedited *The 1883 Philadelphia Athletics: American Association Champions*. Paul is currently the assistant vice president for international affairs at the University of Louisville and teaches in the College of Management at National Changhua University of Education in Taiwan. A native of Detroit, Paul is an avid baseball card collector and a lifelong Detroit Tigers fan. He resides in Lakeville, Minnesota.

**JASON HOROWITZ** is a researcher, writer, and editor. He never saw Willie Mays play in person, though his parents (one a Brooklyn Dodgers fan and the other a New York Giants supporter) filled their home with tales of the great NYC baseball teams of the 1940s and '50s. This is his second publication since joining SABR in 2020. When not researching sports, Jason focuses on the intersection of high tech, business strategy, and international affairs.

**MIKE HUBER** is a professor of mathematics at Muhlenberg College in Allentown, Pennsylvania, where he regularly teaches a course titled Reasoning with Sabermetrics. His sabermetrical research focuses on studying rare baseball events, such as hitting for the cycle, and he enjoys writing for SABR's Games Project. His first book, *West Point's Field of Dreams*, chronicled exhibition games between major-league teams and Army's baseball team at West Point, including a few contests in the 1950s involving the New York Giants and Willie Mays.

**DOUGLAS JORDAN** is a professor emeritus at Sonoma State University in Northern California. He's a member of the Society for American Baseball Research, whose baseball articles have been published in *NINE*, *Baseball Research Journal*, and *The Sport Journal*. He enjoys hiking and chess when he is not watching or writing about baseball. You can contact him at jordand@sonoma.edu.

**DAVID KAISER** first experienced Willie Mays on television during the 1954 World Series, at the age of 7, when he saw Willie's famous catch in the first game. A historian, he taught for 37 years at Harvard, Carnegie Mellon, the Naval War College, and Williams College. He is the author of two baseball books, *Epic Season, the 1948 American League Pennant Race,* and *Baseball Greatness: The Best Players and Teams According to Wins Above Average.* He has given numerous presentations at local SABR chapters and at a number of national conventions. He lives with his wife, Patti Cassidy, in Watertown, Massachusetts.

A six-year SABR member, **BRENT KALLESTAD** spent his career in journalism, including a four-year period in the mid-'70s when he covered the Minnesota Twins as the beat writer early in his 40-year career with the Associated Press. It was at a time Harmon Killebrew and Tony Oliva were winding down Hall of Fame careers and Cooperstown-bound Rod Carew was nearing the end of his days in Minnesota with a streak of American League batting titles. A memorable highlight for Brent before AP days was a story written in 1969 for the *Florida Times-Union* following his interview with Elmer Smith, who hit the first World Series grand slam. Brent has a Bachelor of Arts in mass communications from the University of South Dakota and two diplomas from the Department of Defense Information School obtained during his service in the US Navy. He is a member of the Buck O'Neil SABR chapter. based in Tallahassee.

**DAVE LANDE** lives with his wife, Pam, in Oakdale, Minnesota. They were born with baseball in their genes as both of their fathers played town baseball, his father in North Dakota and hers in Minnesota and Wisconsin. Originally from North Dakota, he moved to the Twin Cities over 40 years ago to live in a warmer climate. An active member of the Halsey Hall SABR Chapter, he is a lifelong Twins fan and also cheers for the Cardinals, his second-favorite baseball team. He went to his first baseball game with his father to watch the Williston Oilers in the Manitoba-Dakota (ManDak) League.

For over 20 years, **KEVIN LARKIN** patrolled the highways and byways of the roads in his home town of Great Barrington, Massachusetts. When not at work keeping the citizens of his hometown safe, inevitably Larkin was listening to a baseball game on the radio. He has been going to baseball games since he was 5 years old. His baseball life is the only thing he loves more than his children and grandchildren. One day while he was browsing through the local bookstore, the owner asked him if he was interested in writing a book about baseball. Larkin's first effort was *Baseball in the Bay State: A History of Baseball in Massachusetts.* He then took quite an interest in the history of the game, authoring a book on one of his heroes, Lou Gehrig, called *Gehrig: Game by Game*, a look at every game the Iron Horse played during his major-league career. He has since written a number of other books and articles on the sport and has a number of others ready for future publication. His latest book, *Big Time Baseball in a Small Berkshire County Town,* has led to his heading an effort to erect a historical marker in the town where this semipro team played a number of major-league teams, Black baseball teams, and the House of David touring team, with the plaque being dedicated on July 6, 2022. Kevin and Jesse Stewart also cohost a monthly radio show that talks about baseball history with a focus on Berkshire County baseball and its players. He writes and fact-checks for SABR, an experience he considers the best decision he has ever made. According to Larkin, writing about baseball is a great way to keep the memory of the sport alive and he will continue to delve into sports history with more to come.

**BOB LEMOINE** is a high-school librarian and adjunct professor at White Mountains Community College and Emporia State University. He lives in New Hampshire and has contributed to several SABR projects. Bob is the author of the book *When the Babe Went Back to Boston: Babe Ruth, Judge Fuchs, and the Hapless 1935 Boston Braves* (McFarland & Co., 2023).

**LEN LEVIN** is a longtime newspaper editor in New England, now retired. He lives in Providence with his wife, Linda, and an overachieving orange cat. He now (Len, not the cat) is the grammarian for the Rhode Island Supreme Court and edits its decisions. He also copy-edits many SABR books, including this one. He is just down the interstate from Fenway Park, where he has spent many happy hours.

**CHAD MOODY** is a nearly lifelong resident of the Detroit area, where he has been a fan of the Detroit Tigers from birth. An alumnus of the University of Michigan and Michigan State University, he has spent 30 years working in the automotive industry. Chad has contributed to numerous SABR and Professional Football Researchers Association projects. He and his wife, Lisa, live in Plymouth, Michigan, with their dog, Daisy.

**ROB NEYER** is the author or coauthor of eight baseball books, including the CASEY Award-winning *Power Ball: Anatomy of a Modern Baseball Game*. Rob lives in Oregon with his wife and daughter, and has been the commissioner of the West Coast League, the West's premier summer collegiate baseball league, since 2018. He's been a SABR member since 1985.

**BILL NOWLIN** pretty much only saw American League games while growing up in the Boston area, so never saw Willie Mays play. He does wish the Red Sox had signed Mays when they had the opportunity, but there are a lot of things to regret from that era. He has worked as a political science professor, cofounded the Rounder Records label, and has written or edited a lot of books and articles about baseball.

**TIM ODZER** grew up in the Minneapolis area, where Willie Mays played before being recalled to the Giants. He recalls thinking as a child how cool it was that the great Willie Mays played in the Twin Cities. Tim has a law degree from the University of Chicago and now practices commercial litigation in Miami. In his free time, he enjoys writing articles for SABR.

**TIM OTTO** grew up in northeast Ohio, 35 miles from Cleveland's Municipal Stadium. His first memories of major-league baseball date to the spring of 1960 when, as a second-grader, he was fascinated by the controversy surrounding the trade of Rocky Colavito to the Tigers for Harvey Kuenn. Shortly thereafter he started monopolizing the sports section of the *Cleveland Plain Dealer* each morning at breakfast, and that June attended his first major-league game. He remembers closely following the 1962 Dodgers-Giants pennant race and was excited to learn that his article on the deciding playoff game would be included in this book.

**RICHARD J. PUERZER** is the chairperson of the Department of Engineering at Hofstra University. His writing on baseball has appeared in several SABR books, including *Bittersweet Goodbye: The Black Barons, The Grays, and the 1948 Negro League World Series* (2017) and *Pride of Smoketown: The 1935 Pittsburgh Crawfords* (2020), as well as in *Nine: A Journal of Baseball History and Culture; Black Ball; The National Pastime; The Cooperstown Symposium on Baseball and American Culture proceedings; Zisk;* and *Spitball.* He and his wife, Clare, have four children: Casey, Aaron, Josh, and Addie.

**STEPHEN V. RICE**, Ph.D., is a native of Detroit and resides in Collierville, Tennessee. From 2013 to 2022 he authored more than 150 articles for the SABR BioProject and Games Project. A computer scientist and software developer for more than 40 years, he currently develops genomics software for cancer diagnosis and research at St. Jude Children's Research Hospital in Memphis.

**CARL RIECHERS** retired from United Parcel Service in 2012 after 35 years of service. With more free time, he became a SABR member that same year. Born and raised in the suburbs of St. Louis, he became a big fan of the Cardinals. He and his wife, Janet, have three children and he is the proud grandpa of two.

**HOWARD ROSENBERG** has been a baseball fan since the Dodgers played in Brooklyn. His baseball interests include writing SABR game stories, editing BioProject articles, tweeting about the Mets (@Metbaseball), and doing statistical analyses using R. He received his Ph.D. from Syracuse University, where he investigated complex systems using system dynamics. A college teacher, he teaches a course on Sports Communication, Culture, and Identity, enjoys writing poems about baseball, including one that was the Baseball Poem of the Month in *Spitball Magazine* in July 2010, and drawing baseball-related pictures.

**JOHN T. SACCOMAN** is a professor and chair of Mathematics and Computer Science at Seton Hall University in New Jersey. An avid fan of the New York Mets, Willie Mays, and Gil Hodges, he has team-taught one of the earliest known Sabermetrics courses (1988) there with its founder, Rev. Gabe Costa, Ph.D. They, along with Dr. Mike Huber, have coauthored three books published by McFarland – *Understanding Sabermetrics, Practicing Sabermetrics*, and *Reasoning with Sabermetrics.* John has contributed 10 articles to the SABR BioProject, and several articles to the Games Project and the *Baseball Research Journal.* He resides in northern New Jersey with his Bosox-loving wife, Mary, and tries to get to Citi Field whenever possible with his Boston-area son, Ryan, whom he interviewed for the SABR book *The Fenway Project.*

**MARK SIMON** works in content creation for Sports Info Solutions, where he often writes about the defensive excellence of current MLB players. He previously worked at the *Trenton Times* and ESPN. His father's all-time favorite players are Willie Mays and Keith Hernandez.

**GLEN SPARKS** is a lifelong Dodgers fan and also a fan of Giants great Willie Mays. He has worked on many books for SABR and wrote *Pee Wee Reese: The Life of a Brooklyn Dodger,* published in 2022 by McFarland. Sparks has a bachelor's degree in journalism from the University of Missouri. His wife, Pam, is a professional horticulturist. They live with their three cats (Lucy, Buster, and Kasper) and an assortment of tropical fish.

**CREG STEPHENSON** has written about sports, mostly college football, for a variety of print and online publications since 1994. He lives in Mobile, Alabama, birthplace of five Baseball Hall of Famers and many "Hall of Very Good"-ers. After years of procrastination, he finally joined SABR in 2019.

The first World Series that **MARK S. STERNMAN** dimly recalls involved Willie

Mays and the 1973 Mets. At the age of 5, Sternman watched some of the games on a small television. He regrets not having had the chance to see Mays play in the prime of his career.

**JEB STEWART** is a lawyer in Birmingham, Alabama, whose favorite pastime has always been taking his sons, Nolan and Ryan, and his wife, Stephanie, to the Rickwood Classic each year. He has been a SABR member since 2012 and is co-president of the Rickwood Field SABR Chapter. He is an executive committee member on the Board of the Friends of Rickwood Field and is a regular contributor to the *Rickwood Times*. He also edits the Friends' quarterly newsletter, "Rickwood Tales." He has written several biographies for SABR's Biography Project.

**STEW THORNLEY** joined SABR in 1979 and became motivated to do research and writing. He began researching the history of the Minneapolis Millers, whom Willie Mays played for in 1951, and in 1988 had his first book published, *On to Nicollet: The Glory and Fame of the Minneapolis Millers*.

**TOM THRESS** is president of Retrosheet. He has been published in the *Baseball Research Journal* and is the author of *Player Won-Lost Records in Baseball: Measuring Performance in Context* (McFarland, 2017) as well as two other self-published books. Tom lives in Portland, Maine, with his wife and sons after spending most of his adult life on the North Side of Chicago, where he and his family attended Game Four of the 2016 World Series (the last World Series game ever lost by the Chicago Cubs). In his day job, Tom is an economist.

**THEO TOBEL** is a senior at Santa Monica High School. In his spare time, Theo enjoys watching Dodgers baseball and making wood baseball bats on his lathe at home. He combines his love for baseball and mathematics by studying baseball analytics. Theo can be reached at theotobel@yahoo.com and his baseball blog can be found at theobaseballblog.wordpress.com.

**BOB WEBSTER** grew up in northwestern Indiana and has been a Cubs fan since 1963. After moving to Portland, Oregon, in 1980, Bob spends his time working on baseball research and writing and is a contributor to quite a few SABR projects. He worked as a stats stringer on the MLB Gameday app for three years. He is a member of the Pacific Northwest Chapter of SABR and is on the board of directors of the Old-Timers Baseball Association of Portland.

**DANIEL WINKLER** is a committed Baltimore Orioles fan, and he most enjoys the team when it is mediocre. Hopefully, the Birds never again make the playoffs, as modern playoff baseball is too nerve-wracking to be enjoyed. Cathartic, meaningless games are preferable to such high-stakes affairs. He is a lifelong fan of Willie Mays, though he never saw the Star play. Five-tool players are gifts, and this is doubly so for the spectacular ones. Daniel has researched and published on a number of topics ranging from educational history to blowout baseball games. He annually conducts a Hall of Fame ballot among SABR members, and has contributed to SABR publications. He eagerly awaits the Orioles' spring-training games, the year's most purposeless and profound sporting events.

**GREGORY H. WOLF** was born in Pittsburgh, but now resides in the Chicagoland area with his wife, Margaret, and daughter, Gabriela. A professor of German studies and holder of the Dennis and Jean Bauman Endowed Chair in the Humanities at North Central College in Naperville, Illinois, he has edited more than a dozen books for SABR. Since January 2017 he has been co-director of SABR's BioProject, which you can follow on Facebook and Twitter.

# SABR Books on the Negro Leagues and Black Baseball

## From Rube to Robinson: SABR's Best Articles on Black Baseball

*From Rube to Robinson* brings together the best Negro League baseball scholarship that the Society of American Baseball Research (SABR) has ever produced, culled from its journals, Biography Project, and award-winning essays. The book includes a star-studded list of scholars and historians, from the late Jerry Malloy and Jules Tygiel, to award winners Larry Lester, Geri Strecker, and Jeremy Beer, and a host of other talented writers. The essays cover topics ranging over nearly a century, from 1866 and the earliest known Black baseball championship, to 1962 and the end of the Negro American League.

**Edited by John Graf; Associate Editors Duke Goldman and Larry Lester**
**$24.95 paperback (ISBN 978-1-970159-41-7)**
**$9.99 ebook (ISBN 978-1-970159-40-0)**
**8.5"X11", 220 pages**

## Pride of Smoketown: The 1935 Pittsburgh Crawfords

The 1935 Pittsburgh Crawfords team, one of the dominant teams in Negro League history, is often compared to the legendary 1927 "Murderer's Row" New York Yankees. The squad from "Smoketown"—a nickname that the *Pittsburgh Courier* often applied to the metropolis better-known as "Steel City"—boasted four Hall-of-Fame players in outfielder James "Cool Papa" Bell, first baseman/manager Oscar Charleston, catcher Josh Gibson, and third baseman William "Judy" Johnson. This volume contains exhaustively-researched articles about the players, front office personnel, Greenlee Field, and the exciting games and history of the team that were written and edited by 25 SABR members. The inclusion of historical photos about every subject in the book helps to shine a spotlight on the 1935 Pittsburgh Crawfords, who truly were the Pride of Smoketown.

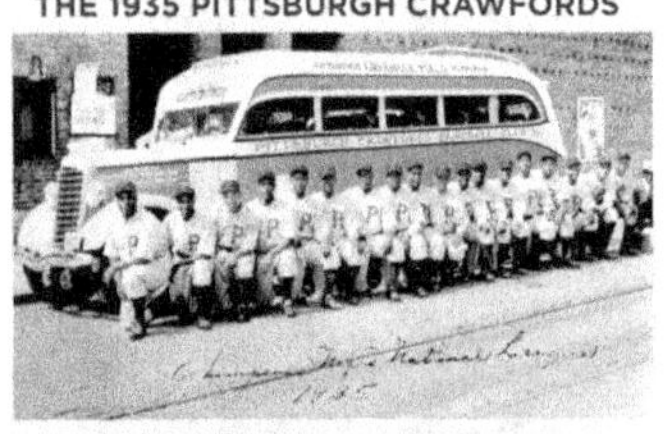

**Edited by Frederick C. Bush and Bill Nowlin**
**$29.95 paperback (ISBN 978-1-970159-25-7)**
**$9.99 ebook (ISBN 978-1-970159-24-0)**
**8.5"X11", 340 pages, over 60 photos**

Edited By FREDERICK C. BUSH & BILL NOWLIN
Associate Editors LEN LEVIN & CARL RIECHERS

## The Newark Eagles Take Flight: The Story of the 1946 Negro League Champions

The Newark Eagles won only one Negro National League pennant during the franchise's 15-year tenure in the Garden State, but the 1946 squad that ran away with the NNL and then triumphed over the Kansas City Monarchs in a seven-game World Series was a team for the ages. The returning WWII veterans composed a veritable "Who's Who in the Negro Leagues" and included Leon Day, Larry Doby, Monte Irvin, and Max Manning, as well as numerous role players. Four of the Eagles' stars—Day, Doby, Irvin, and player/manager Raleigh "Biz" Mackey, as well as co-owner Effa Manley—have been enshrined in the National Baseball Hall of Fame in Cooperstown. In addition to biographies of the players, co-owners, and P.A. announcer, there are also articles about Newark's Ruppert Stadium, Leon Day's Opening Day no-hitter, a sensational midseason game, the season's two East-West All-Star Games, and the 1946 Negro League World Series between the Eagles and the renowned Kansas City Monarchs.

**Edited by Frederick C. Bush and Bill Nowlin**
**$24.95 paperback (ISBN 978-1-970159-07-3)**
**$9.99 ebook (ISBN 978-1-970159-06-6)**
**8.5"X11", 228 pages, over 60 photos**

## Bittersweet Goodbye: The Black Barons, The Grays, and the 1948 Negro League World Series

This book was inspired by the last Negro League World Series ever played and presents biographies of the players on the two contending teams in 1948—the Birmingham Black Barons and the Homestead Grays—as well as the managers, the owners, and articles on the ballparks the teams called home. Also included are articles that recap the season's two East-West All-Star Games, the Negro National League and Negro American League playoff series, and the World Series itself. Additional context is provided in essays about the effects of baseball's integration on the Negro Leagues, the exodus of Negro League players to Canada, and the signing away of top Negro League players, specifically Willie Mays. Many of the players' lives and careers have been presented to a much greater extent than previously possible.

**Edited by Frederick C. Bush and Bill Nowlin**
**$21.95 paperback (ISBN 978-1-943816-55-2)**
**$9.99 ebook (ISBN 978-1-943816-54-5)**
**8.5"X11", 442 pages, over 100 photos and images**

# The SABR Digital Library

**Available wherever books are sold**

**The First Negro League Champion: The 1920 Chicago American Giants**

*Edited by Frederick C. Bush and Bill Nowlin*

Paperback $29.95 244 pages • Ebook $9.99

This book chronicles the team which won the title of champion in the Negro National League's inaugural season. Rube Foster, a Hall of Famer, and his White business partner John Schorling are featured along with biographies of every player on the team include Cristóbal Torriente, a member of both the National Baseball Hall of Fame and the Cuban Baseball Hall of Fame, as well as early Blackball stalwarts Dave "Lefty" Brown, Bingo DeMoss, Judy Gans, Dave Malarcher, Frank Warfield, and Frank Wickware. A comprehensive timeline of the 1920 season and a history of the founding of the Negro National League are included.

**We Are, We Can, We Will: The 1992 World Champion Toronto Blue Jays**

*Edited by Adrian Fung and Bill Nowlin*

**Forewords by Buck Martinez and Dave Winfield**

Paperback US $34.95/Canada $41.95 394 pages • Ebook $9.99

The 1992 Toronto Blue Jays will always be remembered as the first World Series-winning club from Canada. After a near miss in 1991, the 1992 club confidently adopted "We Are, We Can, We Will" as their team motto. This book features biographies of every player who played for the 1992 Toronto Blue Jays including Hall of Famers Dave Winfield, Jack Morris, and Roberto Alomar. Manager Cito Gaston, Hall of Fame general manager Pat Gillick, and radio broadcaster Tom Cheek are also included, as well as a "ballpark biography" of SkyDome. Ten reports describe significant games from the 1992 season illustrating Toronto's championship journey from Opening Day to the last game of the World Series.

**From Shibe Park to Connie Mack Stadium: Great Games in Philadelphia's Lost Ballpark**

*Edited by Gregory H. Wolf*

Paperback $39.95 398 pages • Ebook $9.99

This collection evokes memories and the exciting history of the celebrated ballpark through stories of 100 games played there and several feature essays. The games included in this volume reflect every decade in the ballpark's history, from the inaugural game in 1909, to the last in 1970.

Shibe Park was the home of the Philadelphia A's from 1909 until their relocation to Kansas City and the Philadelphia Phillies from 1938 until the ballpark's closure at the end 1970. In 1953 it was renamed Connie Mack Stadium. The ballpark hosted big-league baseball for 62 seasons and more than 6,000 games—over 3,500 games by the A's and 2,500 by the Phillies—and was home to Frank Baker, Del Ennis, Chief Bender, and Robin Roberts.

**¡Arriba!: The Heroic Life of Roberto Clemente**

*edited by Bill Nowlin and Glen Sparks*

Paperback $34.95 338 pages • Ebook $9.99

2022 marks the 50th anniversary year of Roberto Clemente's passing. This book celebrates his life and baseball career. Named to 15 All-Star Game squads, Clemente won 12 Gold Gloves, four batting titles, and was the National League's Most Valuable Player in 1966. The first Latino inducted into the National Baseball Hall of Fame, Clemente played 18 seasons for the Pittsburgh Pirates and became the 11th player to reach the 3,000-hit milestone, hitting number 3000 on the season's last day. At the time no one knew he would never play baseball again. Clemente was known for his charitable work. He lost his life on the final day of 1972 while working to provide relief for victims of an earthquake in Nicaragua.

**SABR publishes up to a dozen new books per year on baseball history and culture. Researched and written by SABR members, these collaborative projects cover some of the game's greatest players, classic ballparks, and teams.**

**SABR members can download all Digital Library publications for free or get 50% off the purchase of paperback editions.**